THE BEST OF

Gourmet

THE BEST OF

Gourmet

FROM THE EDITORS OF GOURMET

CONDÉ NAST BOOKS
RANDOM HOUSE, NEW YORK

ISBN 1-4000-6519-4
ISSN 1046-1760

Random House website address: www.atrandom.com
Gourmet Books website address: www.Gourmetbks.com

All of the recipes in this work were published previously in
Gourmet Magazine.

Printed in the United States of America on acid-free paper.

987654321
First Edition

All informative text in this book was written by Diane Abrams, Kate Winslow,
Jane Daniels Lear, Nichol Nelson, Lesley Porcelli, and Eric Hastie.

The text of this book was set in Trade Gothic. The four-color separations
were provided by North Market Graphics and Quad/Graphics, Inc. The book
was printed and bound at R. R. Donnelley and Sons. Stock is Sterling Ultra
Web Gloss, MeadWestvaco.

FOR RANDOM HOUSE
Lisa Faith Phillips, Vice President/General Manager
Tom Downing, Marketing Director
Deborah Williams, Operations Director
Lyn Barris Hastings, Associate Marketing Director
Eric Killer, Assistant Direct Marketing Manager
Angela Donadic, Direct Marketing Assistant
Richard Elman, Production Manager

FOR *GOURMET* BOOKS
Diane Abrams, Director
Kate Winslow, Senior Associate Editor

FOR *GOURMET* MAGAZINE
Ruth Reichl, Editor-in-Chief
Richard Ferretti, Creative Director

Zanne Early Stewart, Executive Food Editor
Kemp Miles Minifie, Senior Food Editor
Alexis M. Touchet, Associate Food Editor
Paul Grimes, Food Editor/Stylist
Shelton Wiseman, Food Editor
Ruth Cousineau, Food Editor
Gina Marie Miraglia Eriquez, Food Editor
Melissa Roberts-Matar, Food Editor
Maggie Ruggiero, Food Editor
Lillian Chou, Food Editor
Ian Knauer, Food Editor

Romulo A. Yanes, Photographer

Index illustrations copyright © 2002 and 2005 by Tobie Giddio

Produced in association with Anne B. Wright and John W. Kern

Jacket: Macaroni and Eggplant (page 60)
Frontispiece: Pickled Peaches (page 270)

ACKNOWLEDGMENTS

Every year we look forward to working on *The Best of Gourmet*, knowing we have a solid core of colleagues and professionals behind us. We would like to thank those who made this book look so beautiful, as well as those who ensured its recipes were delicious and easy to follow.

On the artistic front, *Gourmet* creative director Richard Ferretti has once again designed a book that reflects the sensibilities of the magazine and is a joy to peruse. The talented photographers whose images bring this book to life are Quentin Bacon, Matthew Hranek, John Kernick, David Loftus, Geoff Lung, Martyn Thompson (who also contributed the cover image), Mikkel Vang, and staff photographer Romulo Yanes. Photo editor Amy Koblenzer helped gather their images throughout this process.

Editors and wordsmiths also play a big role in this book. We relied on Shannon Rodgers Fox and her scrupulous eye to edit all of this book's recipes for consistency, while Jane Daniels Lear, Nichol Nelson, Lesley Porcelli, and Eric Hastie contributed to the helpful "Kitchen Notes" sprinkled throughout The Recipe Compendium.

Developing, testing, and tasting all the tempting menus and recipes that appear in this annual is an enormous endeavor, and the magazine's entire food department tackled the job with creativity and grace: Zanne Stewart, Kemp Minifie, Alexis Touchet, Paul Grimes, Shelley Wiseman, Ruth Cousineau, Gina Marie Miraglia Eriquez, Melissa Roberts-Matar, Maggie Ruggiero, Lillian Chou, and Ian Knauer.

The production aspects of putting this book together are time-consuming and, at times, complicated. We appreciate the hours Stephanie Stehofsky spent retrieving electronic files and solving computer glitches. Thanks also to Richard Elman for handling the flow of color photography, and to Marilyn Flaig, who once again compiled a clear and easy-to-use index.

Long-time project director Anne Wright and production editor John Kern complete our team. We thank them not only for their conscientious work but for their indispensable good cheer, which made the everyday work of this book go so smoothly.

TABLE OF CONTENTS

TIPS FOR USING GOURMET'S RECIPES

MEASURE LIQUIDS in glass or clear plastic liquid-measuring cups. **MEASURE DRY INGREDIENTS** in nesting dry-measuring cups (usually made of metal or plastic) that can be leveled off with a knife.

MEASURE FLOUR by spooning (not scooping) it into a dry-measuring cup and leveling off with a knife without tapping or shaking cup. **SIFT FLOUR** only when specified in recipe. If sifted flour is called for, sift flour before measuring. (Many brands say "presifted" on the label; disregard this.)

A SHALLOW BAKING PAN means an old-fashioned jelly-roll or four-sided cookie pan.

MEASURE SKILLETS AND BAKING PANS across the top, not across the bottom.

A WATER BATH for baking is prepared by putting your filled pan in a larger pan and adding enough boiling-hot water to the larger pan to reach halfway up the side of the smaller pan.

METAL PANS used for baking should be light-colored, unless otherwise specified. If using dark metal pans, including nonstick, your baked goods will likely brown more and the cooking times may be shorter.

ALL PRODUCE must be washed and dried before using. **FRESH HERBS OR GREENS** are prepped by first removing the leaves or fronds from the stems. The exception is cilantro, which has tender stems.

SALTED WATER for cooking requires 1 tablespoon of salt for every 4 quarts of water.

BLACK PEPPER in recipes is always freshly ground.

CHILES require protective gloves when handling.

CHEESES should be grated just before using. To finely grate Parmigiano-Reggiano and similar cheeses, use the small (1/8-inch) teardrop-shaped holes (not the ragged-edged holes) of a box or similar handheld grater. Other shaped holes, a microplane rasp, and pregrated cheese yield different volumes.

ZEST CITRUS FRUITS by removing the colored part of the rind only (avoid the bitter white pith). For strips, use a vegetable peeler. For grated zest, we prefer using a rasplike Microplane zester, which results in fluffier zest, so pack to measure.

TOAST SPICES in a dry heavy skillet over moderate heat, stirring, until fragrant and a shade or two darker. **TOAST NUTS** in a shallow baking pan in a 350°F oven until golden, 5 to 10 minutes. **TOAST SEEDS** as you would toast spices or nuts.

IF USING A CHARCOAL GRILL, open vents on bottom of grill, then light charcoal. When charcoal turns grayish white (about 15 minutes from lighting), hold your hand 5 inches above grill rack to determine heat for charcoal as follows:
Hot: When you can hold your hand there for 1 to 2 seconds.
Medium-hot: 3 to 4 seconds.
Low: 5 to 6 seconds.
IF USING A GAS GRILL, preheat burners on high, covered, 10 minutes, then, if necessary, reduce to heat specified in the recipe.

INTRODUCTION

For those of us who work at *Gourmet*, foreign travel means visiting every farmers market, specialty foods shop, winery, cooking school, and bistro that promises an exciting new taste. Adventures such as these tend to inspire our food editors to create breathtaking menus. This year, because so many different international flavors emerged from our kitchen, we decided to gather them all in a special new section, *The World at Your Table*.

If bucolic settings have anything to do with creative flow, Gina Marie Miraglia Eriquez knew that she could depend on her ancestral Sicily. Last spring, she studied with Sicilian cooking authority Anna Tasca Lanza on her winery estate near Palermo before spending time with cousins in the village of Fiumara di Piraino. Many of the exquisite dishes in her streetside *La Dolce Via* menu (page 52) will look familiar to you, while others, like the perciatelli and eggplant dish, might come as a surprise.

For years, Ruth Cousineau has drawn inspiration from Spain. Back in 1999, she went to Barcelona on a research trip and was so intrigued by the Mediterranean ingredients and how they were used that she returned again and again, adding Madrid and Seville to her itinerary. Along the way, tapas became a passion, and thoughts of combining these little dishes in a menu began to percolate. Then, as fate would have it, Ruth's son married a lovely Spanish woman. At the wedding in the Pyrenees, roasted red bell peppers with white anchovies were served, and Ruth's *Sketches of Spain* tapas menu (page 12) took shape.

And, once in awhile, a restaurant experience comes along that's so special it must be shared. Such is the case with a London hot spot that Maggie Ruggiero fell in love with and returned to several times. *Dinner at Moro* (page 46), by chefs Samuel and Samantha Clark, showcases some of the most delicious and accessible Spanish-Moroccan fusion dishes imaginable. Likewise, during research trips to Veracruz and Mexico City, Shelley Wiseman was impressed by chef Ricardo Muñoz Zurita's ability to combine Mexican village ingredients in sophisticated dishes. His creative gems (like black-bean stuffed plantain croqettes) can be found in the exciting menu *Passion Pink* (page 64).

Years of foreign travel have also taught us that the most authentic native tastes can be found in humble street food. When executive editor Doc Willoughby traveled to Turkey, his friend Ihsan lead him to his favorite kebab stand on the banks of the Bosporus in the Asian section of Istanbul. Many addictive lamb kebabs later, Doc and fellow cookbook author Chris Schlesinger re-created them from memory. Their recipe and those for other snacks from our travels are now yours for the taking (page 76).

As always, this volume also contains many exciting entertaining menus and recipes that were developed in *Gourmet*'s test kitchens last year. We hope that you will enjoy them all, in due season, and in the happy spirit in which they were created.

THE EDITORS OF GOURMET BOOKS

THE WORLD AT YOUR TABLE

Since 1941, *Gourmet* has explored the world's cuisines, bringing home tales of sultan's delight from Istanbul, white truffles from Italy, and salty fish sauce from Vietnam. Our readers today are just as savvy—they think nothing of going out for pad Thai one night, tacos the next, and sushi the third. The next frontier is learning to prepare these foods at home. And so we invite you on a whirlwind culinary tour, featuring eight exceptional menus and snacks from around the globe.

Our voyage starts in Spain, where we throw a lavish tapas party of tender salt cod in tomato garlic confit, unctuous short rib terrine, roasted red peppers strewn with plump white anchovies, and much more. Because this menu is so involved, we suggest dividing the recipes among friends.

South of the equator—where it's summer during our coldest months—we encounter a colorful Brazilian supper sparkling with warm, local flavor. Caipirinha cocktails, lamb with malagueta peppers and farofa crust, and billowy caramel coffee meringues prove a delicious antidote to the winter doldrums.

From there, we move on to Paris and a comforting bistro dinner that begins with an ethereal salmon and scallop terrine and ends with prune Armagnac sorbet. Conveniently, every course can be prepared at least one day ahead.

London, newly recognized as one of the world's premier food cities, provides two of our dinners. The first, an update of classic English cookery, includes mustard fennel pork loin and pistachio rhubarb trifle, a perfect balance of worldly decadence and British restraint. The other, from the celebrated restaurant Moro, sings with the complex flavors of Spain and Morocco.

No trip around the world is complete without a stop in Italy, and our alfresco meal transports you to the sun-drenched shores of Sicily. Think caponata, chickpea fritters, baby octopus salad, and veal involtini, plus plenty of good Italian cheeses, crusty bread, and sweet cannoli. Be sure to follow the detailed game plan if making this feast on your own.

The cuisine of Mexico City is sophisticated and wildly flavorful, as seen in dishes like black-bean-stuffed plantain croquettes and Veracruz-style shrimp. This colorful meal calls for bouquets of tropical blooms and your very best tequila.

A casual little South Indian supper yields big flavor in the guise of chicken and green bean coconut curry and a cooling carrot pachadi (see photo, opposite). Wedges of watermelon sprinkled with fennel salt make a refreshing—and easy—finale. In fact, if you prepare the curry a day ahead, this meal comes together very quickly.

If you're stumped by where to find guanabana purée, green cardamom pods, or other items called for in these recipes, turn to our Sources page at the back of the book. Though some of the ingredients may be exotic, you'll be pleasantly surprised by how easy it is to create these authentic dishes at home.

SKETCHES OF SPAIN

A TAPAS DINNER PARTY

SERVES 12

SALT COD IN TOMATO GARLIC CONFIT

**ROASTED PEPPERS WITH
BOQUERONES**

**CHICKEN EMPANADA WITH CHORIZO,
RAISINS, AND OLIVES**

RICH BEEF BROTH WITH CARROT

SHORT RIB TERRINE

HOT PEPPER AND GARLIC SHRIMP

MINTED EGGPLANT

**CAULIFLOWER WITH SERRANO
HAM AND TOMATO**

**POTATOES WITH PEPPERS
AND CHORIZO**

**ASSORTED SPANISH OLIVES AND
CHEESES**

DOMECQ MANZANILLA DRY SHERRY

BELONDRADE Y LURTON RUEDA '02

SEIS Y AZUL Y GARANZA NAVARRA '02

**DRIED FIGS IN RED WINE WITH
MAHÓN CHEESE ICE CREAM AND
SHERRY VINEGAR SYRUP**

PUMPKIN SEED BRITTLE

Most of the Spanish ingredients in this menu can be found in specialty foods shops and supermarkets. See Sources for other locations and websites.

SALT COD IN TOMATO GARLIC CONFIT

SERVES 12 (AS PART OF TAPAS BUFFET)

Active time: 40 min   Start to finish: 1¾ hr (plus up to 3 days for soaking cod)

1   lb center-cut skinless boneless salt cod (*bacalao*), rinsed well and cut into 1½-inch pieces
8   large garlic cloves, peeled
⅓   cup extra-virgin olive oil
4   (14-oz) cans diced tomatoes, drained
¼   teaspoon sugar
6   tablespoons mayonnaise
¼   cup crème fraîche
1   tablespoon water

Soak and poach cod:

▶ Cover cod with 2 inches of cold water in a large bowl and soak, chilled, changing water 3 times a day, up to 3 days (see cooks' note, below).

▶ Drain cod and transfer to a 3-quart saucepan, then add 6 cups water. Bring just to a simmer and remove from heat. (Cod will just begin to flake; do not boil or it will become tough.) Gently transfer cod with a slotted spatula to a paper-towel-lined plate to drain. Cover with a dampened paper towel and chill while making confit.

Make confit and cook fish:

▶ Cook garlic in oil in a 12-inch heavy skillet over moderately low heat, turning occasionally, until golden, 10 to 15 minutes. Add tomatoes and sugar and cook, stirring frequently, until tomatoes break down into a very thick sauce and oil separates, 45 minutes to 1 hour.

▶ Mash garlic cloves into sauce and add salt and pepper to taste. Spread sauce in a 3-quart gratin dish or other flameproof shallow baking dish and arrange fish over sauce.

▶ Preheat broiler.

▶ Whisk together mayonnaise, crème fraîche, and water and spread over each piece of fish. Broil fish 5 to 6 inches from heat just until mayonnaise mixture is lightly browned, about 2 minutes.

CLOCKWISE FROM TOP LEFT: potatoes with peppers and chorizo; cauliflower with serrano ham and tomato; rich beef broth with carrot; minted eggplant

Cooks' notes:

• Brands of salt cod differ in their degree of saltiness: A less salty variety may need only 1 day of soaking, while another could require up to 3. To test it, simply taste a small piece after 1 day; you want it to be pleasantly salty but not overwhelming.

• Confit can be made 2 days ahead and cooled, uncovered, then chilled, covered. Reheat before using.

ROASTED PEPPERS WITH BOQUERONES

SERVES 12 (AS PART OF TAPAS BUFFET)

Active time: 40 min   Start to finish: 2¾ hr (includes marinating)

In Spain, boquerones *can be a variety of small fish, pickled or not. In the U.S., however, the term always refers to anchovies that have been pickled in vinegar (which whitens them). They have a flavor similar to pickled herring.*

6   large red bell peppers (3 lb total)
1   tablespoon Sherry vinegar
1   teaspoon sugar
12   *boquerones* (white anchovy fillets in vinegar), drained, patted dry, and halved lengthwise

▶ Preheat broiler.

▶ Broil bell peppers on a broiler pan about 5 inches from heat, turning occasionally with tongs, until skins are blackened, 15 to 20 minutes. Transfer to a large bowl and cover bowl tightly with plastic wrap, then let steam 20 minutes.

▶ When peppers are cool enough to handle, peel them, reserving all juices in bowl, and discard stems and seeds. Cut peppers lengthwise into ¼-inch-wide strips. Pour pepper juices through a sieve into another bowl, then add vinegar and sugar to juices, stirring until sugar is dissolved, then stir in peppers. Marinate peppers at room temperature, stirring occasionally, at least 2 hours.

▶ Spoon peppers and juices into a shallow bowl and arrange anchovy strips decoratively on top.

Cooks' note:

• Peppers can marinate (without anchovies), covered and chilled, up to 3 days. Bring to room temperature before serving.

CHICKEN EMPANADA WITH CHORIZO, RAISINS, AND OLIVES

SERVES 12 (AS PART OF TAPAS BUFFET)
Active time: 1 hr   Start to finish: 3 hr (includes cooling)

  3 whole chicken legs, including thighs (2 to 2¼ lb total)
  1 teaspoon salt
  ¼ teaspoon black pepper
4½ tablespoons extra-virgin olive oil
  2 large onions, halved lengthwise, then cut lengthwise into ¼-inch-wide strips
  2 large garlic cloves, minced
  2 Turkish bay leaves or 1 California
  ⅓ cup finely diced Spanish chorizo (cured spiced pork sausage; 1½ oz; casings discarded if desired)
  ½ teaspoon Spanish smoked paprika (not hot)
  ¼ cup chopped pitted green olives
  ¼ cup golden raisins
  ½ cup dry white wine
  ½ cup reduced-sodium chicken broth
  1 lb frozen pizza dough, thawed

Make filling:

▶ Pat chicken dry and sprinkle with salt and pepper. Heat 2 tablespoons oil in a 12-inch heavy skillet over moderately high heat until hot but not smoking, then brown chicken, turning once, about 6 minutes total, and transfer to a plate. Sauté onions, garlic, and bay leaves in fat remaining in skillet, stirring frequently, until onions are softened, 4 to 5 minutes. Add chorizo and paprika and cook, stirring, 1 minute. Add olives, raisins, wine, and broth and bring to a boil, stirring and scraping up any brown bits. Return chicken to skillet along with any juices accumulated on plate, then reduce heat to moderately low and simmer chicken, covered, turning over once, until tender, 25 to 30 minutes total.

▶ Transfer chicken to a clean plate. (Sauce in skillet should be the consistency of heavy cream; if it's not, briskly simmer until slightly thickened, about 5 minutes.) When chicken is cool enough to handle, discard skin and bones and coarsely chop meat. Stir chicken into sauce and discard bay leaves. Season with salt and pepper, then cool filling, uncovered, about 30 minutes.

Form and bake empanada:

▶ Form dough into a ball, then wrap in oiled plastic wrap (oiled side in) and let stand at room temperature 30 minutes.

▶ Put oven rack in middle position and preheat oven to 400°F. Grease a 15- by 10-inch shallow baking pan (1 inch deep) with 1 tablespoon oil.

▶ Divide dough in half, then roll out 1 half (keep remaining dough covered with plastic wrap) on a floured surface with a floured rolling pin into a 15- by 10-inch rectangle and transfer to baking pan. Spread filling evenly over dough, leaving a 1-inch border, and moisten border with water. Roll out remaining dough in same manner, then arrange over filling and press edges together to seal. Roll edges in and press to form a decorative rim. Make a 1-inch hole (a steam vent) in center of empanada.

▶ Bake empanada 15 minutes, then brush crust with ¾ tablespoon oil and bake until crust is golden brown, 20 to 25 minutes more. Remove from oven and brush empanada with remaining ¾ tablespoon oil. Cool 10 minutes in pan on a rack, then slide empanada onto rack using a wide metal spatula and cool to warm.

▶ Cut empanada into squares and serve warm or at room temperature.

Cooks' notes:
• Filling can be made 2 days ahead and cooled, uncovered, then chilled, covered. Bring to room temperature before using.
• Empanada can be made 4 hours ahead and kept, uncovered, at room temperature. If desired, reheat in a preheated 375°F oven 15 minutes.

RICH BEEF BROTH WITH CARROT

MAKES ABOUT 4 CUPS (SERVING 12 AS PART OF TAPAS BUFFET)
Active time: 30 min   Start to finish: 1 day (includes chilling)

Having broth as a tapa is an old custom that's becoming popular again in both Spain and the U.S. Food editor Ruth Cousineau set out to make just the broth, but the resulting short rib meat was so delicious (even after cooking in broth all that time) that she didn't want to waste it, so she came up with a use for it in a terrine (recipe follows). This recipe is traditionally made with oxtails, but we substituted short ribs and beef shanks because they're easier to get in most supermarkets. If you'd like to try it with oxtails instead of ribs and shanks, use 6 pounds of oxtails (preferably from grass-fed beef, such as Niman Ranch).

4 lb short ribs or flanken

2 lb meaty beef shanks

2 onions, left unpeeled, quartered

2 celery ribs, quartered

2 carrots, 1 quartered and 1 cut into ¼-inch dice

4 fresh parsley stems (without leaves)

1 fresh thyme sprig

1 Turkish or ½ California bay leaf

4 whole black peppercorns

14 cups water

1½ teaspoons salt

Special equipment: **cheesecloth; kitchen string; 12 demitasse or espresso cups**

▶ Put oven rack in lower third of oven and preheat oven to 450°F.

▶ Spread short ribs, shanks, onions, celery, and quartered carrot in a large flameproof roasting pan and roast, turning occasionally, until well browned, about 1 hour.

▶ Wrap parsley, thyme, bay leaf, and peppercorns in cheesecloth and tie into a bundle with string to make a bouquet garni.

▶ Transfer meat (with bones) and roasted vegetables to a 6- to 8-quart pot and add 12 cups water, salt, and bouquet garni. Straddle roasting pan across 2 burners, then add remaining 2 cups water and deglaze pan by boiling, stirring and scraping up brown bits, 1 minute. Add deglazing liquid to pot, then bring to a boil, skimming froth. Reduce heat to low and gently simmer, uncovered, until liquid is reduced to about 5 cups, 7 to 8 hours.

▶ Transfer mixture to a bowl and cool completely, uncovered, about 1 hour, then chill, covered, at least 8 hours.

▶ Remove fat. Reheat mixture in cleaned pot over moderate heat until warm. Discard beef shanks (meat and bone), then transfer short ribs to a platter and, when cool enough to handle, discard bones and fat. Finely chop short ribs and reserve for terrine (recipe follows). If not using meat within 1 hour, chill, covered. Pour broth though a cheesecloth-lined sieve into a 1½-quart saucepan and skim off any remaining fat. Bring broth to a simmer and season with salt.

▶ Cook diced carrot in a small saucepan of boiling salted water until just tender, about 4 minutes. Drain in sieve and divide among demitasse cups, then add broth.

Cooks' notes:
• Meat and vegetables can be chilled in broth up to 1 day.
• Broth can be strained 4 days ahead and cooled, uncovered, then chilled, covered. Reheat and season before using. (Chill raw diced carrot in a sealed plastic bag until ready to cook.)

SHORT RIB TERRINE

SERVES 12 (AS PART OF TAPAS BUFFET)
Active time: 20 min   Start to finish: 25 hr (includes preparing short ribs)

If you only have sweet Spanish smoked paprika on hand, you can mix 1½ teaspoons of it with ⅛ teaspoon cayenne as a substitute for hot Spanish smoked paprika.

8 large garlic cloves, peeled

½ cup extra-virgin olive oil

1½ teaspoons hot Spanish smoked paprika

1 teaspoon salt

½ teaspoon black pepper

6 cups finely chopped cooked short rib meat (reserved from rich beef broth; recipe precedes)

Accompaniments: **thin slices of crusty bread; caper berries; sea salt**

▶ Cook garlic in oil in a 10-inch heavy skillet over low heat, turning occasionally, until tender and golden, about 15 minutes. Transfer garlic with a slotted spoon to a cutting board and mash to a paste with a fork. Cook paprika, salt, and pepper in oil remaining in skillet over low heat, stirring, until fragrant, about 1 minute.

▶ Stir together paprika oil, garlic paste, and short rib meat in a large bowl until combined well. Pack mixture into a 5- to 6-cup crock, terrine, or bowl and let stand at room temperature 1 hour to allow flavors to develop. Serve at room temperature.

Cooks' note:
• Terrine can be made 2 days ahead and chilled, covered. Bring to room temperature before serving.

HOT PEPPER AND GARLIC SHRIMP

SERVES 12 (AS PART OF TAPAS BUFFET)

Active time: 35 min   Start to finish: 35 min

  2 lb large shrimp in shell (21 to 25 per lb), peeled, leaving tail and first segment of shell intact, and deveined
 10 large garlic cloves, thinly sliced
 ¼ teaspoon dried hot red pepper flakes
 ½ teaspoon fine sea salt
 ⅓ cup extra-virgin olive oil
  1 tablespoon fresh lemon juice

Accompaniment: **lemon wedges**

▶ Pat shrimp dry. Cook garlic, red pepper flakes, and sea salt in oil in a 12-inch heavy skillet over moderately low heat, stirring occasionally, until garlic is pale golden, 4 to 5 minutes. Increase heat to moderately high, then add shrimp and sauté, turning occasionally, until shrimp are just cooked through, 3 to 4 minutes. Remove from heat and stir in lemon juice, then transfer to a serving bowl. Serve warm or at room temperature.

MINTED EGGPLANT

SERVES 12 (AS PART OF TAPAS BUFFET)

Active time: 15 min   Start to finish: 2½ hr (includes marinating)

Ruth Cousineau learned this technique in Seville; it ensures the eggplant maintains its shape and flavor perfectly.

 ¼ cup Sherry vinegar
  3 medium eggplants (2 lb total), trimmed and each cut lengthwise into 8 wedges
 ¾ teaspoon salt
  1 garlic clove, minced
 ½ teaspoon dried oregano, crumbled
 ⅛ teaspoon black pepper
  6 tablespoons extra-virgin olive oil
  2 tablespoons finely chopped fresh mint
  2 tablespoons finely chopped fresh flat-leaf parsley

Special equipment: **a 12-inch collapsible steamer basket or a pasta pot with a shallow perforated colander-steamer insert**

▶ Bring 1 inch water and 2 tablespoons vinegar to a boil in a large pot (or a deep skillet with a lid). Arrange eggplant, skin sides down, in steamer basket and sprinkle with ½ teaspoon salt, then steam, covered, until tender, 15 to 20 minutes. Transfer basket to sink and let eggplant drain 5 minutes.
▶ Transfer eggplant to a deep platter. Whisk together garlic, oregano, pepper, remaining ¼ teaspoon salt, and remaining 2 tablespoons vinegar in a small bowl, then add oil in a slow stream, whisking until combined. Pour dressing over eggplant while still warm and let marinate at room temperature, basting with dressing several times, 2 hours. Sprinkle with mint and parsley just before serving.

CAULIFLOWER WITH SERRANO HAM AND TOMATO

SERVES 12 (AS PART OF TAPAS BUFFET)

Active time: 30 min   Start to finish: 30 min

  1 large head cauliflower (2½ lb), cored and cut into 1-inch florets
 ⅓ cup chopped red onion
 ⅓ cup extra-virgin olive oil
  1 cup grape or cherry tomatoes, cut into ¼-inch dice
 ¼ lb thinly sliced serrano ham, cut into ¼-inch pieces
1½ tablespoons fresh lemon juice
 ¼ cup finely chopped fresh flat-leaf parsley

▶ Cook cauliflower in a large pot of boiling salted water (see Tips, page 8) until just tender, 4 to 6 minutes. Drain well in a colander, then transfer to a large bowl.
▶ While cauliflower boils, cook onion in oil in a 10-inch heavy skillet over moderate heat, stirring occasionally, 2 minutes. Add tomatoes and ham and cook, stirring frequently, until just heated through, about 2 minutes. Remove from heat and stir in lemon juice and parsley.
▶ Pour tomato mixture over cauliflower and toss to coat, then season with salt and pepper. Serve warm or at room temperature.

Cooks' note:
• Cauliflower can be cut into florets and onion, tomatoes, and ham can be cut 1 day ahead and chilled separately in sealed plastic bags.

POTATOES WITH PEPPERS AND CHORIZO

SERVES 12 (AS PART OF TAPAS BUFFET)
Active time: 45 min   Start to finish: 1 hr

- 2 lb medium boiling potatoes, peeled
- ½ cup extra-virgin olive oil
- ½ teaspoon salt
- 2 fresh jalapeño chiles
- 1 large onion, halved lengthwise, then cut lengthwise into ¼-inch-wide strips
- 1 lb green bell or Italian frying peppers, cut lengthwise into ¼-inch-wide strips
- ½ cup finely chopped Spanish chorizo (cured spiced pork sausage; 2 oz), casings discarded if desired
- ¾ cup dry white wine

▶ Make a crosswise cut halfway through 1 potato, then break it apart. Turn potato cut sides down, then cut and break halves in same manner. Repeat halving and breaking until pieces are about 1½ inches. Repeat with remaining potatoes.

▶ Heat oil in a 12-inch heavy nonstick skillet over moderately high heat until hot but not smoking, then sauté potatoes with salt, turning occasionally, until browned and just cooked through, 15 to 20 minutes. Transfer potatoes with a slotted spoon to a bowl, reserving oil in skillet.

▶ Cut a 1½-inch lengthwise slit in each chile, then add to skillet along with onion, peppers, and chorizo and reduce heat to moderate. Cook, uncovered, stirring frequently, until vegetables are softened, 5 to 6 minutes. Add wine and boil until reduced to about ¼ cup, 3 to 4 minutes. Discard chiles, then add pepper mixture to potatoes along with salt and pepper to taste and toss well. Serve warm or at room temperature.

Cooks' note:

• Onion and peppers can be cut into strips and chorizo can be chopped 1 day ahead and chilled separately in sealed plastic bags.

DRIED FIGS IN RED WINE WITH MAHÓN CHEESE ICE CREAM AND SHERRY VINEGAR SYRUP

SERVES 12 (AS PART OF TAPAS BUFFET)
Active time: 25 min   Start to finish: 7 hr (includes making ice cream and syrup)

- 1½ lb soft dried Mission figs, hard stem ends discarded
- 2 cups dry red wine
- ½ cup sugar
- 3 (3- by 1-inch) strips fresh orange zest, removed with a vegetable peeler
- 2 (3- by 1-inch) strips fresh lemon zest, removed with a vegetable peeler

Special equipment: **parchment paper**
Accompaniments: **Mahón cheese ice cream (recipe follows); Sherry vinegar syrup (page 21)**

▶ Put oven rack in middle position and preheat oven to 350°F.

▶ Put figs in a 3-quart shallow glass or ceramic baking dish. Bring wine with sugar and zests to a boil in a 1-quart heavy saucepan, stirring until sugar is dissolved, then pour over figs (figs will not be covered by liquid). Bake figs, uncovered, stirring occasionally, until figs have absorbed about two thirds of liquid and are very tender but still hold their shape, 50 to 60 minutes.

▶ Put a sheet of parchment directly on figs, pressing them into liquid, then let stand at room temperature 1 hour.

▶ Serve figs with a bit of their juices and small scoops of ice cream, all drizzled with Sherry vinegar syrup.

Cooks' note:

• Figs can be made 1 week ahead and chilled, covered. Bring to room temperature before serving.

MAHÓN CHEESE ICE CREAM
MAKES ABOUT 1 QUART
Active time: 15 min   Start to finish: 7 hr (includes freezing)

  3 cups whole milk
  3 large eggs
 ½ cup sugar
  4 oz cream cheese, softened
  4 oz Spanish Mahón or Danish Fontina cheese, rind
      discarded and cheese coarsely grated (1 cup)
 ½ teaspoon vanilla

Special equipment: **an instant-read thermometer; an ice cream maker**

▶ Bring milk just to a boil in a 1½- to 2-quart heavy saucepan. Whisk together eggs, sugar, and a pinch of salt in a bowl, then add hot milk in a slow stream, whisking. Pour custard back into saucepan and cook over moderately low heat, stirring with a wooden spoon, until it registers 170 to 175°F on thermometer, 2 to 3 minutes. Immediately pour custard through a fine-mesh sieve into a clean bowl, then add cheeses and vanilla, stirring until cheeses are completely melted and incorporated. Cover surface of custard with a round of wax paper and chill until very cold, about 4 hours.
▶ Freeze custard in ice cream maker. Transfer ice cream to an airtight container and freeze at least 2 hours.
▶ Let soften at room temperature 20 minutes before serving.

Cooks' note:
• Ice cream can be made 1 week ahead.

SHERRY VINEGAR SYRUP
MAKES ABOUT ½ CUP
Active time: 5 min   Start to finish: 1 hr (includes cooling)

 ½ cup Sherry vinegar
 ½ cup packed light brown sugar

▶ Bring vinegar and sugar to a boil in a 1-quart heavy nonreactive saucepan over moderate heat, stirring until sugar is dissolved. Reduce heat and simmer until slightly syrupy and reduced to about ½ cup, about 15 minutes. Pour into a heatproof bowl and cool completely.

Cooks' note:
• Syrup can be made 1 week ahead and kept in an airtight container at room temperature.

PUMPKIN SEED BRITTLE
SERVES 12 (AS PART OF TAPAS BUFFET)
Active time: 30 min   Start to finish: 30 min

  1 cup sugar
 ½ cup water
 ⅛ teaspoon fine sea salt
 ¾ cup raw green (hulled) pumpkin seeds
      (not toasted; 4 oz)

Special equipment: **parchment paper; a candy thermometer**

▶ Put a 24- by 12-inch sheet of parchment on a work surface and anchor corners with pieces of tape. Bring sugar, water, and sea salt to a boil in a 2-quart heavy saucepan over moderate heat, stirring until sugar is dissolved. Cook mixture, without stirring, washing down any sugar crystals from side of pan with a pastry brush dipped in cold water, until syrup registers 238°F (soft-ball stage) on thermometer, 10 to 12 minutes (sugar syrup will be colorless). Remove from heat and stir in seeds with a wooden spoon, then continue stirring until syrup crystallizes, 3 to 4 minutes.
▶ Return pan to moderate heat and cook, stirring constantly, until sugar melts completely (sugar will continue to dry and become grainy before melting) and turns a deep caramel color, 4 to 5 minutes more (seeds will be toasted). Carefully pour hot caramel mixture onto parchment and carefully cover with another sheet. Immediately roll out (between sheets of parchment) as thinly as possible with a rolling pin, pressing firmly. Remove top sheet of parchment and immediately cut brittle into pieces with a heavy knife or pizza wheel. Cool brittle completely, then peel paper from bottom. (Alternately, break brittle into pieces once cool.)

Cooks' note:
• Brittle can be made 2 weeks ahead and kept, layers separated by wax paper, in an airtight container.

FOLLOWING PAGES: pumpkin seed brittle; dried figs in red wine with Mahón cheese ice cream and sherry vinegar syrup

GAME PLAN

2 WEEKS AHEAD
-Make pumpkin seed brittle

1 WEEK AHEAD
-Make dried figs in red wine
-Make Mahón cheese ice cream
-Make Sherry vinegar syrup for drizzling on ice cream

4 DAYS AHEAD
-Make rich beef broth

3 DAYS AHEAD
-Start soaking salt cod
-Marinate roasted peppers

2 DAYS AHEAD
-Make tomato garlic confit for salt cod
-Make chicken filling for empanada
-Make short rib terrine

1 DAY AHEAD
-Thaw pizza dough in refrigerator for empanada
-Cut cauliflower into florets and cut onion, tomatoes, and ham for cauliflower dish
-Cut onion and peppers into strips and chop chorizo for potato dish

DAY OF TAPAS BUFFET
-Bring short rib terrine to room temperature
-Bring figs to room temperature
-Broil salt cod with tomato garlic confit
-Bake empanada
-Make cauliflower with serrano ham and tomato
-Make minted eggplant
-Make potatoes with peppers and chorizo
-Make hot pepper and garlic shrimp
-Assemble roasted peppers with *boquerones*
-Reheat rich beef broth and cook diced carrot

SUPPER SAMBA

THE FLAVORS OF BRAZIL

SERVES 8

CAIPIRINHAS

SHRIMP AND BLACK-EYED PEA "CROQUETTES"

CALABAZA, CORN, AND COCONUT SOUP

**ROASTED RACKS OF LAMB WITH
MALAGUETA PEPPER AND FAROFA CRUST**

BRAZILIAN-STYLE COLLARD GREENS

YUCA GRATIN

CASA LAPOSTOLLE CUVÉE ALEXANDRE MERLOT '01

CARAMEL COFFEE MERINGUES

DOMAINE DE LA RECTORIE BANYULS
VIN DOUX NATUREL MUTÉ SUR GRAINS '01

CAIPIRINHAS

MAKES 8 DRINKS
Active time: 20 min   Start to finish: 20 min

Cachaça, *a liquor made from sugarcane, gives these drinks their distinctive flavor. In Brazil it is traditional to make caipirinhas one or two at a time, as we do here. For ease of entertaining, however, you can simply combine all the ingredients in a pitcher.*

  4 **limes**
  ½ **cup sugar**
     Ice cubes
1½ **cups *cachaça* (from a 500-ml bottle)**

▶ Quarter 1 lime lengthwise, then cut each quarter in half crosswise and divide pieces between 2 (6-ounce) glasses.
▶ Add 1 tablespoon sugar to each glass, then muddle lime pieces by pounding and pressing with a wooden spoon until sugar is dissolved. Fill each glass with ice and add 3 tablespoons (1½ ounces) *cachaça* to each, stirring well. Make 6 more cocktails in same manner.

ABOVE: shrimp "croquettes"; caramel coffee meringue

SHRIMP AND BLACK-EYED PEA "CROQUETTES"

MAKES 24 HORS D'OEUVRES
Active time: 1½ hr   Start to finish: 9½ hr (includes soaking peas)

If you substitute regular bread crumbs for the panko, *the coating will be heavier and the texture denser. In this recipe, the peas are soaked but not precooked before grinding, much like in a falafel.*

  ⅔ **cup dried black-eyed peas (¼ lb), picked over**
  1 **medium onion, chopped**
  ½ **cup loosely packed fresh cilantro leaves**
  3 **drained bottled red *malagueta* peppers (see Sources)**
1¼ **teaspoons salt**
 24 **medium shrimp in shell (¾ lb), peeled, leaving tail and first segment of shell intact, and deveined**
  2 **large eggs, lightly beaten**
1½ **cups *panko* (Japanese bread crumbs; see Sources) or plain coarse dry bread crumbs**
     About 6 cups vegetable oil (48 fl oz)

Special equipment: a deep-fat thermometer
Accompaniment: lime wedges

▶ Soak peas in water to cover by 2 inches at least 8 hours and up to 12. Drain in a colander.

▶ Put oven rack in middle position and preheat oven to 250°F. Line a baking sheet with wax paper.

▶ Pulse peas, onion, cilantro, peppers, and 1 teaspoon salt in a food processor until finely chopped, then transfer to a bowl.

▶ Toss shrimp with remaining ¼ teaspoon salt. Press a scant tablespoon pea mixture around each shrimp, encasing shrimp in a thin even layer but leaving tail (and shell) exposed, then transfer to baking sheet.

▶ Put eggs and *panko* in 2 separate shallow bowls. Holding 1 shrimp by the tail, dip coated portion of shrimp first into egg, letting excess drip off, and then into crumbs, returning shrimp to baking sheet. Coat remaining shrimp in same manner.

▶ Line another baking sheet with paper towels. Heat 1¼ inches oil in a 5- to 6-quart heavy pot (9 to 10 inches in diameter) until it registers 350°F on thermometer. Fry croquettes in 4 batches, turning over once or twice, until deep golden, 2 to 3 minutes per batch, transferring with a slotted spoon to paper-towel-lined baking sheet. Keep fried croquettes warm in oven while frying remainder, returning oil to 350°F between batches.

▶ Serve croquettes immediately.

Cooks' note:

• Croquettes can be coated with pea mixture, egg, and *panko* (but not fried) 1 hour ahead and chilled, covered.

CALABAZA, CORN, AND COCONUT SOUP
SERVES 8 (FIRST COURSE)
Active time: 40 min   Start to finish: 40 min

For soup

- 2 tablespoons olive oil
- 1 medium onion, coarsely chopped
- ¼ cup finely chopped fresh cilantro stems
- 2 garlic cloves, coarsely chopped
- 1 (2¼-lb) piece calabaza squash or 1 (2½-lb) whole kabocha squash, peeled, seeded, and cut into ½-inch pieces (6 cups)
- 4 cups water
- 1¼ cups well-stirred canned unsweetened coconut milk (12 oz)
- 3 ears of corn (fresh or thawed frozen), kernels cut off and reserved for relish (below) and cobs halved crosswise
- 2 teaspoons salt
- ¼ teaspoon cayenne

For corn relish

- 4½ teaspoons fresh lime juice
- ¼ teaspoon salt
  Pinch of sugar
- 2 tablespoons olive oil
- 2 cups corn kernels (see above)
- 2 tablespoons coarsely chopped fresh cilantro
- 1 tablespoon finely chopped shallot

Make soup:

▶ Heat oil in a 4- to 5-quart heavy pot over moderately high heat until hot but not smoking, then sauté onion, stirring occasionally, until beginning to soften and edges are browned, about 4 minutes. Add cilantro stems and garlic and cook, stirring occasionally, 3 minutes. Add squash pieces and cook, stirring frequently, 3 minutes. Stir in water, coconut milk, corn cobs, salt, and cayenne and simmer, uncovered, stirring occasionally, until squash is very tender, about 15 minutes.

Prepare corn relish while soup simmers:

▶ Whisk together lime juice, salt, and sugar in a bowl, then add oil and whisk until combined.

▶ Cook corn kernels in a saucepan of boiling salted water (see Tips, page 8) until just tender, 2 to 3 minutes. Drain in a sieve, then rinse under cold water to stop cooking. Drain well, then transfer to dressing along with cilantro and shallot and toss well to coat.

Finish soup:

▶ Discard corn cobs, then purée soup in batches in a blender (use caution when blending hot liquids) until smooth, transferring to a 2-quart measure.

▶ Divide soup among bowls and gently stir ¼ cup corn relish into each.

Cooks' notes:

• Soup (without corn relish) can be made 2 days ahead and chilled, covered. Reheat before serving.

• Corn relish can be made 1 hour ahead and kept, covered, at room temperature.

ROASTED RACKS OF LAMB WITH MALAGUETA PEPPER AND FAROFA CRUST

SERVES 8

Active time: 45 min   Start to finish: 1½ hr

If you're making this entire menu in a single oven, we recommend baking the yuca gratin ahead; while it cooks, brown the lamb and coat with the sauce and farofa. *When the gratin comes out of the oven, the lamb can go in. (The gratin will stay warm while the lamb bakes and stands.)*

½ stick (¼ cup) unsalted butter
¾ cup *farinha de mandioca* (manioc flour; not toasted; see Sources)
1½ cups chopped onion
5 garlic cloves
7 bottled red *malagueta* peppers (see Sources)
1 teaspoon sugar
1 teaspoon cider vinegar
1 tablespoon plus ½ teaspoon salt
3 tablespoons olive oil
3 (1½-lb) frenched racks of lamb (8 ribs each), trimmed of all but a thin layer of fat
3 tablespoons finely chopped fresh flat-leaf parsley

Special equipment: **an instant-read thermometer**

▶ Put oven rack in middle position and preheat oven to 400°F.

▶ Heat butter in a 10-inch heavy skillet over moderate heat until foam subsides, then cook flour, stirring, until golden brown, 3 to 4 minutes. Transfer to a small bowl.

▶ Purée onion, garlic, peppers, sugar, vinegar, and ½ teaspoon salt in a blender until smooth, adding 1 to 2 tablespoons water if needed to facilitate puréeing.

▶ Heat 2 tablespoons oil in a large nonstick skillet over moderate heat until hot but not smoking, then cook purée, stirring, until thickened, 3 to 4 minutes. (Don't worry if mixture turns blue-green; this sometimes results from the interaction of vinegar and immature garlic.) Reserve 5 tablespoons purée in a small bowl (for coating lamb) and transfer remainder to another small bowl (to be served on the side with lamb).

▶ Sprinkle lamb with remaining tablespoon salt. Heat remaining tablespoon oil in cleaned 10-inch skillet over moderately high heat until hot but not smoking, then brown lamb 1 rack at a time, turning over once, about 4 minutes per rack. Transfer racks to a large roasting pan, arranging with bones curving downward.

▶ Spread 1½ tablespoons *malagueta* purée over meaty part of each rack of lamb, excluding ends. Stir parsley into *farofa* mixture, then pat mixture onto lamb (over purée) to coat, pressing gently to adhere.

▶ Roast lamb until thermometer inserted diagonally 2 inches into center (do not touch bone) registers 125°F (for medium-rare), 20 to 25 minutes. Transfer to a cutting board and let racks stand 15 minutes (internal temperature will rise to about 130°F).

▶ Cut each rack into chops and serve remaining purée on the side.

Cooks' notes:
• *Farofa* can be made 1 day ahead and chilled, covered. Bring to room temperature before stirring in parsley.
• *Malagueta* purée can be made 1 day ahead and chilled, covered.

BRAZILIAN-STYLE COLLARD GREENS

SERVES 8

Active time: 15 min   Start to finish: 15 min

2½ lb collard greens, leaves halved lengthwise and stems and center ribs discarded
4 teaspoons olive oil
½ teaspoon salt
¼ teaspoon black pepper

▶ Stack half of collard leaves and roll into a cigar shape. Cut crosswise into very thin strips (⅛ inch wide) with a sharp knife. Repeat with remaining leaves.

▶ Heat 2 teaspoons oil in a heavy 12-inch skillet over moderate heat until hot but not smoking, then cook half of collards, tossing, until just tender and bright green, about 1 minute, and transfer to a serving dish. Cook remaining collards in remaining 2 teaspoons oil in same manner, then toss all of collards with salt and pepper. Serve immediately.

YUCA GRATIN

SERVES 8
Active time: 20 min   Start to finish: 1 hr

1½ lb frozen yuca (not thawed; do not substitute fresh)
 2 cups heavy cream
 2 garlic cloves, finely chopped
 ¾ teaspoon salt
 ¼ teaspoon black pepper

▸ Put oven rack in middle position and preheat oven to 400°F.

▸ Cook yuca in a 4- to 5-quart pot of boiling salted water (see Tips, page 8) until fork-tender, about 25 minutes (thinner pieces may need less time and can be removed early with a slotted spoon).

▸ While yuca cooks, bring cream, garlic, salt, and pepper just to a boil, uncovered, in a 2-quart saucepan over moderate heat, then remove from heat.

▸ Drain yuca. When cool enough to handle, remove and discard thin fibrous cores if necessary, then cut yuca crosswise into ¼-inch-thick slices. Layer slices evenly in a 2- to 2½-quart shallow ovenproof baking dish.

▸ Pour cream mixture over yuca. Bake gratin until cream is thickened and top is golden brown in spots, about 30 minutes.

Cooks' note:
• Gratin can be baked 1 hour ahead and kept, loosely covered with foil, at room temperature.

CARAMEL COFFEE MERINGUES

SERVES 8
Active time: 20 min   Start to finish: 3¼ hr (includes chilling)

1½ cups sugar
 3 tablespoons instant-espresso powder (see Sources)
 5 large egg whites at room temperature 30 minutes
 ½ cup water
1½ cups heavy cream

Special equipment: **8 (5- to 6-oz) ramekins (see Sources)**

Make meringues:

▸ Put oven rack in lower third of oven and preheat oven to 500°F. Lightly oil ramekins.

▸ Stir together 1 cup sugar and 2 tablespoons espresso powder in a small bowl. Beat whites with a pinch of salt in a large bowl with an electric mixer at medium speed until they just hold soft peaks. Add sugar mixture a little at a time, beating, then increase speed to high and continue to beat until whites hold stiff, glossy peaks.

▸ Spoon meringue into ramekins, forming gentle swirling peaks in tops. Arrange ramekins on a baking sheet and bake until meringues are slightly puffed and a shade darker, 4 to 5 minutes (meringues will still be very soft). Transfer ramekins to a rack and cool 30 minutes, then chill at least 3 hours. (Meringues will deflate slightly and pull away from sides of ramekins.)

Make syrup:

▸ Stir together ¼ cup water and remaining tablespoon espresso powder in a small glass.

▸ Bring remaining ½ cup sugar and remaining ¼ cup water to a boil in a 1- to 1½-quart heavy saucepan, stirring until sugar is dissolved and washing down any crystals from side of pan with a pastry brush dipped in water. Boil syrup, without stirring, gently swirling pan, until mixture is a deep golden caramel. Remove from heat and carefully pour in espresso mixture (liquid will bubble and steam), then stir until well combined (if necessary, stir over low heat until caramel is dissolved). Transfer syrup to a heatproof bowl and cool to room temperature, about 20 minutes.

Make topping and serve meringues:

▸ Just before serving, beat heavy cream with cleaned beaters until it just holds soft peaks. Drizzle each meringue with 1 tablespoon syrup and top generously with whipped cream.

Cooks' notes:
• The egg whites in this recipe will not be fully cooked, which may be of concern if salmonella is a problem in your area.
• Meringues can be chilled, loosely covered, up to 6 hours.
• Syrup can be made 1 day ahead and kept, covered, at room temperature.

CHEZ NOUS

A BISTRO DINNER IN PARIS

SERVES 8

**SALMON AND SCALLOP TERRINE
WITH FRISÉE SALAD**

**BRAISED RABBIT WITH GRAINY
MUSTARD SAUCE**

**FRENCH LENTILS WITH CARROTS
AND PEARL ONIONS**

LUNA NAPA COUNTY PINOT GRIGIO '03

PRUNE ARMAGNAC SORBET

ORANGE CORKSCREW TUILES

SALMON AND SCALLOP TERRINE WITH FRISÉE SALAD

SERVES 8
Active time: 1 hr   Start to finish: 2 hr

For terrine

- 2 long medium-thick leeks
- ½ cup dry white wine
- 1½ cups water
- ¼ cup chopped onion (½ small)
- 2 tablespoons finely chopped carrot
- 4 long fresh cilantro sprigs plus 2 tablespoons chopped leaves
- 2 tablespoons minced peeled fresh ginger
- 1 teaspoon coriander seeds, toasted (see Tips, page 8) and crushed
- ½ teaspoon salt
- ⅜ teaspoon white pepper
- ⅓ lb salmon fillet, skin, pin bones, and any dark flesh discarded
- ⅔ lb medium sea scallops (about 13), tough muscle removed from side of each if necessary
- 1 large egg white, lightly beaten (2 tablespoons)
- 6 tablespoons mild olive oil

For salad

- 2 tablespoons white-wine vinegar
- ¼ teaspoon salt
- ⅛ teaspoon white pepper
- ¼ cup extra-virgin olive oil
- ¼ lb frisée (French curly endive), torn into bite-size pieces (4 cups)
- 2 Belgian endives, halved lengthwise, cored, and sliced crosswise
- 1 cup thinly sliced radicchio leaves (from 1 head)
- 1 teaspoon *fleur de sel* or kosher salt
- ½ teaspoon coriander seeds, toasted (see Tips, page 8) and crushed
- 2 tablespoons finely chopped fresh cilantro

Special equipment: a 1-qt loaf pan (preferably 8 by 4 inches; about 2¼ inches deep); a kitchen scale (optional)

Prepare leeks and broth for terrine:

▶ Discard any discolored leaves from leeks, then cut off root end (to expose layers) and discard. Thinly slice enough of dark green ends to measure ¼ cup. Wash sliced leeks well and

reserve for broth. Keep remainder of leeks for lining.
▶ Bring wine and water to a boil in a 2-quart saucepan with sliced leeks, onion, carrot, cilantro sprigs, 1 tablespoon ginger, ½ teaspoon crushed coriander seeds, ⅛ teaspoon salt, and ⅛ teaspoon white pepper, then simmer, partially covered, 20 minutes. Pour broth through a fine-mesh sieve into a bowl, pressing hard on and then discarding solids. (You will have 1 to 1½ cups broth.) Set bowl in a larger bowl of ice and cold water and chill broth until cold, 5 to 10 minutes.
▶ While broth is simmering, slit 1 side of each leek lengthwise, cutting only to center, and peel off layers. Rinse layers in warm water to remove any grit, then cook in a 6- to 8-quart pot of boiling salted water (see Tips, page 8) until tender, about 10 minutes. Transfer with tongs to a bowl of ice and cold water to stop cooking, then spread layers flat on paper towels and pat dry.

Make terrine:

▶ Put oven rack in middle position and preheat oven to 325°F.
▶ Lightly oil loaf pan, then line bottom and long sides of pan by draping some of leeks crosswise over bottom and up long sides of pan, allowing at least 1 inch of leeks to hang over each side.
▶ Cut salmon into 1-inch cubes, then weigh on scale (if using) with enough scallops (about 3) to total ½ lb and set aside together.
▶ Purée remaining ½ lb scallops (about 10) with 1 tablespoon egg white, ⅛ teaspoon salt, and ⅛ teaspoon white pepper in a food processor until smooth. Add ½ cup cooled broth and blend well. With motor running, add 3 tablespoons oil in a slow stream until incorporated. Transfer scallop purée to lined terrine with a rubber spatula and smooth top evenly.
▶ Stir together chopped cilantro leaves, ⅛ teaspoon salt, and remaining tablespoon ginger and ½ teaspoon crushed coriander seeds in a small bowl, then sprinkle evenly over scallop purée.
▶ Purée salmon and scallop mixture with remaining tablespoon egg white, ⅛ teaspoon salt, and ⅛ teaspoon white pepper in processor until smooth. Add ½ cup cooled broth and blend well. With motor running, add remaining 3 tablespoons oil in a slow stream until incorporated. Spoon salmon purée evenly over herb mixture to fill terrine, then smooth top. Fold leeks over purée to cover, filling in any bare spots with additional pieces of remaining leeks. Cover surface of terrine with an oiled piece of wax paper or parchment (oiled side down).
▶ Put loaf pan in a larger baking pan and bake in a hot water

bath (see Tips, page 8) until terrine is just cooked through (terrine will be firm to the touch and will separate easily from sides of pan), about 30 minutes. Let terrine stand in loaf pan on a rack at least 15 minutes before unmolding.

Make salad while terrine stands:

▶ Whisk together vinegar, salt, and white pepper, then add oil in a slow stream, whisking until combined well.

▶ Toss frisée, endive, and radicchio in a large bowl with just enough vinaigrette to coat.

To serve:

▶ Divide salad among 8 plates, then unmold terrine (warm or at room temperature) and cut into 8 slices. Divide among plates, then drizzle with remaining vinaigrette and sprinkle with *fleur de sel*, crushed coriander seeds, and cilantro.

Cooks' notes:

• Terrine can be assembled, but not cooked, 3 hours ahead and chilled, covered.

• Terrine can be cooked 1 day ahead if serving at room temperature. Cool in pan, uncovered, then unmold and chill, covered with plastic wrap. Bring to room temperature before serving (this will take about 1 hour).

BRAISED RABBIT WITH GRAINY MUSTARD SAUCE

SERVES 8

Active time: 50 min   Start to finish: 2½ hr

2 (3-lb) rabbits, each cut into 6 serving pieces
1½ teaspoons salt
1 teaspoon black pepper
3 to 4 tablespoons vegetable oil
1¾ cups reduced-sodium chicken broth (14 fl oz)
2 medium onions, finely chopped (2 cups)
3 large garlic cloves, finely chopped
1 teaspoon chopped fresh thyme
¾ stick (6 tablespoons) cold unsalted butter, cut into tablespoon pieces
2½ cups dry white wine
⅓ cup Dijon mustard
¼ cup whole-grain mustard
2 teaspoons cornstarch
2 tablespoons cold water

Garnish: fresh thyme sprigs

▶ Rinse rabbit pieces and remove any fat, then pat dry and divide into 3 batches. Mix together salt and pepper in a small bowl for seasoning rabbit.

▶ Put oven rack in middle position and preheat oven to 350°F.

▶ Heat a dry 12-inch heavy skillet over moderately high heat until hot. Season first batch of rabbit, then add 3 tablespoons oil to skillet and brown rabbit on all sides, about 5 minutes total. Transfer browned rabbit to a flameproof roasting pan just large enough to hold all 3 batches in 1 layer. Season and brown remaining 2 batches of rabbit in same manner, transferring to roasting pan and adding more oil to skillet between batches if necessary. Reserve skillet.

▶ Add broth to roasting pan, then cover pan tightly with foil and braise rabbit in oven 15 minutes.

▶ While rabbit is braising, pour off any fat from skillet, then add onions, garlic, thyme, and 3 tablespoons butter and cook over moderately low heat, stirring and scraping up any brown bits, until onions are softened, about 5 minutes. Add wine and boil until liquid is reduced by half, about 10 minutes.

▶ Pour mixture over rabbit and continue to braise, covered tightly, until rabbit is tender when pierced with a fork, 45 minutes to 1 hour more. Transfer rabbit to an ovenproof serving dish and keep warm, covered loosely with foil, in turned-off oven.

▶ Straddle roasting pan over 2 burners and boil braising liquid until reduced to about 3¼ cups, about 10 minutes. Transfer ½ cup reduced liquid to a bowl and whisk in mustards. Add mustard mixture to reduced liquid in pan, whisking to incorporate. Dissolve cornstarch in water and whisk into sauce, then simmer, whisking, 2 minutes. Add remaining 3 tablespoons butter to sauce and swirl pan until incorporated. Season sauce with salt and pepper and pour over rabbit.

Cooks' notes:

• Rabbit can be made 1 day ahead and cooled completely, uncovered, then chilled, covered. Reheat in a preheated 350°F oven, covered, 20 to 30 minutes.

• If you have difficulty finding rabbit (see Sources), you can substitute 6 pounds of chicken, cut into 12 serving pieces, with the skin removed from all pieces but wings. Cook as directed above.

FRENCH LENTILS WITH CARROTS AND PEARL ONIONS
SERVES 8
Active time: 45 min   Start to finish: 1¼ hr

The cooking time of lentils varies—the fresher they are, the faster they will cook.

2 (10-oz) packages fresh pearl onions
3 tablespoons unsalted butter
2 large carrots, cut diagonally into ⅛-inch-thick slices
4 large garlic cloves, thinly sliced
2 teaspoons salt
½ teaspoon black pepper
4 fresh thyme sprigs
1 Turkish or ½ California bay leaf
2 cups dried French green lentils (14 oz), rinsed
5 cups water
¼ cup chopped fresh flat-leaf parsley

▸ Blanch pearl onions in a 3- to 4-quart heavy saucepan of boiling water 1 minute, then drain and peel.

▸ Heat butter in dry cleaned saucepan over moderate heat until foam subsides, then cook onions, carrots, garlic, salt, pepper, thyme, and bay leaf, stirring occasionally, until vegetables are softened, 6 to 8 minutes.
▸ Add lentils and water and bring to a boil, then reduce heat and simmer, partially covered, until lentils are just tender, 12 to 20 minutes. Discard thyme and bay leaf. Transfer lentils to a serving dish using a slotted spoon. Sprinkle with parsley.

Cooks' note:
• Lentils can be made 1 day ahead and cooled completely, uncovered, then chilled, covered. Reheat over moderately low heat, covered, stirring occasionally, 10 to 15 minutes.

ABOVE: salmon and scallop terrine with frisée salad; prune Armagnac sorbet with orange corkscrew tuiles

34

PRUNE ARMAGNAC SORBET

SERVES 8
Active time: 20 min   Start to finish: 1 day plus 3½ hr
(includes macerating and freezing)

This fabulous sorbet is a twist on the classic prune Armagnac ice cream. The prunes can macerate in the Armagnac indefinitely if kept in an airtight container in a cool, dark place.

  1 **cup pitted prunes (7 oz)**
  1 **cup Armagnac**
 ¾ **cup sugar**
  2 **cups cold water**
 ½ **cup fresh orange juice**

Special equipment: **an ice cream maker**
Garnish: **slivers of prune**

▸Combine prunes and Armagnac in an airtight container and let macerate at room temperature at least 24 hours.
▸Bring sugar and ¾ cup cold water to a boil in a 1-quart heavy saucepan, stirring until sugar is dissolved, then reduce heat and simmer 2 minutes.
▸Purée prune and Armagnac mixture with sugar syrup in a food processor until very smooth, about 2 minutes. Add orange juice and remaining 1¼ cups cold water and pulse to combine. Force through a fine-mesh sieve into a bowl and discard solids. Chill until cold, about 1 hour. Freeze in ice cream maker, then transfer to an airtight container and put in freezer to harden, at least 2 hours.

Cooks' note:
• Sorbet can be made 1 day ahead.

ORANGE CORKSCREW TUILES

MAKES ABOUT 2 DOZEN SMALL COOKIES
Active time: 40 min   Start to finish: 1¼ hr

A corkscrew shape gives these light cookies a new look.

 ¼ **cup sugar**
  1 **tablespoon finely chopped fresh orange zest**
      (see Tips, page 8)
  2 **tablespoons unsalted butter, softened**
  1 **large egg white**
 ¼ **teaspoon vanilla**
  2 **tablespoons all-purpose flour**

Special equipment: **a nonstick bakeware liner such as a Silpat (see Sources); a small offset spatula; 4 wooden spoons with round handles or 4 pencils**

▸Put oven rack in middle position and preheat oven to 400°F. Put nonstick liner on a baking sheet.
▸Grind together sugar and zest in a food processor 1 minute. Add butter and blend until combined well, then add egg white, vanilla, and a pinch of salt and blend until incorporated. Add flour and pulse until just combined.
▸Spoon ½ teaspoon batter in a 5-inch line at one end of nonstick liner, then spread into a strip (about ¾ inch wide and 5 inches long) with offset spatula. Make 3 more strips on same liner and bake until golden all over, 5 to 7 minutes. Cool strips on baking sheet 30 seconds (to facilitate removal), then carefully remove 1 strip with cleaned spatula and invert onto a work surface. Working quickly, wrap strip twice in a spiral around handle of a wooden spoon and transfer (still wrapped around handle) to a rack to cool and harden, about 1 minute. Repeat with remaining strips. (If strips become too brittle to work with, return to oven a few seconds to soften.) When cool and hard, remove wooden spoons and transfer *tuiles* to a tray. Make more *tuiles* in same manner, cooling and cleaning nonstick liner and spatula between batches.

Cooks' note:
• *Tuiles* can be made 2 days ahead and kept in a large shallow airtight container at room temperature.

REWRITING THE CLASSICS

EASTER DINNER IN LONDON

SERVES 8

ASPARAGUS CUSTARD TART

BIBB AND TARRAGON SALAD

REICHSGRAF VON KESSELSTATT
PIESPORTER GOLDTRÖPFCHEN
RIESLING KABINETT '03

**MUSTARD FENNEL PORK LOIN WITH
CUMBERLAND PAN SAUCE**

PORK CRACKLINGS

**ROASTED POTATOES WITH
LEMON SALT**

SMASHED PEAS WITH MINT BUTTER

CHÂTEAU RAMAFORT MÉDOC '98

PISTACHIO RHUBARB TRIFLE

ASPARAGUS CUSTARD TART

SERVES 8

Active time: 1 hr   Start to finish: 2¾ hr (includes cooling)

For pastry
- 1 cup all-purpose flour
- ½ teaspoon salt
- ¾ stick (6 tablespoons) cold unsalted butter, cut into ½-inch cubes
- 1 large egg, lightly beaten

For filling
- 1 medium leek (white and pale green parts only), quartered lengthwise, then cut crosswise into ⅓-inch pieces
- 1 lb medium asparagus, trimmed
- 1 tablespoon unsalted butter
- ½ teaspoon salt
- ½ teaspoon black pepper
- 1⅓ cups heavy cream
- 3 large eggs
- 2 teaspoons finely chopped fresh tarragon
- 2 teaspoons water

Special equipment: parchment paper; a 9¼-inch flan ring (see Sources and cooks' note, below)

Make pastry:
▸ Blend together flour, salt, and butter in a bowl with your fingertips or a pastry blender (or pulse in a food processor) until most of mixture resembles coarse meal with some small (roughly pea-size) butter lumps. Drizzle evenly with egg and gently stir with a fork (or pulse in processor) just until a dough forms.

▸ Turn out dough onto a lightly floured surface and divide into 4 portions. With heel of your hand, smear each portion once or twice in a forward motion to help distribute fat. Gather dough into a ball, then flatten into a 5-inch disk. Chill dough, wrapped in plastic wrap, until firm, at least 30 minutes.

Make filling while pastry chills:
▸ Wash leek in a bowl of cold water, agitating water, then lift out leek and pat dry.

▸ Cook asparagus in a wide 4- to 5-quart pot of boiling salted water (see Tips, page 8), uncovered, until just tender, about 5 minutes. Transfer asparagus with tongs to a bowl of ice and cold water to stop cooking, then drain and pat dry. Cut off and reserve tips (leave more stalk if asparagus is thin), then thinly slice stalks crosswise.

▸ Heat butter in a 10- to 12-inch heavy skillet over moderately low heat until foam subsides, then cook leek with ¼ teaspoon salt, stirring, until softened, 6 to 8 minutes. Stir in sliced asparagus and ¼ teaspoon pepper and remove from heat.

Finish filling and assemble and bake tart:
▸ Put oven rack in middle position and preheat oven to 375°F.

▸ Line a baking sheet with parchment paper and put flan ring in center of baking sheet. Roll out dough on a lightly floured surface with a floured rolling pin into an 11-inch round, then fit dough inside flan ring, pressing dough against bottom edge and side of ring. Run rolling pin over top edge of ring to cut off excess dough.

▸ Whisk together cream, 2 eggs, tarragon, and remaining ¼ teaspoon salt and ¼ teaspoon pepper. Lightly beat remaining egg with water in a small bowl and brush tart shell all over with some egg wash. Spoon asparagus mixture into shell, spreading evenly, then pour cream mixture over asparagus.

▸ Bake tart until filling is just beginning to set but still loose on top, 20 to 25 minutes. Scatter asparagus tips over top, pressing lightly if necessary to help them settle into filling, then continue to bake until custard is golden and just set but still slightly wobbly in center, about 30 minutes more (custard will continue to set as it cools).

▸ Cool tart on baking sheet on a rack until warm, about 30 minutes. Loosen edge with a small sharp knife, then lift off flan ring. Serve warm or at room temperature, cut into wedges.

Cooks' notes:
• Pastry dough can be chilled up to 1 day. Let stand at room temperature until slightly softened before rolling out.

• If you don't have a flan ring, you can use a 9- to 9¼-inch tart pan with a removable bottom instead. Put a baking sheet in oven while preheating, then bake tart on sheet.

• Tart can be baked 2 hours ahead and cooled completely, then kept, loosely covered with plastic wrap, at room temperature. If desired, reheat in a preheated 350°F oven until warm, 15 to 20 minutes.

OPPOSITE: mustard fennel pork loin with Cumberland pan sauce; smashed peas with mint butter; pork cracklings; and roasted potatoes with lemon salt

BIBB AND TARRAGON SALAD

SERVES 8
Active time: 20 min   Start to finish: 20 min

  2 tablespoons cider vinegar
  1 tablespoon finely chopped shallot
 ½ teaspoon coarse-grain mustard
 ⅜ teaspoon sugar
 ¼ teaspoon salt
 ¼ teaspoon black pepper
 ⅓ cup olive oil
 ¾ lb Bibb lettuce (3 medium heads), larger leaves
      torn into bite-size pieces
 ¼ cup loosely packed small fresh tarragon leaves

▶ Whisk together vinegar, shallot, mustard, sugar, salt, and pepper until sugar and salt are dissolved, then add oil in a stream, whisking until emulsified.
▶ Toss lettuce and tarragon with just enough dressing to coat and serve remaining dressing on the side.

Cooks' note:
• Dressing can be made 2 days ahead and chilled, covered.

MUSTARD FENNEL PORK LOIN WITH CUMBERLAND PAN SAUCE

SERVES 8
Active time: 20 min   Start to finish: 14½ hr (includes marinating)

For pork
  2 California bay leaves
 1½ tablespoons kosher salt
  1 tablespoon fennel seeds
  1 (4- to 4½-lb) center-cut boneless pork loin roast (3 to
      4 inches in diameter; preferably organic; see Sources)
 ¼ cup coarse-grain mustard
  2 teaspoons olive oil plus additional for greasing
For sauce
 ½ cup plus 1 tablespoon water
 ⅓ cup ruby Port
 ⅔ cup fresh orange juice
 1½ tablespoons fresh lemon juice
  3 tablespoons red-currant jelly
 ¼ teaspoon ground ginger
 ¼ teaspoon salt
  1 tablespoon cornstarch
  1 tablespoon unsalted butter

Special equipment: **an electric coffee/spice grinder; kitchen string; a 17- by 12-inch flameproof roasting pan (not glass) with a rack; an instant-read thermometer**
Accompaniment: **pork cracklings (recipe follows)**

Roast pork:

▸ Discard center stem from bay leaves, then crumble leaves into grinder and pulse with kosher salt and fennel seeds until bay leaves are finely chopped.

▸ Discard any strings from loin if tied. Arrange loin, fat side up, lengthwise on a work surface. Holding knife horizontally, make a lengthwise cut about 1½ inches deep along side of loin (do not cut all the way through). Open loin like a book, then pat dry inside and out. Rub 1 tablespoon mustard all over cut sides, then sprinkle with 1 teaspoon seasoned salt. Close loin and tie crosswise at 1-inch intervals with string. Rub olive oil evenly over roast, then rub with remaining mustard and sprinkle with remaining seasoned salt, pressing lightly to help adhere. Oil roasting rack, then transfer pork, fat side up, to rack set in roasting pan and marinate, loosely covered and chilled, at least 12 hours.

▸ Let pork stand at room temperature 30 minutes before roasting.

▸ While pork comes to room temperature, put oven rack in middle position and preheat oven to 450°F.

▸ Roast pork 25 minutes, then reduce oven temperature to 325°F and continue to roast until thermometer inserted diagonally 2 inches into center of meat registers 145°F, 35 to 45 minutes. Transfer pork to a platter (reserve roasting pan) and let stand, uncovered, 25 minutes.

Make sauce while pork stands:

▸ If there is fat in roasting pan, skim all but 1 tablespoon. Straddle roasting pan across 2 burners, then add ½ cup water and deglaze pan by boiling over high heat, stirring and scraping up brown bits, 1 minute. Add Port and boil 1 minute. Add orange and lemon juices, jelly, ginger, and salt, and cook, whisking, until jelly is dissolved. Whisk together remaining tablespoon water and cornstarch in a cup, then add to pan and boil, whisking, 1 minute. Remove from heat and whisk in butter, then pour sauce through a fine-mesh sieve into a bowl.

▸ Discard string from pork. Slice pork and serve with sauce and cracklings.

Cooks' note:
• Pork can be marinated up to 24 hours.

PORK CRACKLINGS
SERVES 8
Active time: 20 min   Start to finish: 2 hr

If you're making this entire menu in a single oven, you will have to make the cracklings ahead (see cooks' note, below) and reheat them in the upper third of oven during the last 10 minutes of roasting the potatoes.

  2 teaspoons kosher salt
1½ teaspoons fennel seeds
  1 (2-lb) piece pork fatback with skin, fat trimmed
       to ⅓ inch thick
¾ cup water

Special equipment: **an electric coffee/spice grinder**

▸ Pulse kosher salt and fennel in grinder until fennel is coarsely ground. Arrange fatback, skin side up, on a work surface with longest side nearest you. Score pork skin (¼ inch deep) crosswise with a sharp knife at ⅓-inch intervals (do not cut through to fat). Pat skin completely dry with paper towels, then rub fennel salt into skin. Let stand, loosely covered, at room temperature 1 hour.

▸ Put oven rack in bottom third of oven and preheat oven to 450°F.

▸ Pat skin completely dry with paper towels again, then cut skin into strips using scored cuts as a guide. Arrange strips close together in a large shallow baking pan (1 inch deep) and slowly pour water into pan (not over skin). Roast, stirring twice (use caution, as fat may splatter), until strips are golden, blistered, and crisp, 30 to 35 minutes. Transfer with a slotted spoon to a paper-towel-lined plate to drain, then discard fat remaining in pan.

Cooks' note:
• Cracklings can be made 6 hours ahead and cooled, uncovered, then kept, covered, at room temperature. Reheat in upper third of a preheated 425°F oven until hot, about 10 minutes.

ROASTED POTATOES WITH LEMON SALT

SERVES 8

Active time: 20 min   Start to finish: 55 min

If you're making this entire menu in a single oven, it's best to roast the potatoes while the pork loin stands (increase the oven temperature as soon as the pork comes out).

4½ lb medium (3-inch) yellow-fleshed potatoes such as Yukon Gold

⅓ cup extra-virgin olive oil

6 garlic cloves, halved

¼ teaspoon table salt

1 tablespoon finely grated fresh lemon zest

2 teaspoons flaky sea salt, such as Maldon, or kosher salt

▸ Put oven rack in lower third of oven and preheat oven to 425°F.

▸ Peel potatoes and quarter. Parboil potatoes in a 5- to 6-quart pot of boiling salted water (see Tips, page 8) 5 minutes, then drain in a colander and let stand in colander 5 minutes.

▸ Transfer potatoes to a 17- by 12-inch shallow baking pan and toss with oil, garlic, and table salt. Roast, stirring and turning once halfway through cooking, until golden brown, 20 to 25 minutes.

▸ Transfer potatoes and garlic to a large bowl, then sprinkle with zest and sea salt and toss well.

SMASHED PEAS WITH MINT BUTTER

SERVES 8

Active time: 20 min   Start to finish: 30 min

This recipe is a variation on mushy peas, a beloved British street food. Ours have a much brighter color and flavor.

4 (10-oz) packages frozen peas, not thawed

⅔ cup water

1¼ teaspoons salt

5 tablespoons unsalted butter, cut into ½-inch cubes and softened

⅓ cup finely chopped fresh mint

3 tablespoons finely chopped fresh flat-leaf parsley

½ teaspoon coarsely ground black pepper

▸ Cook peas with water and ½ teaspoon salt in a 5-quart heavy pot over moderate heat, covered, stirring occasionally, until heated through and tender, about 8 minutes.

▸ While peas cook, stir together butter, mint, parsley, pepper, and remaining ¾ teaspoon salt until combined well.

▸ Pulse peas (with cooking water) in 2 batches in a food processor until coarsely puréed, transferring to a large bowl. Stir in herb butter until melted.

PISTACHIO RHUBARB TRIFLE

SERVES 8

Active time: 1¼ hr   Start to finish: 12½ hr (includes chilling)

Don't be tempted to use a dark dry Sherry for the syrup or topping—it will muddy the beautiful green-gold color of the cake and tint the cream topping brown.

For cake

  ½ cup all-purpose flour plus additional for dusting

1½ cups sugar

  ½ cup unsalted shelled pistachios

  ½ teaspoon salt

  8 large egg yolks

  3 tablespoons whole milk

  1 teaspoon vanilla extract

  ½ teaspoon almond extract

  4 large egg whites

For assembling trifle

    Sherry syrup (page 44)

    Vanilla custard (page 44)

    Rhubarb purée (page 44)

For topping

  1 cup chilled heavy cream

  1 tablespoon sugar

  1 tablespoon light Fino Sherry

  2 tablespoons unsalted shelled pistachios, chopped

Special equipment: **a 15- by 10- by 1-inch baking pan; parchment paper; a 3- to 3½-qt glass trifle or soufflé dish**

Make cake:

▸ Put oven rack in middle position and preheat oven to 350°F. Butter baking pan, then line bottom with parchment paper and butter paper. Dust pan with flour, knocking out excess.

▸ Pulse together ½ cup flour, 1 cup sugar, pistachios, and salt in a food processor until pistachios are very finely ground (mixture will resemble a slightly grainy flour). Transfer mixture to a large bowl and whisk in yolks, milk, and extracts.

▸ Beat egg whites with a pinch of salt using an electric mixer at medium-high speed until they hold soft peaks. Reduce speed to low, then add remaining ½ cup sugar, a little at a time. Increase speed to high and beat until whites hold stiff, glossy peaks. Fold one third of whites into batter to lighten, then fold in remaining whites gently but thoroughly.

▸ Pour batter into baking pan, spreading evenly, and rap pan against counter to release any air bubbles. Bake cake until golden and springy to the touch, 20 to 25 minutes.

▸ Cool cake in pan on a rack 20 minutes. Remove pan (with cake) from rack and cover rack with a sheet of parchment, then invert rack over cake and flip cake onto rack. Carefully peel off parchment from bottom of cake and cool completely.

Assemble trifle:

▸ Slide cake (on parchment) onto a work surface and arrange with a long side nearest you. Trim cake with a serrated knife to make a 12- by 9-inch rectangle, reserving trimmings, then brush cake and trimmings with Sherry syrup. Halve cake crosswise, then cut each half into thirds first lengthwise and then crosswise to total 18 (3- by 2-inch) pieces. Halve each piece diagonally to form triangles.

▸ Spoon ½ cup custard into bottom of trifle dish. Arrange half of triangles over custard in 2 layers, pressing short ends of triangles against side of dish (there should be small spaces in between slices for custard to run through). Arrange half of trimmings in the center, cutting them as needed to fit. Spread 1½ cups custard over cake, then spread 1 cup rhubarb purée over custard. Cover with remaining cake and trimmings in same manner, then spread remaining custard over. Spread remaining rhubarb purée over custard, leaving a 1-inch border around edge. Chill, covered tightly with plastic wrap, at least 8 hours.

Make topping just before serving:

▸ Beat cream with sugar and Sherry using cleaned beaters until it just holds soft peaks. Spoon cream over top of trifle, then sprinkle with pistachios.

Cooks' note:

• Trifle can be chilled up to 2 days.

SHERRY SYRUP

MAKES ABOUT ¾ CUP
Active time: 5 min   Start to finish: 1¼ hr (includes cooling)

½ cup water
½ cup sugar
6 tablespoons light Fino Sherry

▶ Bring water, sugar, and Sherry to a boil in a small heavy saucepan, stirring until sugar is dissolved, then boil until reduced to about ¾ cup, about 5 minutes. Cool syrup completely before using, about 1 hour.

Cooks' note:
• Syrup can be made 1 week ahead and chilled in an airtight container.

VANILLA CUSTARD

MAKES ABOUT 4 CUPS
Active time: 20 min   Start to finish: 3¼ hr (includes chilling)

This custard isn't meant to be eaten on its own. Food editor Melissa Roberts-Matar wanted the trifle's cake layers (page 43) to soak up the custard, so this one has a much looser consistency than most puddings.

3 cups whole milk
8 large egg yolks
⅔ cup sugar
¼ cup cornstarch
¼ teaspoon salt
1 tablespoon unsalted butter, softened
1 teaspoon vanilla

Special equipment: **an instant-read thermometer**

▶ Heat milk in a 2½- to 3-quart heavy saucepan over moderate heat until hot but not boiling.
▶ While milk heats, whisk together yolks, sugar, cornstarch, and salt in a heatproof bowl until smooth.
▶ Add 1 cup hot milk to yolk mixture in a stream, whisking, then add remaining milk, whisking constantly. Transfer mixture to saucepan and cook over moderately low heat, stirring constantly, until thickened and registers 170°F on thermometer, 6 to 10 minutes (do not boil).

▶ Immediately force custard through a fine-mesh sieve into a clean bowl and stir in butter and vanilla. Chill custard, its surface covered with wax paper, until cold and thickened, at least 3 hours.

Cooks' notes:
• Custard can be cooled quickly by setting bowl in a larger bowl of ice and cold water and stirring occasionally.
• Custard can be chilled, its surface covered with wax paper and bowl covered tightly with plastic wrap, up to 2 days.

RHUBARB PURÉE

MAKES ABOUT 2 CUPS
Active time: 15 min   Start to finish: 1¾ hr (includes cooling)

Vegetable oil for greasing pan
2 lb rhubarb stalks, cut into 1-inch pieces
⅔ cup confectioners sugar

▶ Put oven rack in middle position and preheat oven to 375°F. Lightly oil a large shallow baking pan with vegetable oil.
▶ Arrange rhubarb in 1 layer in pan and sift confectioners sugar evenly over top. Bake, stirring occasionally, until rhubarb is very tender, 25 to 30 minutes.
▶ Transfer rhubarb to a food processor and purée until smooth. Force through a medium-mesh sieve into a bowl, discarding solids, and cool completely.

Cooks' notes:
• Rhubarb purée can be cooled quickly by setting bowl in a larger bowl of ice and cold water and stirring occasionally.
• Rhubarb purée can be made 3 days ahead and chilled in an airtight container.

DINNER AT MORO

A SPANISH-MOROCCAN FEAST BY SAMUEL AND SAMANTHA CLARK

SERVES 4

**GRILLED ENDIVE WITH SHERRY
VINEGAR AND HAM**

**ROASTED WHOLE SEA BASS WITH
PISTACHIO SAUCE**

WINTER TABBOULEH

DOMAINE DE L'ORATOIRE SAINT-MARTIN
CÔTES DU RHÔNE BLANC '03

DATES WITH COFFEE AND CARDAMOM

This menu is the creation of chefs Samuel and Samantha
Clark of Moro restaurant in London. The recipes, a mélange of
Spanish and Moroccan flavors, are adapted from Moro: The
Cookbook and Casa Moro: The Second Cookbook.

GRILLED ENDIVE WITH SHERRY VINEGAR AND HAM

SERVES 4
Active time: 30 min   Start to finish: 30 min

¼   cup Sherry vinegar
½   garlic clove
½   teaspoon fresh thyme leaves
⅛   teaspoon fine sea salt
    Pinch of coarsely ground black pepper
3   tablespoons extra-virgin olive oil
2   large Belgian endives (10 oz total), each cut lengthwise
    into 6 wedges
5   oz thinly sliced *jamón de pata negra* or serrano ham
    (see Sources)
3   tablespoons coarsely chopped fresh flat-leaf parsley

▶ Simmer vinegar in a small heavy saucepan over moderate
heat until reduced to about 1 tablespoon, 1 to 2 minutes.
Transfer to a large bowl.
▶ Mince garlic and thyme with a large heavy knife, then mash
to a paste with sea salt using flat side of knife. Stir paste into
vinegar along with pepper. Whisk in oil until combined.
▶ Heat a well-seasoned ridged grill pan over moderate heat
until hot but not smoking, then grill endives, cut sides down,
in 2 batches, turning, until charred and slightly softened,
about 6 minutes per batch. Toss with dressing in bowl, then
arrange on a platter alongside ham. Sprinkle with parsley and
serve warm or at room temperature.

Cooks' note:
• Dressing can be made 2 hours ahead and kept at room
temperature.

ABOVE: making pistachio sauce; roasted whole sea bass

ROASTED WHOLE SEA BASS WITH PISTACHIO SAUCE

SERVES 4
Active time: 35 min   Start to finish: 45 min (includes making pistachio sauce)

 1   (3-lb) whole sea bass, cleaned, leaving head and
      tail intact
 2   teaspoons flaky sea salt such as Maldon (see Sources)
 ½   teaspoon coarsely ground black pepper
 4   fresh flat-leaf parsley stems
 4   thin lemon slices
 ½   fennel bulb, stalks discarded and bulb thinly sliced
 ½   tablespoon fennel seeds
 ½   red onion, thinly sliced
 2   Turkish bay leaves or 1 California (preferably fresh),
      halved lengthwise
 ½   cup dry white wine
 6   tablespoons extra-virgin olive oil

Accompaniment: **pistachio sauce (recipe follows)**

▸ Put oven rack in middle position and preheat oven to 425°F.
▸ Rinse fish inside and out, then pat dry and put in a large shallow baking or roasting pan. Sprinkle fish inside and out with some of sea salt and pepper. Place parsley stems, lemon, fennel bulb and seeds, onion, and bay leaves in cavity of fish. (Aromatics may spill into baking pan.) Drizzle some of wine and extra-virgin olive oil over fish, then add remainder of both to pan. Sprinkle fish with remaining sea salt and pepper.
▸ Roast until fish is just cooked through, 25 to 30 minutes. Discard bay leaves. Transfer to a platter and pour any juices in pan around fish.

PISTACHIO SAUCE

MAKES ABOUT 1 1/2 CUPS
Active time: 20 min   Start to finish: 20 min

The Clarks refer to this condiment as a sauce, but it's more of a chunky relish—so intense a little bit goes a long way. It would pair nicely with quail, grilled lamb, chicken, or fish.

1¼   cups shelled unsalted pistachios
       (preferably Persian (see Sources); 5¼ oz)
 1   small garlic clove
 ¼   teaspoon finely grated fresh lemon zest
 5   tablespoons extra-virgin olive oil
 2   tablespoons fresh lemon juice
 1   tablespoon water
 1   to 3 teaspoons orange-flower water (also called
       orange-blossom water; see Sources)
 ½   cup coarsely chopped fresh flat-leaf parsley
 1   tablespoon coarsely chopped fresh mint
 ¼   teaspoon sea salt
 ⅛   teaspoon black pepper

▸ Pulse pistachios in a food processor until coarsely chopped, then transfer to a bowl.
▸ Mince garlic with a large heavy knife, then mash to a paste with a pinch of sea salt using flat side of knife.
▸ Stir garlic paste into pistachios along with remaining ingredients until combined well.

Cooks' note:
• Sauce can be made 2 hours ahead and kept at room temperature.

WINTER TABBOULEH

SERVES 4 TO 6

Active time: 45 min   Start to finish: 45 min

This winter version of the famous Middle Eastern bulgur salad replaces tomato and cucumber with endive, fennel, cauliflower, walnuts, and pomegranate seeds.

For tabbouleh

- 1¼ cups coarse bulgur (cracked wheat; 7 oz)
- 1 large Belgian endive (5 to 6 oz), halved lengthwise, cored, and coarsely chopped
- 1 medium fennel bulb, stalks discarded and bulb quartered lengthwise, cored, and coarsely chopped
- 1½ cups tiny cauliflower florets (no larger than ½ inch in diameter; 6 oz total)
- 6 tablespoons coarsely chopped fresh flat-leaf parsley
- 3 tablespoons coarsely chopped fresh mint
- 3 tablespoons walnuts, coarsely chopped
  Seeds from 1 large pomegranate (about 1⅓ cups), bitter white membranes discarded
- ½ teaspoon fine sea salt
- ¼ teaspoon black pepper

For dressing

- 1 garlic clove, minced
- ¼ teaspoon cinnamon
- 3 tablespoons pomegranate molasses
- 1 tablespoon water
- ¼ teaspoon fine sea salt
  Pinch of black pepper
- 6 tablespoons extra-virgin olive oil
- ½ teaspoon sugar (optional)

Prepare salad:

▶ Cover bulgur with warm water by 2 inches in a bowl and soak 10 minutes. Drain well in a sieve, then transfer to a large bowl and stir in endive, fennel, cauliflower, parsley, mint, walnuts, and pomegranate seeds until combined.

Make dressing:

▶ Stir together garlic, cinnamon, molasses, water, sea salt, and pepper in a small bowl, then add oil in a slow stream, whisking until emulsified. (Dressing will be very tart; add sugar to sweeten if desired.)

Finish salad:

▶ Just before serving, toss tabbouleh with dressing, sea salt, and pepper.

Cooks' notes:
- Tabbouleh, without herbs and dressing, can be prepared 4 hours ahead and kept at room temperature.
- Dressing can also be made 4 hours ahead and kept at room temperature. Just before serving, toss tabbouleh with herbs and dressing.

DATES WITH COFFEE AND CARDAMOM

SERVES 4

Active time: 10 min   Start to finish: 1 day (includes steeping)

Be certain to use Medjool dates—they tend to be sweeter and will make the espresso more syrupy. Steeping them overnight allows the flavors to develop fully.

- 1 cup plain whole-milk yogurt (preferably Greek)
- 2 cups whole or pitted Medjool dates (14 oz)
- 2 cups freshly made espresso, or 5 rounded teaspoons instant-espresso powder mixed with 2 cups boiling-hot water
- 1 teaspoon sugar
- 20 whole green cardamom pods (see Sources), lightly crushed
- 1 (3-inch) cinnamon stick, broken in half

▶ If using a regular supermarket brand of yogurt (not Greek), drain in a paper-towel-lined sieve set over a bowl 1 hour. Discard liquid.

▶ If necessary to pit dates, slit dates lengthwise along 1 side and remove and discard pits. Put dates in a heatproof bowl.

▶ Bring espresso, sugar, cardamom pods, and cinnamon stick just to a boil in a small saucepan, then pour over dates and cool to room temperature. Steep dates, covered and chilled, overnight.

▶ Serve chilled dates with a little espresso syrup and yogurt.

Cooks' note:
- Dates can steep up to 2 days.

LA DOLCE VIA

ALFRESCO DINING SICILIAN-STYLE

SWEET-AND-SOUR EGGPLANT
(*Caponata*)
MAKES ABOUT 1 QUART; SERVES 10 (AS PART OF ANTIPASTI)
Active time: 1½ hr   Start to finish: 10½ hr (includes chilling)

This recipe makes a lot of caponata, so you'll definitely have leftovers. But it keeps well and is so addictive you'll be happy to have extra on hand.

  2 lb eggplant (preferably small but not Asian)
  2 tablespoons plus 1 teaspoon coarse sea salt (preferably Sicilian; see Sources)
2¼ to 2½ cups olive oil
11 garlic cloves (from 2 heads), chopped
  2 tablespoons tomato paste (preferably from a tube)
  1 (28-oz) can whole Italian tomatoes, finely chopped and juice reserved
  5 celery ribs, cut into ½-inch pieces
  1 large onion, chopped
  1 large red or yellow bell pepper, cut into ½-inch pieces
  1 cup large green Sicilian olives (6 oz; see Sources), pitted and cut into ¼-inch pieces
 ¼ cup drained bottled capers, rinsed
 ⅓ cup red-wine vinegar
 ¼ cup sugar
 ½ teaspoon black pepper
 ¼ cup chopped fresh flat-leaf parsley
 ¼ cup chopped fresh basil

Special equipment: a deep-fat thermometer

▶ Cut eggplant into ½-inch cubes and transfer to a colander. Toss with 2 tablespoons sea salt. Let drain 1 hour.

▶ While eggplant drains, heat 2 tablespoons oil in a 4- to 5-quart heavy pot over moderately high heat until hot but not smoking, then sauté three fourths of garlic, stirring, until golden, about 1 minute. Add tomato paste and cook, stirring, 1 minute. Add tomatoes with their juice, then reduce heat and simmer, uncovered, stirring occasionally, until thickened, 20 to 25 minutes.

▶ Bring 3 cups salted water (see Tips, page 8) to a boil in a 1- to 1½-quart saucepan, then cook celery until tender, 5 to 7 minutes. Drain in a colander and rinse under cold water to stop cooking.

▶ Gently squeeze eggplant to remove excess moisture and pat dry. Heat ¼ inch oil (about 2 cups) in a 12-inch heavy skillet over moderately high heat until it registers 360°F on thermometer, then fry eggplant in 4 batches, stirring and turning constantly with a slotted spoon, until browned and tender, 3 to 5 minutes per batch. (Return oil to 360°F between batches.) Transfer to paper towels.

▶ Pour off all but 2 tablespoons oil from skillet, then reduce heat to moderate and cook onion, bell pepper, and remaining garlic, stirring occasionally, until golden, about 10 minutes. Add tomato sauce, eggplant, celery, olives, capers, vinegar, sugar, pepper, and remaining teaspoon sea salt and simmer, uncovered, stirring occasionally, 15 minutes. Cool to room temperature, uncovered, then chill, covered, at least 8 hours.

▶ Just before serving, stir in parsley and basil. Serve cold or at room temperature.

Cooks' notes:
• If your sea salt is very granular and pebblelike, crush it using the flat side of a large heavy knife or the bottom of a heavy skillet.
• To take the temperature of a shallow amount of oil, put bulb in skillet and turn thermometer facedown, resting other end against rim of skillet. Check temperature frequently.
• Caponata can be chilled up to 1 week.

OPPOSITE: grilled oyster mushrooms; sautéed escarole; and veal *involtini*.
FOLLOWING PAGES: chickpea fritters; Sicilian cured olives; Italian cured meats; roasted red bell peppers; Italian cheeses; sweet-and-sour eggplant; and rustic Italian bread

GAME PLAN

1 WEEK AHEAD
-Make sweet-and-sour eggplant

3 DAYS AHEAD
-Make dough for cannoli shells

2 DAYS AHEAD
-Roast peppers and cut into strips
-Make tomato sauce for macaroni and eggplant
-Make cannoli shells

1 DAY AHEAD
-Prepare and chill chickpea mixture
-Cook and cut octopuses
-Assemble macaroni and eggplant
-Assemble veal *involtini*
-Sauté escarole
-Wash and tear greens for salad

4 HOURS AHEAD
-Fry chickpea fritters

CHICKPEA FRITTERS
(Panelle)

SERVES 10 (AS PART OF ANTIPASTI)
Active time: 1 hr   Start to finish: 4 hr (includes chilling)

This is a popular street food in Sicily where warm panelle *are served between two pieces of country bread.*

  3 cups water
  2 cups Italian chickpea flour (see Sources)
  1 teaspoon coarse sea salt (preferably Sicilian)
2¼ to 2½ cups olive oil
  ¼ cup chopped fresh flat-leaf parsley
  2 tablespoons finely grated Parmigiano-Reggiano

Special equipment: parchment paper; a deep-fat thermometer

▸ Lightly oil an 8- by 4-inch loaf pan (6-cup capacity) and line with parchment paper, leaving a 2-inch overhang at each end.
▸ Whisk together water, chickpea flour, sea salt, and 2 tablespoons oil in a 2½- to 3-quart heavy saucepan until smooth, then cook over moderate heat, stirring constantly with a wooden spoon (to prevent lumps from forming), until very thick and mixture pulls away from side of pan, 20 to 25 minutes. Transfer mixture to loaf pan, smoothing top. Cool, uncovered, then chill, surface of mixture covered with plastic wrap, until firm, at least 3 hours.
▸ Lift chickpea block out of pan using parchment and transfer to a work surface. Gently flip over block and discard parchment, then pat dry. Cut block crosswise into ¼-inch-thick slices for *panelle.*
▸ Preheat oven to 300°F.
▸ Heat ½ inch oil (about 2 cups) in a deep 10-inch heavy skillet until it registers 375°F on thermometer, then fry *panelle* in 5 batches, carefully turning occasionally with tongs, until golden and puffed, 3 to 5 minutes per batch, and transfer to paper towels to drain. Keep warm on a baking sheet in oven while frying remaining batches.
▸ Arrange *panelle* on a platter and sprinkle with parsley and cheese. Serve immediately.

Cooks' notes:
• If your sea salt is very granular and pebblelike, crush it using the flat side of a large heavy knife.

• To take the temperature of a shallow amount of oil, put bulb in skillet and turn thermometer facedown, resting other end against rim of skillet. Check temperature frequently.
• Chickpea mixture can be chilled in loaf pan up to 1 day.
• *Panelle* can be fried 4 hours ahead and kept, uncovered, at room temperature. Reheat on a baking sheet in a preheated 350°F oven 10 to 15 minutes.

ROASTED RED BELL PEPPERS
(Peperoni Rossi Arrostiti)
SERVES 10 (AS PART OF ANTIPASTI)
Active time: 35 min   Start to finish: 1¼ hr

  5 red bell peppers
  2 small garlic cloves, very thinly sliced
  2 tablespoons extra-virgin olive oil
  ½ teaspoon balsamic vinegar
  1 tablespoon finely chopped fresh oregano
  ¾ teaspoon coarse sea salt (preferably Sicilian)
  ¼ teaspoon black pepper

▶ Prepare grill for cooking. If using a charcoal grill, open vents on bottom of grill, then light charcoal. Charcoal fire is hot when you can hold your hand 5 inches above rack for 1 to 2 seconds. If using a gas grill, preheat burners on high, covered, 10 minutes, then reduce heat to moderately high.
▶ Lay bell peppers on their sides on lightly oiled grill rack and roast, turning occasionally with tongs, until skins are blackened, 10 to 12 minutes.
▶ Transfer to a bowl, then cover and let steam 10 minutes. Peel and seed peppers (reserving juices), then cut into ¼-inch-thick strips.
▶ Stir together peppers (with their juices), garlic, oil, vinegar, oregano, sea salt, and pepper and marinate 30 minutes at room temperature.

Cooks' notes:
• If your sea salt is very granular and pebblelike, crush it using the flat side of a large heavy knife.
• If you're unable to grill outdoors, peppers can be broiled on rack of a broiler pan about 2 inches from heat 10 to 20 minutes.
• Peppers can be roasted and cut into strips (but not marinated) 2 days ahead and chilled, covered.

BABY OCTOPUS SALAD
SERVES 10 (AS PART OF ANTIPASTI)
Active time: 30 min   Start to finish: 2 hr

2½ lb cleaned baby octopuses (see Sources; see
      cooks' note, below), thawed if frozen
  1 Turkish or ½ California bay leaf
 ⅓ cup extra-virgin olive oil
  2 tablespoons fresh lemon juice
  1 teaspoon coarse sea salt (preferably Sicilian)
  ½ teaspoon black pepper
  1 tablespoon chopped fresh oregano

▶ Rinse octopuses under cold water, then cover with water by 2 inches in a 5- to 6-quart heavy pot. Bring to a boil with bay leaf, then reduce heat and simmer, covered, until octopuses are tender (tentacles can easily be pierced with a fork), about 45 minutes.
▶ Transfer octopuses to a colander with tongs, then discard cooking liquid and bay leaf. When cool enough to handle, cut off and discard heads and halve octopuses lengthwise. Cool to room temperature.
▶ Whisk together oil, lemon juice, sea salt, pepper, and oregano. Toss octopuses with dressing and marinate, stirring occasionally, 20 minutes at room temperature.

Cooks' notes:
• If you can't find baby octopuses, you can substitute a 2½-lb regular octopus, though the texture will not be as delicate. Discard head of regular octopus, then cut body and tentacles into 2-inch pieces; follow baby octopus cooking procedure (above), but simmer about 1½ hours rather than 45 minutes.
• If your sea salt is very granular and pebblelike, crush it using the flat side of a large heavy knife or the bottom of a heavy skillet.
• Octopuses can be cooked and cut (but not tossed with dressing) 1 day ahead and chilled, covered. Bring to room temperature before proceeding.

MACARONI AND EGGPLANT
(Maccheroni e Melanzane)

SERVES 10 (FIRST COURSE)
Active time: 1½ hr Start to finish: 2½ hr

This is a pasta dish that is served in Sicilian homes and home-style restaurants, rather than upscale places. The recipe calls for perciatelli *or* bucatini, *which is what Italians consider* maccheroni.

- 2 (1½-lb) large eggplants (not Asian), trimmed
- 2 tablespoons plus ½ teaspoon coarse sea salt (preferably Sicilian)
- 2¼ to 2½ cups olive oil
- 1 medium onion, finely chopped
- 3 garlic cloves, finely chopped
- 1 (28-oz) can whole Italian tomatoes, finely chopped and juice reserved
- ¼ cup chopped fresh basil
- ¾ lb *perciatelli* or *bucatini* (long tubular pasta)

Special equipment: **a deep-fat thermometer**
Accompaniment: **finely grated Pecorino Romano or Parmigiano-Reggiano**

▸ Cut eggplants lengthwise into 20 (¼-inch-thick) slices total with a long serrated knife and transfer to a colander. Toss with 2 tablespoons sea salt, then let drain 1 hour.
▸ While eggplant drains, heat 2 tablespoons oil in a 4- to 5-quart heavy pot over moderately high heat until hot but not smoking, then sauté onion and garlic, stirring, until golden, about 6 minutes. Add tomatoes with their juice and remaining ½ teaspoon sea salt, then reduce heat and simmer, uncovered, stirring occasionally, until thickened, 20 to 25 minutes. Stir in basil.
▸ Gently squeeze eggplant to remove excess moisture (this helps reduce any bitter flavor) and pat dry. Heat ¼ inch oil (about 2 cups) in a 12-inch heavy skillet over moderately high heat until it registers 360°F on thermometer, then fry eggplant in 4 batches, turning over once with tongs, until golden, about 4 minutes per batch. Transfer with tongs to paper towels to drain.
▸ Cook pasta in a large pot of boiling salted water (see Tips, page 8) until al dente, then drain in colander and rinse under cold water to stop cooking. Drain well and toss pasta with 1 tablespoon oil.

▸ Put oven rack in middle position and preheat oven to 350°F. Spread ½ cup tomato sauce in bottom of a 13- by 9-inch glass or ceramic baking dish.
▸ Line up 5 pasta strands parallel to one another on a work surface and cut crosswise into thirds. Put 1 fried eggplant slice on work surface and stack cut pasta (15 pieces) across 1 end of slice. Roll up eggplant, leaving ends of pasta exposed, and transfer to baking dish, seam side down. Make more rolls in same manner with remaining eggplant and pasta, transferring to dish (rolls will fit snugly). Spoon remaining sauce over eggplant, then cover dish loosely with foil. Bake until rolls are heated through, about 15 minutes.

Cooks' notes:
• Tomato sauce, without basil, can be made 2 days ahead and cooled, uncovered, then chilled, covered. Stir in basil before proceeding.
• To take the temperature of a shallow amount of oil, put bulb in skillet and turn thermometer facedown, resting other end against rim of skillet. Check temperature frequently.
• Dish can be assembled (but not baked) 1 day ahead and chilled, covered (basil may discolor). Bring to room temperature to bake.

VEAL INVOLTINI

SERVES 10 (MAIN COURSE)
Active time: 2 hr Start to finish: 2¼ hr

With so many courses in a single dinner, you don't need huge portions of meat for the main course. Top-quality veal really makes a difference in this dish; meat should be cut from the leg for scaloppine.

- 4 cups fine fresh bread crumbs (from 10 slices firm white sandwich bread)
- 2 lb veal cutlets (no more than ¼ inch thick)
- ½ cup chopped fresh flat-leaf parsley
- 5 garlic cloves, minced
- 4½ oz finely grated Pecorino Romano or Parmigiano-Reggiano (1¼ cups; see Tips, page 8)
- 1¼ cups olive oil
- 1 teaspoon black pepper
- 1 large white onion, cut into 8 wedges and layers separated

Special equipment: **7 (10- to 12-inch) metal skewers**

▸Put oven rack in middle position and preheat oven to 350°F.

▸Spread bread crumbs in a shallow baking pan and toast, stirring once or twice, until golden, 8 to 10 minutes.

▸Gently pound veal cutlets to slightly less than ⅛ inch thick between 2 sheets of plastic wrap with flat side of a meat pounder or with a rolling pin, then cut into roughly 4- by 3-inch pieces.

▸Stir together parsley, garlic, ¾ cup cheese, ¼ cup oil, and ½ teaspoon pepper until a paste forms.

▸Stir together bread crumbs, remaining ½ cup cheese, and remaining ½ teaspoon pepper.

▸Season cutlets lightly with salt and pepper and spread 1 side of each piece with 1 teaspoon parsley-garlic paste.

▸Line a baking sheet with wax paper. Roll up veal pieces (paste sides up), starting from a short side. Put remaining cup oil in a bowl and dip each roll in it, letting excess drip off, then dredge in bread-crumb mixture, pressing gently to help crumbs adhere. Transfer to baking sheet.

▸Thread 1 veal roll onto a skewer, then 1 piece of onion, leaving about ¼ inch between. Repeat on same skewer 2 more times, then transfer skewer to baking sheet. Assemble 6 more skewers in same manner (last skewer will have only 2 rolls).

▸Prepare grill for cooking. If using a charcoal grill, open vents on bottom of grill, then light charcoal. Charcoal fire is hot when you can hold your hand 5 inches above rack for 1 to 2 seconds. If using a gas grill, preheat burners on high, covered, 10 minutes, then reduce heat to moderately high.

▸Grill veal on a lightly oiled grill rack, covered only if using gas grill, turning over once, until rolls are golden, about 6 minutes total.

▸Remove veal and onion from skewers and serve immediately.

Cooks' notes:
• Veal and onion can be threaded onto skewers 1 day ahead and chilled, loosely covered.
• If you're unable to grill outdoors, you can broil veal and onion skewers. Preheat broiler and lightly oil rack of a broiler pan. Broil skewers in 2 batches 4 to 6 inches from heat, turning over once, until golden, about 6 minutes per batch.

SICILIAN SALAD
SERVES 10
Active time: 30 min   Start to finish: 30 min

This Sicilian-style salad is more heavily dressed than other green salads, so that there's extra oil and vinegar to soak up with bread.

- 3 bunches arugula (¾ lb), coarse stems discarded and leaves torn into pieces
- ½ lb Bibb lettuce (2 small heads), leaves torn if large
- 1 celery heart (½ lb), thinly sliced on a sharp diagonal
- 1 small red onion, halved lengthwise and very thinly sliced crosswise
- ½ lb cherry tomatoes, halved
- ½ lb brine-cured black olives (1 cup), drained
- 2 tablespoons drained bottled capers, rinsed
- ⅓ cup extra-virgin olive oil
- 1 teaspoon coarse sea salt (preferably Sicilian)
- 2 tablespoons red-wine vinegar

▸Combine arugula, lettuce, celery, onion, tomatoes, olives, and capers in a large bowl. Drizzle with oil and sprinkle with sea salt, then toss. Drizzle with vinegar and toss again.

Cooks' notes:
• If your sea salt is very granular and pebblelike, crush it using the flat side of a large heavy knife or the bottom of a heavy skillet.
• Greens can be washed and torn 1 day ahead and chilled in sealed plastic bags lined with dampened paper towels.

THE BEST OF GOURMET

SAUTÉED ESCAROLE

SERVES 10

Active time: 30 min   Start to finish: 45 min

4   lb escarole (about 4 heads), cored and coarsely chopped
¼   cup extra-virgin olive oil plus additional for drizzling
5   garlic cloves, thinly sliced
½   teaspoon dried hot red pepper flakes
1   (2-oz) can anchovy fillets in olive oil, drained, patted dry, and chopped

▶Wash escarole well in a sinkful of water, then lift out and drain. Cook escarole in a 7- to 8-quart heavy pot of boiling salted water (see Tips, page 8) until tender, about 10 minutes, then drain in a colander.
▶Heat oil in same pot over moderately high heat until hot but not smoking, then sauté garlic and red pepper flakes, stirring, until garlic is golden, about 1 minute. Add anchovies, then reduce heat to moderate and cook, stirring, until dissolved, about 1 minute. Add escarole, stirring to coat with oil, then increase heat to moderately high and cook, uncovered, stirring occasionally, until escarole is tender and most of liquid is evaporated, 8 to 10 minutes. Season lightly with salt.
▶Spoon onto a platter and drizzle with oil to taste.

Cooks' note:
• Escarole can be sautéed (but not drizzled with oil) 1 day ahead and cooled completely, uncovered, then chilled, covered. Reheat in a large pot over moderately low heat, stirring, until hot.

GRILLED OYSTER MUSHROOMS

(Funghi alla Griglia)

SERVES 10

Active time: 30 min   Start to finish: 55 min

2   tablespoons fresh orange juice
1   tablespoon fresh lemon juice
2   teaspoons red-wine vinegar
6   tablespoons olive oil
2   lb large oyster mushrooms, stems trimmed
½   teaspoon coarse sea salt (preferably Sicilian)

Special equipment: **a perforated grill sheet**

▶Whisk together juices, vinegar, and oil in a large bowl. Toss mushrooms with vinaigrette and marinate 15 minutes. Transfer mushrooms to another bowl with tongs, reserving vinaigrette.
▶Prepare grill for cooking. If using a charcoal grill, open vents on bottom of grill, then light charcoal. Charcoal fire is hot when you can hold your hand 5 inches above rack for 1 to 2 seconds. If using a gas grill, preheat burners on high, covered, 10 minutes, then reduce heat to moderately high.
▶Grill mushrooms in 3 batches on oiled grill sheet set on grill rack, with grill covered only if using gas grill, turning frequently, until golden brown, about 5 minutes per batch. Transfer to vinaigrette as grilled, then toss with sea salt.

Cooks' notes:
• If your sea salt is very granular and pebblelike, crush it using the flat side of a large heavy knife or the bottom of a heavy skillet.
• If you're unable to grill outdoors, mushrooms can be grilled in batches in a lightly oiled well-seasoned ridged grill pan over moderately high heat, turning frequently, about 5 minutes per batch.

STRAWBERRIES WITH MARSALA

(Fragole al Marsala)

SERVES 10

Active time: 15 min   Start to finish: 45 min

2   lb strawberries (2 qt), trimmed, halved if large
¼   cup sugar
¼   cup sweet Marsala wine

▶Toss together strawberries, sugar, and Marsala until sugar is dissolved.
▶Let macerate at room temperature, tossing occasionally, 30 minutes before serving.

SICILIAN CANNOLI

MAKES ABOUT 10 DESSERTS
Active time: 2 hr   Start to finish: 3 hr

Sicilian cannoli are made using fresh sheep's-milk ricotta. We've substituted fresh cow's-milk ricotta and goat cheese. If you don't like goat cheese, use additional ricotta instead.

For cannoli shells

- 1 cup all-purpose flour plus additional for dusting
- 3 tablespoons sugar
- 1 teaspoon unsweetened cocoa powder (not Dutch-process)
- ¼ teaspoon cinnamon
- ¼ teaspoon salt
- ⅛ teaspoon baking soda
- 1 lb cold lard
- 2 tablespoons sweet Marsala wine
- 1 large egg, separated
  - About 3 cups vegetable oil

For filling

- 1 lb fresh ricotta (2 cups)
- 2 oz soft mild goat cheese
- ¼ cup confectioners sugar
- 1 tablespoon minced candied orange peel
- ½ teaspoon orange-flower water (also called orange-blossom water; see Sources)
- ¼ teaspoon cinnamon
- ⅓ cup shelled unsalted pistachios (not dyed red), chopped
- 2 oz bittersweet chocolate (not unsweetened), chopped (½ cup)

Special equipment: a pasta maker; a 4- to 4¼-inch round cookie cutter; a deep-fat thermometer; 6 (roughly 5⅝- by ⅝-inch) metal cannoli tubes (see Sources); 2 heavy-duty oven mitts; a pastry bag fitted with a ¾-inch plain tip
Garnish: confectioners sugar

Make dough for shells:

▶ Whisk together flour, sugar, cocoa, cinnamon, salt, and baking soda. Add 2 tablespoons lard and blend in with your fingertips until combined. Add wine and yolk and stir until a dough forms.

▶ Turn out dough onto a lightly floured surface and knead until smooth and elastic, 5 to 7 minutes. Form dough into a disk and wrap tightly in plastic wrap, then let stand at room temperature 1 hour.

Make filling while dough stands:

▶ Beat together ricotta, goat cheese, sugar, orange peel, orange-flower water, and cinnamon in a bowl with an electric mixer at medium speed 1 minute (do not overbeat). Fold in nuts and chocolate until combined and chill.

Make shells:

▶ Set smooth rollers of pasta maker at widest setting. Unwrap dough and cut in half, then lightly flour 1 piece (keep remaining half covered with plastic wrap). Flatten floured dough into an oval and feed through rollers. Turn dial down 2 notches and feed dough through rollers again. Continue to feed dough through rollers, making space between rollers narrower by 2 notches each time, until narrowest setting is used.

▶ Line a baking sheet with plastic wrap. Transfer rolled dough to a lightly floured surface and cut out 4 or 5 rounds with floured cutter. Transfer rounds to baking sheet and keep covered with more plastic wrap. Roll out remaining dough and cut rounds in same manner. Gather scraps and let stand 10 minutes. Roll out scraps and cut in same manner.

▶ Heat remaining lard with 1¼ inches oil in a 4-quart heavy pot over moderate heat until it registers 350°F on thermometer.

▶ Meanwhile, lightly oil cannoli tubes. Lightly beat egg white, then brush bottom edge of 1 dough round with egg white. Wrap dough around a tube, overlapping ends (egg-white edge should go on top), then press edges together to seal. Make 5 more shells in same manner (keep remaining rounds covered with plastic).

▶ Fry dough on tubes 1 at a time, turning with metal tongs, until 1 shade darker, about 45 seconds. Wearing oven mitts, clamp end of hot tubes, 1 at a time, with tongs and, holding tube vertically, allow shell to slide off tube onto paper towels, gently shaking tube and wiggling shell as needed to loosen. (If you allow shell to cool it will stick to tube and shatter when you try to remove it.) Transfer shells to paper towels to drain and cool tubes before reusing. Wrap remaining dough around tubes and fry in same manner.

▶ Spoon filling into pastry bag and pipe some into 1 end of a cannoli shell, filling shell halfway, then pipe into other end. Repeat with remaining shells. Serve immediately.

Cooks' note:

• Shells can be fried 2 days ahead and cooled completely, then kept, layered between paper towels, in an airtight container at room temperature.

PASSION PINK

A MODERN MEXICAN DINNER

SERVES 8

CHILE-DUSTED ORANGES, JICAMA, AND CUCUMBER

CHINACO REPOSADO TEQUILA

BLACK-BEAN-STUFFED PLANTAIN CROQUETTES WITH TOMATO SAUCE

VERACRUZ-STYLE SHRIMP OVER TORTILLAS IN PUMPKIN SEED SAUCE

MONTE XANIC VIÑA KRISTEL '03

GUANABANA SORBET WITH MANGO LIME COULIS

CHILE-DUSTED ORANGES, JICAMA, AND CUCUMBER

SERVES 8 (HORS D'OEUVRE)
Active time: 20 min   Start to finish: 20 min

This dish—meant to be eaten with your fingers or with wooden picks—is a light, refreshing hors d'oeuvre to complement tequila. The recipe is a take on the jicama and cucumber spears that are a popular Mexican street snack.

  4 **navel oranges**
  1 **small jicama (1 lb), peeled and quartered lengthwise**
  ½ **seedless cucumber (usually plastic-wrapped), peeled and halved lengthwise**
      Cayenne to taste

▶ Cut off peel and white pith from 3 oranges with a sharp knife. Cut peeled fruit in half lengthwise, then cut crosswise into ¼-inch-thick slices. Cut remaining orange in half crosswise, then cut each half into 6 to 8 wedges for squeezing.
▶ Cut jicama wedges and cucumber crosswise into ¼-inch-thick slices.

▶ Squeeze juice from 4 to 6 orange wedges into a bowl, then add jicama, cucumber, and salt to taste and toss well. Season orange slices with salt and arrange on a platter with jicama and cucumber. Lightly sprinkle with cayenne.
▶ Serve with remaining orange wedges.

Cooks' note:
• Oranges, jicama, and cucumber can be cut 3 hours ahead and chilled separately in sealed plastic bags.

BLACK-BEAN-STUFFED PLANTAIN CROQUETTES WITH TOMATO SAUCE

SERVES 8 (FIRST COURSE)
Active time: 1¼ hr   Start to finish: 2½ hr

Ripe (yellow, black-mottled) plantains are best for this recipe by Mexico City chef Ricardo Muñoz Zurita because they have the perfect balance of sweetness and starch. If they are very ripe (predominantly black or brown), the dough may be too sticky and not come together properly; if this happens, you can correct the dough's texture by adding bread crumbs.

4 ripe (yellow, black-mottled) plantains (3 lb total),
  left unpeeled
2 tablespoons minced white onion
6 to 8 cups vegetable oil (preferably corn oil)
1 small garlic clove, minced
1 (14- to 15-oz) can black beans, rinsed and drained
⅓ cup water
¼ teaspoon salt, or to taste
¼ to ¾ cup plain dry bread crumbs (if needed)
  Tomato sauce (recipe follows), heated
¼ cup crumbled *queso fresco* (Mexican fresh cheese)
  or ricotta salata (1¼ oz)
½ cup Mexican *crema* or crème fraîche (4 oz)

Special equipment: **a deep-fat thermometer**

Bake plantains:
▸ Put oven rack in middle position and preheat oven to
425°F. Line a shallow baking pan with foil.
▸ Cut a lengthwise slit through peel of each plantain from
tip to tip along inner curve and put plantains in baking
pan. Bake until tender when pierced with a knife, 30 to
50 minutes. Cool completely in pan on a rack, about 1 hour.
Make bean filling while plantains cool:
▸ Cook onion in 2 tablespoons oil in an 8- to 9-inch heavy
skillet over moderately low heat, stirring occasionally, until
pale golden, 3 to 5 minutes. Add garlic and cook, stirring,
until golden, about 1 minute. Add beans and water, then
increase heat to moderate and cook beans, mashing with
a potato masher in a circular pattern around skillet, until a
cohesive doughlike mass forms that sticks to masher and
lifts away from skillet, 8 to 10 minutes. Stir in salt and
transfer to a bowl.
▸ Line a tray with wax paper. When filling is cool enough to
handle, form bean mixture into 8 (2½- by 1-inch) ovals with
your hands, transferring to tray, and cover with plastic wrap.
Form croquettes:
▸ Peel and slice cooled plantains, then purée in a food
processor just until they come together as a dough. If purée
does not come together, pulse with just enough bread
crumbs so that mixture will not stick to oiled hands.
▸ Roll ¼ cup plantain dough between palms of oiled hands
to form a ball, then flatten between your hands to a 4-inch
round (¼ inch thick). Put a bean oval in center of round,
then fold dough around it and seal edges. Shape croquette
lengthwise between slightly cupped palms to smooth surface

and form a football shape, using heels of hands to make ends
pointed, and transfer to tray. Make 7 more croquettes in
same manner and cover with plastic wrap.
Fry croquettes:
▸ Heat 2 inches oil in a deep 4- to 5-quart heavy pot over
moderately high heat until thermometer registers 350°F.
▸ Fry croquettes in 2 batches, gently turning occasionally
with a slotted spoon, until golden brown, 2 to 3 minutes
per batch, and transfer to paper towels. (Return oil to
350°F between batches.)
▸ Divide warm tomato sauce among 8 plates. Gently cut
croquettes in half diagonally and arrange on top of sauce.
Sprinkle with cheese and serve with a small dollop of *crema*.

Cooks' note:
• Croquettes can be formed (but not fried) 2 hours ahead
and kept, covered with plastic wrap, at room temperature.

TOMATO SAUCE
MAKES ABOUT 2 CUPS
Active time: 15 min Start to finish: 30 min

This sauce, called caldillo de jitomate *("tomato broth"), has a
consistency similar to a light tomato soup.*

1½ lb tomatoes, coarsely chopped, or 1 (14- to 15-oz) can
  whole tomatoes in juice, including juice
⅓ cup water (¾ cup if using canned tomatoes)
2 teaspoons chopped garlic
3 tablespoons chopped white onion
1 large fresh green serrano chile, coarsely chopped
  (including seeds)
1½ teaspoons sugar
1 teaspoon salt, or to taste

▸ Blend all ingredients in a blender until very smooth, 1 to
2 minutes. Pour through a medium-mesh sieve into a
1½- to 2-quart heavy saucepan, pressing hard on and then
discarding solids. Gently simmer sauce, uncovered, stirring
occasionally and skimming froth, until sauce is slightly
thickened and reduced to about 2 cups, 10 to 15 minutes.

Cooks' note:
• Sauce can be made 1 day ahead and cooled, uncovered,
then chilled, covered.

VERACRUZ-STYLE SHRIMP OVER TORTILLAS IN PUMPKIN SEED SAUCE

SERVES 8

Active time: 2½ hr   Start to finish: 3 hr (includes making pumpkin seed sauce)

Although chef Ricardo Muñoz Zurita serves these shrimp with tortillas, feel free to serve them with rice instead.

For Veracruz sauce

3	lb tomatoes (9 or 10 medium), cored
⅓	cup extra-virgin olive oil
½	cup finely chopped white onion
1½	tablespoons finely chopped garlic
1	teaspoon sugar, or to taste
1	teaspoon salt, or to taste
2	Turkish bay leaves or 1 California
¼	cup small to medium green olives, pitted and quartered lengthwise
2	tablespoons raisins, chopped
1	tablespoon bottled capers, rinsed and drained
2	teaspoons dried oregano, crumbled

For tortillas

	Pumpkin seed sauce (recipe follows), heated
½	cup vegetable oil (preferably corn oil)
16	(6- to 7-inch) corn tortillas

For shrimp

40	large shrimp in shell (about 2 lb; 21 to 25 per lb), peeled and deveined
1	tablespoon finely chopped garlic
1	teaspoon salt
¼	cup olive oil
3	tablespoons finely chopped fresh flat-leaf parsley

Make Veracruz sauce:

▸ Blanch tomatoes in 3 batches in a pot of boiling water 10 seconds per batch, transferring with a slotted spoon to a bowl of cold water. Peel, seed, and finely chop tomatoes.

▸ Heat oil in a deep 12- to 13-inch heavy skillet over moderately high heat until hot but not smoking, then sauté onion (without browning), stirring, 3 minutes. Add garlic and sauté, stirring, until garlic and onion are pale golden, about 1 minute. Stir in tomatoes, sugar, salt, and bay leaves and bring to a boil. Reduce heat to moderately low and cook, uncovered, stirring occasionally, until most of liquid is evaporated, 20 to 30 minutes.

▸ While sauce cooks, put oven racks in upper and lower thirds of oven and preheat oven to 200°F.

▸ Add olives, raisins, capers, and oregano to sauce and cook, stirring, 1 minute. Transfer sauce to a baking dish, discarding bay leaves, and keep warm, covered, in oven.

Prepare tortillas:

▸ Transfer 2 cups hot pumpkin seed sauce to a pie plate. Keep remainder warm, covered, on stovetop over low heat or in oven.

▸ Heat oil in a 7- to 8-inch heavy skillet over moderate heat until hot but not smoking, then pass tortillas 1 at a time through oil with tongs to soften, about 2 seconds per side. Blot both sides with paper towels and stack on a plate.

▸ Flip stack so slightly cooler tortillas are on top. Working with 1 tortilla at a time, dredge in pumpkin seed sauce (in pie plate) to coat both sides, then roll up like a cigar in a shallow baking pan, arranging tortillas side by side in pan as rolled. Cover tortillas with foil and keep warm in oven.

Sauté shrimp:

▸ Pat shrimp dry, then toss with garlic and salt. Heat oil in a 12-inch heavy skillet over moderately high heat until hot but not smoking, then sauté shrimp mixture, stirring and turning shrimp, until just cooked through, 3 to 5 minutes.

▸ Stir shrimp and parsley into Veracruz sauce. Put 2 tortillas on each of 8 plates and spoon more pumpkin seed sauce over them. Spoon shrimp mixture over tortillas.

Cooks' notes:

• Veracruz sauce can be made 1 day ahead and cooled, uncovered, then chilled, covered. Reheat before proceeding.

• Shrimp can be tossed with garlic and salt 1 hour ahead and chilled, covered.

• Tortillas can be prepared no more than 30 minutes ahead and kept warm in a 200°F oven, covered with foil. Keep remaining pumpkin seed sauce warm on stovetop over low heat or in oven, covered. Thin with water if necessary before serving.

• If you're making this entire menu, the tortillas can be softened in the same oil used to deep-fry the plantain croquettes (page 66).

PREVIOUS PAGES: **Veracruz-style shrimp over tortillas in pumpkin seed sauce; guanabana sorbet with mango lime coulis**

PUMPKIN SEED SAUCE
MAKES ABOUT 6 CUPS
Active time: 1¼ hr   Start to finish: 1¼ hr

*There are versions of this sauce all across central Mexico,
from the highlands (Mexico City and Puebla) to the
neighboring states of Veracruz and Oaxaca.*

- ½ lb raw green (hulled) pumpkin seeds (1⅔ cups)
- 1 lb fresh tomatillos
- ½ cup chopped white onion
- 2 tablespoons chopped garlic
- 2 to 3 fresh green serrano chiles, coarsely chopped (including seeds)
- 2 tablespoons chopped fresh or 1 teaspoon crumbled dried epazote (see Sources)
- 1 tablespoon salt, or to taste
- 1 cup coarsely chopped fresh cilantro
- 4½ to 5½ cups water
- ⅓ cup mild olive oil or vegetable oil (preferably corn oil)

Special equipment: **an electric coffee/spice grinder**

▶ Heat a wide 4- to 5-quart heavy pot over moderate heat
until hot, about 5 minutes, then toast pumpkin seeds,
stirring constantly, until puffed and beginning to pop,
3 to 6 minutes. Transfer to a plate to cool completely.
▶ While seeds cool, discard husks from tomatillos and rinse
tomatillos under warm water to remove any stickiness.
Coarsely chop tomatillos, then purée in a blender with onion,
garlic, chiles (to taste), epazote, salt, ½ cup cilantro, and
½ cup water until very smooth.
▶ Grind pumpkin seeds to a fine powder in 8 small batches in
grinder, then stir together with 2 cups water in a bowl. Heat
oil in cleaned pot over moderate heat until hot but not
smoking, then cook pumpkin seed mixture, stirring
constantly, until thickened to a soft, dry paste that pulls
away from side of pot, 10 to 15 minutes (do not let brown).
▶ Add tomatillo purée and simmer, stirring, 2 minutes. Stir in
1½ cups water and simmer, uncovered, stirring frequently,
10 minutes (large streaks or pools of green oil from pumpkin
seeds will appear on surface).
▶ Just before using, purée remaining ½ cup cilantro with
½ cup water in blender until smooth and add to sauce. If
necessary, add more water for a pourable sauce, then return
to a simmer.

Cooks' note:
• Sauce can be made (without adding puréed cilantro) 1 day
ahead and cooled completely, uncovered, then chilled,
covered. Make and add cilantro purée just before serving.

GUANABANA SORBET WITH MANGO LIME COULIS
SERVES 8
Active time: 20 min   Start to finish: 3¼ hr (includes freezing)

- 1½ cups sugar
- 1¾ cups water
- 2 (14-oz) packages frozen guanabana (soursop) purée such as Goya brand, thawed (3 cups; see Sources)
- 1½ cups fresh mango purée (from 1½ lb mangoes) or 1 (14-oz) package frozen mango purée, thawed
- 3 tablespoons fresh lime juice, or to taste
- ½ teaspoon finely grated fresh lime zest

Special equipment: **an ice cream maker**
Garnish: **lime zest**

▶ Bring sugar and 1½ cups water to a boil in a 1½- to 2-quart
saucepan, stirring until sugar is dissolved, then reduce heat
and simmer, uncovered, until reduced to about 2 cups, 3 to
5 minutes. Transfer syrup to a bowl and cool completely.
▶ Whisk together guanabana purée and 1½ cups syrup, then
freeze in ice cream maker. Transfer to an airtight container
and put in freezer to harden, about 2 hours.
▶ Blend mango purée, lime juice, 6 tablespoons of remaining
syrup, and remaining ¼ cup water in a blender until very
smooth. Force through a fine-mesh sieve into a bowl,
pressing on and then discarding solids, then whisk in zest
and, if necessary, additional water for a thin purée.
▶ Serve sorbet with coulis.

Cooks' notes:
• Sorbet can be made 2 days ahead.
• Coulis can be made 8 hours ahead and chilled, covered.

MASALA MAGIC

A CASUAL DINNER IN SOUTHERN INDIA

SERVES 6

**CHICKEN AND GREEN BEAN
COCONUT CURRY**

BASMATI RICE

CARROT PACHADI

CLAIBORNE & CHURCHILL CENTRAL
COAST GEWÜRZTRAMINER '04

**WATERMELON WITH
FENNEL SALT**

CHICKEN AND GREEN BEAN COCONUT CURRY

SERVES 6

Active time: 1¾ hr   Start to finish: 2 hr

This recipe uses what is known in Indian cooking as a tarka— *hot oil seasoned with spices, which are added in sequence to infuse their flavors. The* tarka *is either incorporated at the beginning of a recipe or poured, sizzling, over a finished dish, as we do here, to impart another layer of flavor.*

2	tablespoons tamarind (not concentrate; see Sources) from a pliable block
½	cup boiling-hot water
2	tablespoons coriander seeds
1½	teaspoons cumin seeds
27	fresh curry leaves (see Sources)
6	(3-inch-long) dried hot Indian red chiles (see Sources)
6	chicken breast halves with skin and bones (5 lb total)
2	teaspoons salt
3	tablespoons vegetable oil
3	medium onions, halved lengthwise, then thinly sliced crosswise
3	garlic cloves, thinly sliced
1	teaspoon turmeric
2	(14-oz) cans unsweetened coconut milk (not low-fat)
1½	lb green beans, trimmed and halved crosswise
1½	teaspoons black mustard seeds

Special equipment: an electric coffee/spice grinder

▶ Break up tamarind, then add to boiling-hot water (½ cup) in a heatproof bowl and soak 15 minutes. Mash tamarind with a fork until pulp is dissolved, then pour tamarind mixture through a fine-mesh sieve into a small bowl, pressing hard on solids to extract as much liquid as possible. Discard solids.

▶ Heat a dry 10-inch heavy skillet (preferably cast-iron) over moderately low heat until hot, about 2 minutes, then toast coriander and cumin seeds, stirring constantly, 2 minutes. Add 12 curry leaves and toast, stirring constantly, until leaves curl and darken, 3 to 4 minutes. Add 4 chiles and toast, stirring constantly, until a shade darker, 1 to 2 minutes. Transfer to a plate and cool completely, then finely grind in grinder.

▶ Pat chicken dry and sprinkle with 1 teaspoon salt. Heat 2 tablespoons oil in a wide 6-quart heavy pot over moderately high heat until hot but not smoking, then brown chicken in 2 batches, skin sides down first, turning over once, about 8 minutes per batch. Transfer to a plate.

▶ Pour off all but 2 tablespoons fat from pot, then cook onions over moderate heat, stirring occasionally, until edges are golden, 5 to 8 minutes. Reduce heat to moderately low, then add ground-spice mixture, garlic, turmeric, and remaining teaspoon salt and cook, stirring frequently (to prevent scorching), about 3 minutes. Add coconut milk and tamarind liquid and simmer, stirring, until any coconut-milk solids are dissolved, about 1 minute. Add chicken, skin sides up, in 1 layer (chicken will not be completely covered with liquid) and simmer, covered, until chicken is just cooked through, about 15 minutes.

▶ While chicken simmers, cook green beans in an 8-quart pot of boiling salted water until crisp-tender, 3 to 4 minutes. Drain and transfer to a bowl of ice water to stop cooking. Drain well.

▶ When chicken is done cooking, transfer with tongs to a cutting board, reserving sauce in pot, and halve each chicken breast diagonally through bone. Put chicken in a deep serving dish and keep warm, covered with foil. Add green beans to coconut sauce and simmer until just tender, about 1 minute.

▶ While beans simmer, heat remaining tablespoon oil in 10-inch heavy skillet over moderate heat until hot but not smoking. Add mustard seeds, then cover skillet and cook until seeds make popping sounds, about 5 seconds. Remove lid, then add remaining 15 curry leaves and 2 chiles and cook, stirring, until leaves crackle and chiles darken slightly, about 5 seconds. Pour hot oil mixture over coconut sauce and beans, then stir to combine. Season with salt, then spoon sauce and beans around chicken. Discard whole chiles if desired.

Cooks' notes:
• Chicken and coconut sauce, without green beans and spice oil, can be made 1 day ahead and cooled completely, uncovered, then chilled, covered.
• Green beans can be cooked and refreshed 1 day ahead and chilled in a sealed plastic bag.

BASMATI RICE

SERVES 6

Active time: 15 min   Start to finish: 40 min

Traditional Indian recipes for basmati rice call for soaking the rice, but we find that it isn't necessary in this case.

- 2 cups basmati rice (14 oz)
- 2 tablespoons unsalted butter
- 3⅓ cups water
- 1 teaspoon salt

▶ Rinse rice in several changes of cold water until water runs clear. Drain well in a fine-mesh sieve. Melt butter in a 4-quart heavy pot over moderate heat, then add rice and cook, stirring, 2 minutes. Stir in water and salt and bring to a boil over high heat. Reduce heat to low and cook, covered, until rice is tender and liquid is absorbed, about 20 minutes. Remove from heat. Let stand, covered and undisturbed, 5 minutes. Fluff rice gently with a fork.

Cooks' note:
• Rice can be made 1 day ahead and cooled completely, uncovered, then chilled in an airtight container. Reheat rice, its surface covered with a dampened paper towel, in a colander set over a saucepan of boiling water, covered, 5 to 10 minutes.

CARROT PACHADI

SERVES 6 (MAKES ABOUT 3½ CUPS)

Active time: 30 min   Start to finish: 1 hr

- 1½ cups plain whole-milk yogurt
- 1 lb carrots
- 1 tablespoon vegetable oil
- 1 teaspoon black mustard seeds (see Sources)
- 8 fresh curry leaves (see Sources)
- 1 cup finely chopped red onion
- 1 teaspoon ground cumin
- ½ teaspoon salt
- ⅛ teaspoon cayenne
- ¼ cup chopped fresh cilantro

Special equipment: **a food processor fitted with shredding disk**

▶ Drain yogurt in a large fine-mesh sieve set over a bowl about 30 minutes. Meanwhile, finely shred carrots using food processor.
▶ Heat oil in a 12-inch heavy skillet over moderately high heat until hot but not smoking, then add mustard seeds and cook, covered, until they make popping sounds, about 15 seconds. Add curry leaves and cook, stirring constantly, until fragrant, about 3 seconds. Add carrots, onion, cumin, salt, and cayenne and cook over moderate heat, stirring frequently, until carrots are crisp-tender, 2 to 3 minutes. Transfer to a shallow bowl and cool about 30 minutes. Stir in yogurt and cilantro.

Cooks' note:
• *Pachadi*, without cilantro, can be made 1 day ahead and chilled, covered.

WATERMELON WITH FENNEL SALT

SERVES 6

Active time: 10 min   Start to finish: 20 min

- 1 tablespoon fennel seeds
- 2 teaspoons kosher salt
- 12 (1-inch-thick) slices from a 5-lb quartered chilled watermelon
- 6 lime wedges

▶ Heat a dry small heavy skillet over moderately low heat until hot, about 3 minutes, then toast fennel seeds, stirring constantly, until lightly browned, 3 to 4 minutes. Transfer seeds to a work surface and cool 10 minutes. Coarsely crush seeds using bottom of skillet, then stir together with salt and sprinkle over watermelon. Serve with lime wedges.

STREET FOOD

FAVORITE SNACKS FROM OUR TRAVELS

JAMAICAN HOT PEPPER SHRIMP

SERVES 4
Active time: 10 min   Start to finish: 1½ hr (includes cooling)

Pepper shrimp are sold by the bagful in the Jamaican village of Middle Quarters. Peel them as you eat them.

- 4 cups water
- ½ cup chopped scallion
- 4 garlic cloves, crushed
- 3 fresh thyme sprigs
- 3 fresh Scotch bonnet or habanero chiles, halved and seeded
- 2 tablespoons salt
- ½ teaspoon black pepper
- 10 whole allspice
- 1 lb large shrimp in shell (21 to 25 per lb)

▶ Combine all ingredients except shrimp in a 4-quart heavy pot and bring to a boil, then reduce heat and simmer, covered, 20 minutes.

▶ Stir in shrimp, making sure they are just covered by liquid, and remove pot from heat. Cool shrimp in liquid to room temperature, uncovered, about 1 hour. Transfer shrimp with a slotted spoon to a bowl and drizzle some of liquid on top.

BEEF POT STICKERS

MAKES 24 DUMPLINGS
Active time: 50 min   Start to finish: 1 hr

In deference to the prohibition of pork by the Muslims who populate Xian, China, these pot stickers, adapted from Fuschia Dunlap, are made with beef.

For dough
- 1¾ to 2 cups all-purpose flour
- ¾ cup boiling-hot water

For filling
- ¼ lb ground beef chuck (½ cup)
- 1½ tablespoons soy sauce
- 1 tablespoon Asian sesame oil
- 1 tablespoon peanut oil
- 1 tablespoon minced peeled fresh ginger
- 1 teaspoon Chinese sweet bean paste (see Sources)
- 2 cups finely chopped garlic chives (6 oz; see Sources)

For panfrying
- 1 tablespoon peanut oil
- ⅓ cup warm water

Special equipment: a 6-inch (¾-inch-diameter) rolling pin

Make dough:
▶ Put 1¾ cups flour in a large bowl, then add boiling-hot water, stirring with a wooden spoon until a shaggy dough forms. When just cool enough to handle, turn out dough (including any loose flour) onto a work surface and knead, incorporating some of remaining ¼ cup flour if dough is sticky, until smooth, about 5 minutes.

▶ Form into a ball and wrap in plastic wrap. Let stand at room temperature at least 10 minutes and up to 30.

Make filling while dough stands:
▶ Stir together beef, soy sauce, oils, ginger, and bean paste in a medium bowl, then stir in chives.

Form and fry dumplings:
▶ Form dough into a log (24 inches long and about 1 inch wide), then cut dough crosswise into 24 (1-inch-wide) pieces. Put 6 pieces, cut sides down, on a lightly floured surface (keep remaining pieces loosely covered with plastic wrap) and flatten slightly with your hand. Roll out each flattened piece into a 3¼-inch round with lightly floured rolling pin. Put a level tablespoon of filling in center of each round, then brush or dab halfway around edge with a little water and fold in half, pressing edges together to seal and leaving a small opening at each end of semicircle. Stand each dumpling, sealed edge up, on a wax-paper-lined tray, then press dumplings slightly onto 1 side so more of dumpling touches tray. Make more dumplings in same manner.

▶ Heat oil in a 12-inch nonstick skillet over moderate heat until hot, then remove from heat and arrange dumplings in a tight circular pattern standing up in oil (they should touch one another). Cook, uncovered, over moderate heat until oil sizzles, then drizzle warm water (⅓ cup) over pot stickers and cook, covered, until bottoms are browned, 8 to 10 minutes. Add 2 tablespoons more water if skillet looks dry before bottoms are browned.

▶ Remove lid and cook, shaking skillet to loosen pot stickers, until steam dissipates, 1 to 2 minutes. Invert a large plate with a rim over skillet. Using pot holders, hold plate and skillet together and invert skillet. Remove skillet and serve pot stickers warm.

YAKITORI
(Chicken and Scallion Skewers)

MAKES 12 SKEWERS
Active time: 30 min Start to finish: 40 min

These savory skewers are sold from yatai *(street stalls)*
throughout Tokyo.

    Vegetable oil for brushing
¼ cup mirin (Japanese sweet rice wine; see Sources)
3 tablespoons soy sauce
3 tablespoons sake or dry Sherry
2 teaspoons sugar
3 bunches large scallions
1 lb skinless boneless chicken thighs (about 3),
    cut into 1-inch pieces

Special equipment: **12 (8-inch) wooden skewers, soaked
in water for 30 minutes**

▶ Line bottom of a broiler pan with foil and cover with rack.
Lightly brush rack with oil.
▶ Bring mirin, soy sauce, sake, and sugar to a boil in a
1-quart saucepan over moderately high heat, stirring until
sugar is dissolved. Boil, uncovered, until reduced to about
⅓ cup, about 5 minutes. Remove from heat and reserve
1½ tablespoons sauce in a small bowl for brushing after
skewers are cooked.
▶ Cut white and pale green parts of scallions crosswise into
1½-inch pieces (reserve scallion greens for another use).
▶ Cook scallions in a 2-quart saucepan of boiling (unsalted)
water 1 minute, then drain in a colander. Immediately
transfer to a bowl of ice and cold water to stop cooking.
Drain, then pat scallions dry with paper towels.
▶ Preheat broiler.
▶ Thread 1 skewer alternately with chicken and scallions,
using 3 pieces of each and piercing scallions crosswise
through center. Place skewer on rack of broiler pan, then
brush both sides generously with sauce. Repeat with
remaining skewers, arranging all skewers in same direction.
▶ Cover exposed skewers (but not chicken or scallions) with
a strip of foil to prevent scorching.
▶ Broil skewers 4 to 6 inches from heat until chicken is
slightly charred, about 4 minutes. Remove foil and brush
both sides with more sauce, then turn skewers over and
replace foil. Broil until other side of chicken is slightly

charred and cooked through, about 4 minutes more.
▶ Serve warm or at room temperature. Just before serving,
coat skewers with reserved sauce using cleaned brush.

Cooks' note:
• Skewers can be assembled, but not brushed with sauce,
1 day ahead and chilled, covered. Brush with sauce before
broiling as directed.

GRILLED WHITE CHEESE WITH OREGANO OIL

MAKES 6 SKEWERS
Active time: 30 min Start to finish: 1¼ hr

These skewers, a favorite in Rio, are traditionally made with
Brazilian queijo de coalho, *a dense, salty white cheese very*
similar in taste and texture to the Haloumi we use here.
Soaking the cheese on the skewers removes some of the salt
and prevents the skewers from burning.

½ lb Haloumi cheese, cut into 12 rectangular blocks
2 tablespoons extra-virgin olive oil
1 teaspoon dried oregano, crumbled

Special equipment: **6 (6- to 8-inch) wooden skewers**

▶ Thread 2 blocks of cheese lengthwise onto each skewer,
then cover skewers with cold water and soak 1 hour.
▶ Stir together oil and oregano in a 13- by 9-inch dish.
▶ While cheese soaks, prepare grill for cooking over medium-
hot charcoal or moderately high heat for gas (see Tips,
page 8).
▶ Drain cheese skewers on paper towels and pat dry, then
grill, covered only if using a gas grill, on a well-oiled grill
rack, turning (use a metal spatula to scrape under cheese
to loosen before turning each time), until evenly browned,
3 to 7 minutes total.
▶ Add cheese skewers to oregano oil and turn to coat.

Cooks' note:
• Cheese may also be cooked in an oiled well-seasoned large
ridged grill pan over moderate heat.

PREVIOUS PAGES: **Jamaican hot pepper shrimp; grilled white cheese with
oregano oil; warm peanut salad; Belgian fries with sauce andalouse;
beef pot stickers**

WARM PEANUT SALAD

SERVES 4 TO 6 (SNACK)
Active time: 40 min   Start to finish: 1½ hr

As a child, Padma Lakshmi enjoyed a boiled peanut snack on the beach in Madras, India. We adapted her recipe.

- 1   lb raw peanuts in shell, shelled (1¾ cups; see Sources)
- 1   Turkish or ½ California bay leaf
- 2   medium tomatoes, seeded and chopped
- 1   cup chopped fresh cilantro (from 2 bunches)
- 2   fresh small green Thai or serrano chiles (about 2 inches long), minced
- 2   tablespoons fresh lemon juice
- ¾   teaspoon fine sea salt

▶ To skin peanuts, blanch in a 3-quart saucepan of boiling salted water (see Tips, page 8) 1 minute, then drain well. Slip off and discard skins using your fingers and transfer peanuts to a bowl.

▶ Bring 5 cups water to a boil with bay leaf in same saucepan. Add peanuts and reduce heat to moderate, then simmer, covered, until peanuts are soft enough to crumble easily when pressed with tines of a fork, 30 to 45 minutes. (Test 1 or 2 peanuts, leaving the rest intact.) Drain well.

▶ When peanuts are almost finished cooking, stir together tomatoes, cilantro, chiles, lemon juice, and sea salt in a bowl. Add drained peanuts and stir to combine.

PASSION-FRUIT NIEVE

MAKES ABOUT 3 CUPS
Active time: 5 min   Start to finish: 3 hr (includes chilling nectar)

Nieve, or "snow," is Mexico's sorbet, sold from carts throughout the country.

- 3   cups passion-fruit nectar (24 fl oz), chilled
- ⅔   cup light corn syrup
- 2   tablespoons fresh lime juice

Special equipment: an ice cream maker

▶ Stir together all ingredients and freeze in ice cream maker. Transfer sorbet to an airtight container and put in freezer to harden, at least 1 hour.

BELGIAN FRIES WITH SAUCE ANDALOUSE

SERVES 4 TO 6
Active time: 1 hr   Start to finish: 1½ hr

Fries are a national obsession in Belgium, and they come with a variety of condiments. We chose andalouse, *a tomatoey mayo.*

For sauce
- 1   cup mayonnaise
- 2   tablespoons tomato paste
- 2   tablespoons finely chopped onion
- 1   tablespoon finely chopped green bell pepper
- 1   tablespoon finely chopped red bell pepper
- 1   tablespoon fresh lemon juice
- ¼   teaspoon salt

For fries
- 4   to 6 cups vegetable oil for deep-frying
- 3   lb russet (baking) potatoes (5 or 6)

Special equipment: a deep-fat thermometer

Make sauce:

▶ Stir together all sauce ingredients and chill, covered, at least 1 hour to allow flavors to develop. Bring to room temperature before serving.

Make fries:

▶ Heat 2 inches of oil slowly in a 5- to 6-quart heavy pot over moderately low heat until thermometer registers 300°F.

▶ While oil is heating, peel potatoes, then cut lengthwise into ⅓-inch-thick sticks and submerge in a large bowl of ice and cold water. Rinse potatoes in several changes of cold water in bowl until water is clear. Drain in a colander and spread potatoes out in 1 layer on paper towels to drain, then pat dry.

▶ When oil is ready, increase heat to moderately high and fry potatoes in 4 batches, turning, until just cooked through but still white, about 3 minutes. (Return oil to 300°F between batches.) Transfer as fried with a slotted spoon to dry paper towels to drain. Cool potatoes to room temperature, about 30 minutes.

▶ Reheat oil over moderately high heat until thermometer registers 375°F. Fry potatoes again in 4 batches, turning, until deep golden, 3 to 4 minutes. (Return oil to 375°F between batches.) Transfer as fried with a slotted spoon to dry paper towels to drain briefly, then season with salt and serve immediately, with sauce for dipping.

TURKISH LAMB KEBABS

MAKES 4 WRAPS
Active time: 45 min   Start to finish: 50 min

These addictive snacks from Istanbul give grilled lamb new meaning. Ground Urfa and Maras peppers are flavorful without being fiery. If you find only one, use 1 tablespoon of it. For sources for these spices and the lavash *bread, see Sources.*

1	medium red onion, finely chopped (½ cup)
½	cup coarsely chopped fresh flat-leaf parsley
1	medium tomato, diced (¾ cup)
1	teaspoon dried oregano
½	tablespoon Urfa pepper
½	tablespoon Maras pepper
6	tablespoons olive oil
¾	teaspoon salt
1	(1½-lb) piece boneless leg of lamb, trimmed and cut into 32 (1-inch) cubes
½	teaspoon black pepper
4	(10-inch) square pieces soft *lavash* bread

Special equipment: **8 (10-inch) wooden skewers, soaked in water 30 minutes**

▶ Prepare grill for cooking over medium-hot charcoal or moderate heat for gas (see Tips, page 8).
▶ Stir together onion, parsley, tomato, oregano, Urfa and Maras peppers, 2 tablespoons oil, and ¼ teaspoon salt.
▶ Pat lamb dry, then toss with black pepper, 1 tablespoon oil, and remaining ½ teaspoon salt and thread 4 lamb cubes onto each skewer, leaving a little space in between cubes. Brush *lavash* (on both sides) with remaining 3 tablespoons oil and transfer to a platter.
▶ Grill lamb, covered only if using a gas grill, on lightly oiled grill rack, turning over once, until medium-rare, 6 to 8 minutes total. Transfer lamb skewers to a platter and cover with foil to keep warm.
▶ Grill *lavash*, covered only if using a gas grill, turning over once, until just heated through and lightly browned but still flexible, about 45 seconds total.
▶ Remove lamb from skewers and divide among pieces of *lavash*. Top lamb with tomato mixture and roll up *lavash* to enclose lamb. Serve immediately.

Cooks' note:
• If you aren't able to grill outdoors, lamb can be grilled in a large well-seasoned ridged grill pan (without crowding) over moderately high heat, turning over once, about 8 minutes total for medium-rare. *Lavash* can be heated in 4 batches in grill pan over moderately high heat, turning over once, about 1 minute total per batch. Wrap in foil to keep warm.

BUTTER MOCHI
(Sweet Rice-Flour and Coconut Cake)

MAKES 24 SQUARES
Active time: 15 min   Start to finish: 3¾ hr (includes cooling)

This chewy Hawaiian cake gets its distinctive gelatinous texture from mochiko, a very soft Japanese rice flour. Coconut milk and butter add rich, creamy flavor to this cake, which we adapted from Rachel Laudan's The Food of Paradise.

3	cups mochiko (sweet rice flour; 1 lb; see Sources)
2½	cups sugar
2	teaspoons baking powder
¼	teaspoon salt
2	(14-oz) cans unsweetened coconut milk (not low-fat)
5	large eggs
½	stick (¼ cup) unsalted butter, melted and cooled
1	teaspoon vanilla

▶ Put oven rack in middle position and preheat oven to 350°F.
▶ Whisk together mochiko, sugar, baking powder, and salt in a large bowl. Whisk together coconut milk, eggs, butter, and vanilla in another bowl. Add coconut mixture to flour mixture, whisking until batter is combined.
▶ Pour batter into an ungreased 13- by 9-inch baking pan, smoothing top, and bake until top is golden and cake begins to pull away from sides of pan, about 1½ hours. Cool cake completely in pan on a rack, about 2 hours. Cut mochi into 24 squares before serving.

Cooks' note:
• Mochi keeps, covered and chilled, 3 days.

THE MENU COLLECTION

Each year, *Gourmet*'s food editors anticipate spring's tender spears of asparagus, sweet ears of farmstand corn, and the chubby winter squashes that appear when the weather turns crisp. Working with such peak ingredients, they create dishes that sparkle with seasonality. These sixteen menus—from grand and elegant to fun and casual—all celebrate freshness. In addition, you'll see helpful ideas for time-saving make-ahead suggestions, wine pairings, and table decorations.

In January, a crate of cheery clementines just might be the best way to perk up a gloomy evening. *Orange Crush* includes a trio of dishes that highlight the fruit's many dimensions: juicy wedges in an endive salad, a beautiful glaze for roasted duck, and candied peel dotting a rich chocolate tart. This lovely meal proves that wintry comfort food need not be stodgy.

As warm breezes melt away the frost, rejoice with *Fresh*, which begins with a herald of spring: artichokes braised with garlic and thyme. If you've never braised artichokes, you'll be surprised by their tenderness and the tremendous pan sauce they produce. Anchovy and rosemary roasted leg of lamb, souffléed gnocchi, and a tangle of roasted fennel and baby carrots continue the spring theme, which concludes with a show-stopping confection of almond macaroons, apricot compote, praline almonds, and mascarpone cream.

When the mercury starts to climb, life moves outdoors. For these dog days, we offer three alfresco meals packed with treasures from the garden that lead you easily through a long weekend, including brunch (*Beginning to See the Light*), lunch (*A Plateful of Summer*), and a supper of steamed blue crabs (*Dinner Gets Crackin'*). Most dishes require less than 30 minutes active work, leaving lots of time to enjoy the fleeting summer sun.

Start *A New Tradition* with our huge Thanksgiving dinner menu, which includes miso-rubbed turkey, chickpea, eggplant, and tomato tarts, and a bevy of side dishes and desserts. All of your guests, including vegetarians, will remember this meal for a long time to come. If you're spending Thanksgiving dinner at someone else's home but still want to entertain over the long weekend, peruse *A Midday Feast* and imagine how good orange cinnamon sweet rolls with orange butter will smell on a chilly November morning.

Although these menus were designed for entertaining, you'll also discover great ideas for weeknight suppers. For example, *Twilight Zone* features grilled beef, shrimp, chicken, and mushroom skewers served with a variety of dipping sauces. Why not choose just one type of skewer and one sauce for an easy family dinner? Or, try pairing the skillet corn from *A Little Bit Country* with grilled hamburgers. And the pasta and chicken gratin from our casual Christmas buffet *All Aglow* is sure to become a weekly staple in many homes.

Fabulous entertaining—or even a wholesome dinner for your family—shouldn't sap your energy, so look to these menus for inspiration and then make them your own. From good food and good company come wonderful memories.

ORANGE CRUSH

A WINTRY DINNER FEATURING CLEMENTINES

SERVES 8

CLEMENTINE, OLIVE, AND ENDIVE SALAD

QUIVIRA DRY CREEK SAUVIGNON BLANC '02

GLAZED DUCK WITH CLEMENTINE SAUCE

**WILD RICE AND BULGUR WITH
BRAISED VEGETABLES**

COOPER-GARROD FRANCVILLE VINEYARD
CABERNET FRANC '00

**CHOCOLATE TART WITH CANDIED
CLEMENTINE PEEL**

FONTANEL MAURY VIN DOUX NATUREL '00

CLEMENTINE, OLIVE, AND ENDIVE SALAD

SERVES 8
Active time: 1 hr   Start to finish: 1 hr

Combining sweet, sour, salty, and bitter ingredients with a tangy vinaigrette, this salad almost explodes with flavor.

  2 tablespoons red-wine vinegar
  1 teaspoon sugar, or to taste
  ½ teaspoon salt, or to taste
  ¼ cup extra-virgin olive oil
1¾ lb clementines (7 to 11)
  2 lb Belgian endives (6 to 8)
  4 pale inner ribs of celery, including leaves
  ½ cup Kalamata or other brine-cured black olives, pitted
       and cut lengthwise into slivers
  1 cup drained cocktail (pickled) onions (5 oz), quartered
  ¾ cup loosely packed fresh flat-leaf parsley leaves

▶ Whisk together vinegar, sugar, and salt in a small bowl until sugar and salt are dissolved, then add oil in a slow stream, whisking until emulsified. Season with pepper.
▶ Cut off tops and bottoms from clementines to expose fruit, then, resting fruit on a cutting board, remove peel, including all white pith, by cutting off vertical strips with a sharp paring knife. Cut segments free from inner membranes.
▶ Halve endives lengthwise, then cut out and discard cores. Cut endives diagonally into ½-inch-wide strips and put in a large salad bowl.
▶ Separate celery leaves from ribs and cut ribs diagonally into very thin slices, then add leaves and ribs to endives along with olives, onions, parsley, and clementine segments. Whisk dressing, then gently toss salad with enough dressing to coat.

Cooks' notes:
• Salad ingredients can be prepared 4 hours ahead and chilled separately in sealed plastic bags.
• Dressing can also be made 4 hours ahead and chilled, covered.

GLAZED DUCK WITH CLEMENTINE SAUCE

SERVES 8
Active time: 1½ hr   Start to finish: 7½ hr (includes chilling)

Clementines take the place of oranges in this variation on the French classic duck à l'orange. Borrowing the "twice cooked" approach from Chinese cuisine, we braise the ducks first for tender, unctuous meat, then roast them in a hot oven to crisp the skin. Part of the secret in getting duck skin crisp lies in successfully separating the skin and fat from the meat, which helps to drain off some fat.

  2 (6- to 7-lb) Pekin ducks (sometimes called Long Island
       ducks), thawed if necessary and excess fat discarded
  2 tablespoons kosher salt
  2 medium onions, quartered lengthwise
  1 large celery rib, cut crosswise into 4 pieces
  ½ cup plus 2 tablespoons sugar
  3 lb clementines (12 to 20)
  ½ cup red-wine vinegar
  ⅓ cup finely chopped shallot
  3 tablespoons Mandarine Napoléon liqueur or Cointreau
1½ tablespoons arrowroot

Special equipment: **heavy-duty foil**

Braise ducks:
▶ Put oven rack in middle position and preheat oven to 350°F.
▶ Working from large cavity end, separate duck skin (including fat) from breast meat as much as possible by working your fingers between skin and meat, being careful not to tear skin, then prick skin all over ducks with a fork. Put ducks, breast sides up, side by side in a large flameproof roasting pan and rub each duck inside and out with kosher salt. Divide onions and celery between duck cavities and sprinkle ½ cup sugar around ducks. Pour enough boiling-hot water over ducks (to help tighten skin) to reach about halfway up ducks (don't fill roasting pan more than 1 inch from rim). Cover pan tightly with heavy-duty foil, then carefully transfer to oven and braise ducks 1 hour.
▶ Remove pan from oven and remove foil (do not discard), then carefully turn ducks over (breast sides down) using one large wooden spoon to turn and another inside cavity. Cover with foil, then carefully return to oven and braise until meat is very tender but not falling off the bone, about 1 hour more.

Chill ducks:

▶ Remove pan from oven and discard foil. Transfer ducks with wooden spoons to 2 large plates, draining any juices inside ducks back into pan, then transfer cooking liquid to a large bowl. Return ducks to roasting pan, breast sides up, and cool ducks and cooking liquid (separately), uncovered, then chill, uncovered, at least 4 hours (to firm up duck before roasting and to solidify fat on cooking liquid).

Prepare glaze and start sauce:

▶ Discard all fat from chilled cooking liquid.

▶ Remove zest from 2 large or 4 small clementines in strips with a vegetable peeler, then trim any white pith from zest with a sharp paring knife and cut zest into fine julienne strips. Blanch strips in a small saucepan of boiling water 5 minutes, then drain.

▶ Squeeze enough juice from remaining clementines to measure 2 cups and pour through a fine-mesh sieve into a 3-quart heavy saucepan. Add vinegar and remaining 2 tablespoons sugar and boil until reduced to about ⅓ cup (glaze will bubble up and darken), about 15 minutes. Reserve 1 tablespoon glaze in a cup to brush on ducks, then stir julienned zest and 1 cup cooking liquid into glaze remaining in saucepan and reserve for sauce. Reserve remaining cooking liquid.

Roast ducks and finish sauce:

▶ Put oven rack in middle position and preheat oven to 500°F.

▶ Roast ducks until skin is crisp, 25 to 35 minutes. Brush reserved glaze (from cup) on ducks, then transfer ducks to a platter and let stand while finishing sauce, at least 10 minutes.

▶ Pour off all but 1 tablespoon fat from roasting pan and straddle pan over 2 burners. Add shallot and cook over moderately low heat, stirring, until softened and pale golden, 3 to 5 minutes. Add 2 cups reserved cooking liquid and deglaze pan by boiling, scraping up brown bits, 2 minutes, then pour through fine-mesh sieve into sauce (containing julienned zest) and bring to a boil.

▶ Stir together liqueur and arrowroot and whisk into sauce. Simmer, whisking occasionally, until thickened, 3 to 5 minutes, then season sauce with salt and pepper. Serve ducks, whole or carved into serving pieces, with sauce.

Cooks' notes:

• Ducks can be braised and chilled 1 day ahead. Chill cooking liquid separately.

• Glaze can be made and sauce can be started 6 hours ahead. Cool separately, uncovered, then chill, covered. Reheat glaze and stir before using.

WILD RICE AND BULGUR WITH BRAISED VEGETABLES

SERVES 8 (SIDE DISH)
Active time: 45 min   Start to finish: 2 hr

2   qt water
2½   teaspoons salt
1   cup bulgur (cracked wheat)
1   cup wild rice
2   medium leeks (white and pale green parts only), cut into ¼-inch dice
3   tablespoons unsalted butter
1   cup finely chopped onion (1 large)
1   cup diced (¼ inch) carrots (about 2)
1   cup diced (¼ inch) celery (about 2 ribs)

▶ Bring 2 quarts water with 2 teaspoons salt to a boil in a 3-quart saucepan. Put bulgur in a large bowl, then pour half of boiling water over it and soak, uncovered, until tender, about 1 hour. Add wild rice to water remaining in pan and simmer, covered, until tender and grains are split open, 1 to 1¼ hours.

▶ Drain bulgur and wild rice together in a large colander.

▶ Wash leeks in a bowl of cold water, agitating leeks, then lift out and drain in a sieve.

▶ Melt butter in a 3- to 4-quart wide heavy saucepan over moderately low heat. Add leeks, onion, carrots, celery, and remaining ½ teaspoon salt and cook, stirring occasionally, until tender, about 10 minutes. Stir in rice and bulgur and cook, covered, stirring occasionally, until heated through, 5 to 10 minutes. Season with salt and pepper.

Cooks' note:

• Bulgur can be soaked and rice can be cooked 1 day ahead. Drain and cool, uncovered, then chill, covered.

CHOCOLATE TART WITH CANDIED CLEMENTINE PEEL

SERVES 8 TO 10

Active time: 1¼ hr   Start to finish: 6 hr (includes making candied peel and chilling)

This tart was inspired by the torta di cioccolata *at Florence's Trattoria Garga.*

For crust

    Vegetable oil for greasing pan
5 **oz wheatmeal biscuits such as Carr's whole-wheat crackers, finely ground (1⅓ cups)**
2 **tablespoons sugar**
5 **tablespoons unsalted butter, melted**

For filling

2 **large egg yolks**
1⅓ **cups heavy cream**
10½ **oz fine-quality bittersweet chocolate (not unsweetened), finely chopped**
½ **cup candied clementine peel (not sugarcoated; recipe follows), finely chopped**

Special equipment: **a 9- or 10-inch fluted round tart pan (1 inch deep) with a removable bottom; an instant-read thermometer**
Garnish: **candied clementine peel (recipe follows)**

Make crust:

▸Put oven rack in middle position and preheat oven to 350°F. Lightly oil tart pan.

▸Stir together biscuit crumbs, sugar, and butter in a bowl, then press crumb mixture evenly onto bottom of tart pan. Bake crust 10 minutes, then cool completely in pan on a rack.

Make filling:

▸Lightly beat yolks in a small bowl. Bring cream to a simmer in a 2-quart heavy saucepan and remove from heat. Add about one third of hot cream to yolks in a slow stream, whisking constantly, then pour yolk mixture into remaining cream, whisking.

▸Cook custard over moderately low heat, stirring constantly with a wooden spoon, until it is thick enough to coat back of spoon and registers 170°F on thermometer, 1 to 2 minutes (do not let boil). Remove from heat and add chopped chocolate, whisking until smooth, then whisk in chopped candied peel.

▸Pour filling evenly over crust and chill tart, uncovered, until firm, at least 2 hours. Remove side of pan and serve tart chilled or at cool room temperature.

Cooks' note:

• Tart can be chilled up to 1 day. Cover loosely once firm.

CANDIED CLEMENTINE PEEL

MAKES ABOUT 1 CUP

Active time: 30 min   Start to finish: 3¾ hr

1 **lb clementines (4 to 7)**
1 **teaspoon salt**
2 **cups regular granulated sugar**
1½ **cups water**
    Vegetable oil for greasing rack
1 **cup superfine granulated sugar**

▸Halve clementines crosswise and juice them with a citrus juicer, reserving juice for another use. Discard any membranes still attached to peel, then cut each half into eighths.

▸Bring peel to a boil in a 3-quart saucepan three-fourths full of cold water with ½ teaspoon salt and boil, uncovered, 10 minutes, then drain and rinse peel. Repeat procedure with more water and salt, draining and rinsing peel again.

▸Bring regular sugar and 1½ cups water to a boil in a 2- to 3-quart heavy saucepan, stirring until sugar is dissolved, then reduce heat and simmer 5 minutes. Add peel and gently simmer, uncovered, until tender and translucent and syrup is thickened, about 1 hour.

▸Transfer candied peel with a slotted spoon to a lightly oiled rack set in a shallow baking pan, spreading it out so pieces don't touch, and let drain 30 minutes. If using peel for chocolate tart (recipe precedes), reserve ½ cup candied peel before coating remainder with sugar.

Coat peel with sugar:

▸Put superfine sugar in a small bowl and toss peel, a few pieces at a time, in sugar to coat, then transfer with a dry slotted spoon to a sheet of wax paper to dry slightly, about 1 hour.

Cooks' note:

• Candied peel can be left in syrup and cooled, then chilled, covered, 2 weeks.

FRESH
AN EARLY SPRING DINNER

SERVES 6

ARTICHOKES BRAISED WITH GARLIC AND THYME

ANCHOVY AND ROSEMARY ROASTED LAMB WITH SALSA VERDE

ROASTED FENNEL AND BABY CARROTS

SOUFFLÉED GNOCCHI

CHIFFONADE OF ROMAINE AND BIBB LETTUCES

PRESTON OF DRY CREEK OLD VINES/OLD CLONES ZINFANDEL '02

APRICOT ALMOND LAYER CAKE

ARTICHOKES BRAISED WITH GARLIC AND THYME

SERVES 6
Active time: 25 min   Start to finish: 1 hr

- 6 medium artichokes (½ lb each)
- 18 fresh flat-leaf parsley sprigs
- ¼ cup olive oil
- 8 fresh thyme sprigs
- 1 head of garlic, cloves separated and left unpeeled
- 1 cup water
- ¼ teaspoon black pepper
- 1 teaspoon salt
- 1 tablespoon extra-virgin olive oil

Special equipment: **a 6- to 8-qt heavy pot wide enough to hold artichokes in a single layer (about 11 inches in diameter)**
Accompaniment: **crusty bread**

▶ Working with 1 artichoke at a time, cut off top inch of artichoke and gently pull open center. Scoop out sharp leaves and fuzzy choke from center with a melon-ball cutter or a spoon. Trim bottom ¼ inch of stem (if present), keeping stem attached, and peel stem. Put artichoke in a large bowl of cold water. Repeat with remaining artichokes.
▶ Remove artichokes from water and push 3 parsley sprigs into center of each. Heat ¼ cup olive oil in pot over moderate heat until hot but not smoking, then add artichokes, thyme sprigs, garlic, ¼ cup water, pepper, and ½ teaspoon salt. Cover pot and braise artichokes, turning occasionally, until artichokes are browned in spots and bases are tender when pierced with a knife, about 35 minutes.
▶ Transfer artichokes, thyme, and garlic to a platter. Add remaining ¾ cup water to pot and deglaze by boiling over high heat, stirring and scraping up brown bits, 1 minute. Pour pan juices (they will be dark) into a small bowl and stir in extra-virgin olive oil and remaining ½ teaspoon salt. Squeeze pulp from 2 of garlic cloves into juices and mash into sauce with a fork.
▶ Divide artichokes and remaining garlic cloves among 6 plates and drizzle with sauce. Garlic cloves can be peeled and spread on crusty bread.

Cooks' note:
• Artichokes can be cleaned and trimmed 8 hours ahead and kept in bowl of water in refrigerator.

ANCHOVY AND ROSEMARY ROASTED LAMB WITH SALSA VERDE

SERVES 6
Active time: 30 min   Start to finish: 3½ hr (includes marinating)

Lamb with anchovy herb paste is a classic Italian preparation. The anchovy doesn't come across as fishy tasting—it simply lends a savory note that blends beautifully with the meat.

- 6 garlic cloves
- 9 flat anchovy fillets, drained and patted dry
- ¼ cup olive oil
- 2½ tablespoons chopped fresh rosemary
- 1 (6- to 7-lb) semiboneless leg of lamb (aitchbone removed), all but a thin layer of fat discarded and lamb tied
- 2 teaspoons salt
- ¾ teaspoon black pepper

Special equipment: **a 17- by 11-inch roasting pan (or larger) with a rack; an instant-read thermometer**
Accompaniment: **Salsa Verde (page 94)**

Marinate lamb:
▶ Mince garlic and anchovies and mash to a paste with a large heavy knife, then stir together with oil and rosemary in a small bowl. Pat lamb dry and transfer, fat side up, to rack in pan. Make several small 1-inch-deep slits in lamb with a paring knife, then rub marinade over entire surface of lamb, pushing some marinade into slits. Marinate lamb, loosely covered, at room temperature 1 hour.
Roast lamb:
▶ Put oven rack in middle position and preheat oven to 400°F.
▶ Sprinkle lamb all over with salt and pepper, then roast until thermometer inserted into thickest part of lamb (almost to the bone but not touching it) registers 125°F for medium-rare, 1½ to 1¾ hours (temperatures in thinner parts of leg may register up to 160°F). Let stand 30 minutes before slicing.

Cooks' note:
• Lamb can be marinated, covered and chilled, up to 5 hours. Bring to room temperature, about 1 hour, before roasting.

93

SALSA VERDE

MAKES ABOUT ¾ CUP
Active time: 15 min Start to finish: 15 min

½   cup extra-virgin olive oil
9   flat anchovy fillets, drained, patted dry, and minced
2½ tablespoons drained bottled capers (preferably
        nonpareil), rinsed and finely chopped
6   tablespoons finely chopped fresh flat-leaf parsley
3   tablespoons finely chopped fresh mint
1   teaspoon white-wine vinegar
⅛   teaspoon black pepper

▶ Stir together all ingredients in a bowl.

Cooks' note:
• Salsa verde can be made 1 day ahead and chilled, covered.

ROASTED FENNEL AND BABY CARROTS

SERVES 6
Active time: 15 min Start to finish: 45 min

*If you're making this entire menu in a single oven, roast the
vegetables and bake the souffléed gnocchi (recipe follows)
while the lamb stands (increase the oven temperature as soon
as the lamb comes out).*

6   bunches baby carrots, peeled and trimmed, leaving
        ½ inch of stems intact
2   medium fennel bulbs, stalks discarded and bulbs cut
        into ½-inch-thick wedges
3   tablespoons olive oil
3   tablespoons water
1   teaspoon fennel seeds
¾   teaspoon salt
¼   teaspoon black pepper

▶ Put oven racks in upper and lower thirds of oven and
preheat oven to 450°F. (If you are making just this dish, you
can put oven rack in middle position and roast vegetables on
that rack throughout.)

Toss carrots and fennel with olive oil, water, fennel seeds, salt, and pepper and arrange in 1 layer in a 17- by 11-inch shallow baking pan. Cover pan with foil and roast vegetables in lower third of oven 10 minutes, then uncover and roast, turning occasionally, 10 minutes more. Switch pan to upper third of oven and roast until vegetables are tender and browned, about 10 minutes more.

SOUFFLÉED GNOCCHI
SERVES 6
Active time: 35 min   Start to finish: 2 hr (includes chilling)

If you're making this entire menu in a single oven, put the souffléed gnocchi in the oven to bake after the fennel and carrots have been roasting for 10 minutes.

  3 cups whole milk
 ¾ teaspoon salt
 ¾ cup semolina (3 oz; sometimes labeled "semolina flour"; see Sources)
  3 large eggs
 ¾ oz finely grated Parmigiano-Reggiano (7 tablespoons; see Tips, page 8)
4½ tablespoons unsalted butter, softened

Special equipment: **a 2-inch round cookie cutter; a 2-qt shallow baking dish**

Bring milk with salt to a simmer in a 2- to 3-quart heavy saucepan over moderately low heat. Add semolina in a slow stream, whisking, then simmer, stirring constantly with a wooden spoon, 12 minutes (mixture will be very stiff). Remove from heat and stir in eggs 1 at a time, then stir in 6 tablespoons cheese and 3 tablespoons butter. Spread gnocchi mixture into a ½-inch-thick slab on an oiled baking sheet using a lightly oiled rubber spatula, then chill, uncovered, until cool to the touch, about 10 minutes.
Cut out rounds from gnocchi mixture with cookie cutter dipped in cool water (incorporating scraps as you work) and gently transfer rounds (they will be very soft), slightly overlapping, to buttered baking dish. Chill gnocchi, uncovered, 1 hour.
Put oven racks in upper and lower thirds of oven and preheat oven to 450°F.
Melt remaining 1½ tablespoons butter and brush over

gnocchi, then sprinkle with remaining tablespoon cheese. Bake in upper third of oven 10 minutes, then switch dish to lower third of oven and continue to bake until gnocchi are slightly puffed and lightly browned, about 10 minutes more. Let stand 5 minutes before serving.

Cooks' note:
• Unbaked gnocchi can be chilled up to 1 day, covered after 1 hour.

CHIFFONADE OF ROMAINE AND BIBB LETTUCES
SERVES 6
Active time: 20 min   Start to finish: 20 min

1½ tablespoons fresh lemon juice
 ¼ teaspoon Dijon mustard
 ⅜ teaspoon salt (preferably fine sea salt)
 ⅛ teaspoon black pepper
 ⅓ cup extra-virgin olive oil
  2 hearts of romaine, trimmed, quartered lengthwise, then sliced crosswise into ¼-inch strips (8 cups)
 ¾ lb Bibb lettuce (3 medium heads), trimmed, quartered lengthwise, then sliced crosswise into ¼-inch strips

Whisk together lemon juice, mustard, salt, and pepper in a small bowl, then add oil in a slow stream, whisking until emulsified.
Toss lettuces with just enough dressing to coat.

OPPOSITE: roasted fennel and baby carrots; souffléed gnocchi and anchovy and rosemary roasted lamb with salsa verde

APRICOT ALMOND LAYER CAKE
SERVES 6
Active time: 45 min   Start to finish: 2½ hr (includes cooling)

California dried apricots are essential for this recipe—they have the tartness needed to balance the sweet filling and macaroon layers. Don't assemble this cake ahead or the crisp macaroon layers will get soggy.

For almond macaroon layers
- 12 oz sliced blanched almonds (3¾ cups) or blanched slivered almonds (2¾ cups)
- 3⅓ cups confectioners sugar
- 6 large egg whites
- ¼ teaspoon salt
- 6 tablespoons granulated sugar

For apricot compote
- 6 oz dried California apricots (1½ cups; see Sources), finely chopped
- 1½ cups water
- 3 tablespoons apricot preserves

For praline almonds
- 1 cup sliced blanched almonds (3 oz)
- ½ cup confectioners sugar

For mascarpone cream
- 1½ cups imported Italian mascarpone cheese (10 oz)
- ¼ cup well-chilled heavy cream
- ¼ cup Disaronno Amaretto or other almond-flavored liqueur

Special equipment: **parchment paper**

Make macaroon layers:
▶ Trace 2 (8-inch) circles on 1 sheet of parchment paper and a third circle on second sheet. Turn sheets over and put on 2 baking sheets.
▶ Pulse almonds with 1⅓ cups confectioners sugar in a food processor until very finely ground (mixture will resemble sand), 2 to 3 minutes. Transfer to a large bowl and sift in remaining 2 cups confectioners sugar, then stir until combined well.
▶ Beat egg whites with salt in a large bowl with an electric mixer at medium speed until they just hold soft peaks. Add granulated sugar a little at a time, beating, then increase speed to high and continue to beat until whites hold stiff, glossy peaks, about 3 minutes.
▶ Stir whites into almond mixture until completely

incorporated (batter will be thick), then divide batter evenly among traced circles on baking sheets (about 1⅔ cups per circle), smoothing into ½-inch-thick rounds. Let rounds stand, uncovered, at room temperature until tops are no longer sticky and a light crust forms, about 30 minutes.
▶ Put oven racks in upper and lower thirds of oven and preheat oven to 300°F.
▶ Bake macaroon layers, switching position of baking sheets halfway through cooking, until macaroons are crisp and edges are just barely pale golden, about 25 minutes. Turn off oven and let macaroons stand in oven 10 minutes. Cool completely on baking sheets on racks, about 1 hour.

Make compote while macaroon layers bake:
▶ Simmer dried apricots in water in a 2- to 3-quart heavy saucepan, uncovered, over moderate heat, stirring occasionally, until apricots are very soft and most of liquid is evaporated, about 15 minutes. Stir in preserves, then cool completely.

Make praline almonds:
▶ Heat almonds in a 12-inch dry heavy skillet over moderate heat, stirring frequently, until almonds are hot but not yet colored, about 2 minutes. Add confectioners sugar and continue cooking, stirring and tossing, until almonds are lightly toasted and sugar glaze is caramelized, about 3 minutes. Immediately transfer almonds to a large sheet of foil and spread into 1 layer with a fork. Cool completely.

Make mascarpone cream:
▶ Just before serving, beat together mascarpone, heavy cream, and Amaretto with cleaned beaters at medium speed until thick and smooth, about 2 minutes. Reserve ¼ cup praline almonds, then fold remainder into cream.
▶ Put 1 macaroon layer on a platter and spread with one third of compote (about ½ cup), then spread one fourth of mascarpone cream (about ¾ cup) on top. Make another layer with second macaroon in same manner. Top with remaining macaroon, remaining compote, and remaining cream (1½ cups), then sprinkle with reserved praline almonds.

Cooks' notes:
• Macaroon layers can be made 2 days ahead and kept in an airtight container, layered between parchment paper, at room temperature.
• Apricot compote can be made 5 days ahead and chilled, covered.
• Praline almonds can be made 1 week ahead and kept in an airtight container at room temperature.

IN BLOOM

LUNCH AMONG THE LILACS

SERVES 6

DANDELION SALAD WITH LARDONS AND GOAT CHEESE PHYLLO BLOSSOMS

WILD SALMON WITH PEARL COUSCOUS, SLOW-ROASTED TOMATOES, AND LEMON OREGANO OIL

REX HILL MARESH VINEYARD OREGON CHARDONNAY '03

BLACKBERRY BUTTERMILK PANNA COTTAS WITH BLACKBERRY COMPOTE

DANDELION SALAD WITH LARDONS AND GOAT CHEESE PHYLLO BLOSSOMS

SERVES 6

Active time: 50 min   Start to finish: 1½ hr

This dish is a take on the bistro classic frisée salad with lardons. We recommend removing the ribs from the dandelion greens; though it's time-consuming, the result will be much more delicate.

For goat cheese blossoms

- 2   tablespoons unsalted butter, melted
- 8   oz soft mild goat cheese (1 cup) at room temperature
- 3   tablespoons heavy cream
- 1   large egg
- 1   teaspoon Dijon mustard
- ¼   teaspoon black pepper
- 3   (17- by 12-inch) sheets phyllo dough, thawed if frozen

For salad

- 6   oz slab bacon (see Sources), rind discarded if necessary and bacon cut into ⅛-inch-thick slices, then cut into 1-inch-wide pieces (to form lardons)
- 1   tablespoon olive oil
- 2   tablespoons finely chopped shallot
- 2½ tablespoons Sherry vinegar
- ½   teaspoon sugar
- ¼   teaspoon salt
- 1½ lb dandelion greens (see Sources), stems and center ribs discarded and leaves cut into 2-inch pieces (10 cups)

Special equipment: **a muffin tin with 6 (½- or ⅓-cup) muffin cups**

Make goat cheese blossoms:

▶ Put oven rack in middle position and preheat oven to 375°F. Brush muffin cups with some melted butter.

▶ Stir together goat cheese, cream, egg, mustard, and pepper in a bowl until combined well.

▶ Cover phyllo with 2 overlapping sheets of plastic wrap and then a dampened kitchen towel. Arrange 1 sheet of phyllo on a work surface, then brush with some melted butter. Cut phyllo into 4 (8½- by 6-inch) rectangles and arrange 2 of them one over the other in a crisscross pattern, then line a muffin cup with overlapping phyllo. Line another muffin cup

with remaining 2 phyllo rectangles in same manner. Repeat procedure with remaining 2 phyllo sheets and melted butter, lining remaining 4 muffin cups.

▶ Spoon goat cheese filling into cups and loosely gather edges of phyllo over center (if pieces of phyllo break off, arrange in center).

▶ Bake phyllo blossoms until tops are golden brown and sides are golden, 25 to 35 minutes, then transfer from pan to a rack to cool slightly.

Prepare salad while goat cheese blossoms bake:

▶ Cook bacon in a 12-inch heavy skillet over moderate heat, stirring occasionally, until browned and crisp, about 12 minutes. If necessary pour off all but 1 tablespoon fat. Add oil and shallot to skillet and cook, stirring, until softened, about 2 minutes. Add vinegar, quickly stirring and scraping up brown bits, then stir in sugar and salt. Immediately pour hot dressing and bacon over dandelion greens in a large bowl and toss well.

▶ Divide salad among plates and put a warm goat cheese blossom alongside each salad. Serve immediately.

Cooks' notes:

• Dandelion greens can be washed and trimmed 1 day ahead and chilled in a sealed plastic bag lined with dampened paper towels. Bacon can be cut 1 day ahead and chilled, covered.

• Goat cheese phyllo blossoms can be baked 3 hours ahead and kept at room temperature. Reheat in a preheated 350°F oven until warmed through, about 10 minutes.

WILD SALMON WITH PEARL COUSCOUS, SLOW-ROASTED TOMATOES, AND LEMON OREGANO OIL

SERVES 6

Active time: 40 min   Start to finish: 3¼ hr (includes roasting tomatoes)

We prefer wild salmon both for ecological reasons and for its flavor, which is milder than farm raised. Limited varieties are available year-round, but peak season begins in the spring.

For tomatoes and lemon oregano oil

- 6 plum tomatoes (1 lb), halved lengthwise
- 1¼ teaspoons sugar
- ¾ teaspoon salt
- ½ teaspoon black pepper
- ⅓ cup extra-virgin olive oil
- 2 garlic cloves, finely chopped
- 10 fresh basil leaves
- 12 whole fresh oregano leaves plus 3 tablespoons finely chopped
- 2 teaspoons fresh lemon zest, removed in strips with a vegetable peeler and finely minced
- 2 tablespoons fresh lemon juice

For couscous

- 2 teaspoons olive oil
- 2¼ cups pearl (Israeli) couscous (see Sources; 12 oz)
- 1¾ cups reduced-sodium chicken broth (14 fl oz)
- 1 cup water
- ¼ teaspoon salt

For salmon

- 6 (6-oz) pieces wild salmon fillet with skin (see Sources; preferably center cut)
- 1 teaspoon olive oil
- ½ teaspoon salt
- ½ cup Kalamata or other brine-cured black olives (3 oz), pitted and quartered lengthwise

Roast tomatoes and prepare oil:

▶ Put oven rack in middle position and preheat oven to 250°F.

▶ Toss tomatoes with sugar, ½ teaspoon salt, and ¼ teaspoon pepper and arrange, cut sides down, in a small shallow baking pan. Heat oil in a 9- to 10-inch heavy skillet over moderate heat until hot but not smoking, then cook garlic, stirring occasionally, until pale golden, 1 to 2 minutes. Stir in basil and whole oregano leaves, then pour oil over tomatoes. Roast tomatoes until very tender but not falling apart, 2¼ to 2½ hours.

▶ Transfer tomatoes with a spatula to a large plate, then pour oil through a fine-mesh sieve into a small bowl or measuring cup, discarding solids. Stir in chopped oregano, zest, juice, and remaining ¼ teaspoon salt and pepper.

Cook couscous:

▶ Heat 2 teaspoons olive oil in a 3-quart heavy saucepan over moderate heat until hot but not smoking, then toast couscous, stirring occasionally, until fragrant and pale golden, 3 to 5 minutes. Add broth, water, and salt and simmer, covered, until liquid is absorbed and couscous is al dente, 10 to 12 minutes. Remove from heat and let stand, covered, 10 minutes, then stir in 2½ tablespoons lemon oregano oil. Season with salt.

Roast salmon while couscous stands:

▶ Put oven rack in upper third of oven and preheat oven to 500°F. Line a 17- by 12-inch shallow baking pan with foil.
▶ Arrange salmon, skin sides down, in baking pan, then drizzle with olive oil, rubbing it over tops of fillets, and sprinkle with salt. Roast salmon until just cooked through, 12 to 14 minutes.
▶ Divide couscous among 6 plates. Lift salmon flesh from skin with a slotted spatula and transfer a fillet to each bed of couscous. Put 2 tomato halves on each plate, then sprinkle salmon with olives and drizzle with some lemon oregano oil.

Cooks' note:

• Tomatoes can be roasted 3 days ahead and chilled in oil in an airtight container. Bring to room temperature before proceeding.

BLACKBERRY BUTTERMILK PANNA COTTAS WITH BLACKBERRY COMPOTE

SERVES 6

Active time: 30 min Start to finish: 8½ hr (includes chilling)

For panna cottas

¾   lb blackberries (about 3 cups)
1¼ cups well-shaken buttermilk
2¾ teaspoons unflavored gelatin (from two ¼-oz envelopes)
¼   cup water
1½ cups heavy cream
⅔   cup sugar
2   tablespoons blackberry syrup, store-bought (see Sources) or homemade (see cooks' note, below)

For compote

½   cup water
½   cup crème de cassis
2   tablespoons sugar
1½ tablespoons fresh lemon juice
½   lb blackberries (about 2 cups)

Special equipment: 6 (6-oz) molds (preferably nonreactive)

Make panna cottas:

▶ Purée blackberries with buttermilk in a blender until very smooth, then pour through a fine-mesh sieve into a bowl, pressing on and then discarding solids.
▶ Sprinkle gelatin over water in a small bowl and let stand 1 minute to soften.
▶ While gelatin softens, heat cream and sugar in a saucepan over moderate heat until hot, stirring until sugar is dissolved. Remove from heat and add gelatin mixture, stirring until dissolved. Stir cream mixture and syrup into blackberry purée, then pour through cleaned sieve into a bowl. Pour mixture into molds and chill, covered, until firm, at least 8 hours.

Make compote while panna cottas finish chilling:

▶ Boil water, crème de cassis, and sugar in a small saucepan, stirring occasionally, until syrupy and reduced to about ⅓ cup, 10 to 12 minutes. Stir in lemon juice, then pour syrup over blackberries and gently stir to combine.
▶ To serve panna cottas, run a thin knife along edge of molds to loosen if necessary and dip molds in a small bowl of warm water 3 to 5 seconds, then invert panna cottas onto plates and gently lift off molds. Spoon berries and syrup over and around each panna cotta.

Cooks' notes:

• If you're using reactive metal molds, make sure there are no rust spots—the acid in the buttermilk and the fruit will react to the exposed rust and cause the panna cotta to discolor. We had the best luck with molds made of nonreactive materials such as stainless steel, glass, and ceramic.
• To make blackberry syrup, heat ¼ cup blackberry jam with 1 tablespoon water in a small saucepan over moderately low heat, stirring, until jam is dissolved. Pour mixture through a fine-mesh sieve into a small bowl, pressing on and then discarding solids.
• Panna cottas can be chilled in molds up to 1 day.
• Compote can be made 2 hours ahead and kept at room temperature.

COOL AND BRIGHT

DINNER IN A TRANQUIL GARDEN

SERVES 8

CHIVE AND PINE NUT DIP WITH SOURDOUGH TOASTS

ABUNDANCE VINEYARD TALMAGE BLOCK VIOGNIER '01

HORSERADISH-CRUSTED BEEF TENDERLOIN

BLOODY MARY ASPIC

POTATOES AND HARICOTS VERTS WITH VINAIGRETTE

JUSTIN VINEYARDS SYRAH '02

PASSION-FRUIT MERINGUE TART

TREFETHEN LATE-HARVEST RIESLING '02

CHIVE AND PINE NUT DIP WITH SOURDOUGH TOASTS

SERVES 8 (HORS D'OEUVRE)
Active time: 15 min   Start to finish: 1¼ hr

¾ cup coarsely chopped fresh chives plus 2 tablespoons
   finely chopped fresh chives (2 to 3 bunches)
¼ cup vegetable oil
⅜ teaspoon salt
1 (12-inch-long) sourdough baguette, sliced diagonally
   ⅛ inch thick
¼ cup pine nuts (1 oz)
⅔ cup mascarpone (4¾ oz) at room temperature
2 tablespoons cream cheese at room temperature

▸ Purée ¾ cup chives with oil and ⅛ teaspoon salt in a blender until smooth, then chill 1 hour.
▸ While chive oil stands, put oven racks in upper and lower thirds of oven and preheat oven to 375°F. Divide bread slices between 2 baking sheets and toast, switching position of sheets halfway through toasting, until golden, 8 to 10 minutes. Leave oven on.
▸ Toast pine nuts in a shallow baking pan in lower third of oven, shaking pan occasionally, until pale golden, 4 to 5 minutes. Cool, then coarsely chop.
▸ Pour chive oil through a fine-mesh sieve into a small bowl, pressing on and then discarding solids. Stir in pine nuts and remaining 2 tablespoons chives.
▸ Whisk together mascarpone, cream cheese, and remaining ¼ teaspoon salt in a bowl until smooth. Fold in chive oil with pine nuts until cream is streaked (do not mix in thoroughly). Transfer dip to a shallow bowl and serve with toasts.

Cooks' note:
• Dip can be made 6 hours ahead and chilled, covered. Bring to room temperature before serving (this will take about 30 minutes).

HORSERADISH-CRUSTED BEEF TENDERLOIN

SERVES 8
Active time: 15 min   Start to finish: 1¾ hr

1 (3½-lb) trimmed center-cut beef tenderloin
   roast, tied
1¼ teaspoons salt
½ teaspoon black pepper
6 tablespoons olive oil
1 lb fresh horseradish, peeled and coarsely grated
   (1 cup; see cooks' note, below)
2 tablespoons Dijon mustard

Special equipment: an instant-read thermometer
Accompaniment: Bloody Mary aspic (recipe follows)

▸ Put oven rack in middle position and preheat oven to 400°F.
▸ Pat tenderloin dry, then sprinkle with salt and pepper.
▸ Straddle a 17- by 12-inch flameproof heavy roasting pan across 2 burners and heat 3 tablespoons oil in pan over high heat until hot but not smoking, then brown tenderloin on all sides, about 10 minutes total. Remove from heat and transfer meat to a cutting board to cool slightly, about 5 minutes. Put a lightly oiled metal rack inside roasting pan.
▸ While meat cools, toss horseradish with remaining 3 tablespoons oil. Rub meat all over with mustard, then transfer to rack in roasting pan and coat top and sides of meat with horseradish, pressing to help adhere.
▸ Roast tenderloin until thermometer inserted diagonally 2 inches into center of meat registers 120°F, 25 to 35 minutes for medium-rare. Transfer to cutting board and cool, uncovered, to room temperature, about 45 minutes. (Internal temperature will rise to at least 130°F before cooling.)
▸ Remove and discard string. Cut tenderloin into thick slices.

Cooks' note:
• If fresh horseradish is unavailable, substitute ¾ cup drained bottled white horseradish. Rinse well in a sieve, then squeeze very dry in 3 or 4 layers of paper towels.

BLOODY MARY ASPIC
SERVES 8
Active time: 45 min   Start to finish: 7¼ hr (includes chilling)

½ cup coarsely chopped shallots
3 celery ribs, coarsely chopped
2 tablespoons olive oil
5 lb plum tomatoes, cored, quartered, and puréed
   in a blender
2 tablespoons sugar
1¾ teaspoons salt
¾ teaspoon black pepper
½ teaspoon ground celery seeds
2 teaspoons Worcestershire sauce
¼ cup fresh lemon juice
¼ cup vodka
2 tablespoons gelatin (from three ¼-oz envelopes)
   Vegetable oil for greasing pan

Special equipment: **a double layer of rinsed and squeezed cheesecloth**

▶ Cook shallots and celery in olive oil in a 4-quart heavy pot over moderate heat, stirring occasionally, until softened, about 10 minutes. Add puréed tomatoes, sugar, salt, pepper, and celery seeds and simmer, partially covered, stirring occasionally, 25 minutes. Pour tomato mixture through a sieve lined with dampened cheesecloth into a clean 3-quart saucepan, pressing hard on solids to extract as much liquid as possible. Discard solids. Bring tomato broth just to a boil, then remove from heat and stir in Worcestershire sauce.
▶ While tomato broth comes to a boil, stir together lemon juice and vodka in a small bowl. Sprinkle gelatin over vodka mixture. (Spoon vodka mixture over any powdered gelatin remaining on top.) Let stand until softened, about 5 minutes.
▶ Lightly oil a 1½- to 2-quart nonreactive shallow baking pan (2 inches deep).
▶ Add gelatin mixture to hot tomato broth, stirring until gelatin is dissolved. Pour into baking pan and chill, uncovered, until firm, at least 6 hours.
▶ To unmold aspic, run a small sharp knife around edge, then dip baking pan into a larger pan of warm water, 15 to 20 seconds. Put a cutting board over baking pan, then carefully invert aspic onto board and cut into ½-inch cubes.

POTATOES AND HARICOTS VERTS WITH VINAIGRETTE
SERVES 8
Active time: 30 min   Start to finish: 1½ hr

3 tablespoons Champagne vinegar or white-wine vinegar
½ teaspoon Dijon mustard
¼ teaspoon black pepper
¼ teaspoon sugar
2 teaspoons salt
½ cup olive oil
3 lb small (1½- to 2-inch) yellow-fleshed potatoes
   such as Yukon Gold, scrubbed well
¾ cup diced (¼-inch) red onion
¾ lb haricots verts or other thin green beans, trimmed
   and cut into 2-inch pieces
3 celery ribs, cut into ¼-inch dice
⅓ cup finely chopped fresh flat-leaf parsley

▶ Whisk together vinegar, mustard, pepper, sugar, and 1 teaspoon salt in a small bowl. Add oil in a slow stream, whisking until emulsified.
▶ Quarter potatoes, then cover with cold water by 1 inch in a 4- to 5-quart pot and bring to a boil with remaining teaspoon salt. Reduce heat and simmer, uncovered, until potatoes are tender, 8 to 10 minutes. Drain, then transfer hot potatoes to a bowl and toss with onion and all but ¼ cup vinaigrette. Cool to room temperature, about 1 hour.
▶ While potatoes cool, cook beans in a 3-quart saucepan of boiling salted water, uncovered, until crisp-tender, 3 to 4 minutes, then drain and transfer to a bowl of ice water to stop cooking. Let stand 2 minutes. Drain and pat dry.
▶ Just before serving, toss potato mixture with beans, celery, parsley, and remaining ¼ cup vinaigrette.

Cooks' notes:
• If you're making your vinaigrette with white-wine vinegar, use ½ teaspoon sugar to balance the higher acidity.
• Potatoes can be cooked and combined with onion and vinaigrette 1 day ahead and chilled, covered. Bring to room temperature (this will take about 1 hour), then add remaining ingredients.
• Green beans can be cooked and celery can be diced 1 day ahead and chilled separately, wrapped well in dampened paper towels, in sealed plastic bags.

PASSION-FRUIT MERINGUE TART

SERVES 8

Active time: 1¼ hr   Start to finish: 8¾ hr (includes chilling)

For passion-fruit curd

- 6 large eggs
- 1 cup sugar
- 1 tablespoon cornstarch
- ⅛ teaspoon salt
- ⅔ cup thawed unsweetened passion-fruit (*maracuyá*) purée such as Goya brand (see Sources)
- 1 stick (½ cup) unsalted butter, cut into ½-inch cubes

For pastry

- 1⅓ cups all-purpose flour plus additional for dusting
- 2 tablespoons sugar
- ¼ teaspoon salt
- 1 stick (½ cup) cold unsalted butter, cut into ½-inch cubes
- 1 large egg yolk
- 1½ tablespoons ice water plus additional if necessary

For meringue

- 4 large egg whites at room temperature 30 minutes
- ⅛ teaspoon salt
- ¾ cup sugar
- ¼ cup water

Special equipment: a pastry or bench scraper; a 9- to 9½-inch fluted round tart pan with removable bottom; pie weights or raw rice; a candy thermometer; a pastry brush; a small blowtorch

Make curd:

▶ Whisk together eggs, sugar, cornstarch, and salt in a bowl until smooth.

▶ Heat passion-fruit purée in a 1½- to 2-quart heavy saucepan over moderate heat until heated through, then add hot purée to egg mixture in a slow stream, whisking until combined. Return to saucepan. Whisk in butter, 1 cube at a time, over moderate heat and cook, whisking frequently, until mixture is thickened and just comes to a boil, about

6 minutes. Cook, whisking constantly, 2 minutes more. Force curd through a fine-mesh sieve into a bowl and chill, its surface covered with wax paper, at least 8 hours.

Make pastry while curd chills:

▶ Whisk together flour, sugar, and salt in a large bowl (or pulse in a food processor). Blend in butter with your fingertips or a pastry blender (or pulse) until mixture resembles coarse meal with some roughly pea-size butter lumps. Beat together yolk and water with a fork and stir into flour mixture (or pulse) until combined well.

▶ Squeeze a small handful: If it doesn't hold together, add more water, ½ tablespoon at a time, to dough, stirring (or pulsing) until just combined. (Do not overwork, or pastry will be tough.)

▶ Turn out dough onto a lightly floured surface and divide into 8 portions. With heel of your hand, smear each portion once in a forward motion to help distribute fat. Gather all of dough together with scraper and press into a ball, then flatten into a 5-inch disk. Chill, wrapped tightly in plastic wrap, until firm, at least 1 hour.

▶ Bring dough to cool room temperature before rolling out, about 30 minutes.

▶ Lightly dust dough with flour and roll out between 2 sheets of wax paper into a 12-inch round. Fit dough into tart pan (discard paper), pressing with floured fingers onto bottom and up side of pan. Trim overhang to ½ inch and fold inside, pressing against rim of pan, then chill shell 30 minutes.

▶ Put oven rack in middle position and preheat oven to 350°F.

▶ Line shell with foil and fill with pie weights. Bake until edge is pale golden, about 20 minutes. Remove foil and weights and bake shell until bottom and side are golden, 20 to 25 minutes more. Cool completely in pan on a rack. Remove side of pan.

Make meringue and assemble tart:

▶ Combine whites and salt in a bowl.

▶ Bring sugar and water to a boil in a 1- to 1½-quart heavy saucepan over moderate heat, stirring until sugar is dissolved. Put thermometer facedown into sugar syrup, resting other end against rim of saucepan, and continue to boil (but do not stir), brushing any sugar crystals down side of pan with pastry brush dipped in water.

▶ When syrup reaches about 235°F, beat egg whites with salt at medium-high speed until they just hold soft peaks.

▶ When syrup reaches 238 to 242°F, immediately remove syrup from heat and pour in a slow, thin stream down side of bowl into whites (avoid beaters), beating at high speed until meringue is cool to the touch, about 10 minutes in a stand mixer or 15 with a handheld.

▶ Transfer shell to a cake plate. Spoon curd into shell and spread evenly. Dollop meringue on top of curd, then spread to edge of crust. Draw meringue up into peaks with a rubber spatula.

▶ Move blowtorch flame evenly back and forth over meringue peaks, holding flame 1 to 2 inches from meringue to avoid burning, until lightly browned in spots.

Cooks' notes:
• The egg whites will not be fully cooked.
• Curd can be chilled up to 3 days.
• Dough can be made 5 days ahead and chilled, wrapped well in plastic wrap.
• Tart shell can be baked 1 day ahead and cooled completely, uncovered, then kept at room temperature, wrapped in plastic wrap.
• Tart can be assembled and meringue browned 1 hour ahead, then kept at cool room temperature.

OPPOSITE: chive and pine nut dip with sourdough toasts; passion-fruit meringue tart

EASY LIVING

A LAKESIDE GRILLED SUPPER

SERVES 8

**CRAB SALAD WITH WONTON CRISPS
AND LIME**

DOMAINE DES MAILLETTES EN POMMARD
SAINT-VÉRAN '03

**GRILLED CORNISH HENS WITH COCONUT
CURRY SAUCE**

**PICKLED NAPA CABBAGE, CARROTS,
AND SNOW PEAS**

**JASMINE RICE WITH PEANUTS AND
SCALLIONS**

MCDOWELL GRENACHE '03

**GRILLED COCONUT POUND-CAKE
SUNDAES WITH TROPICAL FRUIT**

CRAB SALAD WITH WONTON CRISPS AND LIME

SERVES 8
Active time: 35 min   Start to finish: 35 min

Traditionally used to enclose a savory filling, wonton wrappers are cut and fried into crisp triangles here, lending crunchy texture to soft crabmeat.

For wonton crisps

- 8 square wonton wrappers, thawed if frozen
  About 6 cups vegetable oil

For crab salad

- 1 teaspoon finely grated fresh lime zest
- 1½ tablespoons fresh lime juice
- ¼ teaspoon salt
- ¼ teaspoon black pepper
- 2½ tablespoons olive oil
- 1 lb jumbo lump crabmeat, picked over
- 2 celery ribs, cut into ¼-inch dice
- ¼ cup thinly sliced white and pale green parts of scallions (reserve dark green parts for jasmine rice with peanuts and scallions, page 113)

Special equipment: **a deep-fat thermometer**
Accompaniment: **lime wedges**

Make wonton crisps:

▶ Halve each wonton wrapper to make 2 rectangles, then halve each rectangle diagonally to make 2 triangles. Heat 1¼ inches vegetable oil in a 4- to 5-quart heavy pot over moderately high heat until thermometer registers 360°F. Gently lay 4 triangles on oil (do not drop in, or triangles will lose their shape) and fry, turning over once, until just golden, 15 to 30 seconds total. Transfer with a slotted spoon to paper towels to drain and season with salt. Fry remaining triangles in same manner.

Make crab salad:

▶ Whisk together zest, juice, salt, and pepper in a bowl until salt is dissolved. Add olive oil, whisking until combined well.
▶ Add crab, celery, and scallions to dressing and toss gently to combine.
▶ Serve crab salad in glasses topped with wonton crisps.

Cooks' note:

• Wontons can be fried 1 day ahead and kept in an airtight container at room temperature.

GRILLED CORNISH HENS WITH COCONUT CURRY SAUCE

SERVES 8
Active time: 1 hr   Start to finish: 14½ hr (includes marinating)

For this recipe, we prefer Thai Kitchen coconut milk (available at many supermarkets) because it has a higher coconut-cream content than other brands, giving the sauce and marinade a much thicker consistency. Other brands will work but are thinner; use about half a can more than we call for here.

- ½ cup finely chopped shallots (2 large)
- ¼ cup vegetable oil
- 2 large garlic cloves, minced
- 2 teaspoons minced peeled fresh ginger
- 2 tablespoons Thai red curry paste (see Sources)
- 2 (14-oz) cans unsweetened coconut milk
- 1½ teaspoons packed light brown sugar
- 1 teaspoon salt
- 2 teaspoons Asian fish sauce
- 4 (1¼- to 1½-lb) Cornish hens, halved lengthwise

Garnish: **fresh cilantro sprigs**

▶ Cook shallots in oil in a wide 4- to 5-quart heavy pot over moderately low heat, stirring occasionally, until softened, 4 to 5 minutes. Add garlic and ginger and cook, stirring occasionally, 2 minutes. Add curry paste and cook, mashing paste to combine with oil and stirring constantly, 3 minutes (paste will begin sticking to bottom of pot). Add coconut milk, brown sugar, and salt and simmer, uncovered, stirring occasionally, until reduced to about 3 cups, 25 to 30 minutes. Remove from heat, then stir in fish sauce and cool to room temperature, stirring occasionally, about 30 minutes. Reserve 1½ cups curry sauce (for serving) in a bowl and chill, covered.
▶ Trim and discard any excess fat from hens (to prevent flare-ups on grill), then rinse and pat dry. Coat hens well with remaining curry sauce in a large bowl, then divide hens between 2 large sealable plastic bags and seal bags, pressing out excess air. Marinate hens, chilled, at least 12 and up to 24 hours.
▶ Let hens stand at room temperature 30 minutes before grilling.
▶ Prepare grill for cooking over medium-hot charcoal or moderate heat for gas (see Tips, page 8).

▶ Remove hens from marinade, shaking off excess, and transfer to a large platter. Discard marinade. Season hens with salt, then grill, starting with skin sides down, covered only if using a gas grill, on lightly oiled grill rack, turning occasionally to prevent overbrowning, until cooked through, 25 to 30 minutes total.

▶ Heat reserved curry sauce in a small saucepan over moderate heat, stirring, until hot. Serve hens with curry sauce.

Cooks' note:

• If you aren't able to grill outdoors, hens can be roasted in a lightly oiled large shallow baking pan (1 inch deep) in middle of a preheated 450°F oven, skin sides up and without turning, until cooked through, about 35 minutes. (If, after roasting hens, you prefer the skin slightly darker, broil them 4 to 5 inches from heat 1 to 2 minutes.)

PICKLED NAPA CABBAGE, CARROTS, AND SNOW PEAS
SERVES 8
Active time: 1 hr Start to finish: 1 hr

In Malaysian cuisine, at least one pickled dish (acar) is offered with every meal—it provides a bold flavor contrast to the other dishes. Our recipe isn't traditional, but it serves the same purpose.

½ cup rice vinegar (not seasoned)
¼ cup plus 2 tablespoons sugar
1 tablespoon finely chopped peeled fresh ginger
2 teaspoons salt
1½ teaspoons finely chopped garlic
3 whole cloves
5 medium carrots, cut into 3- by ⅛-inch matchsticks
¾ lb snow peas, trimmed and strings discarded
1¼ lb Napa cabbage, leaves halved lengthwise, then cut crosswise into ¼-inch strips
2 tablespoons thinly sliced seeded fresh mild red chile, such as red jalapeño

▶ Bring vinegar, sugar, ginger, salt, garlic, and cloves to a boil in a small saucepan, stirring until sugar is dissolved, then remove from heat and let steep, uncovered, 30 minutes. Discard cloves.

▶ While pickling liquid steeps, blanch carrots in a 6- to 8-quart pot of boiling salted water (see Tips, page 8) 30 seconds, then transfer with a large slotted spoon to a bowl of ice and cold water to stop cooking. Lift out carrots with slotted spoon and drain in a colander. Transfer to paper towels and pat dry.

▶ Blanch snow peas in same pot of boiling water 30 seconds, then transfer to ice water, drain, and pat dry in same manner. Cut each snow pea lengthwise into 4 strips.

▶ Blanch cabbage in same pot of boiling water 5 seconds, then transfer to ice water, drain, and pat dry.

▶ Just before serving, toss vegetables with pickling liquid and chile in a large bowl.

Cooks' notes:

• Pickling liquid can be made 1 day ahead and chilled, covered.

• Vegetables can be blanched 1 day ahead and chilled separately in sealed plastic bags lined with paper towels.

JASMINE RICE WITH PEANUTS AND SCALLIONS
SERVES 8
Active time: 10 min Start to finish: 30 min

2 cups jasmine rice (13 oz)
2 cups water
1 cup reduced-sodium chicken broth
½ cup salted roasted peanuts (2½ oz), finely chopped
⅔ cup thinly sliced scallion greens

▶ Wash rice in several changes of cold water in a bowl until water is almost clear, then drain rice well in a sieve. Bring rice, water, and broth to a boil in a 3- to 4-quart heavy saucepan, then reduce heat to low and cook, covered, until rice is tender and water is absorbed, 12 to 15 minutes. Remove from heat and let stand, covered, 5 minutes. Fluff with a fork, then stir in peanuts and scallion greens.

COCONUT POUND CAKE

MAKES 1 LOAF

Active time: 30 min   Start to finish: 4 hr (includes cooling)

Although this cake, used in the grilled coconut pound-cake sundaes with tropical fruit (recipe follows), calls for flaked coconut, don't be tempted to omit the coconut extract—it really adds depth to the coconut flavor.

  2 cups all-purpose flour plus additional for dusting
  1 teaspoon baking powder
 ½ teaspoon salt
  2 sticks (1 cup) unsalted butter, softened
1½ cups sugar
  4 large eggs
  1 teaspoon vanilla extract
 ½ teaspoon coconut extract
1½ cups sweetened flaked coconut (6 oz), toasted
    (see Tips, page 8) and cooled

▸ Put oven rack in middle position and preheat oven to 325°F.
▸ Butter a 9- by 5- by 3-inch loaf pan and dust with flour, knocking out excess flour.
▸ Whisk together flour (2 cups), baking powder, and salt in a bowl.
▸ Beat together butter and sugar in a large bowl with an electric mixer at medium-high speed until pale and fluffy, about 5 minutes with a stand mixer or 8 to 10 minutes with a handheld. Add eggs 1 at a time, beating well after each addition, then beat in extracts. Reduce speed to low, then mix in flour mixture until just combined. Fold in coconut gently but thoroughly with a rubber spatula.
▸ Spoon batter evenly into loaf pan, smoothing top. Bake until golden and a wooden pick or skewer inserted into center comes out clean, 1 to 1¼ hours.
▸ Cool cake in pan on a rack 15 minutes. Run a thin knife around edge of cake, then invert onto rack and cool completely.

Cooks' note:
• Cake can be made 3 days ahead and kept, wrapped well in plastic wrap, at room temperature.

GRILLED COCONUT POUND-CAKE SUNDAES WITH TROPICAL FRUIT

SERVES 8

Active time: 1 hr   Start to finish: 5 hr (includes making cake)

Be sure to clean the grill rack thoroughly with a metal brush to remove any bits of grilled food that might impart an off flavor to the cake. If you're making this entire menu, we recommend grilling the cake before cooking the Cornish hens. Reheat the cake on a baking sheet in a 350°F oven before serving.

 ½ cup packed light brown sugar
 ¼ cup fresh lemon juice
 ¼ cup water
  4 (⅛-inch-thick) slices fresh ginger, smashed
 ½ pineapple, trimmed, peeled, and halved lengthwise
  8 (½-inch-thick) slices coconut pound cake (recipe
    precedes)
  2 pt premium ice cream (vanilla, banana, or mango)
  2 mangoes, peeled, pitted, and cut lengthwise into
    ¼-inch pieces

▸ Bring sugar, lemon juice, water, and ginger to a boil in a 1-quart heavy saucepan, stirring until sugar is dissolved, then remove from heat and let steep, uncovered, 15 minutes. Pour syrup through a sieve into a bowl and cool to room temperature, about 15 minutes.
▸ Prepare grill for cooking over medium-hot charcoal or moderate heat for gas (see Tips, page 8).
▸ While grill heats, cut core from pineapple and discard. Cut each piece of pineapple lengthwise into 8 wedges, then halve each wedge diagonally (use caution; peeled pineapple is slippery).
▸ Grill pound cake, covered only if using a gas grill, on lightly oiled grill rack, turning over once with a metal spatula, until grill marks appear, about 1½ minutes total.
▸ Divide coconut pound cake among 8 shallow bowls, then top each slice with a generous scoop of ice cream and some pineapple and mango. Drizzle each serving with 1½ tablespoons lemon ginger syrup.

Cooks' note:
• Syrup can be made 3 days ahead and chilled, covered.

BEGINNING TO SEE THE LIGHT

BRUNCH ALFRESCO

SERVES 6

MANGO MINT SPARKLERS

SMOKED-SALMON QUESADILLAS WITH WARM TOMATOES AND ARUGULA

CHERRY-APRICOT YOGURT SUNDAES

MAPLE GRANOLA BRITTLE

MANGO MINT SPARKLERS

SERVES 6

Active time: 15 min   Start to finish: 1¼ hr

Brunch is a wonderful time to indulge in this refreshing Mimosa alternative. It's important to use pure mango nectar here (though it may not be labeled "pure"); nectar mixed with other fruit juices or high-fructose corn syrup makes the drink too sweet.

¼ cup packed fresh mint leaves
1 tablespoon fresh lime juice
3 cups (24 fl oz) pure mango nectar, chilled
1 (750-ml) bottle Moscato d'Asti sparkling wine or
    sparkling water, chilled

Garnish: cucumber spears and fresh mint leaves

▶ Crush mint leaves with lime juice in a bowl with a pestle or wooden spoon until bruised and beginning to break up. Stir in mango nectar, then chill, covered, at least 1 hour.
▶ Pour mango mixture through a sieve into a large glass measure, discarding solids, then pour about ½ cup mango mixture into each of 6 (10-ounce) glasses and top off with Moscato d'Asti (or sparkling water).

Cooks' note:
• Mango mixture can be chilled, covered, up to 1 day.

SMOKED-SALMON QUESADILLAS WITH WARM TOMATOES AND ARUGULA

SERVES 6

Active time: 45 min   Start to finish: 45 min

We prefer Nova salmon for this particular recipe because it's the mildest and least salty. Although Nova has become a general term for smoked salmon, it really describes the delicacy made from fish descended from wild Nova Scotia salmon.

1 small red onion, thinly sliced crosswise
6 oz cream cheese, softened
6 oz soft mild goat cheese at room temperature
2 teaspoons finely chopped fresh chives
½ teaspoon finely grated fresh lemon zest
¼ teaspoon black pepper
12 (8-inch) flour tortillas (not low-fat)
1 lb sliced smoked salmon (preferably Nova)
1 firm-ripe California avocado
2 teaspoons fresh lemon juice
3 tablespoons extra-virgin olive oil
1 lb cherry tomatoes, halved lengthwise (2⅔ cups)
4 cups loosely packed arugula leaves (2 to 3 bunches)

Special equipment: a large (2-burner) cast-iron griddle

▶ Soak sliced onion in a bowl of ice and cold water 15 minutes, then drain well and pat dry.
▶ While onion soaks, stir together cheeses, chives, zest, and pepper in a bowl with a rubber spatula until combined well.
▶ Spread about 1½ tablespoons cheese mixture evenly over each of 2 tortillas (keep remaining tortillas covered with plastic wrap). Top 1 tortilla with an even layer of salmon, covering cream cheese completely, then top with other tortilla, cheese side down. Make 5 more quesadillas in same manner, then stack on a plate and chill, covered with plastic wrap, until ready to heat.
▶ Halve, pit, and peel avocado, then cut lengthwise into ⅛-inch-thick slices. Lightly brush avocado slices with lemon juice.
▶ Heat griddle over high heat until very hot, then reduce heat to moderate. Lightly brush 2 quesadillas on both sides with some oil, then toast on griddle (1 at a time if necessary) until undersides are golden with some blackened spots, about 1 minute. Flip quesadillas over with a spatula and toast until undersides are golden with some blackened spots, 1 to 2 minutes, then transfer to a baking sheet, arranging in 1 layer, and cover with foil to keep warm. Toast remaining quesadillas in same manner, using a second baking sheet.
▶ Heat remaining oil in a 12-inch heavy skillet over high heat until hot but not smoking, then cook tomatoes, stirring occasionally and seasoning with salt and pepper, until just beginning to soften, about 1 minute.
▶ Transfer quesadillas to plates, then top with onion, avocado, tomatoes, and arugula.

CHERRY-APRICOT YOGURT SUNDAES

SERVES 6

Active time: 20 min   Start to finish: 1 hr

Though you could certainly use regular red cherries in this recipe, we prefer yellow cherries such as Royal Ann or Rainier, available in supermarkets, for their lovely yellow color, as well as their bright flavor and mild sweetness.

We use Greek yogurt because it has a much thicker texture than other yogurts and holds its shape nicely.

- ⅓ cup sugar
- ½ cup water
- 5 fresh bay leaves (see Sources), halved lengthwise, or 2 large dried California bay leaves
- 2 (3- by 1-inch) strips fresh lemon zest (see Tips, page 8)
- 2 (3- by 1-inch) strips fresh orange zest
- 6 fresh apricots
- 1 lb fresh cherries (preferably Royal Ann or Rainier)
- 2 teaspoons fresh lemon juice
- 2 cups plain yogurt (preferably Greek)

Accompaniment: **maple granola brittle (recipe follows)**

▶ Simmer sugar, water, bay leaves, and zests in a 1-quart heavy saucepan 5 minutes, then remove from heat and let steep 20 minutes.

▶ While syrup steeps, halve apricots lengthwise and remove pits. Run a paring knife crosswise around each cherry, touching pit, then twist cherry halves to separate. Remove pits with tip of knife.

▶ Toss apricots and cherries with lemon juice in a large shallow bowl. Return syrup to a boil, then pour over fruit, tossing to coat. Cover and let stand, stirring occasionally, at least 30 minutes.

▶ Put ⅓ cup yogurt on each of 6 plates and serve with fruit.

Cooks' notes:
• Apricots and cherries can stand in syrup up to 2 hours (cherries will start to discolor after that time).
• Bay-leaf syrup can be made 3 days ahead and cooled completely, uncovered, then chilled, covered. Bring to a boil before tossing with apricots and cherries.

MAPLE GRANOLA BRITTLE

SERVES 6

Active time: 30 min   Start to finish: 1¼ hr

- 1 cup old-fashioned rolled oats
- ½ cup whole almonds (2½ oz)
- ½ cup pecans (2 oz)
- ½ cup shelled sunflower seeds (2 oz)
- ½ cup roasted pumpkin seeds (2½ oz)
- 1 teaspoon finely grated fresh orange zest (see Tips, page 8)
- 1 cup packed light brown sugar
- ½ cup pure maple syrup
- ½ cup fresh orange juice
- ¼ teaspoon salt
- ½ stick (¼ cup) cold unsalted butter, softened

Special equipment: **a nonstick bakeware liner such as Silpat; a candy thermometer; parchment paper**

▶ Put oven rack in middle position and preheat oven to 350°F.

▶ Spread oats, almonds, pecans, and sunflower seeds in an even layer in a large shallow baking pan and bake, stirring occasionally, until oats are pale golden, about 15 minutes. Transfer to a bowl and toss with pumpkin seeds and zest.

▶ Line a baking sheet with nonstick liner. Cook brown sugar, syrup, juice, and salt in a 4- to 6-quart heavy saucepan over moderately high heat, stirring with a wooden spoon (be careful not to splash or splatter while stirring; mixture will become extremely hot), until it registers 290°F on thermometer, 8 to 10 minutes. Stir in butter until melted (mixture will thicken and become opaque), then quickly add nut mixture and stir until coated well. Immediately pour onto liner, then cover mixture with a sheet of parchment paper.

▶ Roll out brittle as thin as possible with a rolling pin. Carefully peel off parchment paper and discard (don't worry if some caramel sticks to parchment).

▶ Cool to room temperature, about 30 minutes. Break brittle into large pieces.

Cooks' note:
• Brittle can be made 2 weeks ahead and kept, layered between sheets of parchment paper, in an airtight container at room temperature.

A PLATEFUL OF SUMMER

DINING WATERSIDE

SERVES 6

CHILLED ZUCCHINI SOUP

**LONDON BROIL WITH SOY CITRUS
MAYONNAISE**

SUMMER TOMATOES

CHÂTEAU MAS NEUF ROSÉ '04

**LEMON SUN CAKES WITH BERRIES
AND CREAM**

ELIO PERRONE SOURGAL '04

CHILLED ZUCCHINI SOUP

SERVES 6

Active time: 20 min   Start to finish: 40 min

This creamy chilled soup will make you hope for an abundance of zucchini in your garden this year. Thin-sliced zucchini blossoms, available at produce markets and specialty foods shops, add a beautiful hint of color while lending texture to the soup's smoothness.

¼ lb shallots, thinly sliced crosswise (1 cup)
2 tablespoons extra-virgin olive oil
1½ lb zucchini (3 to 4 medium), peeled and
     halved lengthwise, then cut crosswise
     into ⅛-inch-thick slices
2 (2- by 1½-inch) strips fresh lemon zest
    (see Tips, page 8)
1 teaspoon salt
¼ teaspoon black pepper
1¾ cups reduced-sodium chicken broth (14 fl oz)
1¾ cups water
1 cup loosely packed fresh flat-leaf parsley leaves
1 tablespoon finely chopped fresh dill
½ cup well-shaken buttermilk or plain yogurt

Garnish: **thinly sliced or torn zucchini blossoms**

▶ Cook shallots in oil in a 4-quart heavy saucepan over moderate heat, stirring occasionally, until softened, about 5 minutes.
▶ Add zucchini, zest, salt, and pepper and cook, stirring occasionally, until zucchini is softened, about 5 minutes. Add broth and water and simmer until zucchini is tender, about 3 minutes.
▶ Purée zucchini mixture, including zest, along with parsley and dill in a blender (in 2 batches if necessary) until smooth (use caution when blending hot liquids). Transfer to a metal bowl, then set bowl into a larger bowl of ice and cold water. Cool, stirring occasionally, about 20 minutes.
▶ Stir in buttermilk and season with salt.

Cooks' note:
• Soup (with buttermilk or yogurt) can be made 1 day ahead and chilled, covered. (If making soup ahead, cooling in ice bath is not necessary.) Stir well before serving.

LONDON BROIL WITH SOY CITRUS MAYONNAISE

SERVES 6

Active time: 25 min   Start to finish: 5¼ hr (includes marinating)

London broil comes in different weights and thicknesses; it may be necessary to use two pieces to get the proper amount.

¾ cup fine-quality fermented soy sauce (see Sources)
½ cup dry red wine
¼ cup fresh lemon juice
⅓ cup fresh orange juice
3 tablespoons olive oil
1 bunch scallions, cut into 3-inch lengths
5 garlic cloves, smashed and peeled
½ teaspoon white pepper
    Pinch of cayenne
2½ to 3 lb top-round London broil (1 to 1½ inches thick)
1 cup mayonnaise

Special equipment: **an instant-read thermometer**
Accompaniment: **toasted or grilled country bread**

▶ Combine soy sauce, red wine, juices, 2 tablespoons oil, scallions, garlic, white pepper, and cayenne in a 1-quart heavy-duty sealable plastic bag. Add steak and seal bag, pressing out air. Turn bag to coat steak, then marinate, chilled, turning bag occasionally, at least 4 hours.
▶ Transfer steak to a plate and pour 2 tablespoons marinade through a fine-mesh sieve into a 1-quart heavy saucepan, discarding remainder. Bring steak to room temperature, about 30 minutes.
▶ Heat remaining tablespoon oil in a 12-inch heavy skillet over moderately high heat until hot but not smoking, then cook steak, uncovered, until underside is browned, about 5 minutes. Turn steak over, then reduce heat to moderately low and cover skillet. Continue cooking until thermometer inserted horizontally 2 inches into center of steak registers 120°F, 10 to 12 minutes. Transfer to a cutting board and let stand at least 15 minutes (internal temperature of steak will rise to 130–135°F for medium-rare).
▶ While steak cooks and stands, bring marinade in saucepan to a boil, then pour into a bowl and cool completely. Whisk in mayonnaise until combined well and chill, covered.
▶ Holding knife at a 45-degree angle, cut steak across the grain into very thin slices and transfer to a platter, then

drizzle with any juices accumulated on cutting board. Serve at room temperature or slightly chilled, with mayonnaise.

Cooks' notes:
• Steak can be marinated up to 1 day.
• Soy citrus mayonnaise can be chilled up to 5 days.

SUMMER TOMATOES

SERVES 6
Active time: 10 min   Start to finish: 10 min

Whether you use heirloom, beefsteak, or cherry, this dish is all about the tomatoes. Use the ripest ones you can find.

3   tablespoons extra-virgin olive oil
2   tablespoons malt vinegar
¾   teaspoon packed light brown sugar
½   teaspoon salt (preferably flaky sea salt or *fleur de sel*)
½   teaspoon coarsely ground black pepper
2   lb ripe tomatoes, cut crosswise into ½-inch-thick slices
1   scallion, thinly sliced diagonally

▶ Whisk together oil, vinegar, brown sugar, salt, and pepper in a small bowl. Arrange one third of tomatoes in 1 layer on a large plate, then drizzle with some dressing and sprinkle with some scallion. Make 2 more layers of tomatoes, drizzling each with dressing and sprinkling with scallion.

Cooks' note:
• Tomatoes can be sliced and dressed, without scallion, 6 hours ahead and chilled, covered with plastic wrap. Sprinkle scallion over tomatoes just before serving.

LEMON SUN CAKES WITH BERRIES AND CREAM

MAKES 6 INDIVIDUAL CAKES
Active time: 20 min   Start to finish: 1¼ hr (includes cooling)

¾   cup plus 2 tablespoons all-purpose flour
1   teaspoon baking powder
½   teaspoon finely grated fresh lemon zest
¼   teaspoon salt
½   stick (¼ cup) unsalted butter, softened
½   cup sugar
1   large egg
½   teaspoon vanilla
½   cup whole milk
1   cup raspberries (4 oz)
1   cup blueberries (5 oz)
1   cup blackberries (5 oz)
1   cup strawberries (4 oz), sliced ¼ inch thick
3   tablespoons superfine granulated sugar
½   cup chilled heavy cream

Special equipment: 6 (5-oz) fluted brioche molds (4 inches across top) or a muffin tin with 6 (5- to 6-oz) muffin cups
Garnish: white and red currants or other fresh berries

▶ Put oven rack in middle position and preheat oven to 350°F. Generously butter molds and put on a baking sheet.
▶ Whisk together flour, baking powder, zest, and salt.
▶ Beat together butter and sugar with an electric mixer at high speed until pale and fluffy, about 2 minutes. Beat in egg and vanilla until just incorporated. Add milk and beat until just combined (mixture will appear curdled). Reduce speed to low, then add flour mixture in 3 batches, beating until just combined after each addition.
▶ Divide batter among molds, filling each mold about two-thirds full. Bake until edges of cakes are golden and a wooden pick inserted in center of a cake comes out clean, about 25 minutes. Cool cakes in molds on a rack 5 minutes, then turn out onto rack and cool completely.
▶ While cakes cool, pulse ½ cup each of raspberries, blueberries, blackberries, and strawberries (all together) with 2 tablespoons superfine sugar in a food processor until fruit is just crushed. Chill, covered, up to 2 hours.
▶ Beat cream with remaining tablespoon superfine sugar using cleaned beaters at medium-high speed until it just forms soft peaks. Chill, covered, until ready to serve (but no longer than 2 hours).
▶ Arrange cakes upside down on 6 plates and top each with 2 rounded tablespoons whipped cream and 1 rounded tablespoon crushed berries. Scatter remaining whole berries over top and serve remaining crushed berries on the side.

Cooks' note:
• Cakes can be made 2 days ahead and kept in an airtight container at room temperature, or 2 weeks ahead and frozen, wrapped in plastic wrap and then foil. Thaw frozen cakes in refrigerator and bring to room temperature before serving.

DINNER GETS CRACKIN'

FEASTING ON CRAB

SERVES 6

RADISHES WITH TRIPLE-CRÈME CHEESE

**STEAMED BLUE CRABS WITH
BLACK GINGER DIPPING SAUCE**

HERB-TOSSED CORN

FARMERS MARKET GREENS

MACROSTIE WILDCAT MOUNTAIN
CHARDONNAY '03

**WARM SKILLET SOUR CHERRIES
WITH VANILLA ICE CREAM**

129

STEAMED BLUE CRABS WITH BLACK GINGER DIPPING SAUCE

SERVES 6

Active time: 20 min   Start to finish: 35 min

½   cup fresh cilantro stems, coarsely chopped

36 live blue crabs (¼ to ⅓ lb each; see Sources),
    well rinsed

1½ to 2 tablespoons finely chopped peeled fresh ginger

½   cup fermented fine-quality soy sauce

¼   cup sugar

¼   cup water

3   tablespoons Chinese black vinegar (preferably
    Chinkiang; see Sources) or cider vinegar

¼   teaspoon salt

Special equipment: a wide 6- to 8-qt heavy pot with a lid

▶ Bring 1½ inches water to a boil in pot. Add cilantro stems, then carefully add half of crabs using tongs and return to a boil. Cook, covered with lid, 8 minutes (for ¼-pound crabs) to 10 minutes (for ⅓-pound crabs) from time they enter water. (Break shell of 1 claw to check for doneness;

crabmeat should be opaque.) Transfer crabs with long-handled tongs to a large platter, reserving cooking liquid in pot, and keep warm, loosely covered with foil. Cook remaining crabs in same manner.

▶ While crabs cook, stir together ginger (to taste), soy sauce, sugar, water, vinegar, and salt in a small bowl until sugar and salt are dissolved.

▶ If necessary, dip crabs in cooking liquid to remove any external residue, then transfer to another large platter. Serve crabs hot, with dipping sauce.

HERB-TOSSED CORN

SERVES 6

Active time: 15 min   Start to finish: 25 min

6   ears fresh corn, shucked

½   stick (¼ cup) unsalted butter

1½ teaspoons fresh lemon juice

½   teaspoon salt

¼   teaspoon coarsely ground black pepper

⅛   teaspoon cayenne

¼   cup chopped fresh cilantro

Special equipment: a wide 6- to 8-qt heavy pot with a tight-fitting lid
Garnish: **fresh cilantro leaves**

▶ Bring 1½ inches water (do not salt water) to a boil in pot, then add corn. Cook corn (water may not cover it), covered with lid, turning occasionally, until tender, 3 to 5 minutes. Transfer with tongs to a large platter.
▶ While corn cooks, melt butter in a 1-quart heavy saucepan, then remove from heat and stir in lemon juice, salt, black pepper, and cayenne.
▶ When corn is just cool enough to handle, cut kernels off cobs in long, wide strokes with a large heavy knife, leaving kernels in clusters. Transfer to a serving bowl.
▶ Add butter mixture and cilantro to corn, stirring gently to keep kernel clusters intact. Serve warm or at room temperature.

FARMERS MARKET GREENS

SERVES 6
Active time: 15 min   Start to finish: 15 min

2	tablespoons extra-virgin olive oil
1½	tablespoons finely chopped shallot
2	teaspoons fresh lemon juice
½	teaspoon salt
½	teaspoon coarsely ground black pepper
½	lb summer lettuces such as baby red oak, Bibb, and baby romaine (12 cups total)

▶ Whisk together oil, shallot, lemon juice, salt, and pepper in a large serving bowl.
▶ Just before serving, add lettuces to dressing and toss to coat.

Cooks' note:
• Greens can be washed and dried 1 day ahead and chilled in sealed plastic bags lined with dampened paper towels.

WARM SKILLET SOUR CHERRIES WITH VANILLA ICE CREAM

SERVES 6 (MAKES 3 CUPS)
Active time: 20 min   Start to finish: 30 min

We found a significant difference in the amount of liquid exuded by fresh versus frozen sour cherries when cooked. If your cherries give off a lot of liquid, you may have to reduce your syrup a little longer.

1	cup sugar
1	teaspoon fresh lemon juice
1	tablespoon unsalted butter
1½	lb fresh or thawed frozen sour cherries (see Sources), pitted (2½ cups)
2	tablespoons kirsch
	Premium vanilla ice cream

Accompaniment: **bakery butter cookies**

▶ Rub together sugar and lemon juice in a 12-inch heavy skillet with your fingertips until mixture resembles wet sand. Heat over moderately high heat, swirling skillet slowly, until sugar is melted and pale golden, 5 to 6 minutes. Add butter and swirl skillet until incorporated, about 30 seconds (mixture will bubble up). Add cherries, swirling skillet to coat, and bring to a boil (cherries will exude liquid; caramel will harden). Cook cherries, swirling skillet, until caramel is dissolved, 5 to 8 minutes. Pour through a medium-mesh sieve set over a bowl, then return liquid to skillet and boil until reduced to about ¾ cup, 6 to 8 minutes. Remove from heat, then add cherries and kirsch. Return to stove and boil 30 seconds.
▶ Spoon warm cherries into shallow bowls and top with scoops of ice cream.

Cooks' note:
• Cherries can be cooked 3 hours ahead and kept, covered, at room temperature. Bring to a boil just before serving.

OPPOSITE: **herb-tossed corn; warm skillet sour cherries with vanilla ice cream**

TWILIGHT ZONE

A COCKTAIL PARTY ON THE BEACH

SERVES 10 TO 12

JEALOUS MARYS

**GRILLED BEEF, CHICKEN, SHRIMP,
AND MUSHROOM SKEWERS**

ASSORTED VEGETABLES

**ANCHOVY MAYONNAISE,
CILANTRO CHUTNEY, AND
ROMESCO SAUCE**

STRAWBERRIES WITH PORT-WINE DIP

ALMOND BUTTER COOKIES

C. MENDES VINHO VERDE

JEALOUS MARYS
MAKES 6 DRINKS
Active time: 10 min   Start to finish: 10 min

This recipe combines the cool taste of cucumber with the flavors of a Bloody Mary.

- 2 large seedless cucumbers (usually plastic-wrapped; 2 lb total), peeled and coarsely chopped
- ½ cup chopped celery
- ⅓ cup fresh lemon juice
- 1 tablespoon drained bottled horseradish
- 1 teaspoon salt
- ½ teaspoon Worcestershire sauce
- ¼ teaspoon black pepper
- ⅛ teaspoon green Tabasco sauce
- ¾ cup vodka (6 fl oz)

Garnish: **6 small pale inner celery ribs with leaves, halved lengthwise if desired**

▶ Purée all ingredients in a blender until very smooth, about 1 minute. Force through a fine-mesh sieve set into a bowl, discarding solids. (You will have about 3¾ cups liquid.)
▶ Serve drinks over ice in small glasses.

GRILLED BEEF, CHICKEN, SHRIMP, AND MUSHROOM SKEWERS
MAKES 80 TO 100 SMALL SKEWERS
Active time: 2¼ hr   Start to finish: 2½ hr (does not include soaking skewers)

To make your cocktail party more participatory, have your guests grill their own skewers. A hibachi is even more user-friendly than a grill, since the ends of the skewers hang out over the edge, eliminating the need for tongs. If you're cooking everything yourself, it's easiest to use a large grill and serve the skewers in batches.

For marinade

- 4 large garlic cloves
- 2 teaspoons salt
- 2 tablespoons fresh lemon juice
- ½ teaspoon black pepper
- ⅓ cup extra-virgin olive oil

For skewers

- 1 lb sirloin steak (1 inch thick), trimmed of excess fat
- 2 medium skinless boneless chicken breast halves (1 lb total)
- 1¼ lb medium shrimp in shell (31 to 35 per lb; about 40), peeled and deveined
- 1 lb mushrooms, trimmed and halved through stem if large

Special equipment: **about 100 (6-inch) wooden skewers, soaked in water 1 hour**

Make marinade:
▶ Mince garlic and mash to a paste with salt using a large heavy knife. Transfer to a small bowl and whisk in lemon juice and pepper, then add oil in a stream, whisking until emulsified. Divide marinade among 4 (1- to 2-quart) bowls.

Prepare skewers:
▶ Cut steak into 20 to 25 (¼-inch-thick) slices (about 4 inches long and 1 inch wide), then toss with marinade in one of bowls and thread each slice lengthwise onto a skewer.
▶ Cut chicken breast halves diagonally into 20 to 25 (¼-inch-thick) slices (about 4 inches long and 1 inch wide; if breasts are thin, hold knife at a 45-degree angle to get 1-inch-wide slices). Toss with marinade in another bowl and thread each slice lengthwise onto a skewer.
▶ Toss shrimp with marinade in another bowl, then thread 2 shrimp onto each of 20 to 25 skewers.
▶ Toss mushrooms with marinade in remaining bowl and thread 2 small mushrooms or 2 large halves onto each of 20 to 25 skewers.
▶ Prepare grill for cooking over hot charcoal or high heat for gas (see Tips, page 8).
▶ Grill skewers in batches on lightly oiled grill rack, covered only if using a gas grill, turning over once with tongs, until beef is medium-rare, about 3 minutes total; chicken is just cooked through, about 3 minutes; shrimp is just cooked through, about 2 minutes; and mushrooms are tender, about 4 minutes.

Cooks' note:
• Skewers can be threaded up to 2 hours ahead and chilled separately, covered with plastic wrap.

OPPOSITE: three dipping sauces: *romesco* sauce, cilantro chutney, and anchovy mayonnaise; grilled chicken, shrimp, mushroom, and beef skewers

ASSORTED VEGETABLES

SERVES 10 TO 12
Active time: 30 min   Start to finish: 30 min

- 1   lb small red potatoes
- 1   lb asparagus, trimmed
- ½   lb sugar snap peas, trimmed
- 1   small head cauliflower (1¼ lb)
- 1   tablespoon olive oil
- 3   mixed red and yellow bell peppers, cut into
        ½-inch-wide strips
- 1   pt assorted cherry tomatoes

Accompaniment: assorted dips (recipes follow)

▶ Cover potatoes with salted cold water (see Tips, page 8) by 1 inch in a 4-quart pot and boil, uncovered, until tender, 10 to 15 minutes. Drain in a colander and halve if large.

▶ While potatoes boil, steam asparagus in a steamer set over boiling water, covered, until crisp-tender, 3 to 5 minutes. Transfer with a slotted spoon to a bowl of ice and cold water to stop cooking, then pat dry.

▶ Steam sugar snaps in steamer set over boiling water,

covered, until crisp-tender, about 1 minute. Transfer with slotted spoon to ice water to stop cooking, then pat dry.

▶ Preheat broiler.

▶ Cut cauliflower into large florets (about 3 inches long and 2 inches wide), then cut florets lengthwise through stem into flat ½-inch-wide slices. Gently toss with oil and salt to taste in a bowl and arrange in 1 layer on a broiler pan. Broil 3 inches from heat, turning over once, until cauliflower is crisp-tender and edges are brown, about 5 minutes total.

▶ Arrange cooked vegetables (warm or at room temperature), bell peppers, and tomatoes separately or mixed on 1 or 2 platters and serve with dips (recipes follow): anchovy mayonnaise, cilantro chutney, and *romesco* sauce.

Cooks' notes:

• Asparagus and sugar snaps can be steamed 4 hours ahead and chilled separately, wrapped in dampened paper towels in a sealed plastic bag. Bring to room temperature before serving.

• Potatoes can be boiled 2 hours ahead and kept at room temperature.

• Cauliflower is best broiled just before serving.

ANCHOVY MAYONNAISE

MAKES ABOUT 1¼ CUPS
Active time: 5 min   Start to finish: 30 min

12 large garlic cloves, peeled and smashed with side
      of a large heavy knife
¾   cup whole milk plus additional for thinning sauce
1   (2-oz) can flat anchovies (56 g; about 12 fillets), drained
¼   cup extra-virgin olive oil
¼   cup mayonnaise

▶ Combine garlic and milk in a 1- to 1½-quart heavy saucepan and gently simmer over low heat, uncovered, until garlic is very tender, about 20 minutes. Cool slightly, about 5 minutes, then purée mixture with anchovies, oil, and mayonnaise in a blender until smooth. (Use caution when blending hot liquids.) Add more milk to thin if necessary.

Cooks' note:
• Anchovy mayonnaise can be made 1 day ahead and chilled, covered. Bring to room temperature before serving.

CILANTRO CHUTNEY

MAKES ABOUT 1½ CUPS
Active time: 15 min   Start to finish: 15 min

2   cups firmly packed fresh cilantro sprigs
6   scallions, coarsely chopped
1½ to 2 teaspoons finely chopped small hot green chile,
      such as serrano or Thai, including seeds
2   teaspoons sugar
1½ teaspoons ground cumin
1½ teaspoons salt
¼   to ⅓ cup fresh lime juice
¼   cup olive oil

▶ Purée all ingredients in a food processor until smooth.

Cooks' note:
• Chutney can be made up to 1 day ahead and chilled, covered. Bring to room temperature before serving.

ROMESCO SAUCE

MAKES ABOUT 1½ CUPS
Active time: 20 min   Start to finish: 40 min

This dip is our version of a Catalan sauce that has many variations and tastes great with almost any type of grilled meat or fish. Even though 2 tablespoons of hazelnuts seems a small amount, they round out the flavor.

1   large tomato (½ lb), cored
1   (½-oz) dried ancho chile (see Sources)
⅓   cup extra-virgin olive oil
2   tablespoons hazelnuts, toasted (see Tips, page 8) and
      loose skins rubbed off with a kitchen towel while warm
2   tablespoons blanched almonds
1   (½-inch-thick) slice firm white bread, cut into
      ½-inch cubes
2   large garlic cloves, sliced
⅛   teaspoon dried hot red pepper flakes
¼   cup drained bottled pimientos, rinsed
2   tablespoons water
1   tablespoon red-wine vinegar
¼   teaspoon salt, or to taste

▶ Put oven rack in middle position and preheat oven to 400°F. Line a small baking pan with foil.
▶ Roast tomato in pan until tender and skin peels off easily, about 30 minutes.
▶ While tomato is roasting, slit chile open lengthwise and discard stem and seeds, then tear chile into small pieces. Heat oil in an 8- to 10-inch heavy skillet over moderate heat until hot but not smoking, then add chile and cook, stirring, until fragrant and chile turns a brighter red, 30 seconds to 1 minute. Transfer chile with a slotted spoon to a heatproof bowl. Add hazelnuts to skillet along with almonds, bread, garlic, and red pepper flakes and cook, stirring, until bread and garlic are golden, 2 to 3 minutes. Add mixture (including oil) to chile in bowl and cool slightly.
▶ Peel tomato, then coarsely chop and transfer (with juices) to a food processor. Add bread and chile mixture, pimientos, water, vinegar, and ¼ teaspoon salt and purée until smooth. Thin with water if desired and season with salt.

Cooks' note:
• Sauce can be made 1 day ahead and chilled, covered. Bring to room temperature before serving.

STRAWBERRIES WITH PORT-WINE DIP

SERVES 10 TO 12
Active time: 10 min Start to finish: 1 hr

  1   (750-ml) bottle Tawny Port
  1   cup sugar
  2   to 3 lb whole medium strawberries, stems left intact
      and berries rinsed and patted dry

▶ Bring Port and sugar to a boil in a 2- to 3-quart heavy
saucepan over moderate heat, stirring until sugar is dissolved,
and boil, uncovered, until slightly syrupy and reduced to 1 to
1¼ cups, about 20 minutes. Cool to room temperature, about
30 minutes (sauce will thicken as it cools). Transfer to a small
bowl and serve with berries for dipping.

Cooks' note:
• Port-wine dip can be made 1 day ahead and cooled to room
temperature, uncovered, then chilled, covered. Bring to room
temperature before serving.

ALMOND BUTTER COOKIES

MAKES ABOUT 5 DOZEN COOKIES
Active time: 20 min Start to finish: 3 hr (includes chilling)

*These icebox cookies are perfect for a party because the
dough can be made ahead and chilled or frozen until you
are ready to slice and bake.*

  1   cup all-purpose flour
  ½   teaspoon baking soda
  ⅛   teaspoon salt
  ¾   stick (6 tablespoons) unsalted butter, softened
  ¼   cup granulated sugar
  ¼   cup packed light brown sugar
  1   tablespoon corn syrup
  ½   teaspoon vanilla
  ¼   teaspoon almond extract
  ½   cup sliced almonds with skins (4½ oz), toasted
      (see Tips, page 8) and cooled completely

▶ Whisk together flour, baking soda, and salt.
▶ Beat together butter, sugars, corn syrup, vanilla, and almond
extract in a large bowl with an electric mixer at medium-high
speed (use paddle attachment if you have a stand mixer) until
pale and fluffy, about 2 minutes. Reduce speed to low, then
add flour mixture and mix just until a dough begins to form.
Add almonds and mix just until incorporated. Form dough into
a rectangular log (about 12 inches long, 2 inches wide, and
¾ inch thick). Wrap in wax paper and chill until firm, about
2 hours.
▶ Put oven rack in middle position and preheat oven to 325°F.
Butter a large baking sheet.
▶ Cut half of log into ⅛-inch-thick slices with a thin sharp
knife and arrange ¾ inch apart on baking sheet. (Keep
remaining dough chilled.)
▶ Bake cookies until golden, about 12 minutes, then transfer
with a thin metal spatula to a rack to cool. Repeat with
remaining dough.

Cooks' notes:
• Dough can be chilled up to 2 days, or frozen, wrapped also
in plastic wrap, 1 month. Transfer frozen dough to refrigerator
to thaw slightly at least 2 hours before slicing.
• Cookies can be baked 3 days ahead and cooled completely,
then kept in an airtight container at room temperature.

LICENSE TO CHILL

COOL FOOD FOR A HOT NIGHT

SERVES 6

**ARCTIC CHAR GRAVLAKS
WITH CUCUMBER JELLY**

**LOBSTER SALAD WITH
GLASS NOODLES AND JICAMA**

DOPFF & IRION SCHOENENBOURG
RIESLING '01

**ICE-WINE SORBET WITH
WHITE PEACHES**

ARCTIC CHAR GRAVLAKS WITH CUCUMBER JELLY

SERVES 6 (FIRST COURSE)

Active time: 30 min   Start to finish: 1½ days (includes curing fish)

Gravlaks—fish cured with salt, sugar, and dill—is usually made with salmon, but we like the milder flavor of arctic char for this particular dish.

Keep in mind before starting to cure your fish that you will need to turn it every 12 hours for a total of 36 hours.

For gravlaks

- 1 (1¼-lb) center-cut piece arctic char fillet with skin, pin bones removed
- ½ cup sugar
- ¼ cup kosher salt
- 1 tablespoon coarsely ground black pepper
- 3 cups coarsely chopped fresh dill (from 2 large bunches)

For cucumber jelly

- 3 seedless cucumbers (usually plastic-wrapped; 3 lb total)
- ¾ teaspoon table salt

- 2 teaspoons unflavored gelatin (from 1 envelope)
- 1 tablespoon distilled white vinegar
- 1 tablespoon tiny fresh dill fronds

Accompaniment: thin Scandinavian crispbread such as Kavli

Make gravlaks:

▸ Pat fish dry, then transfer, skin side up, to a large sheet of plastic wrap. Stir together sugar, salt, and pepper, then rub 3 tablespoons of mixture onto skin of fish. Turn fish over and thickly coat with remaining sugar mixture, then pack dill on top.

▸ Wrap fish tightly in 2 or 3 layers of plastic wrap (to prevent leakage; salt mixture will liquefy as fish cures) and transfer to a large shallow baking pan. Put another baking pan or a cutting board on top of fish and weight down with 3 or 4 full cans (about 3 lb total). Let fish cure, chilled, turning wrapped fillet over roughly every 12 hours and then replacing weight, for 36 hours total.

Make jelly while fish is curing:

▸ Peel cucumbers, making sure to remove all green (for a clearer jelly), then halve lengthwise and core. Coarsely chop cucumbers and purée in a food processor until smooth, then drain in a large fine-mesh sieve set over a bowl, pressing hard on solids to extract 2 cups liquid. Discard solids.

▸ Stir together salt and ½ cup cucumber liquid in a small saucepan and sprinkle with gelatin. Let stand 1 minute to soften, then heat over moderate heat, stirring, just until gelatin is dissolved, about 2 minutes. Cool mixture to room temperature, then stir into remaining 1½ cups cucumber liquid along with vinegar. Pour mixture into an 8-inch square glass baking dish and sprinkle with dill fronds, pressing gently to submerge. Chill, covered, until set, at least 8 hours.

To serve:

▸ Unwrap gravlaks, discarding liquid, and gently scrape off dill. Transfer gravlaks, skin side down, to a cutting board. Holding a very sharp long thin-bladed knife at a 30-degree angle, cut gravlaks across the grain into very thin slices, being careful not to cut through skin. Discard skin.

▸ Cut jelly into 6 pieces and divide among 6 plates with a metal spatula. Serve with several slices of gravlaks.

Cooks' notes:

• Cured gravlaks can be drained, scraped, and wrapped in clean plastic wrap, then chilled up to 5 days.

• Jelly can be chilled up to 4 days.

LOBSTER SALAD WITH GLASS NOODLES AND JICAMA

SERVES 6

Active time: 1¼ hr   Start to finish: 2¼ hr (includes cooking lobsters)

  5 (1¼- to 1½-lb) live lobsters or 1¾ to 2 lb cooked
      lobster meat

  ½ cup fresh lime juice

1½ tablespoons packed light brown sugar

  1 teaspoon dry mustard

  1 teaspoon salt

  ⅓ cup canola oil

  3 to 4 oz very thin bean thread noodles (also known as
      cellophane, glass, or mung bean noodles; see Sources)

  3 tablespoons coarsely chopped fresh basil

  3 tablespoons coarsely chopped fresh cilantro

  2 tablespoons coarsely chopped fresh mint

  1 (½-lb) piece jicama, peeled, then cut into ¹⁄₁₆-inch-thick
      matchsticks with slicer (about 2 cups)
      Flaky sea salt such as Maldon

Special equipment: **an adjustable-blade slicer fitted with julienne blade**

Cook lobsters (if necessary):

▶ Plunge 2 lobsters headfirst into a 10- to 12-quart pot of boiling salted water (see Tips, page 8) and cook, covered, 6 minutes for 1¼-pound lobsters or 7 minutes for 1½-pound lobsters, from time lobsters enter water. Transfer with tongs to sink to drain. Return water to a boil and cook remaining lobsters in 2 batches in same manner.

▶ When lobsters are cool enough to handle, remove meat from tail and claws. Discard tomalley, any roe, and shells, then scrape off any coagulated white albumin from meat with point of a small knife. Cut meat into ¾-inch pieces and chill, covered, at least 1 hour.

Make dressing:

▶ Blend lime juice, brown sugar, mustard, and salt in a blender until combined. With motor running, add oil in a slow, steady stream and blend until dressing is emulsified. Chill, covered, until ready to use.

Prepare noodles:

▶ Soak noodles in cold water until pliable, about 15 minutes, then drain in a colander. Cut noodles in half with kitchen shears.

▶ Cook noodles in a 4-quart pot of boiling salted water, stirring occasionally, until just tender, about 2 minutes. Drain noodles well and rinse under cold water until cool, then drain well again.

Assemble salad:

▶ Stir together lobster, herbs, and 6 tablespoons dressing.

▶ Toss together noodles, jicama, remaining dressing, and table salt to taste, then divide among 6 plates and top each serving with a mound of lobster salad. Sprinkle with sea salt and serve immediately.

Cooks' notes:

• Lobsters can be cooked and meat removed from shell 1 day ahead and chilled, covered.

• Dressing can be made 1 day ahead and chilled, covered.

ICE-WINE SORBET WITH WHITE PEACHES

SERVES 6

Active time: 20 min   Start to finish: 4¾ hr (includes freezing)

Ice wine, or eiswein, is traditionally made from grapes that are handpicked after being allowed to freeze. Less costly bottlings of the concentrated sweet wine are made from grapes frozen in freezers.

  1 (375-ml) bottle ice wine (13 fl oz)

  ¾ cup water

  6 tablespoons sugar

  4 firm-ripe white peaches, cut into ½-inch-thick wedges

Special equipment: **an ice cream maker**

▶ Heat wine, water, and sugar in a 3-quart saucepan over moderate heat, stirring, until sugar is dissolved, then gently simmer 2 minutes. Transfer to a bowl, then set bowl in a larger bowl of ice water and stir until cold, 10 to 15 minutes. Freeze in ice cream maker. Transfer to an airtight container and put in freezer, at least 4 hours. (Texture will be soft.)

▶ Serve sorbet with peaches.

Cooks' note:

• Sorbet can be made 1 day ahead, but texture is best the day it is made.

IN THE MOOD

AN INTIMATE DINNER FOR TWO

SERVES 2

FEVER COCKTAILS

SMOKY PEANUTS

**OYSTERS WITH
CHAMPAGNE-VINEGAR MIGNONNETTE**

**SKATE WITH WILD MUSHROOMS
IN PEARL SAUCE**

PIERRE MOREY MEURSAULT-PERRIÈRES
PREMIER CRU '02

CHOCOLATE MINK

FEVER COCKTAILS
MAKES 2 DRINKS
Active time: 5 min   Start to finish: 5 min

  3 oz (6 tablespoons) gin
  1 oz (2 tablespoons) dry vermouth
  1 teaspoon Dubonnet Rouge
  ½ teaspoon anisette or other anise-flavored liqueur

Garnish: **lemon twists**

▶Fill a cocktail shaker halfway with ice, then add all ingredients and shake or stir well. Strain into chilled glasses.

SMOKY PEANUTS
MAKES ABOUT 1 CUP
Active time: 5 min   Start to finish: 40 min

Lapsang souchong tea imparts a subtle smokiness to these nuts, which will set in as you eat more.

  1 tablespoon lightly beaten egg white
  1 teaspoon sugar
  ¾ teaspoon Lapsang souchong tea leaves (see Sources), crushed if coarse
  ¼ teaspoon salt
  1 cup salted cocktail peanuts

Special equipment: **parchment paper**

▶Put oven rack in middle position and preheat oven to 350°F. Line a baking sheet with parchment paper.
▶Whisk together egg white, sugar, tea, and salt in a small bowl. Stir in peanuts and spread in 1 layer on baking sheet.
▶Bake, stirring occasionally, until nuts are dry, about 7 minutes. Cool on baking sheet on a rack, about 20 minutes. (Nuts will crisp as they cool.)

Cooks' note:
• Smoky peanuts can be made 5 days ahead and cooled completely, then kept in an airtight container at room temperature.

OYSTERS WITH CHAMPAGNE-VINEGAR MIGNONNETTE
SERVES 2 (FIRST COURSE)
Active time: 15 min   Start to finish: 40 min

In this elegant introduction to dinner, oysters are paired with Champagne grapes, whose sweet juice balances the sharpness of the vinegar in the mignonnette.

For *mignonnette*
  2 teaspoons Champagne vinegar
  1½ teaspoons finely chopped shallot
    Pinch of coarsely ground black pepper
    Pinch of sugar
  1 teaspoon finely chopped fresh flat-leaf parsley

For oysters
  1½ cups kosher or other coarse salt
  ½ dozen small oysters, such as Kumamoto or Prince Edward Island, shells scrubbed well and oysters left on the half shell, their liquor reserved and oysters picked over for shell fragments
  ½ tablespoon unsalted butter, cut into 6 pieces
  1 small cluster Champagne table grapes or 2 finely diced seedless red grapes

Make *mignonnette*:
▶Stir together vinegar, shallot, pepper, and sugar and let stand 30 minutes.

Prepare oysters:
▶Preheat broiler.
▶Spread ¾ cup salt in an 8- to 10-inch flameproof shallow baking dish or pan. Arrange oysters on their shells in salt, then top each with a piece of butter.
▶Broil 4 to 6 inches from heat until butter is melted and sizzling and edges of oysters are beginning to curl, 1 to 2 minutes.
▶Stir parsley into *mignonnette*. Divide remaining ¾ cup salt between 2 plates and arrange 3 oysters on each. Spoon ¼ teaspoon *mignonnette* over each oyster and sprinkle oysters with grapes. Serve warm.

Cooks' note:
• *Mignonnette*, without parsley, can be made 1 day ahead and chilled, covered.

SKATE WITH WILD MUSHROOMS IN PEARL SAUCE

SERVES 2

Active time: 45 min   Start to finish: 1¼ hr

In adding translucent pearls of tapioca to the mushroom broth in this recipe, we've borrowed one of chef Daniel Boulud's methods for giving body to a light sauce.

For mushroom sauce

- 1   small leek (white and pale green parts only), chopped
- 1   tablespoon olive oil
- 1   medium carrot, chopped
- ½   medium onion, chopped
- 1   garlic clove
- ¼   cup dry white wine
- 2   cups water
- 1   teaspoon soy sauce
- 1   fresh flat-leaf parsley sprig
- 1   fresh thyme sprig
- 1   Turkish or ½ California bay leaf
- 1   tablespoon crumbled dried porcini (see Sources)
- 1   tablespoon quick-cooking tapioca

For sautéed mushrooms

- ½   tablespoon unsalted butter
- ½   tablespoon olive oil
- 6   oz mixed fresh mushrooms, such as oyster and chanterelle, trimmed and halved lengthwise or quartered if large
- ¼   teaspoon salt
- ⅛   teaspoon black pepper
- 1   celery rib, thinly sliced diagonally

For skate

- 1½   tablespoons all-purpose flour
- ¼   teaspoon curry powder
- 2   (5- to 6-oz) pieces skate fillet, halved crosswise if large
- ½   teaspoon salt
- ⅛   teaspoon black pepper
- 1½   tablespoons unsalted butter

Make broth:

▶ Wash chopped leek well in a bowl of cold water, agitating it, then lift out and pat dry.

▶ Heat oil in a 3- to 4-quart heavy saucepan over moderately high heat until hot but not smoking, then sauté leek, carrot, onion, and garlic clove, stirring frequently, until vegetables are soft and well browned, about 10 minutes. Stir in wine and deglaze saucepan by boiling, stirring and scraping up any brown bits, 1 minute.

▶ Add water, soy sauce, parsley, thyme, bay leaf, and porcini and simmer, uncovered, until liquid is reduced to ¾ cup, about 25 minutes. Pour through a fine-mesh sieve into a glass measure, lightly pressing on and then discarding solids. Transfer to a small saucepan. If you have more than ¾ cup, boil strained liquid a few minutes to reduce.

Sauté fresh mushrooms:

▶ Heat butter and oil in a 10-inch heavy skillet until hot but not smoking, then sauté mushrooms with salt and pepper, stirring, until just tender and golden brown, about 4 minutes. Add celery and sauté until bright green and crisp-tender, about 2 minutes. Remove from heat and keep warm, covered with foil.

Finish sauce and sauté skate:

▶ Bring broth to a simmer, then remove from heat and stir in tapioca. Let stand, covered, 10 to 15 minutes.

▶ While sauce is standing, stir together flour and curry powder in a shallow bowl. Pat fish dry and sprinkle with salt and pepper, then dredge in flour mixture, shaking off excess and transferring to a plate as dredged.

▶ Heat butter in a 12-inch heavy skillet over moderately high heat until foam subsides, then sauté fish, turning over once, until golden brown and just cooked through, about 5 minutes total.

▶ Reheat sauce, then season with salt and pepper. Serve fish with sautéed mushrooms and sauce.

Cooks' note:

• Broth (without tapioca) can be made 2 days ahead and cooled completely, uncovered, then chilled, covered.

CHOCOLATE MINK
SERVES 2
Active time: 15 min   Start to finish: 1¾ hr

These luxurious little desserts are like gooey flourless chocolate pudding cakes.

  2 tablespoons unsalted butter, cut into pieces, plus
     additional for greasing bowls
3½ oz fine-quality bittersweet chocolate (not unsweetened),
     finely chopped
  1 large egg, separated
  1 tablespoon sugar

Special equipment: **2 (5- to 6-oz) ovenproof glass or
ceramic bowls or ramekins**
Accompaniment: **coffee ice cream**

▶ Put oven rack in middle position and preheat oven to
350°F. Butter bowls.
▶ Melt chocolate and butter in a metal bowl set over a
saucepan of barely simmering water, stirring until smooth.
Remove bowl from heat and cool, stirring occasionally,

5 minutes. Whisk in egg yolk and a pinch of salt until
combined.
▶ Beat egg white in a bowl with an electric mixer at medium-
high speed until it holds soft peaks. Gradually add sugar,
beating, and continue to beat until white just holds stiff,
glossy peaks.
▶ Whisk about one fourth of white into chocolate mixture to
lighten, then fold in remaining white gently but thoroughly.
▶ Divide batter between bowls. Cover each bowl with a small
square of foil and crimp foil tightly around rim. Put bowls in
a baking dish, then add enough boiling-hot water to reach
halfway up side of bowls, making sure that foil is above
water. Bake until puddings are just set, about 30 minutes.
(Puddings will be gooey to the touch.) Transfer bowls to a
rack and cool puddings, uncovered, about 1 hour.
▶ Just before serving, unmold puddings into serving bowls.

Cooks' note:
• Puddings can be made 4 hours ahead and kept in bowls at
warm room temperature. Dip in hot water 10 to 15 seconds
to unmold.

ABOVE: **smoky peanuts and a Fever cocktail; skate with wild mushrooms in
pearl sauce.** OPPOSITE: **chocolate mink**

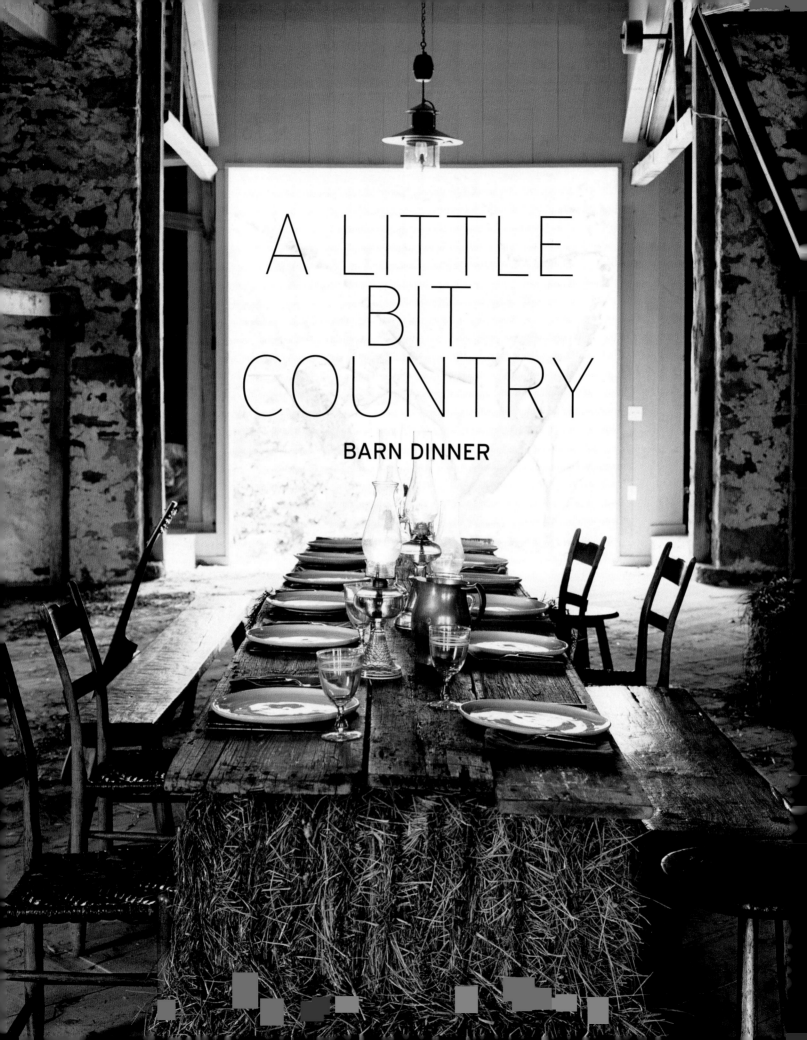

A LITTLE BIT BIT COUNTRY

BARN DINNER

SERVES 12

DEVILED EGGS

**CUCUMBER AND TOMATO SALAD
WITH BUTTERMILK DRESSING**

GARLICKY FRIED CHICKEN

YELLOW SQUASH CASSEROLE

SLOW-COOKED COLLARD GREENS

SKILLET CORN WITH BACON AND ONION

ROSENBLUM HERITAGE CLONES
PETITE SIRAH '03

BLACKBERRY PEACH COBBLER

CHOCOLATE WHISKEY BUNDT CAKE

DEVILED EGGS
SERVES 12 (HORS D'OEUVRE)
Active time: 30 min Start to finish: 40 min

12 large eggs
½ cup mayonnaise
2 teaspoons brown or yellow mustard
¼ cup finely chopped sweet pickles
¼ cup finely chopped celery

Garnish: **finely chopped pimiento-stuffed olives;
paprika**

▸ Cover eggs with cold water by 1½ inches in a 4- to 5-quart pot and bring to a rolling boil, partially covered with lid. Reduce heat to low and cook eggs, covered completely, 30 seconds. Remove pot from heat and let eggs stand in hot water, covered with lid, 15 minutes. Rinse eggs under cold water 5 minutes to stop cooking.
▸ Peel eggs and halve lengthwise. Carefully remove yolks and mash in a bowl with a fork. Add mayonnaise, mustard, pickles, celery, and salt and pepper to taste to yolks and stir with fork until combined well, then spoon into egg whites.

Cooks' note:
• Deviled eggs can be assembled (but not garnished) 2 hours ahead and chilled, covered.

CUCUMBER AND TOMATO SALAD WITH BUTTERMILK DRESSING
SERVES 12
Active time: 30 min Start to finish: 30 min

For more variety, stir in other finely chopped herbs such as basil, thyme, or tarragon.

2 cups mayonnaise
1½ cups well-shaken buttermilk
2 tablespoons white-wine vinegar
½ cup finely chopped fresh chives
6 medium cucumbers, peeled and cut into
   1-inch pieces
8 beefsteak tomatoes, cut into ½-inch wedges
2 heads iceberg lettuce, cored and cut into
   2-inch chunks

▸ Whisk together mayonnaise, buttermilk, vinegar, and salt and pepper to taste until smooth, then whisk in chives.
▸ Put cucumbers, tomatoes, and lettuce into bowls and serve with dressing.

Cooks' note:
• Buttermilk dressing (without chives) can be made 1 day ahead and chilled, covered. Whisk in chives before serving.

GARLICKY FRIED CHICKEN
SERVES 12
Active time: 2 hr Start to finish: 14 hr (includes marinating)

Though the recipe says to keep the fried chicken warm, it's equally good served at room temperature. In fact, if you're making this entire menu using a single oven, you'll need to let the chicken stand at room temperature while the squash casserole bakes.

2 medium onions, chopped
8 large garlic cloves, chopped
⅓ cup plus 2 teaspoons salt
2 tablespoons black pepper
1 tablespoon cayenne
8 cups water
8 chicken breast halves (halved crosswise if large),
   8 drumsticks, and 8 thighs (all with skin and bones;
   8 to 9 lb total)
10 cups all-purpose flour
   About 8 cups vegetable oil (64 fl oz)

Special equipment: **a wide 5- to 6-qt heavy pot (preferably cast-iron; 10 inches wide and 4 inches deep); a deep-fat thermometer**

Marinate chicken:
▸ Purée onions and garlic with ⅓ cup salt, 1 tablespoon black pepper, cayenne, and 1 cup water in a food processor until smooth, then pour into a large bowl and stir in remaining 7 cups water. Divide chicken and marinade among 3 (1-gallon) sealable plastic bags, then seal, forcing out excess air. Marinate chicken, chilled, turning bags over a few times, at least 12 hours and up to 1 day. (If you're concerned about leaks, put bags in a large bowl.)

Dredge and fry chicken:

▶ Whisk together flour, remaining 2 teaspoons salt, and remaining tablespoon black pepper in a large bowl, then divide between 2 large roasting pans. Drain chicken in a colander, discarding marinade, then dredge each piece of chicken in seasoned flour and leave sitting in flour. Let chicken stand 20 minutes.

▶ Preheat oven to 250°F. Line 2 large baking sheets with paper towels and set a cooling rack on each.

▶ Heat 2 inches oil in pot over moderately high heat until it registers 365°F on thermometer. Knocking off excess flour, transfer 4 pieces chicken to oil (keeping batches all white meat or all dark) and fry, turning occasionally with tongs, until golden brown and cooked through, about 8 minutes for breasts or 10 to 12 minutes for drumsticks and thighs. Lift chicken from oil with tongs, letting excess oil drip back into pot, then transfer to a rack and keep warm in oven. Dredge and fry remaining chicken in same manner, keeping it warm in oven. (Return oil to 365°F between batches.)

YELLOW SQUASH CASSEROLE

SERVES 12

Active time: 1 hr   Start to finish: 1½ hr

Resist the temptation to toss together all the squash with the oil, salt, and pepper. If you don't do it in batches, as noted below, the salt will draw out too much liquid from the squash waiting to be roasted, and the casserole will be soupy.

4	lb yellow squash (10 medium), trimmed, halved lengthwise, and sliced crosswise ⅛ inch thick
¼	cup vegetable oil
2	teaspoons salt
2	teaspoons black pepper
2	medium onions, chopped (2 cups)
1	green bell pepper, chopped
1	red bell pepper, chopped
7	tablespoons unsalted butter
4	slices firm white sandwich bread with crust, coarsely ground in a food processor (about 2¼ cups)
¼	cup all-purpose flour
1¾	cups reduced-sodium chicken broth (14 fl oz)
1	cup sour cream

▶ Put oven rack in lower third of oven and put a large shallow baking pan on rack, then preheat oven to 475°F.

▶ Toss one third of squash with 1 tablespoon oil, ½ teaspoon salt, and ½ teaspoon pepper in a bowl, then spread in preheated baking pan in 1 layer and roast in oven, stirring once, until tender, 12 to 15 minutes. Transfer squash to a large bowl. Roast remaining squash in 2 batches in same manner, tossing with 1 tablespoon oil, ½ teaspoon salt, and ½ teaspoon pepper (per batch) just before roasting and adding to bowl when done.

▶ Toss onions and bell peppers with remaining tablespoon oil, remaining ½ teaspoon salt, and remaining ½ teaspoon pepper in another large bowl, then spread in baking pan and roast, stirring once, until onions are golden, 8 to 10 minutes. Transfer to bowl with squash.

▶ Move oven rack to middle position and reduce oven temperature to 400°F.

▶ Melt 3 tablespoons butter in a saucepan and remove from heat, then add bread crumbs and a pinch of salt, tossing to coat crumbs. Spread evenly in cleaned baking pan and bake, without stirring, until pale golden, about 5 minutes.

▶ Melt remaining 4 tablespoons butter in a 3-quart heavy saucepan over moderately low heat, then whisk in flour and cook roux, whisking constantly, 3 minutes. Add broth, whisking, and bring to a boil, whisking. Reduce heat and simmer, whisking occasionally, 3 minutes. Remove from heat and cool 5 minutes, whisking occasionally, then whisk in sour cream and salt and pepper to taste. Pour sauce over squash mixture and stir gently until combined well.

▶ Butter a 13- by 9- by 2-inch glass or ceramic baking dish (3-quart capacity), then spread squash mixture evenly into it and sprinkle with bread crumbs. Bake casserole until golden and bubbling, 15 to 20 minutes. Serve immediately.

Cooks' note:

• Casserole (without bread crumbs) can be assembled 1 day ahead and cooled completely, uncovered, then chilled, covered tightly with plastic wrap. Let stand at room temperature 1 hour before sprinkling with bread crumbs and baking.

are very tender, about 45 minutes. Remove hock from cooking liquid and let stand until cool enough to handle, about 15 minutes. Discard skin and bones and coarsely chop meat. Stir meat and salt to taste into collards.

Cooks' note:
• Collards can be cooked 1 day ahead and cooled completely, uncovered, then chilled, covered.

SKILLET CORN WITH BACON AND ONION
SERVES 12
Active time: 40 min   Start to finish: 45 min

12 ears of corn, shucked
6 bacon slices, cut crosswise into 1-inch pieces
1 large onion, chopped
4 garlic cloves, finely chopped
1 cup water
¾ cup finely chopped scallion

▸ Stand 1 ear of corn upright, pointed end down, in a large bowl and cut kernels from cob using a sharp paring knife. Scrape any remaining corn with its milk from cob into bowl using back edge of knife and discard cob. Remove kernels from remaining ears in same manner.
▸ Cook bacon in a 12-inch heavy skillet (2 inches deep) over moderate heat, stirring occasionally, until crisp, about 8 minutes, then transfer with a slotted spoon to paper towels to drain. Cook onion in fat remaining in skillet over moderately low heat, stirring occasionally, until softened, 2 to 3 minutes. Add corn, garlic, and water (skillet will be very full) and cook over moderately high heat, uncovered, stirring occasionally, until corn is tender, 10 to 15 minutes. Stir in scallion and salt and pepper to taste, then sprinkle with bacon.

Cooks' note:
• Corn can be cooked 6 hours ahead and chilled, covered (without scallion or bacon). Reheat in skillet or a 4-quart heavy saucepan over moderate heat, stirring occasionally, then stir in scallion and salt and pepper to taste. Bacon can be kept at room temperature, then reheated on a small baking sheet in a preheated 400°F oven until hot, about 2 minutes.

OPPOSITE: yellow squash casserole, skillet corn with bacon and onion, and slow-cooked collard greens

SLOW-COOKED COLLARD GREENS
SERVES 12
Active time: 15 min   Start to finish: 2 hr

Cooking collards slowly is the traditional approach in the South, producing tender greens and the bonus of pot likker, the pork-flavored broth left in the pot after the collards are served up. Many people sip the pot likker as a cure for the common cold, while others dunk their corn muffins in it.

4 qt water
1 smoked ham hock (¾ lb), rinsed
4 lb collard greens (preferably small)
½ teaspoon dried hot red pepper flakes

▸ Bring water with ham hock to a boil in an 8-quart pot, uncovered, skimming any froth, then reduce heat and simmer, covered, 1 hour.
▸ While hock simmers, discard coarse stems and center ribs from collards, then wash leaves and drain. Coarsely chop collards.
▸ Add collards and red pepper flakes to ham hock broth, then simmer, partially covered, stirring occasionally, until greens

BLACKBERRY PEACH COBBLER

SERVES 12

Active time: 25 min **Start to finish:** 1½ hr (includes cooling)

If you're making this entire menu in a single oven, we recommend baking the cobbler ahead of time—that way you can reheat it while clearing the table.

2 tablespoons cornstarch
1½ cups plus 1 teaspoon sugar
1¼ lb blackberries (5 cups)
2 lb peaches (6 medium), peeled, pitted, and cut into ½-inch-thick wedges
3 cups all-purpose flour
1 tablespoon baking powder
1 teaspoon salt
2 sticks (1 cup) cold unsalted butter, cut into ½-inch cubes
1 cup plus 3 tablespoons whole milk

▶Put oven rack in middle position and preheat oven to 425°F. Butter a 13- by 9- by 2-inch glass or ceramic baking dish (3-quart capacity).
▶Whisk together cornstarch and 1½ cups sugar in a large bowl, then add blackberries and peaches and toss to combine well. Transfer to baking dish and bake until just bubbling, 10 to 15 minutes.
▶While fruit bakes, whisk together flour, baking powder, and salt in another large bowl, then blend in butter with your fingertips or a pastry blender until mixture resembles coarse meal. Add milk and stir just until a dough forms.
▶Drop dough onto hot fruit mixture in 12 mounds (about ⅓ cup each), then sprinkle dough with remaining teaspoon sugar. Bake cobbler until top is golden, 25 to 35 minutes. Serve warm.

Cooks' note:
• Cobbler can be baked 6 hours ahead and cooled completely, uncovered, then chilled, covered. Before serving, let stand at room temperature 1 hour, then reheat in a preheated 350°F oven until warm, about 20 minutes.

CHOCOLATE WHISKEY BUNDT CAKE

SERVES 12 TO 14

Active time: 30 min **Start to finish:** 3¼ hr (includes cooling)

1 cup unsweetened cocoa powder (not Dutch-process) plus 3 tablespoons for dusting pan
1½ cups brewed coffee
½ cup American whiskey
2 sticks (1 cup) unsalted butter, cut into 1-inch pieces
2 cups sugar
2 cups all-purpose flour
1¼ teaspoons baking soda
½ teaspoon salt
2 large eggs
1 teaspoon vanilla

Special equipment: a 10-inch bundt pan (3¼ inches deep; 3-qt capacity)
Accompaniment: lightly sweetened whipped cream
Garnish: confectioners sugar for dusting

▶Put oven rack in middle position and preheat oven to 325°F. Butter bundt pan well, then dust with 3 tablespoons cocoa powder, knocking out excess.
▶Heat coffee, whiskey, butter, and remaining cup cocoa powder in a 3-quart heavy saucepan over moderate heat, whisking, until butter is melted. Remove from heat, then add sugar and whisk until dissolved, about 1 minute. Transfer mixture to a large bowl and cool 5 minutes.
▶While chocolate mixture cools, whisk together flour, baking soda, and salt in a bowl. Whisk together eggs and vanilla in a small bowl, then whisk into cooled chocolate mixture until combined well. Add flour mixture and whisk until just combined (batter will be thin and bubbly). Pour batter into bundt pan and bake until a wooden pick or skewer inserted in center comes out clean, 40 to 50 minutes.
▶Cool cake completely in pan on a rack, about 2 hours. Loosen cake from pan using tip of a dinner knife, then invert rack over pan and turn cake out onto rack.

Cooks' note:
• This cake improves in flavor if made at least 1 day ahead and kept, in a cake keeper or wrapped well in plastic wrap, at cool room temperature. It can be made up to 5 days ahead and chilled. Bring to room temperature before serving.

A NEW TRADITION

A RUSTIC THANKSGIVING WITH VEGETARIAN CHOICES

SERVES 8 TO 10

EDAMAME DIP WITH CRUDITÉS

TENUTA VILLANOVA ISONZO DEL FRIULI
SAUVIGNON BLANC '04

**CHESTNUT SOUP WITH SOURDOUGH
SAGE CROUTONS**

MASÙT DA RIVE ISONZO DEL FRIULI
SAUVIGNON BLANC '04

MISO-RUBBED TURKEY WITH TURKEY GRAVY

ROASTED MUSHROOM AND BARLEY GRAVY

PERSIMMON CRANBERRY SAUCE

CHICKPEA, EGGPLANT, AND TOMATO TARTS

RUSTIC PORCINI ONION STUFFING

CELERY AND JICAMA SAUTÉ

SWEET-POTATO BRÛLÉE

**BROWN BUTTER AND SCALLION
MASHED POTATOES**

MASÙT DA RIVE ISONZO DEL FRIULI MERLOT '01

APPLE TARTS WITH VANILLA ICE CREAM

**HONEY PECAN TART WITH
CHOCOLATE GLAZE**

CAMPBELLS RUTHERGLEN MUSCAT

EDAMAME DIP WITH CRUDITÉS

SERVES 8 TO 10

Active time: 30 min   Start to finish: 30 min

*This light starter can be prepared ahead of time and is a
smart alternative to fussy holiday hors d'oeuvres. It has
an unbelievably fresh flavor, even when made with
frozen soybeans.*

  4 **large carrots**
  3 **celery ribs, strings removed with a vegetable peeler**
  1 **seedless cucumber (usually plastic-wrapped), halved
     lengthwise and cored**
  1 **bunch radishes**
  1 **lb fresh or frozen shelled *edamame* (soybeans; 3 cups)**
2½ **teaspoons salt**
  1 **tablespoon chopped garlic**
  5 **tablespoons extra-virgin olive oil**
  1 **tablespoon fresh lime juice**
  1 **teaspoon sugar**
 ½ **teaspoon black pepper**
 ¼ **cup chopped fresh cilantro**

▶ Cut carrots, celery, and cucumber into ½-inch-wide sticks
(2½ inches long). Cut radishes lengthwise into ¼-inch-thick
slices. Fill a large bowl with ice and cold water and keep cut
vegetables in ice water (to keep crisp) while making dip.
▶ Cook *edamame* in 1½ quarts boiling water with 1½
teaspoons salt in a 3-quart heavy saucepan 3 minutes, then
reserve ¾ cup cooking liquid and drain *edamame* in a
colander. Rinse under cold water until cool.
▶ Dry saucepan and add garlic and 3 tablespoons oil, then
cook over low heat, stirring occasionally, until garlic is pale
golden, 3 to 5 minutes.
▶ Purée 2 cups *edamame* with garlic-oil mixture in a food
processor until smooth. With motor running, add ½ cup
reserved *edamame*-cooking liquid in a stream. Add
remaining cup *edamame*, lime juice, sugar, pepper,
remaining 2 tablespoons oil, and remaining teaspoon salt
and pulse until slightly lumpy. Add remaining ¼ cup cooking
liquid to thin if desired, then stir in cilantro.
▶ Transfer dip to a serving dish and serve with vegetables,
drained and patted dry, for dipping.

Cooks' notes:

• Vegetables can be cut 1 day ahead and chilled in a sealed plastic bag lined with dampened paper towels. (Ice bath is not necessary if cutting vegetables ahead.)

• Dip, without cilantro, can be made 1 day ahead and chilled, covered. Bring to room temperature and stir in cilantro before serving.

CHESTNUT SOUP WITH SOURDOUGH SAGE CROUTONS

SERVES 8 TO 10

Active time: 1¼ hr   Start to finish: 1¼ hr

Most chestnut soups are fairly substantial. We've made our version lighter and brothier to serve as a first course for a big meal. Chopped chestnuts mixed with tangy croutons add texture and extra layers of complexity.

For soup

2 (7½-oz) jars peeled cooked whole chestnuts (see Sources), rinsed and drained (2⅔ cups)
2 large leeks (white and pale green parts only), coarsely chopped (1¼ cups)
1 tablespoon olive oil
1 tablespoon unsalted butter
1 large onion, coarsely chopped (2 cups)
2 celery ribs, coarsely chopped (1¼ cups)
2 medium carrots, coarsely chopped (1 cup)
1½ Turkish bay leaves or 1 California
1 tablespoon tamari or soy sauce
2½ qt water
2 teaspoons salt, or to taste
⅓ cup chopped fresh flat-leaf parsley
1 teaspoon chopped fresh sage
2 tablespoons medium-dry Sherry or Madeira
½ teaspoon black pepper

For topping

2 tablespoons olive oil
2 tablespoons unsalted butter
½ sourdough loaf, crust discarded and bread cut into ¼-inch cubes (4 cups)
1 teaspoon chopped fresh sage
2 (7½-oz) jars peeled cooked whole chestnuts, chopped (2⅔ cups)
1 teaspoon flaky sea salt (preferably Maldon)

Make soup:

▸ Put oven rack in upper third of oven and preheat oven to 375°F.
▸ Spread chestnuts in 1 layer in a large shallow baking pan, then roast in oven until dry and slightly darkened, about 20 minutes.
▸ While chestnuts roast, wash leeks in a bowl of cold water, agitating them, then lift out and drain well.
▸ Heat oil and butter in a 5- to 6-quart heavy pot over moderately high heat until foam subsides, then sauté leeks, onion, celery, carrots, and bay leaves, stirring occasionally, until vegetables are pale golden, 8 to 10 minutes. Add chestnuts and tamari and cook, stirring, until most of liquid is evaporated, 1 to 2 minutes. Add water (2½ quarts) and salt and simmer, uncovered, stirring occasionally, until vegetables are tender, about 30 minutes. Remove from heat and stir in parsley and sage. Discard bay leaves.
▸ Purée soup in 3 batches in a blender until smooth (use caution when blending hot liquids), transferring to a bowl. Pour purée through a medium-mesh sieve into cleaned pot, pressing hard on and then discarding solids. Bring soup to a simmer and stir in Sherry, pepper, and salt to taste, then remove from heat.

Make topping while soup simmers:

▸ Heat oil and butter in a 12-inch heavy skillet over moderately high heat until foam subsides, then cook bread cubes with sage, turning occasionally, until croutons are golden, 6 to 10 minutes. Add chestnuts and cook, stirring, 2 minutes. Transfer to a large bowl and toss with sea salt.
▸ Ladle soup into bowls and sprinkle each serving with about ⅓ cup topping.

Cooks' notes:

• Topping can be made 3 days ahead and cooled completely, then kept in an airtight container at room temperature. Reheat in 1 layer on a baking sheet in a 350°F oven until bread is crisp, 10 to 20 minutes.

• Soup, without Sherry, can be made 3 days ahead and cooled completely, uncovered, then chilled, covered. Reheat and stir in Sherry before serving.

OPPOSITE: *edamame* dip with crudités; chestnut soup with sourdough sage croutons

MISO-RUBBED TURKEY WITH TURKEY GRAVY
SERVES 8 TO 10
Active time: 1¼ hr   Start to finish: 4½ hr

Using miso on the turkey is a great way to get wonderfully moist meat—always a challenge at Thanksgiving. The skin doesn't get as crisp as it would without, but we think the succulent results are well worth the trade-off. The miso won't give the turkey an Asian flavor, but it will add a rich meatiness to the gravy. Don't use a brined or kosher turkey for this recipe or the bird will be too salty (miso has a high sodium content).

- 1   medium onion, quartered but left unpeeled
- ½   cup miso (white or red fermented-soybean paste)
- 1   stick (½ cup) unsalted butter, softened, plus additional melted butter (from ½ stick) if turkey drippings yield less than ½ cup fat
- 1   teaspoon black pepper
- 1   (12- to 14-lb) turkey, any feathers and quills removed with tweezers or needlenose pliers, and neck and giblets reserved for another use if desired
- ½   teaspoon salt
- 1   cup water
- 9   cups turkey stock (page 164)
- ¾   cup all-purpose flour

Special equipment: **2 small metal picks or skewers; kitchen string; a 19- by 13-inch flameproof roasting pan with a rack; an instant-read thermometer**

▸ Peel and chop 1 onion quarter, then pulse in a food processor until finely chopped. Add miso and purée until smooth. Add ½ stick softened butter and ½ teaspoon pepper and purée until combined (mixture will appear curdled).

▸ Put oven rack in lowest position and preheat oven to 350°F.

▸ Rinse turkey inside and out, then pat dry. Working from large cavity end, gently run your fingers between skin and meat of breast to loosen skin, being careful not to tear skin. Push miso butter under skin, including thighs and drumsticks, and massage skin from outside to spread miso evenly. Sprinkle large cavity with salt and remaining ½ teaspoon pepper. Fold neck skin under body and secure with metal picks or skewers, then stuff large cavity with remaining 3 onion quarters. Tie drumsticks together with string and tuck wings under body.

▸ Put turkey on rack in roasting pan and roast 30 minutes.

▸ Melt remaining ½ stick softened butter and brush over turkey, then add water (1 cup) to roasting pan. Tent turkey with foil and roast, basting every 30 minutes and adding more water to pan if necessary, until thermometer inserted into fleshy part of a thigh (do not touch bone) registers 170°F, 2 to 2½ hours more (total roasting time: 2½ to 3 hours). Remove foil for last 30 minutes of roasting if turkey is pale. Transfer turkey to a platter (reserve roasting pan) and let stand, loosely covered, 25 minutes (temperature will rise to 180°F while turkey stands). Remove picks from turkey.

▸ Pour pan juices through a fine-mesh sieve into a 2-quart glass measure, then skim off and reserve fat. (If there is less than ½ cup fat, add enough melted butter to total ½ cup.) Pour pan juices and 8 cups turkey stock into a 3-quart saucepan and bring to a simmer. Straddle roasting pan across 2 burners, then add remaining cup turkey stock and deglaze roasting pan by boiling over moderately high heat, stirring and scraping up brown bits, 1 minute. Pour through sieve into remaining stock and bring to a simmer.

▸ Cook flour and ½ cup reserved fat in a 4-quart heavy pot over moderately low heat, whisking, 5 minutes. Add hot stock mixture in a fast stream, whisking constantly to prevent lumps, then simmer, whisking occasionally, until gravy is thickened, about 10 minutes. Stir in any turkey juices accumulated on platter and season gravy with salt and pepper.

Cooks' notes:
• Miso butter can be made 4 days ahead and chilled, covered. Soften at room temperature before using.
• Miso butter can be pushed under turkey skin 1 day ahead; chill bird on rack in roasting pan, covered with plastic wrap.

OPPOSITE: chickpea, eggplant, and tomato tarts; brown butter and scallion mashed potatoes; sweet potato brûlée; rustic porcini onion stuffing; miso-rubbed turkey; celery and jicama sauté

knife. Transfer turkey parts, skin sides down, to a dry large heavy roasting pan and roast, turning over once, until golden brown, 30 to 45 minutes total. Transfer to a large stockpot, then add onions, celery, and carrots to roasting pan (arrange onions cut sides down) and roast, stirring once halfway through roasting, until golden, 10 to 20 minutes total. Transfer vegetables to stockpot.

▶ Straddle roasting pan across 2 burners, then add 2 cups water and deglaze pan by boiling over high heat, stirring and scraping up brown bits, 1 minute. Add pan juices to stockpot along with remaining 4½ quarts water and remaining ingredients and bring to a boil, skimming froth as necessary. Reduce heat and gently simmer, partially covered, 3 hours. Cool stock, uncovered, to room temperature, about 1 hour.

▶ Pour stock through a large fine-mesh sieve into a large bowl, discarding solids. Measure stock: If there is more than 9 cups, boil in cleaned pot until reduced. If there is less, add enough water to total 9 cups stock.

▶ If using stock now, let stand until fat rises to top, 1 to 2 minutes, then skim off and discard fat. If not using now, cool completely, uncovered, then chill, covered, before removing fat. Reheat stock before making turkey gravy.

Cooks' note:
• Stock can be chilled in an airtight container 1 week or frozen 3 months.

TURKEY STOCK

MAKES ABOUT 9 CUPS
Active time: 30 min   Start to finish: 5 hr

Using turkey meat rather than just bones adds a deep richness to this stock. Although you have to buy the extra parts, you'll be happy you did; great stock is the key to outstanding gravy, and everyone knows you can never have too much of that at Thanksgiving.

   6 lb turkey parts such as wings, drumsticks, and/or thighs
   3 medium onions, left unpeeled, trimmed and halved
   3 celery ribs, cut into 2-inch lengths
   3 carrots, cut into 2-inch lengths
   5 qt cold water
   6 fresh parsley stems
   1 Turkish or ½ California bay leaf
  10 whole black peppercorns
  1½ teaspoons salt

▶ Put oven rack in lowest position and preheat oven to 500°F.
▶ If using turkey wings, halve at joints with a cleaver or large

ROASTED MUSHROOM AND BARLEY GRAVY

MAKES ABOUT 6 CUPS
Active time: 45 min   Start to finish: 2 hr

This vegetarian gravy is layered with bold flavors—from the onions to the roasted mushrooms and barley—each of which makes a real statement. Even our carnivorous food editors agree it's one of the best gravies they've ever tasted.

  ½ lb portabella mushrooms
  ½ lb fresh shiitake mushrooms
  ½ lb white mushrooms
  ¼ cup olive oil
   3 tablespoons pearl barley
   1 large onion, left unpeeled
   2 celery ribs with leaves
   1 Turkish or ½ California bay leaf

8 cups water
2 fresh thyme sprigs
1 tablespoon tomato paste
½ cup dry white wine
1 teaspoon salt
1 teaspoon black pepper

▶ Put oven racks in upper and lower thirds of oven and preheat oven to 400°F.
▶ Twist off and reserve stems from portabellas. Using a paring knife, scrape off and discard gills from underside of portabella caps, then cut caps into 1-inch pieces. Cut off and reserve stems from shiitakes, then quarter shiitakes and white mushrooms. Toss portabella, shiitake, and white mushrooms (but not reserved stems) with 2 tablespoons oil and spread in a 17- by 11-inch flameproof roasting pan. Roast in upper third of oven, stirring occasionally, until golden, about 1 hour.
▶ Meanwhile, spread barley in a shallow baking pan and roast in lower third of oven, stirring occasionally, 1 hour (barley will be dark brown and smell burned after about 10 minutes, but don't worry—just continue roasting).
▶ While mushrooms and barley roast, peel onion, reserving skin, and coarsely chop onion. Trim celery, reserving trimmings and leaves, and coarsely chop celery. Bring onion skin, celery trimmings, mushroom stems, bay leaf, and 7 cups water to a boil in a 4-quart pot, then reduce heat and simmer 40 minutes.
▶ Add hot roasted barley to broth, then remove from heat and let stand 5 minutes. Pour through a fine-mesh sieve into a 2-quart glass measure, pressing hard on and then discarding solids (you will have about 6 cups broth).
▶ Heat remaining 2 tablespoons oil in a 5- to 6-quart heavy pot over moderately high heat until hot but not smoking, then sauté onion, celery, and thyme, stirring occasionally, until vegetables are golden, about 15 minutes. Add tomato paste and cook, stirring frequently, until paste is very thick, about 1 minute. Add wine and cook, stirring and scraping up any brown bits, 1 minute. Stir in roasted mushrooms (reserve roasting pan) and strained broth and bring to a simmer.
▶ Straddle mushroom-roasting pan across 2 burners and add remaining cup water, then deglaze pan by boiling over high heat, stirring and scraping up any brown bits, 1 minute. Pour into mushroom mixture and stir in salt and pepper, then simmer, partially covered, until vegetables are very tender, about 30 minutes.

▶ Purée in 2 batches in a blender (use caution when blending hot liquids). Force through fine-mesh sieve into a bowl, discarding solids. Season with salt and pepper.

Cooks' note:
• Gravy can be made 5 days ahead and cooled completely, uncovered, then chilled, covered. Bring to a boil just before serving.

PERSIMMON CRANBERRY SAUCE
MAKES ABOUT 2½ CUPS
Active time: 15 min   Start to finish: 15 min

The bright, tender fruit of Fuyu persimmons mellows the intensity of cranberries while lending this sauce a beautiful jewel-like hue. Using Fuyus, which can be eaten hard or soft, removes the guesswork of finding ripe fruit.

¾ lb fresh or frozen cranberries (3½ cups)
¼ cup dry red wine
2 tablespoons water
½ star anise or ¼ teaspoon star-anise pieces
½ to ⅔ cup sugar
3 firm-ripe Fuyu persimmons (about 1 lb total), peeled and cut into ¼-inch dice

▶ Bring cranberries, wine, water, star anise, ½ cup sugar, and a pinch of salt to a boil in a 2-quart heavy saucepan, stirring occasionally, then reduce heat and simmer 5 minutes. Add more sugar, to taste (up to about 2½ tablespoons), and discard star anise. Fold in persimmons.
▶ Transfer to a bowl and serve at room temperature or chilled. Stir gently before serving.

Cooks' note:
• Cranberry sauce, without persimmons, can be made 4 days ahead and chilled, covered. Fold in persimmons before serving.

OPPOSITE: persimmon cranberry sauce. FOLLOWING PAGE: chickpea, eggplant, and tomato tarts

CHICKPEA, EGGPLANT, AND TOMATO TARTS

SERVES 4 (VEGETARIAN MAIN COURSE) OR 8 TO 10 (SIDE DISH)
Active time: 45 min   Start to finish: 1¼ hr

These tarts could be halved (or even quartered) to serve as a side dish. Either way, they are delicious with the roasted mushroom and barley gravy (page 164).

  1 (1-lb) eggplant
1¾ teaspoons salt
  ½ cup extra-virgin olive oil
  1 medium onion, halved lengthwise, then cut
       crosswise into ½-inch-thick slices
  1 Turkish or ½ California bay leaf
  3 garlic cloves, minced
  1 (14½- to 16-oz) can stewed tomatoes, drained,
       reserving juice, and coarsely chopped
  ½ teaspoon paprika (not hot)
  ⅛ teaspoon ground cumin
  1 (15- to 19-oz) can chickpeas, rinsed and drained
  1 teaspoon sugar

1½ teaspoons black pepper
  ¼ cup coarsely chopped fresh flat-leaf parsley
  6 (17- by 12-inch) phyllo sheets (from a 1-lb package),
       thawed if frozen

Garnish: fresh flat-leaf parsley leaves, torn into pieces

Make filling:

▶ Peel eggplant and cut into ½-inch cubes. Toss with 1 teaspoon salt in a large bowl and let stand 15 minutes, then rinse in a colander under cold water and squeeze out excess water.

▶ Heat 2 tablespoons oil in a 12-inch heavy skillet over moderately high heat until hot but not smoking, then cook onion with bay leaf, stirring occasionally, until golden, about 5 minutes. Add 1 tablespoon oil, eggplant, and garlic and cook, stirring, until eggplant is tender, 8 to 10 minutes. Add tomatoes (without juice), paprika, and cumin and cook, stirring, 3 minutes. Add reserved tomato juice, chickpeas, sugar, ½ teaspoon pepper, and remaining ¾ teaspoon salt and simmer, stirring occasionally, until filling is thickened and most of liquid is evaporated, about 5 minutes. Remove from heat and stir in parsley, then discard bay leaf.

Make tarts:

▶ Put oven rack in middle position and preheat oven to 425°F. Line a large baking sheet with foil.

▶ Unroll phyllo and cover stack with plastic wrap and a dampened kitchen towel. Keeping remaining phyllo covered, lightly brush 1 phyllo sheet with some of remaining oil and top with 2 more sheets, brushing each with oil. Sprinkle with ½ teaspoon pepper, then cut stack in half crosswise with a sharp knife. Spoon 1 cup filling into center of each half. Crumple edges of phyllo and shape into a crescent, leaving filling exposed, then transfer to baking sheet using a spatula. Make 2 more tarts in same manner, arranging about ½ inch apart on baking sheet.

▶ Bake, rotating baking sheet 180 degrees after 10 minutes, until edges of tarts are golden, 15 to 20 minutes total. Serve immediately.

Cooks' notes:

• Filling, without parsley, can be made 1 day ahead and chilled, covered. Stir in parsley before using.

• Tarts can be baked 6 hours ahead and kept, uncovered, at room temperature. Reheat in a 350°F oven 15 to 20 minutes (while turkey stands, if making).

RUSTIC PORCINI ONION STUFFING

SERVES 8 TO 10

Active time: 1 hr Start to finish: 1¾ hr

*Unlike many stuffings, this wild mushroom version is
completely vegetarian.*

- 1½ (1-lb) Pullman or round loaves, torn into
      1-inch pieces (20 cups)
- 1   stick (½ cup) unsalted butter plus additional
      for greasing dish
- 4½ cups boiling-hot water
- 2   oz dried porcini mushrooms (sometimes called
      cèpes; see Sources; 54 g)
- 10 oz fresh white mushrooms, cut into ½-inch
      wedges (3 cups)
- 1   large onion, halved lengthwise, then sliced
      crosswise ½ inch thick
- 4   large shallots, quartered
- 2   celery ribs, sliced ¼ inch thick
- 2   medium carrots, halved lengthwise, then sliced
      crosswise ¼ inch thick
- 3   garlic cloves, minced
- 1½ teaspoons chopped fresh thyme
- 1½ teaspoons chopped fresh sage
- 2   tablespoons chopped fresh flat-leaf parsley
- 2¼ teaspoons salt
- ½   teaspoon black pepper

▶ Put oven racks in upper and lower thirds of oven and
preheat oven to 350°F.

▶ Spread bread in 2 large shallow baking pans and bake in
upper and lower thirds of oven, stirring occasionally and
switching position of pans halfway through baking, until
dry, 20 to 25 minutes total. Transfer bread to a large bowl.

▶ Increase oven temperature to 450°F and butter a 13- by
9-inch baking dish (3-quart capacity).

▶ Pour boiling-hot water over porcini and soak 20 minutes,
then drain in a fine-mesh sieve set over a bowl, squeezing
porcini and reserving soaking liquid. Rinse porcini under
cold water to remove any grit, then squeeze out excess water
and coarsely chop.

▶ While porcini soak, heat butter (1 stick) in a 12-inch heavy
skillet over moderately high heat until foam subsides, then
cook white mushrooms, onion, and shallots, stirring
occasionally, until golden, 15 to 20 minutes. Add celery,

carrots, garlic, and porcini and cook, stirring, 5 minutes.
Stir in thyme, sage, parsley, salt, and pepper, then add
vegetables to bread, tossing to combine.

▶ Add 1 cup reserved porcini-soaking liquid to skillet and
deglaze by boiling over high heat, stirring and scraping up
brown bits, 1 minute. Add remaining soaking liquid and salt
and pepper to taste and pour over bread mixture, tossing to
coat evenly.

▶ Spread stuffing in baking dish and cover tightly with
buttered foil (buttered side down), then bake in upper third
of oven until heated through, about 20 minutes. Remove foil
and bake until top is browned, 10 to 15 minutes more.

Cooks' notes:
• Stuffing can be assembled (but not baked) 2 days ahead
and chilled, covered.
• Stuffing can be baked 6 hours ahead and kept, uncovered,
at room temperature. Reheat, uncovered, in a 350°F oven
(with sweet-potato brûlée, if making) until hot, about
30 minutes (test center with a wooden pick for warmth).

CELERY AND JICAMA SAUTÉ

SERVES 8 TO 10

Active time: 25 min Start to finish: 25 min

- 1   (2½-lb) bunch of celery
- 1¼ lb jicama
- 2   tablespoons olive oil
- 2   garlic cloves, smashed
- ⅓   cup coarsely chopped fresh flat-leaf parsley
- 1   teaspoon finely grated fresh lemon zest (see Tips, page 8)
- 2   teaspoons fresh lemon juice
- 1   teaspoon salt
- ¼   teaspoon black pepper

▶ Peel strings from celery with a peeler, then cut celery on a
long diagonal into ¼-inch-thick slices. Peel jicama with a
sharp knife and cut into 2- by ¼-inch matchsticks.

▶ Heat oil in a 6- to 8-quart heavy pot over moderately high
heat until hot but not smoking, then sauté garlic, turning,
until golden on all sides, about 2 minutes. Discard garlic.

▶ Add celery to oil and sauté, stirring, until softened, about
3 minutes. Add jicama and sauté, stirring, until slightly
translucent, about 5 minutes. Stir in remaining ingredients
and remove from heat.

SWEET-POTATO BRÛLÉE

SERVES 8 TO 10 (SIDE DISH)

Active time: 20 min   Start to finish: 3½ hr (includes cooling)

Given the popularity of crème brûlée, this luscious side dish is sure to be a hit. If you're making this entire menu in a single oven, you'll need to make the brûlée ahead and reheat it while the turkey stands (see cooks' note, below).

- 2 lb sweet potatoes (2 or 3 large)
- 7 large egg yolks
- 3 tablespoons packed light brown sugar
- 1 teaspoon fresh lemon juice
- ½ teaspoon freshly grated nutmeg
- ½ teaspoon salt
- 3 cups whole milk
- 5 to 7 tablespoons turbinado sugar such as Sugar in the Raw

Special equipment: **a shallow 2½-qt flameproof baking dish such as a 12-inch quiche dish (1¾ inches deep); a small blowtorch**

▶ Put oven rack in middle position and preheat oven to 400°F.

▶ Pierce potatoes all over with a fork. Bake in a foil-lined shallow baking pan until tender, about 1 hour. Remove from oven and reduce oven temperature to 300°F.

▶ When sweet potatoes are cool enough to handle, peel them. Cut warm potatoes into 2-inch pieces and purée in a food processor until smooth.

▶ Whisk together yolks, brown sugar, lemon juice, nutmeg, and salt in a large bowl until sugar is dissolved. Whisk in sweet-potato purée until combined, then gently stir in milk until combined. Pour mixture into baking dish and bake until custard is just set, about 1 hour. Cool in dish on a rack 1 hour (custard will continue to set as it cools).

▶ Just before serving, gently sprinkle enough turbinado sugar over custard to cover evenly (top of custard may be very soft), then move blowtorch flame evenly back and forth just above sugar until sugar is caramelized, about 3 minutes. Let stand until topping is hardened, 3 to 5 minutes.

Cooks' notes:

• Sweet potatoes can be baked 3 days ahead and chilled, wrapped in foil.

• Sweet-potato custard can be baked (but not topped with sugar) 1 day ahead and cooled completely, then chilled, uncovered (do not cover or condensation will occur). Gently blot any moisture from surface with paper towels, then warm, uncovered, in a 350°F oven 20 to 30 minutes (test center with a wooden pick for warmth) before sprinkling with turbinado sugar.

BROWN BUTTER AND SCALLION MASHED POTATOES

SERVES 8 TO 10

Active time: 25 min   Start to finish: 45 min

It's hard to improve upon the honest goodness of mashed potatoes, but here scallions and brown butter do the trick. The scallions provide sweetness, and the brown butter adds a beguiling nuttiness.

- 5 lb yellow-fleshed potatoes such as Yukon Gold, peeled and cut into 1-inch pieces
- 1 tablespoon salt
- 1 cup whole milk
- ½ cup sour cream
- 1½ sticks (¾ cup) unsalted butter
- 2 bunches scallions, cut crosswise into ½-inch pieces
- ½ teaspoon black pepper

Special equipment: **a potato masher or a food mill fitted with medium disk**

▶ Cover potatoes with cold water by 2 inches in a 5- to 6-quart heavy pot and add 1½ teaspoons salt. Bring to a boil, then reduce heat and simmer, uncovered, until potatoes are tender, 10 to 15 minutes.

▶ Drain potatoes in a colander, then return to pot and cook over moderate heat, shaking pot occasionally, until dry, 1 to 2 minutes. Mash hot potatoes with masher or force through food mill into another pot, then cover to keep warm.

▶ Bring milk with remaining 1½ teaspoons salt just to a boil in a 1-quart saucepan, then remove from heat and stir into potatoes until combined. Stir in sour cream, then cover and keep warm.

▶ Cook butter in a 12-inch heavy skillet over moderately high heat, stirring frequently and scraping up brown bits, until foam subsides and butter is golden brown, about 8 minutes.

Add scallions and pepper and cook, stirring, until slightly softened, about 2 minutes. Fold butter mixture into mashed potatoes and season with salt.

Cooks' note:
• Mashed potatoes can be made 1 day ahead and cooled, uncovered, then chilled, covered. (Scallions may discolor slightly when potatoes are made ahead.) Reheat in a microwave or in a heavy pot over moderate heat, stirring.

APPLE TARTS WITH VANILLA ICE CREAM

SERVES 12
Active time: 40 min   Start to finish: 1½ hr

Easily made with puff pastry, these light, thin apple tarts provide just the right amount of dessert. The skins get added to the syrupy glaze, enhancing the tarts with a bit of sweetness and the faintest blush of pink.

6	Gala apples (preferably red; 2¾ lb)
½	cup water
½	cup sugar
½	vanilla bean, split lengthwise
1	(17¼-oz) package frozen puff pastry sheets, thawed All-purpose flour for dusting
1½	tablespoons unsalted butter, melted

Special equipment: **parchment paper**
Accompaniment: **vanilla ice cream**

▶ Put oven racks in upper and lower thirds of oven and preheat oven to 400°F. Line 2 large baking sheets with parchment paper.
▶ Peel apples, reserving skins. Stir together water and 6 tablespoons sugar in a 1-quart heavy saucepan, then scrape in seeds from vanilla bean and add pod. Add reserved apple skins and bring to a boil, stirring until sugar is dissolved. Remove from heat and let stand 10 minutes. Pour through a medium-mesh sieve into a bowl, pressing hard on and then discarding solids.
▶ Roll out 1 pastry sheet into a 10-inch square on a lightly floured surface with a lightly floured rolling pin, then cut in half and transfer to 1 of the baking sheets. Repeat with remaining pastry sheet, transferring to second baking sheet.

▶ Halve apples lengthwise, then core with a melon-ball cutter or a small spoon and cut crosswise into very thin slices (⅛ inch thick or less), keeping apple halves intact. Fan apple slices slightly, keeping apple shape, then arrange 3 halves in a row on each piece of pastry, leaving a ⅔-inch border on all sides.
▶ Brush border lightly with syrup and fold over about ⅓ inch to touch edges of apples. Crimp edges with a fork, then brush apples and edges of pastry with syrup (reserve remaining syrup). Brush apples completely with melted butter, then sprinkle evenly with remaining 2 tablespoons sugar.
▶ Bake tarts in upper and lower thirds of oven 20 minutes, then switch position of sheets and reduce oven temperature to 375°F. Bake tarts until edges are golden, 15 to 20 minutes more. (If pastry edges aren't browning evenly, rotate tarts 180 degrees on sheets halfway through baking.)
▶ While tarts bake, boil remaining syrup over moderate heat until reduced to about ¼ cup, 30 seconds to 1 minute.
▶ Let tarts stand 5 minutes, then brush warm apples with remaining syrup.

Cooks' notes:
• Tarts can be assembled (but not sprinkled with sugar or baked) 1 day ahead and chilled, covered. Sprinkle apples with sugar just before baking.
• Tarts can be baked 4 hours ahead and kept, uncovered, at room temperature.

HONEY PECAN TART WITH CHOCOLATE GLAZE

SERVES 12 TO 16

Active time: 45 min   Start to finish: 4 hr (includes cooling)

We've made one of America's most famous holiday desserts—pecan pie—even more delicious by adding an unctuous layer of moist caramel, a touch of bittersweet chocolate (to cut the sweetness), and some finely shaved nuts on top.

For filling

4½ cups pecan halves (15 oz)

1 cup sugar

⅓ cup mild honey

1½ cups heavy cream

½ cup whole milk

¾ teaspoon salt

For tart shell

Pastry dough (recipe follows)

For glaze

7 oz fine-quality bittersweet chocolate (not unsweetened; preferably Lindt), finely chopped

¾ cup heavy cream

Special equipment: an 11-inch fluted round tart pan (1¼ inches deep) with removable rim; an adjustable-blade slicer (optional)

Make filling:

▸ Boil 4 cups pecans (reserve remaining ½ cup for garnish) with sugar, honey, cream, milk, and salt in a 4-quart heavy saucepan over moderately high heat, stirring occasionally, until liquid is golden, about 20 minutes (mixture will appear curdled at first, but then become thick and smooth). Remove from heat and transfer mixture to a shallow bowl, then cool completely, about 40 minutes.

Prepare tart shell:

▸ Roll out larger disk of dough (keep remaining piece chilled) between 2 large sheets of parchment paper or plastic wrap into a 13-inch round (⅛ inch thick), then remove parchment from top and invert dough into tart pan set on a baking sheet, pressing onto bottom and side of pan and leaving overhang. Chill shell at least 30 minutes. Roll out remaining disk between 2 large sheets of parchment or plastic wrap into a 12-inch round (⅛ inch thick) and chill on a baking sheet at least 30 minutes.

Bake tart:

▸ Put oven rack in lower third of oven and preheat oven to 425°F.

▸ If nut filling is very firm, warm slightly in a saucepan over low heat until softened but not warm. Spread filling in tart shell, smoothing top. Brush overhang of bottom crust with water. Remove parchment from remaining round of dough and arrange round over tart filling, gently rolling a rolling pin along edge to seal and trim excess.

▸ Bake tart (in pan) on baking sheet until pastry is golden, 30 to 40 minutes. Cool in pan on a rack set on a large plate 15 minutes. Carefully remove side of pan and cool tart completely, about 2 hours.

Make glaze while tart cools:

▸ Put chopped chocolate in a shallow bowl. Bring cream just to a boil and pour over chocolate, then whisk gently (to avoid air bubbles) until chocolate is completely melted.

▸ Pour warm glaze over top of tart and gently spread with an offset spatula to evenly cover top, allowing chocolate to drizzle down side. Let tart stand until glaze is set, at least 30 minutes.

Garnish tart:

▸ Rinse reserved ½ cup pecans in a sieve, then pat dry and carefully shave very thin slices (less than 1/32 inch) using slicer, checking thickness of first shavings on a plate before starting to shave pecans directly onto tart. If you don't have a slicer, finely chop.

Cooks' notes:

• Filling can be made 4 days ahead and cooled completely, then chilled, covered.

• Tart can be baked (but not glazed) 1 day ahead and cooled to room temperature, uncovered, then kept, wrapped in plastic wrap, at room temperature. Glaze and garnish before serving.

PASTRY DOUGH

MAKES ENOUGH FOR 1 DOUBLE-CRUST 11-INCH TART
Active time: 20 min   Start to finish: 1¼ hr

There's a reason that we use this recipe time and time again—it results in a flaky pastry that we think is simply the best.

2½   cups all-purpose flour
1½   sticks (¾ cup) cold unsalted butter, cut into
        ½-inch cubes
¼   cup cold vegetable shortening (preferably
        trans-fat-free)
½   teaspoon salt
7   to 9 tablespoons ice water

Special equipment: **a pastry or bench scraper**

▶ Blend together flour, butter, shortening, and salt in a bowl with your fingertips or a pastry blender (or pulse in a food processor) until most of mixture resembles coarse meal with some small (roughly pea-size) butter lumps. Drizzle evenly with 7 tablespoons ice water and gently stir with a fork (or pulse in processor) until incorporated.

▶ Squeeze a small handful: If it doesn't hold together, add more ice water, 1 tablespoon at a time, stirring (or pulsing) until incorporated, then test again. (Do not overwork mixture, or pastry will be tough.)

▶ Turn mixture out onto a work surface and divide into 8 portions. With heel of your hand, smear each portion once or twice in a forward motion to help distribute fat. Gather two thirds of dough together with scraper and press into a ball. Repeat with remaining dough, then flatten each ball into a 5-inch disk. Wrap disks separately in plastic wrap and chill until firm, at least 1 hour.

Cooks' note:
• Dough can be chilled up to 1 week.

GAME PLAN

1 WEEK AHEAD
-Make turkey stock
-Make pastry dough for honey pecan tart

5 DAYS AHEAD
-Make mushroom and barley gravy

4 DAYS AHEAD
-Make miso butter for turkey
-Make cranberry sauce
-Make filling for honey pecan tart

3 DAYS AHEAD
-Make chestnut soup and croutons
-Bake sweet potatoes for brûlée

2 DAYS AHEAD
-Assemble porcini onion stuffing

1 DAY AHEAD
-Prepare *edamame* dip and cut crudités
-Rub turkey with miso butter
-Make filling for chickpea, eggplant, and tomato tarts
-Bake sweet-potato custard
-Make mashed potatoes
-Cut celery and jicama
-Assemble apple tarts
-Bake honey pecan tart

THANKSGIVING DAY
-Bake stuffing
-Bake chickpea, eggplant, and tomato tarts
-Bake apple tarts
-Reheat croutons for soup
-Roast turkey

WHILE TURKEY ROASTS
-Add persimmons to cranberry sauce
-Glaze and garnish honey pecan tart
-Heat stock for turkey gravy
-Reheat soup
-Reheat mashed potatoes
-Reheat roasted mushroom and barley gravy
-Sauté jicama and celery

WHILE TURKEY STANDS
-Reheat chickpea, eggplant, and tomato tarts
-Reheat stuffing
-Reheat sweet-potato custard, then cook brûlée
  topping on custard
-Finish turkey gravy

A MIDDAY FEAST

AN EASYGOING THANKSGIVING BRUNCH

SERVES 8

**CORN CUSTARD WITH CHORIZO
AND MUSHROOMS**

**GREEN LEAF LETTUCE, POMEGRANATE,
AND ALMOND SALAD**

**ORANGE CINNAMON SWEET ROLLS
WITH ORANGE BUTTER**

PINEAPPLE TANGERINE BATIDO

CAFÉ DE OLLA

CORN CUSTARD WITH CHORIZO AND MUSHROOMS

SERVES 8

Active time: 45 min   Start to finish: 1¾ hr

    Butter for greasing baking dish
2 tablespoons olive oil
½ lb Spanish chorizo (cured spiced pork sausage), casing discarded and sausage quartered lengthwise, then cut crosswise into ⅓-inch-thick slices
¾ lb cremini mushrooms, trimmed and thinly sliced
1 tablespoon finely chopped fresh jalapeño chile including seeds
2 (10-oz) packages frozen corn kernels, thawed (4 cups)
4 oz cream cheese, softened
⅓ cup yellow cornmeal (not coarse)
2 tablespoons sugar
6 large eggs
1 cup whole milk
¾ teaspoon salt
6 scallions, finely chopped (1 cup)
½ lb Monterey Jack cheese, coarsely grated (2½ cups)

Special equipment: **an 11- by 7- by 2-inch shallow baking dish (2-qt capacity)**

▸Put oven rack in middle position and preheat oven to 375°F. Lightly butter baking dish.

▸Heat 1 tablespoon oil in a 12-inch heavy skillet over moderately high heat until hot but not smoking, then sauté chorizo, stirring occasionally, until browned, 6 to 8 minutes. Transfer with a slotted spoon to paper towels to drain briefly, then transfer chorizo to baking dish. Reserve fat in skillet.

▸Add remaining tablespoon oil to fat in skillet and heat over moderately high heat, then sauté mushrooms, stirring occasionally, until liquid mushrooms give off is evaporated and mushrooms are browned, about 8 minutes. Add chile and sauté, stirring, until softened, about 1 minute. Transfer to baking dish with chorizo.

▸Purée 2 cups corn with cream cheese, cornmeal, and sugar in a food processor until as smooth as possible (mixture will still be grainy).

▸Whisk together eggs, milk, and salt in a large bowl until combined well. Whisk in corn purée, scallions, 1½ cups cheese, and remaining 2 cups corn until combined. Pour mixture into baking dish and sprinkle evenly with remaining cup cheese.

▸Bake until puffed, set, and golden, 50 minutes to 1 hour. Cool slightly before serving. Serve warm or at room temperature.

Cooks' note:
• Custard can be baked 1 day ahead, though texture will not be as light. Cool completely, uncovered, then chill, covered. Reheat, uncovered, in a 350°F oven 20 to 25 minutes.

GREEN LEAF LETTUCE, POMEGRANATE, AND ALMOND SALAD

SERVES 8

Active time: 30 min   Start to finish: 30 min

2 tablespoons fresh lime juice
1½ teaspoons sugar
¾ teaspoon salt
¼ teaspoon black pepper
5 tablespoons extra-virgin olive oil
1¼ lb green leaf lettuce (2 heads), trimmed and leaves torn into 2-inch pieces (20 cups)
½ lb watercress (2 bunches), coarse stems discarded and sprigs cut into 1-inch pieces (6 cups)
    Seeds from 1 large pomegranate (1¼ cups), bitter white membranes discarded
¾ cup sliced almonds (2¼ oz), toasted (see Tips, page 8)

▸Whisk together lime juice, sugar, salt, and pepper until sugar and salt are dissolved, then add oil in a steady stream, whisking until combined.

▸Combine lettuce, watercress, and half of pomegranate seeds in a large serving bowl. Toss with just enough dressing to coat, then sprinkle with almonds and remaining pomegranate seeds.

Cooks' notes:
• Lettuce and watercress can be washed and spun dry 1 day ahead and chilled separately, wrapped in dampened paper towels, in sealed plastic bags.
• Pomegranate can be seeded 1 day ahead. Chill seeds in an airtight container.
• Almonds can be toasted 1 day ahead and cooled completely, then kept in an airtight container at room temperature.

ORANGE CINNAMON SWEET ROLLS
MAKES 12 ROLLS
Active time: 30 min   Start to finish: 4¼ hr

Nothing beats buttery sweet rolls fresh from the oven and the warm, yeasty scent as they bake.

  3 tablespoons warm water (105–115°F) plus 2 teaspoons
       water at room temperature
  1 (¼-oz) package active dry yeast (2¼ teaspoons)
  ½ cup plus 1 teaspoon sugar
  5 to 5½ cups unbleached all-purpose flour
  1 tablespoon finely grated fresh orange zest (see Tips,
       page 8)
  2 teaspoons salt
  1 teaspoon cinnamon
  1 cup warm milk (105–115°F)
1½ teaspoons vanilla
  ¾ stick (6 tablespoons) unsalted butter, softened, plus
       additional for greasing bowl
  4 large eggs at room temperature 30 minutes, or
       submerged in a bowl of warm water (105°F) 5 minutes

Special equipment: an instant-read thermometer (for checking water and milk temperatures); a stand mixer with paddle and dough hook attachments; a clean kitchen towel (not terry cloth); parchment paper
Accompaniment: orange butter (recipe follows)

▸Stir together warm water, yeast, and 1 teaspoon sugar in bowl of mixer fitted with paddle attachment and let stand until foamy, about 5 minutes. (If mixture doesn't foam, discard and start over with new yeast.)
▸While yeast is foaming, whisk 4 cups flour with zest, salt, and cinnamon in a bowl.
▸Add milk, vanilla, butter, and remaining ½ cup sugar to yeast, then mix at medium speed until combined. Beat in 3 eggs, 1 at a time, then add orange cinnamon flour and mix until combined well.
▸Replace paddle attachment with dough hook attachment and mix at medium-low speed, adding more flour (1 to 1½ cups), ¼ cup at a time, until a smooth but slightly sticky dough forms, about 5 minutes. Transfer dough to a work surface and knead by hand until smooth and elastic (dough will remain slightly sticky), about 3 minutes. Form dough into a ball and transfer to a large buttered bowl, turning dough to coat with butter.
▸Cover bowl with kitchen towel and let dough rise in a draft-free place at warm room temperature until doubled in bulk, 1½ to 2 hours.
▸Line a 17- by 14-inch baking sheet with parchment paper.
▸Turn out dough onto work surface and knead several times to remove air. Cut dough into 12 equal pieces. Cup your hand over 1 piece and, using your thumb and pinkie to keep ball inside your cupped hand, push dough with heel of your hand against work surface while rolling in a circular motion (clockwise or counterclockwise) to form a smooth ball. Repeat with remaining pieces of dough, arranging balls 1 inch apart on baking sheet.
▸Cover loosely with kitchen towel and let dough rise in a draft-free place at warm room temperature until doubled in bulk, 1 to 1¼ hours.
▸Put oven rack in middle position and preheat oven to 375°F.
▸Whisk together remaining egg with remaining 2 teaspoons water in a small bowl. Cut a 1-inch X (¼ inch deep) in top of each roll with kitchen shears. Brush rolls lightly with egg wash and bake until golden and rolls sound hollow when tapped on bottom, 15 to 20 minutes. Transfer rolls to a rack and cool, at least 15 minutes.

Cooks' note:
• Rolls can be baked 1 day ahead and cooled completely, then kept in sealed plastic bags or a large airtight container at room temperature. Reheat on a baking sheet in a 350°F oven 10 minutes.

ORANGE BUTTER
MAKES ABOUT ¾ CUP
Active time: 5 min   Start to finish: 5 min

Although this orange butter takes only 5 minutes to prepare, it makes the orange cinnamon sweet rolls (recipe precedes) even more spectacular than they already are.

 1   stick (½ cup) salted or unsalted butter, softened
 ⅓   cup orange marmalade

▶ Pulse butter and marmalade in a food processor until combined well. Transfer to a small crock or serving bowl.

Cooks' note:
• Butter can be made 5 days ahead and chilled, covered. Bring to room temperature before serving (this will take about 30 minutes).

PINEAPPLE TANGERINE BATIDO
MAKES ABOUT 12 CUPS
Active time: 15 min   Start to finish: 1¼ hr (includes chilling)

Four fresh fruits bring a sunny taste of the tropics to your table. If you want to make this a virgin drink, simply omit the rum and add an extra cup of tangerine juice.

 2   (4-lb) pineapples (preferably labeled "extra sweet"), trimmed, peeled, quartered lengthwise, cored, and cut into ½-inch pieces (about 10 cups)
 1   medium banana, sliced
 3   cups tangerine juice
 ¼   cup fresh lime juice
 1   cup white rum

▶ Working in 3 batches, purée pineapples, banana, and juices in a blender until very smooth. Transfer as puréed to a large pitcher. (If pineapple is particularly fibrous, pour

through a medium-mesh sieve, pressing hard on and then discarding solids.) Stir in rum. Chill, covered, until cold, about 1 hour. Stir again (or blend for a frothier texture) just before serving.

Cooks' note:
• Batido can be made 1 day ahead and chilled, covered.

CAFÉ DE OLLA
(Mexican-Style Sweetened Black Coffee)
MAKES ABOUT 8 CUPS
Active time: 5 min   Start to finish: 15 min

If you normally take your coffee with milk, you'll find this particular recipe for black coffee a welcome change—the molasses and cinnamon give it a warm and slightly exotic depth that's simply irresistible. Be sure to use coffee that is not finely ground.

 8   cups water
 ⅔   cup packed light brown sugar
 1   teaspoon molasses
 2   (3-inch) cinnamon sticks
 1   cup medium-grind coffee (not espresso)

▶ Bring water, brown sugar, molasses, and cinnamon sticks to a boil in a 4-quart pot over moderate heat, stirring occasionally until sugar is dissolved. Stir in coffee and boil 5 minutes. Pour through a fine-mesh sieve into a heatproof pitcher, discarding coffee grinds and cinnamon sticks.

Cooks' note:
• Coffee can be made 3 hours ahead. Reheat over moderate heat (do not boil).

CHRISTMAS PRESENT

A VERY SPECIAL YULETIDE DINNER

SERVES 10 TO 12

MUSSELS WITH TARRAGON CELERY VINAIGRETTE

CLOS DE LA SÉNAIGERIE CÔTES DE GRANDLIEU MUSCADET '04

CROWN ROAST OF PORK WITH ONION AND BREAD-CRUMB STUFFING

CRANBERRY HORSERADISH SAUCE

CELERY-ROOT AND APPLE PURÉE

POTATO AND LARDON CASSEROLE

FRENCHED GREEN BEANS

CHÂTEAU DE CALADROY CUVÉE LES SCHISTES CÔTES DU ROUSSILLON VILLAGES '03

HAZELNUT PARIS-BREST

POACHED ORANGES WITH CANDIED ZEST AND GINGER

DOMAINE DU MAS BLANC BANYULS BLANC VIN DOUX NATUREL '03

MUSSELS WITH TARRAGON CELERY VINAIGRETTE

SERVES 10 TO 12 (HORS D'OEUVRE)

Active time: 45 min **Start to finish:** 1¾ hr (includes marinating)

2 lb mussels (35 to 45; preferably cultivated), scrubbed
    well and beards removed
⅓ cup dry white wine
2 hard-boiled large eggs
2 tablespoons white-wine vinegar
¼ teaspoon salt
¼ teaspoon black pepper
¼ cup extra-virgin olive oil
½ cup finely chopped celery
½ cup pickled cocktail onions, trimmed and finely chopped
2 tablespoons chopped fresh tarragon

Garnish: seaweed (see Sources)

▸Cook mussels in wine in a 4- to 6-quart pot over moderately
high heat, covered, until mussels just open wide, checking
frequently after 4 minutes and transferring opened mussels
to a large bowl using a slotted spoon. (Discard any unopened
mussels after 8 minutes.)

▸Pour cooking liquid through a fine-mesh sieve into a 1- to
2-quart heavy saucepan and boil until reduced to about
3 tablespoons, about 5 minutes. Transfer to a bowl.

▸Finely chop eggs, then add to reduced liquid along with
vinegar, salt, and pepper. Add oil in a slow stream, whisking,
then whisk in celery, onions, and tarragon. Season vinaigrette
with salt and pepper.

▸Remove mussels from shells and reserve 1 half shell from
each mussel. Stir mussels (but not shells) into vinaigrette
and marinate, covered and chilled, at least 1 hour. Rinse and
dry reserved mussel shells, then chill in a sealed plastic bag
until ready to use.

▸Arrange shells on a large platter lined with seaweed and
spoon a mussel with some vinaigrette into each.

Cooks' note:
• Mussels can be marinated up to 1 day.

CROWN ROAST OF PORK WITH ONION AND BREAD-CRUMB STUFFING

SERVES 10 TO 12
Active time: 1½ hr   Start to finish: 4¼ hr

Nothing is more majestic than this regal cut of meat—and nothing makes your house smell better while it roasts. Here, pork's natural sweetness is coaxed forward by the herbs and onions in the stuffing. You will have to special-order this cut of meat from your butcher.

For stuffing

2   lb onions, finely chopped (6 cups)
2½ teaspoons salt
1½ sticks (¾ cup) unsalted butter
2   tablespoons chopped fresh sage
1   tablespoon chopped fresh marjoram
1   teaspoon black pepper
1½ tablespoons cider vinegar
½   cup dry white wine
1   (1-lb) piece fresh Pullman loaf, *pain de mie*, or country loaf, cut into 1-inch cubes, then pulsed to coarse crumbs in a food processor
¾   lb ground pork (usually comes with roast, see below)
1   cup finely chopped celery

For roast

1   teaspoon finely chopped fresh sage
1   teaspoon finely chopped fresh marjoram or thyme
2   teaspoons salt
½   teaspoon black pepper
1   (9- to 10-lb) crown roast of pork, rib ends frenched (ground pork reserved for stuffing, above)
1½ cups water

For sauce

½   cup dry white wine
1½ cups reduced-sodium chicken broth
2   teaspoons cornstarch, dissolved in 2 tablespoons water
2   tablespoons cold unsalted butter

Special equipment: an instant-read thermometer

Make stuffing:

▸ Cook onions with 1½ teaspoons salt in ¾ stick butter in a 12-inch heavy skillet over moderate heat, covered, stirring occasionally, until tender, about 10 minutes. Continue to cook, uncovered, stirring frequently, until onions are pale golden, about 10 minutes more. Add sage, marjoram, and

pepper and cook, stirring, 5 minutes. Add vinegar and wine and boil, stirring occasionally, until liquid is evaporated, then remove from heat.
▸ Meanwhile, cook bread crumbs and remaining teaspoon salt in remaining ¾ stick butter in a 12-inch nonstick skillet over moderately low heat, stirring, until golden and crisp, 15 to 20 minutes.
▸ Reserve 1 cup onion mixture, covered and chilled, for sauce. Transfer remaining mixture to a large bowl and stir in ground pork, celery, and crumbs.

Cook roast and stuffing:

▸ Put 1 oven rack in lower third of oven and another on bottom of oven and preheat oven to 350°F.
▸ Stir together sage, marjoram, salt, and pepper in a small bowl, then rub over outside and bottom of roast. Put roast in a small flameproof roasting pan and mound 2 cups stuffing loosely in center, then add water to pan. Transfer remaining stuffing to a buttered 2-quart baking dish and chill until ready to bake.
▸ Roast pork in lower third of oven, covering stuffing and tips of ribs with a sheet of foil after about 30 minutes and adding more water if pan becomes dry, until thermometer inserted 2 inches into center of meat (do not touch bones) registers 155°F, 2¼ to 2¾ hours total.
▸ Bake remaining stuffing (next to or under roast, starting 30 minutes before roast is done), covered with foil, 30 minutes. Increase oven temperature to 425°F (after removing roast from oven) and continue to bake stuffing, uncovered, until top is crisp, 15 to 20 minutes more.
▸ Transfer pork to a platter and let stand 30 minutes.

Make sauce while pork stands:

▸ Transfer pan juices from roasting pan to a gravy separator or a glass measure and skim off fat. Straddle roasting pan across 2 burners, then add wine to pan and boil over high heat, stirring and scraping up brown bits, until reduced by about half, about 5 minutes. Add reserved onion mixture, broth, pan juices, and any juices on platter from roast and bring to a simmer. Restir cornstarch mixture and add to pan, whisking, then simmer 2 minutes. Add butter and swirl pan until incorporated. Season with salt and pepper.
▸ Carve pork and serve with stuffing and sauce.

Cooks' notes:

• Stuffing can be made 1 day ahead and chilled, covered.
• Pork can be rubbed with seasoning and stuffed 2 hours before roasting and chilled, covered. Let stand at room temperature 30 minutes before roasting.

CRANBERRY HORSERADISH SAUCE

MAKES ABOUT 2 CUPS
Active time: 10 min   Start to finish: 20 min

Cranberries with horseradish enhance the sweet, sturdy nature of roast pork.

1   (12-oz) bag fresh or frozen cranberries
1   (6-oz) jar prepared horseradish, including juice, or
    ¼ cup firmly packed finely grated peeled fresh
    horseradish
⅔   cup sugar
⅓   cup water

▸ Bring cranberries, horseradish, sugar, and water to a simmer in a 3-quart heavy saucepan over moderate heat, stirring with a wooden spoon until sugar is dissolved. Simmer, uncovered, stirring and mashing berries frequently with spoon, until berries break down, 5 to 10 minutes.
▸ Serve sauce warm or at room temperature.

Cooks' note:
• Sauce can be made 2 days ahead and cooled completely, uncovered, then chilled, covered. Bring to room temperature or reheat over low heat before serving.

GAME PLAN

2 DAYS AHEAD
-Make cranberry horseradish sauce
-Make hazelnut praline and praline "butter" for Paris-Brest
-Make pastry cream for Paris-Brest

1 DAY AHEAD
-Prepare mussels in vinaigrette and clean shells
-Make stuffing for crown roast
-Make celery-root and apple purée
-Assemble potato and lardon casserole
-French or halve green beans
-Make poached oranges with candied zest and ginger

DAY OF MEAL
8 HOURS AHEAD
-Make *choux* pastry ring for Paris-Brest

6 HOURS AHEAD
-Rub crown roast with seasoning, then stuff

3½ HOURS AHEAD
-Put crown roast in oven
-Make hazelnut cream for Paris-Brest

2 HOURS AHEAD
-Bring potato and lardon casserole to room temperature

1 HOUR AHEAD
-Bake potato casserole
-Bake stuffing
-Assemble Paris-Brest (2 hours before serving dessert)
-Assemble mussels in vinaigrette in shells

30 MINUTES BEFORE SERVING
-Make sauce while crown roast stands
-Reheat celery-root and apple purée
-Bring cranberry horseradish sauce to room temperature or reheat
-Cook green beans

ABOVE: potato and lardon casserole; celery-root and apple purée; cranberry horseradish sauce; and frenched green beans

POTATO AND LARDON CASSEROLE

SERVES 10 TO 12

Active time: 45 min   Start to finish: 1½ hr

With ingredients like bacon, garlic, and butter, how could this hearty casserole be anything but wonderful?

 5   lb yellow-fleshed potatoes such as Yukon Gold
 ½   lb slab bacon, any rind discarded, bacon cut lengthwise
        into ¼-inch-thick slices, and then slices cut crosswise
        into ¼-inch-thick strips (lardons)
 1   tablespoon chopped fresh thyme
 1   tablespoon minced garlic
 ½   teaspoon salt
 ½   teaspoon black pepper
 2   tablespoons unsalted butter, cut into bits

▶ Preheat oven to 350°F. If you are also making crown roast of pork with onion and bread-crumb stuffing (page 181), oven racks will already be in lower third and bottom of oven; if not, put oven rack in middle position.

▶ Peel potatoes, then halve lengthwise (quarter if very large) and cut crosswise into ¾-inch-thick pieces. Blanch potatoes in 2 batches in a 6- to 8-quart pot of boiling salted water (see Tips, page 8) 5 minutes per batch (potatoes will not be completely cooked through). Transfer potatoes with a slotted spoon to a large bowl of ice and cold water to stop cooking, then drain in a colander and transfer to another large bowl.

▶ Cook lardons in a 10-inch heavy skillet over moderate heat, stirring occasionally, until pale golden, 5 to 8 minutes. Add lardons and 2 tablespoons fat from skillet to potatoes, then add thyme, garlic, salt, and pepper and toss until combined well. Transfer mixture to a greased 13- by 9-inch shallow baking dish (or other 3-quart shallow baking dish) and dot with butter.

▶ Bake casserole (next to or under crown roast, if making, starting 30 minutes before roast is done), uncovered, 30 minutes. Increase oven temperature to 425°F, then continue to bake until top is golden, about 15 minutes. Season with salt.

Cooks' note:
• Casserole can be assembled (but not baked) 1 day ahead and chilled, covered. Bring to room temperature, 30 minutes to 1 hour, before baking.

CELERY-ROOT AND APPLE PURÉE

SERVES 10 TO 12

Active time: 35 min   Start to finish: 1½ hr

We already know you like applesauce with pork, but this soft, creamy purée is so much better. It's like a bowl of puréed potatoes that yearns to be dessert.

 5   lb celery root (sometimes called celeriac)
 4   Gala, Empire, or McIntosh apples (1½ lb total)
 ½   stick (¼ cup) unsalted butter
 2   teaspoons salt
 1   cup heavy cream
 ½   teaspoon white pepper
 ½   teaspoon freshly grated nutmeg

Garnish: celery leaves

▶ Peel celery root with a sharp knife, then cut into 1-inch cubes. Peel and core apples, then cut into 1-inch pieces.
▶ Melt butter in a 6- to 8-quart heavy pot over moderately low heat, then add celery root, apples, and salt and stir to coat with butter. Cover with a tight-fitting lid and cook (without adding liquid), stirring occasionally, until celery root is tender, 50 minutes to 1 hour.
▶ Purée mixture in batches in a food processor until smooth, about 2 minutes per batch. Return purée to pot and stir in cream, white pepper, and nutmeg. Reheat, covered, over moderate heat, stirring occasionally, until hot, about 5 minutes.

Cooks' note:
• Purée can be made 1 day ahead and cooled completely, uncovered, then chilled, covered. Reheat, covered, over low heat, stirring occasionally, until hot, about 15 minutes.

FRENCHED GREEN BEANS

SERVES 10 TO 12

Active time: 35 min   Start to finish: 45 min

The secret to this dish is the touch of Sherry vinegar, added at the last minute; it lends a sprightly note that complements the rest of the meal.

    2   lb green beans, stem ends trimmed
    ¾   teaspoon salt
    ¼   teaspoon black pepper
    2   teaspoons Sherry vinegar
    1½ tablespoons olive oil

Special equipment: **a green-bean frencher (optional)**

▶ Force beans, trimmed ends first (keeping strings to the side), up through funnel of frencher (if using; see cooks' note, below).

▶ Cook beans in 2 batches in a 6- to 8-quart pot of boiling salted water (see Tips, page 8), uncovered, until just tender, 4 to 5 minutes. Transfer beans with a slotted spoon to a large bowl and toss with salt, pepper, vinegar, and oil. Serve hot or warm.

Cooks' notes:

• If you do not have a frencher, beans can be halved diagonally.

• Beans can be frenched (but not cooked) 1 day ahead and chilled in a sealed plastic bag lined with dampened paper towels.

POACHED ORANGES WITH CANDIED ZEST AND GINGER

SERVES 10 TO 12

Active time: 45 min   Start to finish: 3 hr

    1   (2-oz) piece fresh ginger (2 to 3 inches long)
    12   navel oranges (preferably small)
    1½   cups water
    2   cups sugar
    ¼   teaspoon salt
    1½   cups dry white wine
    1   cup fresh orange juice
    ½   cup plus 2 tablespoons Grand Marnier

▶ Peel ginger and halve crosswise. Cut pieces lengthwise into ¹⁄₁₆-inch-thick slices, then cut slices into ⅛-inch-wide julienne strips and transfer to a 2-quart heavy saucepan.

▶ Remove zest from 3 oranges in long wide strips with a vegetable peeler, removing any white pith from zest with a paring knife, and add to ginger in pan. Fill pan three-fourths full with cold water and bring to a boil. Boil 1 minute, then drain in a sieve. Return zest and ginger to pan and refill with cold water. Bring to a boil, then reduce heat and simmer, uncovered, 10 minutes. Drain zest and ginger. Repeat simmering with more cold water for another 10 minutes, then drain.

▶ Bring 1½ cups water, 1 cup sugar, and salt to a boil in saucepan, stirring until sugar is dissolved. Add zest and ginger and gently simmer, uncovered, stirring occasionally, until zest and ginger are completely translucent and syrup is thickened, 15 to 20 minutes. Drain candied zest and ginger in a sieve, discarding syrup.

▶ Meanwhile, cut ½ inch from top and bottom of all oranges with a sharp knife, exposing fruit at both ends. Cut peel and pith from sides (leaving no white parts) with paring knife, trimming fruit if large (but retaining orange shape) to 2½ to 2¾ inches wide at middle. Discard trimmings.

▶ Bring wine, orange juice, ½ cup Grand Marnier, and remaining cup sugar to a boil in a deep 12-inch heavy skillet, stirring until sugar is dissolved, then boil 3 minutes. Add oranges, arranging in 1 layer, and simmer, covered with a tight-fitting lid, 10 minutes. Transfer oranges with a slotted spoon to a serving dish, inverting them (so syrup coats oranges). Add candied zest and ginger to syrup and boil over moderate heat, uncovered, until syrup is thickened and mixture is reduced to about 1¼ cups, 10 to 15 minutes. Remove from heat and stir in remaining 2 tablespoons Grand Marnier.

▶ When oranges are cool enough to handle, cut each crosswise into thirds on a cutting board, then reassemble "whole" in serving dish. Spoon zest mixture, including syrup, over oranges, arranging zests and ginger decoratively over them. Chill oranges in serving dish until cold, at least 1 hour.

▶ Just before serving, spoon syrup in dish over oranges to coat. Serve chilled or at room temperature.

Cooks' note:

• Oranges can be chilled up to 1 day, covered loosely (preferably with an inverted large bowl) after 1 hour. Spoon syrup over oranges again just before serving.

HAZELNUT PARIS-BREST

SERVES 10 TO 12

Active time: 1½ hr   Start to finish: 3½ hr

For praline
- 1 cup hazelnuts (4½ oz)
- ¼ cup sliced almonds (¾ oz)
- ½ cup granulated sugar

For cream filling
- 1 cup whole milk
- 3 large egg yolks
- ⅓ cup granulated sugar
- 3 tablespoons cornstarch
- ¼ teaspoon salt
- 2 tablespoons unsalted butter
- ½ teaspoon vanilla
- ¾ cup chilled heavy cream

For *choux* pastry
- 1 cup water
- 1 stick (½ cup) unsalted butter, cut into ½-inch cubes
- 1 teaspoon granulated sugar
- ½ teaspoon salt
- 1 cup all-purpose flour
- 4 whole large eggs
- 1 large egg yolk, lightly beaten with 1 tablespoon water
- 3 tablespoons sliced almonds
- 1 tablespoon confectioners sugar plus additional for dusting

Special equipment: a pastry bag; a ⅝-inch plain tip; a ½-inch open-star tip

Make praline:
▶ Put oven rack in middle position and preheat oven to 350°F.

▶ Toast hazelnuts in a shallow baking pan in oven until skins split and nuts are golden, 10 to 15 minutes. Remove from oven (leave oven on), then wrap hazelnuts in a kitchen towel and let steam 5 to 10 minutes. Rub hazelnuts in towel to remove loose skins (some skins may not come off), then transfer hazelnuts to a small bowl, discarding skins. While hazelnuts steam, toast almonds in baking pan until golden, 5 to 8 minutes, then add to bowl with hazelnuts. Lightly grease pan and set aside.

▶ Cook sugar in a dry small heavy skillet over moderate heat, swirling skillet, until sugar begins to melt, about 2 minutes. Continue to cook, swirling skillet, until sugar is melted into a deep golden caramel, 2 to 3 minutes more. Remove from heat and, working quickly, stir in nuts to coat, then transfer mixture to greased baking pan, spreading slightly. Let stand at room temperature until cool, about 30 minutes.

▶ Transfer praline to a heavy-duty sealable plastic bag and seal bag, pressing out excess air. Coarsely crush praline in bag using a rolling pin or bottom of a heavy skillet, then transfer three fourths to a food processor and purée until it becomes a smooth, creamy "butter," 3 to 4 minutes. Reserve remaining crushed praline for garnish.

Make cream filling:

▶ Bring milk to a simmer in a 2½- to 3-quart heavy saucepan over moderate heat. While milk heats, whisk together yolks, sugar, cornstarch, and salt in a heatproof bowl.

▶ Add hot milk to yolk mixture in a stream, whisking, then transfer mixture to saucepan and bring to a simmer over moderate heat, whisking (mixture will become thick and lumpy). Simmer, whisking constantly, 3 minutes (mixture will become smooth). Remove from heat and stir in butter and vanilla. Transfer to a clean bowl and chill pastry cream, its surface covered with wax paper, until cold, at least 1 hour.

▶ Beat heavy cream in a bowl with an electric mixer until it just holds stiff peaks. Beat pastry cream in a large bowl with mixer until smooth, then add praline "butter" and beat until incorporated. Fold in whipped cream, one third at a time, gently but thoroughly, then cover surface of hazelnut cream with wax paper and chill until ready to use.

Make choux pastry:

▶ Put oven rack in middle position and preheat oven to 425°F. Trace a 9-inch circle with a pencil on a 12-inch square of parchment or wax paper, then trace a 5-inch circle inside it. Turn paper over (circles will still be visible) and put on a large baking sheet.

▶ Bring water to a boil with butter, granulated sugar, and salt in a 3-quart heavy saucepan over high heat, then reduce heat to moderate. Add flour all at once and cook, stirring vigorously with a wooden spoon, until mixture pulls away from side of pan, about 1 minute. Continue to cook and stir vigorously (to dry out mixture) 3 minutes more. Remove pan from heat and cool mixture, stirring occasionally, until warm to the touch, 5 to 10 minutes. Add whole eggs 1 at a time, stirring vigorously after each addition until dough is smooth.

▶ Transfer dough to pastry bag fitted with plain tip and pipe 3 concentric rings to fill space between traced circles on parchment, then pipe 2 more on top to cover seams between bottom rings. Lightly brush pastry with some egg wash, then scatter almonds over pastry and dust with 1 tablespoon confectioners sugar.

▶ Bake choux pastry until golden and well puffed, 20 to 25 minutes, then reduce oven temperature to 375°F and continue to bake until deep golden and firm to the touch, about 25 minutes more. Immediately prick top of pastry in 8 to 10 places with tip of a small sharp knife (to release steam) and continue to bake until golden brown, about 10 minutes more. Transfer pastry (on parchment) to a rack and cool completely, about 30 minutes.

▶ Halve pastry horizontally with a serrated knife and carefully invert top onto work surface. Remove and discard any wet dough from interior of top and bottom. Transfer hazelnut cream to cleaned and dried pastry bag fitted with star tip and pipe cream decoratively into bottom half of pastry, then carefully reinvert top half over it. Sprinkle top with reserved praline and dust with additional confectioners sugar.

Cooks' notes:

• Praline and praline "butter" can be made 2 days ahead. Chill butter in an airtight container and keep remaining praline in an airtight container at room temperature.
• Pastry cream (without praline "butter" or whipped cream) can be chilled, its surface covered with wax paper and bowl covered with plastic wrap, up to 2 days.
• Choux ring can be baked (but not halved) 8 hours ahead and cooled completely, uncovered, then kept, loosely covered with foil (not plastic wrap), at room temperature. Cooled choux ring can also be frozen, tightly wrapped in plastic wrap, 1 week. Thaw in wrapping before recrisping in a preheated 350°F oven 10 minutes. Cool to room temperature before proceeding.
• Cream filling can be chilled up to 4 hours.
• Paris-Brest can be assembled 2 hours before serving and kept at cool room temperature.

ALL AGLOW

RELAXED HOLIDAY BUFFET

CRISP PICKLED VEGETABLES

MAKES ABOUT 12 CUPS (HORS D'OEUVRE)
Active time: 45 min   Start to finish: 1 week (includes pickling time)

Hors d'oeuvres like this one are great for entertaining—the vegetables benefit from being prepared in advance, becoming more flavorful as they absorb the pickling liquid. The recipe also yields a large batch, so you'll have plenty on hand.

- 1 large fennel bulb (sometimes called anise), stalks cut off and discarded and bulb sliced lengthwise ½ inch thick, then cut into ½-inch-wide strips
- 1 head cauliflower, cut into 1-inch-wide florets (4 to 6 cups)
- 3 mixed bell peppers (red, orange, and yellow), cut into ¼-inch-wide strips
- 1 lb medium carrots, cut into 3- to 4-inch-long strips (¼ inch thick)
- 3½ cups distilled white vinegar
- 1¾ cups sugar
- 1¾ cups water
- 4 garlic cloves, halved
- 1 tablespoon plus ½ teaspoon salt
- 1 teaspoon dried hot red pepper flakes
- 1 teaspoon fennel seeds, slightly crushed

▶ Add fennel, cauliflower, bell peppers, and carrots to an 8-quart pot half full of unsalted boiling water, then immediately turn off heat and let stand, uncovered, 2 minutes. Drain vegetables in a colander and spread out on a kitchen towel to cool to room temperature.
▶ Bring remaining ingredients to a boil in a 3-quart nonreactive saucepan (see cooks' note, below) over moderate heat, stirring until sugar is dissolved. Transfer pickling liquid to a 4-quart nonreactive bowl and cool to room temperature, about 30 minutes. Discard garlic (don't be alarmed if it has turned blue in reaction to the vinegar) and add vegetables to pickling liquid. Weight vegetables with a plate to keep them submerged in liquid if necessary. Chill, covered, at least 1 week.

Cooks' notes:
• Stainless steel, enameled cast iron, and glass are nonreactive, but avoid pure aluminum and uncoated iron.
• Pickled vegetables keep, covered and chilled, 1 month.

SMOKED-TROUT SPREAD

MAKES ABOUT 4 CUPS (HORS D'OEUVRE)
Active time: 25 min   Start to finish: 8½ hr (includes chilling)

Light and ultrasavory, this is a spread that's definitely worth making—it requires a minimal amount of work and tastes better than any store-bought version. And if you have any left over, you're in luck—it also tastes wonderful on bagels the next morning.

- 1 lb smoked trout fillets, skin discarded and any silver skin scraped off
- 2 sticks (1 cup) unsalted butter, softened
- ⅓ cup finely chopped shallot
- ¼ cup finely chopped fresh dill
- 1 tablespoon fresh lemon juice
- ½ teaspoon hot sauce such as Tabasco
- ¼ teaspoon black pepper
- 1 cup cold water

Accompaniment: **whole-grain crackers**

▶ Flake trout and transfer 2 cups to a food processor, then blend with butter, shallot, dill, lemon juice, hot sauce, and pepper until smooth. Reserve remaining trout.
▶ With motor running, add water to trout purée in a slow stream and process until water is absorbed, about 1 minute. Transfer to a bowl and fold in reserved trout, then pack mixture into a 4-cup glass or ceramic mold or bowl. Cover surface with wax paper, then tightly cover with plastic wrap and chill at least 6 hours to allow flavors to develop. Bring spread to room temperature before serving. (This will take 1 to 2 hours.)

Cooks' note:
• Spread can be chilled up to 5 days.

PASTA AND CHICKEN GRATIN

SERVES 10 TO 12

Active time: 2 hr   Start to finish: 4 hr (includes poaching chicken)

Think macaroni and cheese—only ten times better. This sophisticated version combines the nuttiness of Gruyère with the intense flavor of parmesan, juicy poached chicken, and a crisp, cheesy crust.

For chicken and stock

- 2   (3½- to 4-lb) chickens
- 10 cups cold water
- 1   celery rib, quartered
- 1   carrot, quartered
- 1   medium onion, quartered
- 1   large garlic clove, smashed
- 2   fresh thyme sprigs
- 1   teaspoon salt
- ¼   teaspoon whole black peppercorns

For cheese sauce and casserole

- 1   stick (½ cup) unsalted butter plus additional for greasing gratin dishes
- 1   garlic clove, minced
- ½   cup all-purpose flour
- 3   cups whole milk
- 1   cup crème fraîche (8 oz)
- 1   teaspoon salt
- ½   teaspoon black pepper
- ¼   teaspoon cayenne
- 1   lb Gruyère, coarsely grated (6 cups)
- 1   oz Parmigiano-Reggiano, finely grated with a rasp (1¼ cups)
- 1   lb penne rigate or other short tubular pasta
- 6   cups fine fresh bread crumbs (from 14 slices firm white sandwich bread)

Special equipment: **2 (2½- to 3-qt) shallow gratin dishes (13 by 9 inches)**

Poach chicken and make stock:

▶ Cut backbones, wing tips, and second joints of wings from chickens, then cut each chicken into quarters. Put backbones, wing tips, second joints, and giblets (except livers) in a 6- to 8-quart pot with water, celery, carrot, onion, garlic, thyme, salt, and peppercorns and bring to a boil. Add chicken quarters and return liquid to a boil, skimming off any foam, then reduce heat and simmer, uncovered, 10 minutes. Remove from heat and let stand, covered, 40 minutes.

▶ Transfer chicken quarters with tongs to a shallow baking pan. When chicken is cool enough to handle, remove meat from skin and bones, transferring meat to a cutting board and returning skin and bones to pot. Cut chicken into 1-inch pieces and reserve in a large bowl. Boil stock 40 minutes, then pour through a fine-mesh sieve into a large bowl, discarding solids. Let stand 5 minutes, then skim off fat and set aside 4 cups stock for making sauce. (Reserve remaining stock for another use.)

Make sauce, cook pasta, and assemble casserole:

▶ Put oven rack in middle position and preheat oven to 425°F. Butter gratin dishes.

▶ Heat butter (1 stick) in a 4-quart heavy pot over moderate heat until foam subsides, then add garlic and cook, whisking, 1 minute. Add flour and cook, whisking, 1 minute. Add milk and reserved stock (4 cups) in a slow stream, whisking, then bring to a boil, whisking. Reduce heat and simmer, whisking occasionally, until sauce is slightly thickened, about 10 minutes. Remove from heat and stir in crème fraîche, salt, pepper, cayenne, 2 cups Gruyère, and ½ cup Parmigiano-Reggiano.

▶ While sauce simmers, cook pasta in a 6- to 8-quart pot of boiling salted water (see Tips, page 8), uncovered, until not quite al dente, 8 to 10 minutes (pasta should still be firm), then drain in a colander. Return pasta to pot, then add chicken and sauce, tossing to coat. Divide pasta mixture between gratin dishes.

▶ Toss bread crumbs with remaining 4 cups Gruyère and ¾ cup Parmigiano-Reggiano, then sprinkle evenly over pasta mixture. Bake gratins until crumbs are golden brown and sauce is bubbling, 20 to 30 minutes. Let stand 10 minutes before serving.

Cooks' notes:

• If you're short on time, you can use rotisserie chickens. Pull meat from bones and reserve, then make stock by cooking skin and bones with celery, carrot, onion, garlic, thyme, salt, peppercorns, and 8 cups water 40 minutes total before straining (omit salt in sauce).

• Chicken can be poached and stock can be made 1 day ahead and cooled completely, uncovered, then chilled separately, covered.

BITTER GREEN SALAD WITH ROASTED PEARS

SERVES 10 TO 12

Active time: 35 min Start to finish: 1 hr

Even pears that aren't quite ripe become delicious when roasted until sweet and caramelized. Here, they make the perfect counterpoint to a beautiful mix of bitter greens.

For salad

- 8 firm-ripe Bosc pears (4 lb), peeled, cored, and each cut lengthwise into 8 wedges
- 1½ tablespoons extra-virgin olive oil
- 1 small head chicory
- 1 small head escarole
- 1 small head radicchio
- 1 bunch watercress, coarse stems discarded
- 1 bunch mizuna, coarse stems discarded
- 1 small head romaine

For dressing

- 1 tablespoon finely chopped shallot
- 2½ tablespoons cider vinegar
- ½ teaspoon honey
- ¼ teaspoon salt
- ⅛ teaspoon black pepper
- ¼ cup plus 1 tablespoon extra-virgin olive oil

Roast pears and make salad:

▶ Put oven rack in middle position and preheat oven to 425°F.

▶ Toss pears with oil and spread in 1 layer in a 17- by 12-inch shallow baking pan, then season with salt and pepper. Roast pears, stirring and turning over twice, until pears are tender and beginning to brown, 20 to 30 minutes, then cool about 15 minutes.

▶ While pears are roasting and cooling, tear enough tender chicory and escarole leaves (discard ribs) into bite-size pieces to measure 6 cups total. Tear enough radicchio, watercress, mizuna, and romaine into bite-size pieces to measure 10 cups total. Toss torn greens in a large bowl and reserve remaining greens for another use.

Make dressing and toss salad:

▶ Whisk together shallot, vinegar, honey, salt, and pepper, then add oil in a slow stream, whisking until emulsified.

▶ Just before serving, add roasted pears and dressing to greens and toss to combine well.

Cooks' notes:
- Salad greens can be washed and dried 1 day ahead, then chilled, wrapped in paper towels, in a sealed plastic bag.
- Pears can be roasted 4 hours ahead and kept at room temperature.

BROCCOLINI WITH LEMON OIL

SERVES 10 TO 12

Active time: 15 min Start to finish: 15 min

Delicate with tender stems, Broccolini tastes great simply on its own. Adding a little lemon oil reveals perky new dimensions to its flavor.

- 1 large lemon
- ⅓ cup extra-virgin olive oil
- 3 lb Broccolini (6 bunches), trimmed and thick stalks halved lengthwise

Accompaniment: lemon wedges

▶ Remove zest from lemon in 1-inch-wide strips with a vegetable peeler. Cut off any white pith from zest with a small sharp knife. Halve lemon and set aside.

▶ Heat oil and zest in a 5-quart wide heavy pot over moderate heat until zest is golden, about 3 minutes. Remove from heat and discard zest, reserving oil in pot.

▶ Cook Broccolini in an 8- to 10-quart pot two-thirds full of boiling salted water (see Tips, page 8), uncovered, until crisp-tender, 5 to 7 minutes. Drain well in a large colander.

▶ Reheat lemon oil over moderately high heat until hot but not smoking. Add Broccolini and cook, tossing, until coated well and heated through, about 1 minute. Add salt and pepper to taste, then squeeze half of lemon over Broccolini. (Reserve remaining lemon half for another use.)

OPPOSITE: pasta and chicken gratin and broccolini with lemon oil; bitter green salad with roasted pears

CHOCK-FULL BLONDIE SQUARES

SERVES 10 TO 12

Active time: 30 min   Start to finish: 2 hr (includes cooling)

Loaded with dried fruit, toasted almonds, and bittersweet chocolate, these blondies combine the best of a brownie with what you wish fruitcake could taste like.

- 1   cup boiling-hot water
- 1   cup dried cranberries (5 oz)
- 1   cup dried tart cherries (5 oz)
- 1   cup golden raisins (5 oz)
- 2½ cups all-purpose flour
- 1½ teaspoons baking soda
- 1   teaspoon salt
- ¾   teaspoon cinnamon
- 2   sticks (1 cup) unsalted butter, melted and cooled
- 2   cups sugar
- 3   large eggs
- 1½ teaspoons vanilla
- 1   cup whole almonds with skins (6 oz), toasted (see Tips, page 8) and very coarsely chopped
- 8   oz fine-quality bittersweet chocolate (not unsweetened; preferably 60 to 70% cacao), coarsely chopped

Special equipment: **a 17- by 12-inch shallow baking pan (1 inch deep)**
Accompaniment: **eggnog ice cream (optional)**

▸ Put oven rack in middle position and preheat oven to 325°F. Butter and flour baking pan, knocking out excess flour.

▸ Pour boiling-hot water over dried fruit in a small bowl and soak 20 minutes, then drain well in a sieve.

▸ Stir together flour, baking soda, salt, and cinnamon in another bowl.

▸ Beat together melted butter, sugar, eggs, and vanilla in a large bowl with an electric mixer at high speed until creamy, about 1 minute. Reduce speed to low, then add flour mixture and mix until just combined. Mix in dried fruit, almonds, and chocolate.

▸ Spread batter evenly in baking pan and bake until golden brown and a wooden pick or skewer inserted in center comes out clean, 25 to 30 minutes. Cool completely in pan on a rack. Run a thin knife around edges of pan to loosen blondie, then cut blondie into roughly 3-inch squares.

Cooks' note:
• Blondie can be baked (but not cut into squares) 2 days ahead and cooled completely, then kept, wrapped well in plastic wrap, at room temperature.

EGGNOG ICE CREAM

MAKES ABOUT 1½ QUARTS

Active time: 30 min   Start to finish: 5 hr (includes chilling and freezing)

- 1   cup whole milk
- ¼   teaspoon salt
- 7   large egg yolks
- ¾   cup sugar
- 2   cups chilled heavy cream
- 3   tablespoons dark rum
- 1   teaspoon vanilla
- ¼   teaspoon freshly grated nutmeg

Special equipment: **an instant-read thermometer; an ice cream maker**
Garnish: **freshly grated nutmeg**

▸ Bring milk and salt to a boil in a 2- to 3-quart heavy saucepan over moderate heat. Remove from heat.

▸ Whisk together yolks and sugar in a bowl, then gradually add ¼ cup hot milk, whisking. Add yolk mixture to milk remaining in pan in a slow stream, whisking, and cook over low heat, stirring constantly with a wooden spoon, until mixture is slightly thickened, coats back of spoon, and registers 175°F on thermometer, 3 to 5 minutes. Immediately pour through a fine-mesh sieve set into a clean bowl and stir in cream, rum, vanilla, and nutmeg. Chill custard, covered, until cold, at least 2 hours.

▸ Freeze in ice cream maker, then transfer to an airtight container and put in freezer to harden, at least 2 hours. Soften slightly in refrigerator before serving, about 20 minutes.

Cooks' notes:
• Custard can be chilled up to 1 day.
• Ice cream can be made 1 week ahead.

THE RECIPE COMPENDIUM

These recipes, culled from the Gourmet Every Day, Last Touch, and Seasonal Kitchen columns, were created in *Gourmet*'s test kitchens, which you might be surprised to learn are not so different from your own. Our food editors bake in standard ovens, cook with regular gas stoves, and use the same sorts of pots and pans that are banged around all over the country. But once a recipe is developed, they test it over and over until it is just right. After all, our goal is to ensure that every *Gourmet* recipe will work beautifully when you make it at home.

Busy people need quick, dependable recipes, and that's what you'll find here. In fact, almost all the recipes in this section take just 30 minutes active time or less, making them ideal for hectic weeknights. As you peruse these pages, think seasonally and create your own menus: grilled lemon chicken, barley and corn salad with basil chive dressing, and homey apricot pandowdy is the essence of summer, while braised beef and onions, buttered egg noodles, and a fennel and endive salad with orange vinaigrette will surely warm up a wintry night. Perhaps you only have time for a one-dish dinner. That's when meals like lemony lentil soup with cilantro or a crisp spinach salad with bacon come in handy. Quick recipes are indicated in the index by a clock icon.

This section also includes several recipes for the diet-conscious. Imagine a dinner that begins with cauliflower soup with almonds, moves on to unctuous rosemary lamb chops with Swiss chard and balsamic syrup, and finishes with broiled plums paired with mango sorbet—who would ever suspect that such full-flavor recipes are low-fat?

Look for the feather icon in the index to find more lighter/leaner recipes. Also, if you're a vegetarian or simply enjoy a meatless meal now and then, you'll find plenty of recipes to satisfy that need, including tasty dishes like grilled eggplant stacks with tomato and feta and a hearty red wine spaghetti with broccoli. These, too, are marked in the index, with a "V."

While most of the recipes in this compendium were created with everyday meals in mind, dozens of fine entertaining menus can be put together from these pages. For example, as summer draws to a close, why not set the patio table one more time and invite your neighbors over for peach and tomato gazpacho, beef pinwheels with arugula salad, roasted corn with chipotle mayonnaise, and orange coeurs à la crème with strawberry raspberry sauce. Your guests will be impressed, and you'll be in and out of the kitchen in no time.

From our kitchen to yours, this well-rounded collection of foolproof recipes offers plenty of delicious options—dig in and enjoy!

HORS D'OEUVRES

ASPARAGUS CIGARS
MAKES 24 HORS D'OEUVRES
Active time: 45 min   Start to finish: 45 min

24 medium asparagus (1 lb)
12 (7-inch) flour tortillas (not low-fat)
 1 large egg, beaten with a pinch of salt
 2 tablespoons white sesame seeds
    About 2 cups vegetable oil
 2 tablespoons soy sauce
 2 tablespoons fresh lime juice
 2 tablespoons water
 1 teaspoon sugar
 1 scallion, finely chopped

Special equipment: **wooden picks; a deep-fat thermometer**

▸ Trim asparagus to 6-inch lengths.
▸ Halve tortillas. Brush 1 half with some of egg mixture and place 1 piece asparagus along cut side. Tightly roll up tortilla. Insert 1 pick crosswise to secure. Brush outside of roll with more of egg mixture and sprinkle with some sesame seeds. Make 23 more rolls in same manner.
▸ Heat ½ inch oil in a 10-inch heavy skillet until thermometer registers 350°F.
▸ Fry rolls in batches of 3, turning over once, until golden brown, about 3 minutes per batch, returning oil to 350°F between batches. Transfer to paper towels to drain.
▸ Stir together remaining ingredients until sugar is dissolved. Serve with rolls.

Cooks' note:
• To take the temperature of a shallow amount of oil with a metal flat-framed deep-fat thermometer, put bulb of thermometer in skillet. Turn thermometer facedown, resting other end (not plastic handle) against rim of skillet. Check temperature frequently.

CHICKEN AND CILANTRO BITES
MAKES ABOUT 30 HORS D'OEUVRES
Active time: 35 min   Start to finish: 35 min

¼ cup soy sauce
¼ cup rice vinegar (not seasoned)
 1 lb ground chicken (not breast meat)
 1 large egg
½ cup finely chopped fresh cilantro
 2 scallions, finely chopped
 2 teaspoons Asian sesame oil
 1 teaspoon salt
¾ cup cornstarch
½ cup vegetable oil

▸ Stir together soy sauce and rice vinegar in a bowl for dipping sauce.
▸ Stir together chicken, egg, cilantro, scallions, sesame oil, and salt with a fork until just blended.
▸ Spread cornstarch in a shallow baking pan. With wet hands form chicken mixture into 1-inch balls, transferring them to baking pan as formed. Wash and dry your hands, then gently roll balls in cornstarch until coated. (Balls will be soft.)
▸ Heat ¼ cup vegetable oil in a 12-inch heavy skillet over moderately high heat until hot but not smoking, then cook half of balls, turning over occasionally, until firm and golden (they will flatten slightly), 2 to 3 minutes. Transfer with a slotted spoon to paper towels to drain. Add remaining ¼ cup oil to skillet and cook remaining balls in same manner. Serve meatballs with dipping sauce.

KITCHEN NOTE

CILANTRO, ALSO KNOWN AS CORIANDER, INDIAN PARSLEY, AND CHINESE PARSLEY, RESEMBLES FLAT-LEAF PARSLEY IN FOLIAGE, BUT IT IS A LARGER PLANT, AND HAS A UNIQUE MINTY-FRESH FLAVOR. LONG BEFORE THE HERB BECAME A CULINARY INGREDIENT, IT WAS USED AS A DIGESTIVE AID.

ORANGE SOY BABY BACK RIBS

SERVES 4 TO 6
Active time: 15 min Start to finish: 2¼ hr

- 2 racks baby back pork ribs (2 to 3 lb total), cut into individual ribs
- ¼ cup fresh orange juice
- ¼ cup soy sauce
- ¼ cup packed dark brown sugar
- 1 teaspoon ground cumin

▶ Put ribs in a large sealable plastic bag. Stir together orange juice, soy sauce, brown sugar, and cumin in a bowl until sugar is dissolved, then pour marinade over ribs in bag and seal bag, pressing out excess air. Marinate ribs, chilled, turning bag over after 30 minutes, 1 hour total.

▶ Put oven rack in middle position and preheat oven to 375°F.

▶ Transfer ribs and marinade to a 13- by 9-inch glass baking dish and arrange ribs in 1 layer, not touching. Roast ribs 30 minutes, then turn over ribs with tongs and continue roasting until they are tender and well browned and marinade is thick and syrupy, about 30 minutes more.

TUNA AND CAPER BRANDADE CROSTINI

MAKES 20 TO 25 HORS D'OEUVRES
Active time: 25 min Start to finish: 30 min (includes making crostini)

For brandade

- ½ lb potatoes, peeled and cut into ½-inch cubes (1 cup)
- ¾ cup whole milk
- 2 large garlic cloves, finely chopped
- 1 Turkish or ½ California bay leaf
- ½ teaspoon chopped fresh thyme or ⅛ teaspoon dried thyme, crumbled
- ¼ teaspoon salt
- ⅛ teaspoon black pepper
- 1 (6-oz) can solid white tuna packed in olive oil
- 2 tablespoons bottled capers (not salt-packed), rinsed, drained, and chopped
- 3 tablespoons extra-virgin olive oil

Accompaniment: **crostini (recipe follows)**

Make brandade:

▶ Combine potatoes, milk, garlic, bay leaf, thyme, salt, and pepper in a 1- to 1½-quart heavy saucepan and bring to a simmer, stirring. Reduce heat to low and gently simmer, partially covered, stirring occasionally, until potatoes are very tender, about 10 minutes. Discard bay leaf and transfer to a large bowl.

▶ Add tuna and capers to hot potato mixture, then mix with an electric mixer at low speed, adding oil in a slow stream, until potatoes and tuna are broken up but not smooth and oil is incorporated. Season with salt and pepper.

Cooks' note:

• *Brandade* can be made 2 days ahead and cooled completely, uncovered, then chilled, covered. Reheat, uncovered, in a preheated 400°F oven 10 to 15 minutes.

KITCHEN NOTE

RAID THE FRIDGE FOR **QUICK CROSTINI TOPPING IDEAS:** TRY A SMEAR OF GOAT CHEESE WITH A DAB OF FIG JAM, OR A SLICE OF SHARP CHEDDAR CHEESE WITH A DOLLOP OF MANGO CHUTNEY. JARRED ROASTED RED PEPPERS OR PESTO ARE ALSO GREAT.

CROSTINI

MAKES 20 TO 25 SMALL TOASTS
Active time: 5 min Start to finish: 15 min

Use a leftover baguette to make these crostini; they will keep well in an airtight container for a week.

- ½ baguette, cut into ¼-inch-thick slices
- 1 to 2 tablespoons extra-virgin olive oil
- 1 garlic clove, halved crosswise

▶ Put oven rack in upper third of oven and preheat oven to 350°F.

▶ Put bread slices in a large shallow baking pan and brush slices with oil. Season lightly with salt and pepper, then bake until pale golden, about 10 minutes. Rub toasts with cut sides of garlic.

STUFFED EGGS WITH GOAT CHEESE AND DILL

MAKES 12 HORS D'OEUVRES

Active time: 10 min Start to finish: 35 min

- 6   hard-boiled large eggs
- 2½ oz fresh mild goat cheese (⅓ cup) at room temperature
- 3   tablespoons milk
- ¾   teaspoon Dijon mustard
- ¼   teaspoon coarsely ground black pepper
- ⅛   teaspoon salt
- 2½ tablespoons chopped fresh dill

▸ Halve eggs lengthwise and carefully remove yolks. Purée yolks, goat cheese, milk, mustard, pepper, and salt in a food processor until smooth. Add dill and pulse until finely chopped.
▸ Spoon (or pipe using a pastry bag) goat cheese mixture into egg whites.

DIPS AND SPREADS

CHEDDAR, RED PEPPER, AND HORSERADISH SPREAD

MAKES ABOUT 2 CUPS

Active time: 15 min Start to finish: 15 min

- ½   lb finely grated extra-sharp Cheddar (2¼ cups)
- 1   (7-oz) bottle roasted red peppers, rinsed, drained, patted dry, and finely chopped (½ cup)
- ⅓   cup mayonnaise
- 1   rounded tablespoon drained bottled horseradish
- ½   teaspoon Worcestershire sauce
- ¼   teaspoon salt
- ¼   teaspoon black pepper

Accompaniment: **toasted pita or crackers**

▸ Stir together all ingredients in a bowl until combined well.

HAM AND CHEESE SPREAD

MAKES ABOUT 1½ CUPS

Active time: 15 min Start to finish: 15 min

- ½   lb sliced good-quality cooked smoked ham
- 1½ oz finely shredded Gruyère (½ cup)
- ¾   stick (6 tablespoons) unsalted butter, softened
- 1   rounded tablespoon whole-grain mustard
- 4   cornichons (French sour gherkins), finely chopped
- ¼   teaspoon black pepper

Accompaniment: **toasted pita or crackers**

▸ Pulse ham in a food processor until finely chopped, then transfer to a bowl. Stir in remaining ingredients with a rubber spatula until combined well.

LEBNEH WITH SESAME AND HERBS
(Middle Eastern Style Yogurt)

MAKES ABOUT 1⅔ CUPS

Active time: 10 min Start to finish: 1 day (includes draining yogurt)

- 4   cups whole-milk plain yogurt
- ¾   teaspoon salt
- 1½ tablespoons sesame seeds
- 3   tablespoons extra-virgin olive oil
- 1   teaspoon dried mint, crumbled
- ¾   teaspoon dried thyme, crumbled

Accompaniment: **toasted pita or crackers**

▸ Line a sieve with a double layer of paper towels and set over a bowl. Whisk yogurt with salt and spoon into sieve. Let drain, covered and chilled, at least 12 hours and up to 24.
▸ Meanwhile, toast sesame seeds in a dry small heavy skillet, shaking skillet occasionally, until golden, about 2 minutes. Whisk together oil, mint, and thyme in a bowl, then add toasted sesame seeds and chill, covered, up to 24 hours.
▸ Bring sesame mixture to room temperature, then drizzle it over *lebneh* (thickened yogurt).

FIRST COURSES

GRILLED ZUCCHINI AND TOMATOES WITH FETA SAUCE
SERVES 4

Active time: 20 min   Start to finish: 30 min

  3   oz mild feta (preferably French; ½ cup)
  ¼   cup sour cream
  2   tablespoons water
  2   teaspoons fresh lemon juice
  ½   teaspoon minced garlic
2½   tablespoons extra-virgin olive oil
  2   tablespoons finely chopped fresh basil
  2   medium zucchini (1 lb total)
  ¾   lb cherry tomatoes (preferably on the vine, cut into 4 bunches)
  ¼   teaspoon salt

Special equipment: **an adjustable-blade slicer**

▸ Prepare grill for cooking over medium-hot charcoal or moderate heat for gas (see Tips, page 8).
▸ Purée feta, sour cream, water, lemon juice, and garlic in a food processor until smooth, then, with motor running, add 1½ tablespoons oil in a slow stream. Add basil and salt and pepper to taste and pulse until just combined.
▸ Thinly slice zucchini lengthwise (just under ⅛ inch thick) using slicer. Toss zucchini and tomatoes (on the vine) in a large bowl with salt and remaining tablespoon oil. If using loose cherry tomatoes, thread onto skewers. Grill vegetables, in batches if necessary, on oiled grill rack, turning over once with tongs, until just tender, 3 to 5 minutes total per batch. Serve with sauce.

KITCHEN NOTE

A TANGY WHITE CHEESE THAT IS SOMETIMES SOFT, BUT MORE OFTEN CRUMBLY, **FETA** IS MADE FROM SHEEP'S MILK AND PRESERVED IN BRINE, WHICH IMPARTS ITS CHARACTERISTIC SALTY TASTE. FETA DOES NOT HAVE TO BE GREEK TO BE GOOD; WE HAVE FOUND MANY FRENCH FETAS TO BE QUITE TASTY.

BEER-BATTERED ASPARAGUS
SERVES 4

Active time: 30 min   Start to finish: 30 min

For lemon dipping sauce
  ½   cup mayonnaise
  ½   teaspoon finely grated fresh lemon zest (see Tips, page 8)
  1   teaspoon fresh lemon juice
  ¼   teaspoon black pepper
For asparagus
  1   cup all-purpose flour
  1   teaspoon salt
  1   tablespoon finely grated fresh lemon zest
  ¼   teaspoon black pepper
  1   cup lager such as Harp (pour beer slowly into a measure; do not measure foam)
      About 4 cups vegetable oil
  1   lb medium asparagus, trimmed and cut into 3-inch pieces

Special equipment: **a deep-fat thermometer**

Make dipping sauce:
▸ Stir together mayonnaise, zest, lemon juice, and pepper in a small bowl. Chill, covered, until ready to use.
Make batter and fry asparagus:
▸ Put oven rack in middle position and preheat oven to 200°F.
▸ Whisk together flour, salt, zest, and pepper in a bowl until combined, then add beer, whisking until smooth.
▸ Heat 3 inches oil in a 3- to 4-quart heavy saucepan over moderately high heat until it registers 375°F on thermometer.
▸ Submerge asparagus spears in batter to coat. Working in batches of 10, drag spears 1 at a time gently against rim to remove excess batter, then transfer to oil and fry, stirring gently to keep asparagus from sticking together, until golden, 2 to 3 minutes. Transfer as fried with a slotted spoon to a paper-towel-lined baking sheet and keep warm in oven. Return oil to 375°F between batches. Serve with lemon dipping sauce.

Cooks' note:
• Asparagus can be kept warm in oven up to 30 minutes.

AVOCADO MOUSSE WITH PAPAYA TOMATO RELISH

SERVES 8

Active time: 40 min   Start to finish: 2¾ hr

For mousse

  3 firm-ripe California avocados (1½ to 1¾ lb total)
  1 (500-mg) vitamin C tablet, crushed to a powder
  ½ teaspoon salt
  1 tablespoon plus 1 teaspoon fresh lemon juice
1¼ teaspoons unflavored gelatin (from a ¼-oz envelope)
  3 tablespoons whole milk
  ⅓ cup chilled heavy cream

For relish

  3 tablespoons tarragon white-wine vinegar
  1 to 2 tablespoons sugar
  ¼ teaspoon salt
  ⅛ teaspoon black pepper
  ¼ lb grape tomatoes, cut into ¼-inch dice (½ cup)
  ½ lb papaya, peeled, seeded, and cut into ¼-inch dice (½ cup)
  2 tablespoons chopped red onion
  1 teaspoon finely chopped fresh tarragon

Special equipment: 8 (3-oz) ramekins

Make mousse:

▶ Lightly oil ramekins and line bottoms with wax paper or parchment, then oil paper.
▶ Quarter, pit, and peel 2 avocados. Purée avocado quarters with vitamin C, salt, and 1 tablespoon lemon juice in a food processor until smooth.
▶ Sprinkle gelatin over milk in a small heavy saucepan and let soften 1 minute. Heat over low heat, stirring, until gelatin is dissolved, 1 to 2 minutes, then remove from heat. Add to avocado purée and blend until smooth.
▶ Halve, pit, and peel remaining avocado. Cut into ¼-inch dice and toss with remaining teaspoon lemon juice in a small bowl. Beat cream in a bowl with an electric mixer at medium speed until it just holds soft peaks. Fold in avocado purée gently but thoroughly, then fold in diced avocado. Spoon mousse into ramekins, smoothing tops. Cover surface of each mousse with a piece of plastic wrap, then cover ramekins with plastic wrap. Chill mousse until set, at least 2 hours.

Make relish:

▶ Whisk together vinegar, sugar (to taste), salt, and pepper in

a bowl until sugar is dissolved, then stir in tomatoes, papaya, onion, and tarragon. Let stand at room temperature 1 hour (for flavors to develop).
▶ Unmold mousse by running a knife around edge of each ramekin, then invert each onto a plate, discarding paper. Serve with relish.

Cooks' notes:
• Mousse can be chilled up to 2 days.
• Relish can be made 2 days ahead and chilled, covered.

KITCHEN NOTE

WE FIND THE CREAMY TEXTURE AND NUTTY FLAVOR OF **CALIFORNIA AVOCADOS** TO BE SUPERIOR TO THOSE GROWN IN FLORIDA. THE MOST WIDELY AVAILABLE CALIFORNIA VARIETY IS THE HAAS, WHICH IS DARK GREEN, OVAL-SHAPED AND LEATHERY-SKINNED.

WHITE FISH TERRINE WITH SALMON ROE AND DILL

SERVES 8

Active time: 1¼ hr   Start to finish: 2¼ hr

Even though this terrine is labor-intensive, it's not as fussy and last-minute as quenelles, and its ethereal texture rivals theirs.

    Vegetable oil for greasing terrine and wax paper
1¼ lb skinless cod, scrod, or gray sole fillets, well chilled
  2 teaspoons kosher salt or 1 teaspoon table salt
  ¼ teaspoon white pepper
  ¼ teaspoon freshly grated nutmeg
  1 large egg white
  2 cups chilled heavy cream
  2 tablespoons minced fresh dill
  3 tablespoons salmon roe

Special equipment: a 4-cup terrine mold or loaf pan; a *tamis* (drum sieve) with 30 to 40 holes per square centimeter (see Sources); a slightly flexible bowl scraper; a kitchen scale; an offset spatula; an instant-read thermometer
Accompaniment: beurre blanc (page 268)

▶ Put oven rack in middle position and preheat oven to 325°F. Oil terrine mold and line bottom with a sheet of wax paper (cut to fit), then oil paper.

▶ Remove any visible silver skin or sinew from fish and remove pin bones (cut out entire strip of pin bones), then cut fish into 1-inch pieces. Purée fish with salt, white pepper, and nutmeg in a food processor until very smooth. Add egg white and purée until incorporated, then transfer mixture to a bowl set in a larger bowl of ice.

▶ Set *tamis*, screen side up, on a work surface and work fish mixture through sieve about 2 tablespoons at a time with scraper until all that remains is sinews. As you work fish through sieve, scrape strained fish from underside of *tamis* from time to time and transfer to a large bowl set in another bowl of ice.

▶ Weigh strained fish to determine equal amount of cream (1 cup cream weighs 8 ounces). Then, keeping fish mixture over ice, stir cream into fish mixture, about ¼ cup at a time, with a large rubber spatula until all cream is incorporated.

▶ Transfer one fourth of mixture to a small bowl and stir in dill. Gently fold salmon roe into remaining fish mixture.

▶ Spread about two thirds of roe mixture in terrine and create a wide trough lengthwise along the middle with back of a spoon. Fill trough with dill mixture, mounding it slightly and smoothing surface. Cover with remaining roe mixture and rap mold firmly on counter to compact terrine. Smooth top with offset spatula and cover surface with an oiled sheet of wax paper (oiled side down).

▶ Bake in a water bath (see Kitchen Note, below) until terrine is firm to the touch and separates easily from sides of mold and thermometer inserted diagonally through wax paper into center of terrine registers 110 to 120°F (a metal skewer or thin knife plunged to bottom of terrine for 5 seconds and removed will feel hot), 40 to 45 minutes.

▶ Transfer terrine in mold to a rack and cool 10 to 15 minutes before unmolding.

▶ To unmold, remove wax paper and run a thin knife around inside edge of mold. Invert a cutting board or serving dish over terrine, then reinvert and remove mold and wax paper, blotting any excess liquid. Cut terrine into slices with a sharp knife, supporting each slice as cut with a flat metal spatula and transferring as cut to small plates. Serve each slice drizzled with 2 tablespoons beurre blanc.

Cooks' note:
• Terrine may be assembled (but not baked) 1 day ahead and chilled, covered.

KITCHEN NOTE

A **WATER BATH** FOR BAKING IS PREPARED BY PUTTING YOUR FILLED PAN IN A LARGER PAN AND ADDING ENOUGH BOILING WATER TO THE LARGER PAN TO REACH HALFWAY UP THE SIDE OF THE SMALLER PAN.

STEAMED CLAMS WITH BACON, TOMATO, AND SPINACH

SERVES 4 TO 6
Active time: 20 min   Start to finish: 45 min

½ lb sliced bacon, chopped
1 medium onion, chopped
2 garlic cloves, finely chopped
½ teaspoon dried hot red pepper flakes
2½ lb tomatoes, chopped
3 dozen small hard-shelled clams (2 to 2½ inches in diameter; 3½ lb total), scrubbed well
5 oz baby spinach (4 cups packed)

Accompaniment: **crusty bread**

▶ Cook bacon in a 5- to 6-quart heavy pot over moderate heat, stirring occasionally, until beginning to brown, about 5 minutes. Add onion, garlic, and red pepper flakes and cook, stirring occasionally, until onion is golden, about 6 minutes. Add tomatoes and cook, stirring occasionally, until they begin to break down and sauce thickens slightly, about 8 minutes.

▶ Increase heat to moderately high, then add clams and bring to a boil, covered. Cook, covered, stirring occasionally, until clams just open wide, about 6 minutes (discard clams that do not open after 10 minutes). Stir in spinach and cook until wilted, about 1 minute. Season with salt and pepper.

GRILLED EGGPLANT STACKS
WITH TOMATO AND FETA

SERVES 4

Active time: 45 min   Start to finish: 50 min

Tapered eggplants and a mix of large and medium tomatoes will give your stacks a more graceful appearance.

- 1   cup loosely packed fresh basil leaves
- ½   cup extra-virgin olive oil
- 1   teaspoon salt
- 2   medium eggplants (1¾ to 2 lb total)
- 1   large tomato (about 4 inches in diameter) and 2 medium tomatoes (about 2½ inches in diameter)
- ¼   teaspoon black pepper
- 3   oz feta, crumbled (about ¾ cup)

Garnish: **finely shredded fresh basil leaves**

▸ Blend basil with oil and ½ teaspoon salt in a blender until finely chopped. Pour into a paper-towel- or coffee-filter-lined sieve set over a bowl and let drain 20 minutes. Gather together sides of towel or filter and press gently to extract more oil. (You will have a generous ⅓ cup oil.) Reserve 1 tablespoon basil oil separately for serving. Scrape basil solids into a small bowl and reserve.

▸ Prepare grill for cooking over medium-hot charcoal or moderate heat for gas (see Tips, page 8).

▸ Meanwhile, cut off bottoms of eggplants, then cut 6 (½-inch-thick) crosswise rounds from each, starting from cut end. Reserve remainder for another use. Cut 4 (⅓-inch-thick) rounds from large tomato and 2 center slices (⅓ inch thick) from each medium tomato. Reserve remainder for another use.

▸ Lightly brush eggplant rounds on both sides with basil oil and sprinkle with pepper and remaining ½ teaspoon salt. Grill on lightly oiled grill rack, covered only if using a gas grill, turning over occasionally and lightly brushing eggplant with more basil oil occasionally if it looks dry, until eggplant is very tender, 6 to 10 minutes. (Leave gas grill on.)

Make stacks:

▸ On baking pan, arrange 4 largest eggplant rounds side by side and spread each with a generous ½ teaspoon of reserved basil solids, then top each with 1 of 4 largest tomato rounds. Season tomatoes with salt and pepper and top each with about 1 tablespoon feta. Make another layer with medium-size eggplant rounds, basil solids, medium tomato rounds, salt, pepper, and feta, then top with remaining eggplant and feta.

▸ Set baking pan on grill and cook stacks, with grill cover closed, until heated through and cheese on top is softened, about 3 minutes. Transfer stacks to 4 plates and drizzle plates with reserved basil oil.

Cooks' note:

• If you aren't able to grill outdoors, eggplant can be cooked in a hot lightly oiled large (2-burner) ridged grill pan over moderately high heat, turning over once, about 20 to 25 minutes total. Bake stacks in shallow baking pan in a preheated 450°F oven, about 8 minutes.

BREADS

OATMEAL WHEAT BREAD

MAKES 2 LOAVES
Active time: 30 min   Start to finish: 5¼ hr

This wheat loaf is nothing like your standard "health bread"—the oats make it soft and slightly sweet, ideal for sandwiches or buttered toast.

  2   cups whole milk
  1   cup old-fashioned rolled oats (not quick-cooking) plus
        additional for topping
  ½   cup warm water (105–115°F)
  2   tablespoons active dry yeast (from three ¼-oz packages)
  ½   cup mild honey
  ½   stick (¼ cup) unsalted butter, melted and cooled, plus
        additional for buttering pans
  3   cups stone-ground whole-wheat flour
  1   tablespoon salt
        About 2 cups unbleached all-purpose flour
        Vegetable oil for oiling bowl
  1   large egg, lightly beaten with 1 tablespoon water

Special equipment: **2 (8- by 4-inch) loaf pans**

▶ Heat milk in a 1½- to 2-quart saucepan over low heat until hot but not boiling, then remove pan from heat and stir in oats. Let stand, uncovered, stirring occasionally, until cooled to warm.

▶ Stir together warm water, yeast, and 1 teaspoon honey in a small bowl until yeast is dissolved, then let stand until foamy, 5 minutes. (If mixture doesn't foam, discard and start over with new yeast.) Stir yeast mixture, melted butter, and remaining honey into cooled oatmeal.

▶ Stir together whole-wheat flour, salt, and 1½ cups unbleached flour in a large bowl. Add oat mixture, stirring with a wooden spoon until a soft dough forms. Turn out onto a well-floured surface and knead with floured hands, adding just enough of remaining unbleached flour to keep from sticking, until dough is smooth, soft, and elastic, about 10 minutes (dough will be slightly sticky). Form dough into a ball and transfer to an oiled large bowl, turning to coat. Cover bowl loosely with plastic wrap and a kitchen towel, then let rise in a draft-free place at warm room temperature until doubled in bulk, 1 to 1½ hours.

▶ Lightly butter loaf pans. Turn out dough onto a lightly floured surface and knead several times to remove air. Divide dough in half and shape each half into a loaf, then place 1 loaf in each buttered pan, seam side down, tucking ends gently to fit. Cover loaf pans loosely with a kitchen towel and let dough rise in a draft-free place at warm room temperature until doubled in bulk, about 1 hour.

▶ Put oven rack in middle position and preheat oven to 375°F. Lightly brush tops of loaves with some of egg wash and sprinkle with oats, then bake until bread is golden and loaves sound hollow when tapped on bottom, 35 to 40 minutes. (Remove 1 loaf from pan to test for doneness. Run a knife around edge of pan to loosen.)

▶ Remove bread from pans and transfer to a rack to cool completely, about 1½ hours.

Cooks' note:
• Bread keeps, wrapped in plastic wrap at room temperature, 4 days.

KITCHEN NOTE

LEAN BREADS, LIKE BAGUETTES, GET STALE QUICKLY; OTHERS, SUCH AS SOURDOUGHS AND BREADS MADE WITH EGGS, FATS, MILK, POTATOES, AND/OR SUGAR, KEEP THREE OR FOUR DAYS AT ROOM TEMPERATURE, WRAPPED IN PLASTIC. **FRESH BREAD** CAN BE FROZEN, WRAPPED FIRST IN PLASTIC AND THEN IN FOIL; BEFORE REHEATING IT IN THE OVEN (TO RETAIN CRUSTINESS), REMOVE THE PLASTIC AND REWRAP IT IN THE FOIL.

OATMEAL SCONES

MAKES 18 SCONES

Active time: 20 min   Start to finish: 40 min

1⅔   cups all-purpose flour
¾   teaspoon cinnamon
1   tablespoon baking powder
¾   teaspoon baking soda
½   teaspoon salt
¼   cup plus 2 tablespoons packed light brown sugar
1⅓   cups plus 2 tablespoons old-fashioned rolled oats
1½   sticks (¾ cup) cold unsalted butter, cut into
      tablespoon pieces
⅔   cup well-shaken buttermilk plus additional for brushing

▶ Put oven rack in middle position and preheat oven to 425°F.

▶ Sift together flour, cinnamon, baking powder, baking soda, salt, and ¼ cup brown sugar into a food processor. Add 1⅓ cups oats and pulse 15 times. Add butter and pulse until mixture resembles coarse meal with some roughly pea-size butter lumps. Transfer to a bowl.

▶ Add buttermilk and stir with a fork until a dough just forms. Gently knead on a floured surface 6 times.

▶ Pat dough into a 9-inch square (½ inch thick). Cut into 9 (3-inch) squares. Cut each square diagonally to form 2 triangles. Transfer to an ungreased baking sheet.

▶ Brush dough with buttermilk and sprinkle with remaining 2 tablespoons each of brown sugar and oats. Bake until golden brown, about 16 minutes. Transfer to racks to cool.

CHEDDAR DILL BISCUITS

MAKES 12 BISCUITS

Active time: 20 min   Start to finish: 30 min

2   cups all-purpose flour
2   teaspoons baking powder
1   teaspoon sugar
½   teaspoon baking soda
½   teaspoon salt
5   tablespoons cold unsalted butter, cut into ½-inch cubes
2   oz coarsely grated extra-sharp Cheddar (¾ cup)
1½   tablespoons chopped fresh dill
¾   cup whole-milk plain yogurt
⅓   cup whole milk

▶ Put oven rack in middle position and preheat oven to 400°F.

▶ Pulse flour, baking powder, sugar, baking soda, and salt in a food processor until combined. Add butter and pulse until mixture resembles coarse meal. Add Cheddar and dill and pulse until just combined. Whisk together yogurt and milk, then add to food processor and pulse until dough just comes together. Spoon 12 (¼-cup) mounds of dough about 2 inches apart onto an ungreased large baking sheet and bake until puffed and pale golden, 12 to 15 minutes.

KITCHEN NOTE

MEASURE **FLOUR** BY SPOONING (NOT SCOOPING) IT INTO A DRY-MEASURING CUP AND LEVELING OFF WITH A KNIFE WITHOUT TAPPING OR SHAKING CUP. SIFT FLOUR ONLY WHEN SPECIFIED IN A RECIPE.

CINNAMON SUGAR BISCUITS

MAKES ABOUT 12 BISCUITS

Active time: 25 min   Start to finish: 50 min

2   cups all-purpose flour
1   tablespoon baking powder
2   tablespoons granulated sugar
½   teaspoon salt
1¼   sticks (½ cup plus 2 tablespoons) unsalted butter,
      1 stick cold and cut into ½-inch cubes and
      2 tablespoons melted
1   large egg
½   cup well-shaken chilled buttermilk
3   tablespoons turbinado sugar such as Sugar in the Raw
¾   teaspoon cinnamon

Special equipment: **parchment paper; a 2½-inch round biscuit or cookie cutter**
Accompaniments: **softened butter and jam**

▶ Put oven rack in middle position and preheat oven to 400°F. Line a large baking sheet with parchment paper.

▶ Whisk together flour, baking powder, granulated sugar, and salt in a bowl. Blend in butter cubes with your fingertips or a pastry blender until mixture resembles coarse meal. Stir together egg and buttermilk in another bowl, then add to flour mixture, stirring with a fork until a dough forms.

▶ Gather dough into a ball, then turn out onto a floured surface and gently knead 7 or 8 times. Roll out dough with a floured rolling pin into a ½-inch-thick round and cut out as many biscuits as possible with biscuit cutter. Gather scraps and knead once, then pat out into a ½-inch-thick round and cut out more biscuits.

▶ Arrange biscuits 1 inch apart on baking sheet and brush tops and sides with melted butter. Stir together turbinado sugar and cinnamon and sprinkle over biscuits (sugar will form a crust).

▶ Bake until golden brown and cooked through, about 15 minutes. Transfer biscuits to a rack and cool to warm, about 10 minutes.

LINZER MUFFINS
MAKES 12 MUFFINS
Active time: 30 min   Start to finish: 1¼ hr

- 1   cup whole almonds, toasted (see Tips, page 8) and cooled completely
- ¾   cup granulated sugar
- ½   teaspoon finely grated fresh lemon zest (see Tips, page 8)
- 1½   cups all-purpose flour
- 2   teaspoons baking powder
- ½   teaspoon salt
- ¼   teaspoon cinnamon
- 1   cup whole milk
- ¾   stick (6 tablespoons) unsalted butter, melted and cooled
- 1   large egg
- ⅛   teaspoon almond extract
     About ⅓ cup seedless raspberry jam
     Confectioners sugar for dusting

Special equipment: **a muffin tin with 12 (½-cup) muffin cups**

▶ Put oven rack in middle position and preheat oven to 400°F. Grease muffin cups.

▶ Grind almonds with granulated sugar and zest in a food processor until almonds are finely ground.

▶ Whisk together flour, almond mixture, baking powder, salt, and cinnamon in a large bowl. Whisk together milk, butter, egg, and almond extract in a small bowl, then stir into dry ingredients until combined.

▶ Put a scant ¼ cup batter into each muffin cup. Top each with 1 rounded teaspoon jam. Divide remaining batter among cups. Bake until golden and muffins pull away from edges of cups, about 20 minutes. Cool in pan on a rack 5 to 10 minutes, then turn out onto rack. Dust with confectioners sugar before serving.

BACON CORN MUFFINS
MAKES 12 MUFFINS
Active time: 25 min   Start to finish: 1 hr

- 1¼   cups whole milk
- 1   large egg
- ¾   stick (6 tablespoons) unsalted butter, melted and cooled
- 1   cup yellow cornmeal
- ¾   cup all-purpose flour
- 1   cup chopped scallions
- 8   bacon slices (½ lb), cooked and crumbled
- 2   tablespoons sugar
- 1   tablespoon baking powder
- ¾   teaspoon salt

Special equipment: **a muffin tin with 12 (½-cup) cups**

▶ Put oven rack in middle position and preheat oven to 400°F. Grease muffin cups.

▶ Whisk together milk, egg, and butter in a small bowl. Whisk together remaining ingredients in a large bowl, then add milk mixture to dry ingredients. Stir until just combined.

▶ Divide batter among muffin cups. Bake until golden and a wooden pick or skewer inserted in a center comes out clean, about 20 minutes. Cool in pan on a rack 5 to 10 minutes.

SOUPS

CHILLED CARROT HONEY SOUP

SERVES 6 (FIRST COURSE)
Active time: 20 min   Start to finish: 1½ hr (includes chilling)

  1 lb carrots, peeled and cut into ½-inch pieces
       (2¼ cups)
  3 cups water
1¾ cups reduced-sodium fat-free chicken broth
       (14 fl oz)
  1 cup chopped onion (1 medium)
  1 teaspoon salt
  ¼ teaspoon ground coriander
  ¼ teaspoon ground cumin
  ¼ teaspoon paprika (not hot)
  ⅛ teaspoon cayenne
  2 tablespoons mild honey
2½ tablespoons fresh lemon juice

Garnish: **6 thin lemon slices and 1 tablespoon mild honey
for drizzling**

▸Combine all ingredients except ½ tablespoon lemon
juice in a 3-quart heavy saucepan and bring to a boil over
moderate heat, stirring occasionally. Reduce heat and
simmer, covered, until carrots are tender, 30 to 40 minutes.
▸Purée soup in 2 batches in a blender (use caution when
blending hot liquids) until very smooth, then chill soup
quickly, stirring occasionally, in a metal bowl set in a larger
bowl of ice and cold water, about 30 minutes. (Alternatively,
cool soup, uncovered, 30 to 40 minutes, then chill, covered,
until cold, about 4 hours.)
▸Stir in remaining ½ tablespoon lemon juice and salt to
taste. Divide soup among 6 bowls with a ladle. Float a
lemon slice on top of each serving, then drizzle with honey
and serve.

Cooks' note:
• Soup can be made 3 days ahead and kept chilled, covered.
EACH SERVING ABOUT 77 CALORIES AND LESS THAN 1 GRAM FAT

PEACH AND TOMATO GAZPACHO

SERVES 4 (FIRST COURSE)
Active time: 20 min   Start to finish: 20 min

*We use ice in this recipe because it gives the gazpacho just
the right chill without the soup having to be refrigerated for
any length of time. If you don't have precrushed ice, crush
about ¼ cup ice in a blender.*

1½ lb tomatoes, chopped (4 cups)
  1 lb peaches, pitted and chopped (2 cups)
  ¼ cup crushed ice
  2 tablespoons chopped shallot (1 medium)
  2 tablespoons olive oil
1½ tablespoons white-wine vinegar
  1 tablespoon chopped fresh tarragon
  1 teaspoon salt
  ½ teaspoon black pepper
  ¼ to ½ cup water

▸Purée two thirds of tomatoes and half of peaches with ice,
shallot, 1 tablespoon oil, 1 tablespoon vinegar, 2 teaspoons
tarragon, ¾ teaspoon salt, and ¼ teaspoon pepper in a
blender until very smooth, about 1 minute. Force through a
medium-mesh sieve into a large glass measure, discarding
solids. Stir in water to desired consistency.
▸Toss together remaining tomatoes and peaches with
remaining tablespoon oil, remaining ½ tablespoon vinegar,
remaining teaspoon tarragon, and remaining ¼ teaspoon
each of salt and pepper in a bowl.
▸Serve soup in bowls topped with tomato peach salsa.

KITCHEN NOTE

NOTHING WILL RUIN GOOD **TOMATOES** FASTER
THAN REFRIGERATION. A SUNNY WINDOWSILL
ISN'T THE BEST PLACE EITHER; THEY DO BEST AT
ROOM TEMPERATURE AND IN INDIRECT LIGHT.

BARLEY SOUP WITH DUCK CONFIT AND ROOT VEGETABLES

SERVES 6 (FIRST COURSE)

Active time: 1 hr   Start to finish: 1¼ hr

½ cup pearl barley
7 cups water
2 confit duck legs (see Sources)
2 medium carrots, peeled, quartered lengthwise, then cut crosswise into ¼-inch-thick pieces (1 cup)
2 medium parsnips, peeled, quartered lengthwise, then cut crosswise into ¼-inch-thick pieces (1¾ cups)
1 garlic clove, finely chopped
3 cups reduced-sodium chicken broth (24 fl oz)
¾ teaspoon salt
¼ teaspoon black pepper
1 teaspoon chopped fresh thyme

▸ Simmer barley in 4 cups water in a 5- to 6-quart heavy pot, uncovered, until almost tender, 20 to 40 minutes. Drain in a sieve.

▸ Remove skin and any fat from duck legs. Cook skin and fat in a 1- to 1½-quart heavy saucepan over low heat, stirring occasionally, until fat is rendered, about 8 minutes, then strain through a fine-mesh sieve into a small bowl, discarding skin. Reserve fat.

▸ While fat is rendering, remove duck meat from bones, reserving bones, and shred meat into small pieces.

▸ Heat 1 tablespoon duck fat (reserving any remainder for another use) in cleaned 5- to 6-quart pot over moderately high heat until hot but not smoking, then sauté carrots and parsnips, stirring frequently, until just golden, about 8 minutes. Add garlic and cook, stirring, 1 minute.

▸ Stir in broth, parboiled barley, salt, pepper, duck bones, and remaining 3 cups water and bring to a boil. Reduce heat and simmer, uncovered, stirring occasionally, until vegetables and barley are tender, 15 to 20 minutes. Discard bones and stir in shredded duck meat. Skim any excess fat from soup, then stir in thyme. Season with salt and pepper.

Cooks' notes:
• Pearl barley, by definition, has had some of its bran removed, but we found that different brands varied widely. Higher-fiber varieties will have a slightly longer cooking time.
• Soup can be made 4 days ahead. Cool to room temperature, uncovered, then chill, covered. Reheat before serving.

CREAM OF BARLEY SOUP WITH DILL

SERVES 4 TO 6 (FIRST COURSE)

Active time: 20 min   Start to finish: 30 min

1 cup chopped shallots (2 large)
3 tablespoons unsalted butter
1 teaspoon salt
¾ cup quick-cooking barley
1¾ cups reduced-sodium chicken broth (14 fl oz)
3 cups plus 1 tablespoon water
3 tablespoons sour cream
⅛ teaspoon white pepper
2 tablespoons chopped fresh dill

▸ Cook shallots in butter with ½ teaspoon salt in a 3-quart heavy saucepan over moderate heat, stirring occasionally, until beginning to brown, about 5 minutes. Add barley and cook, stirring frequently, 1 minute. Add broth and 3 cups water and boil, covered, until barley is tender, about 10 minutes.

▸ Pour broth through a medium-mesh sieve into a bowl and set aside half of barley mixture. Transfer broth and remaining barley mixture to a blender, then add 2 tablespoons sour cream and blend until very smooth (use caution when blending hot liquids). Return soup to saucepan, then stir in white pepper, remaining ½ teaspoon salt, and remaining barley mixture.

▸ Divide soup among serving bowls. Thin remaining tablespoon sour cream with remaining tablespoon water and drizzle over soup. Sprinkle with dill.

KITCHEN NOTE

GRAINS LIKE **BARLEY** CAN GET MUSTY WITH AGE. IT'S BEST TO BUY THEM FROM A SOURCE WITH HIGH TURNOVER, LIKE NATURAL FOODS STORES.

CAULIFLOWER SOUP WITH ALMONDS

SERVES 4 (FIRST COURSE)

Active time: 20 min   Start to finish: 45 min

  1 medium leek (white and pale green parts only), halved
     lengthwise, then cut crosswise into ½-inch-thick slices
     (¾ cup)
  1 teaspoon unsalted butter
  1 tablespoon water
  1 (2-lb) head cauliflower, cored and cut into 1-inch pieces
     (6 cups)
  ¾ teaspoon ground coriander
  1¾ cups fat-free reduced-sodium chicken broth (14 fl oz)
  1¼ cups 1% milk
  1¼ teaspoons salt
  ¼ teaspoon black pepper
  1 tablespoon sliced almonds

▶ Wash leek slices in a bowl of cold water, agitating them, then lift out and pat dry.

▶ Melt butter with water in a 4- to 5-quart heavy pot over moderate heat. Add cauliflower and leek and cook, uncovered, stirring occasionally, until cauliflower begins to soften (do not let brown), about 5 minutes. Add coriander and cook, stirring, 1 minute, then add broth, milk, salt, and pepper and bring to a simmer, stirring occasionally. Reduce heat and gently simmer, covered, stirring occasionally, until cauliflower is very tender, 15 to 20 minutes.

▶ While soup simmers, toast almonds in a dry skillet over moderately low heat, stirring frequently, until fragrant and a shade darker, about 3 minutes.

▶ Purée soup in 2 batches in a blender (use caution when blending hot liquids) until very smooth. Serve soup topped with almonds.

Cooks' note:
• Soup can be made 2 days ahead and cooled completely, uncovered, then chilled, covered. Almonds can be toasted 2 days ahead and kept separately in an airtight container at room temperature. Reheat soup before serving.

EACH SERVING ABOUT 96 CALORIES AND 3 GRAMS FAT

TAIWANESE BEEF NOODLE SOUP

SERVES 4 (MAIN COURSE)

Active time: 40 min   Start to finish: 4½ hr

Dried tangerine peel and star anise impart an exotic note to this hearty soup, and pickled mustard greens provide contrast to the beefy broth. For sources for the Asian ingredients, see Sources.

  5 cups water
  1 cup soy sauce
  1 cup Chinese rice wine or medium-dry Sherry
  ¼ cup packed light brown sugar
  1 (1-inch) cube peeled fresh ginger, smashed
  1 bunch scallions, white parts smashed with flat side of
     a large knife and green parts chopped
  3 garlic cloves, smashed
 10 fresh cilantro stems plus ½ cup loosely packed fresh
     cilantro sprigs
  2 (2-inch-long) pieces Asian dried tangerine peel
  4 whole star anise
  ¼ teaspoon dried hot red pepper flakes
  2½ lb meaty beef short ribs
  1¾ cups reduced-sodium chicken broth (14 fl oz)
 10 oz dried Chinese wheat noodles or linguine
  1 cup fresh mung bean sprouts
  4 tablespoons Chinese pickled mustard greens
  1 (4-inch-long) fresh red chile (optional), thinly sliced

Special equipment: **cheesecloth**

▶ Bring water, soy sauce, rice wine, brown sugar, ginger, white parts of scallions, garlic, cilantro stems, tangerine peel, star anise, and red pepper flakes to a boil in a 5- to 6-quart pot, then reduce heat and simmer, uncovered, 10 minutes. Add short ribs and gently simmer, covered, turning occasionally, until meat is very tender but not falling apart, 2¼ to 2½ hours. Let meat stand in cooking liquid, uncovered, 1 hour.

▶ Transfer meat to a cutting board with tongs and remove meat from bones, discarding bones and membranes, then cut meat across the grain into ½-inch-thick slices.

▶ Pour beef broth through a cheesecloth-lined sieve into a bowl and discard solids. Skim fat from cooking liquid and transfer liquid to a 3-quart saucepan. Add chicken broth and meat and reheat soup over moderately low heat.

▶ Meanwhile, cook noodles in a 6- to 8-quart pot of boiling water, uncovered, until tender, about 7 minutes (14 to 15 minutes for linguine). Drain noodles well in a colander and divide among 4 large soup bowls.

▶ Ladle broth over noodles and top with meat, scallion greens, bean sprouts, pickled mustard greens, cilantro sprigs, and red chile (if using).

Cooks' note:

• Meat and beef broth can be cooked and strained 3 days ahead. Cool completely, uncovered, then chill meat in broth, covered. Skim fat before adding chicken broth.

ASIAN DUMPLING SOUP
SERVES 4 (MAIN COURSE)
Active time: 10 min   Start to finish: 25 min

1 (15- to 16-oz) package frozen Asian dumplings (also called pot stickers; about 20 to 24)
5 cups reduced-sodium chicken broth (40 fl oz)
3 cups thinly sliced Napa cabbage (from 1 head)
2 cups sliced shiitake mushroom caps
1 cup shredded or matchstick (⅛-inch-thick) carrots (from a 10-oz bag)
½ cup frozen peas
½ cup chopped scallions
1 teaspoon Asian sesame oil
½ teaspoon salt
⅛ teaspoon black pepper

▶ Cook dumplings in a 6- to 8-quart pot of boiling water, uncovered, stirring occasionally, until cooked through, 5 to 8 minutes. (Cut into a dumpling to check filling.) Remove pot from heat and keep dumplings warm in hot water.

▶ While dumplings cook, bring broth to a boil in a 4- to 6-quart heavy pot. Add cabbage, mushrooms, and carrots and boil, uncovered, stirring occasionally, 3 minutes, then add peas and cook 2 minutes. Stir in scallions, sesame oil, salt, and pepper and boil until all vegetables are tender, about 1 minute.

▶ Divide dumplings among 4 soup bowls with a slotted spoon. Ladle soup over dumplings.

HERBED BEAN AND PASTA SOUP
SERVES 4 (MAIN COURSE)
Active time: 20 min   Start to finish: 45 min

This delicious vegetarian soup is a take on the Persian dish ash-e reshteh.

3 tablespoons olive oil
2 medium onions, halved lengthwise, then thinly sliced crosswise
1½ teaspoons salt
¼ teaspoon turmeric
6 cups water
¼ lb dried linguine, broken into 2-inch pieces (1 cup)
12 fresh chard leaves, stems and center ribs discarded and leaves coarsely chopped (8 cups)
1 (15- to 19-oz) can kidney beans, rinsed and drained
½ cup finely chopped fresh cilantro
½ cup finely chopped fresh dill
½ cup finely chopped fresh flat-leaf parsley
½ cup finely chopped scallion greens

Accompaniments: **sour cream; lemon wedges**

▶ Heat oil in a 4-quart wide heavy pot over moderately high heat until hot but not smoking. Add onions and salt, then reduce heat to moderate and cook, stirring occasionally, until golden, 15 to 20 minutes. Reserve ¼ cup onion.

▶ Add turmeric to onions in pot and cook, stirring, 1 minute. Add water and bring to a boil. Add linguine and boil, uncovered, until tender, about 10 minutes. Stir in chard and beans and simmer, stirring occasionally, until chard is tender, about 5 minutes. Remove from heat. Stir in herbs, scallion greens, and salt and pepper to taste.

▶ Serve soup topped with reserved onion.

LEMONY LENTIL SOUP WITH CILANTRO

SERVES 6 (FIRST COURSE)

Active time: 20 min   Start to finish: 55 min

½ cup chopped fresh cilantro
7 tablespoons olive oil
1 teaspoon salt
1 medium onion, chopped
½ teaspoon ground allspice
1 cup brown lentils, picked over and rinsed
3½ cups reduced-sodium chicken broth (28 fl oz)
3 cups water
2 tablespoons fresh lemon juice

▶ Purée cilantro with 6 tablespoons oil and ¼ teaspoon salt in a blender until smooth. Transfer purée to a bowl and set blender aside.

▶ Cook onion in remaining tablespoon oil in a 3-quart heavy saucepan over moderate heat, stirring occasionally, until beginning to brown, 4 to 5 minutes. Add allspice and remaining ¾ teaspoon salt and cook, stirring frequently, 1 minute. Add lentils, broth, and water and bring to a boil, then reduce heat and simmer, covered, until lentils are very soft, about 30 minutes. Transfer 1 cup lentils with some of broth to blender and purée until smooth (use caution when blending hot liquids), then return to saucepan. Add lemon juice and pepper to taste. Stir in cilantro purée.

KITCHEN NOTE

ALL **BEER** IS EITHER LAGER (PILSNER AND BOCK, FOR EXAMPLE) OR ALE (PALE ALE, BRITISH BITTER, PORTER, AND STOUT, AMONG MANY OTHERS). ALE IS BREWED WITH POWERFUL YEASTS THAT WORK QUICKLY AND CONTRIBUTE FULL, FRUITY FLAVORS. LAGER YEASTS, ON THE OTHER HAND, LET THE BEER FERMENT MORE SLOWLY AND DON'T ADD AS MUCH FLAVOR. AS A RESULT, LAGERS TEND TO SHOWCASE THE OTHER INGREDIENTS MORE.

CHEDDAR BEER SOUP

SERVES 4 TO 6 (MAIN COURSE)

Active time: 40 min   Start to finish: 40 min

2 medium leeks (white and pale green parts only), cut into ¼-inch dice (2 cups)
2 medium carrots, cut into ¼-inch dice (1 cup)
2 celery ribs, cut into ¼-inch dice (1 cup)
2 teaspoons finely chopped garlic
1 Turkish or ½ California bay leaf
½ stick (¼ cup) unsalted butter
⅓ cup all-purpose flour
2 cups whole milk
1¾ cups reduced-sodium chicken broth (14 fl oz)
1 (12-oz) bottle ale such as Bass
1 tablespoon Worcestershire sauce
1 teaspoon dry mustard
1 teaspoon salt
¼ teaspoon black pepper
1 lb extra-sharp Cheddar (preferably English; rind removed if necessary), grated (4 cups)
4 bacon slices (3½ oz total), cooked and crumbled

▶ Wash leeks in a bowl of cold water, agitating them, then lift out leeks and drain in a colander.

▶ Cook leeks, carrots, celery, garlic, and bay leaf in butter in a 4-quart heavy pot over moderate heat, stirring occasionally, until vegetables begin to soften, about 5 minutes. Reduce heat to moderately low and sprinkle flour over vegetables, then cook, stirring occasionally, 3 minutes. Add milk, broth, and beer in a stream, whisking, then simmer, whisking occasionally, 5 minutes. Stir in Worcestershire sauce, mustard, salt, and pepper.

▶ Add cheese by handfuls, stirring constantly, and cook until cheese is melted, 3 to 4 minutes (do not boil). Discard bay leaf.

▶ Serve sprinkled with bacon.

CURRIED PUMPKIN SOUP

SERVES 10 TO 12 (FIRST COURSE)

Active time: 20 min   Start to finish: 50 min

2	medium onions, finely chopped (2 cups)
2	tablespoons unsalted butter
2	large garlic cloves, minced
1½	tablespoons minced peeled fresh ginger
2	teaspoons ground cumin
1	teaspoon ground coriander
⅛	teaspoon ground cardamom
1½	teaspoons salt
¾	teaspoon dried hot red pepper flakes
2	(15-oz) cans solid-pack pumpkin (3½ cups; not pie filling)
7	cups water
1½	cups reduced-sodium chicken broth (12 fl oz)
1	(14-oz) can unsweetened coconut milk (not low-fat)
¼	cup olive oil
2	teaspoons brown mustard seeds
8	fresh curry leaves

► Cook onions in butter in a 6-quart wide heavy pot over moderately low heat, stirring occasionally, until softened, 3 to 5 minutes. Add garlic and ginger and cook, stirring, 1 minute. Add cumin, coriander, and cardamom and cook, stirring, 1 minute. Stir in salt, red pepper flakes, pumpkin, water, broth, and coconut milk and simmer, uncovered, stirring occasionally, 30 minutes. Purée soup in batches in a blender until smooth (use caution when blending hot liquids), transferring to a large bowl, and return soup to pot. Keep soup warm over low heat.

► Heat oil in a small heavy skillet over moderately high heat until hot but not smoking, then cook mustard seeds until they begin to pop, about 15 seconds. Add curry leaves and cook 5 seconds, then pour mixture into pumpkin soup. Stir until combined well, then season soup with salt. Thin with additional water if desired.

Cooks' note:

• Soup can be made 1 day ahead and cooled completely, uncovered, then chilled, covered.

FISH AND SHELLFISH

FISH

FLOUNDER WITH CHAMPAGNE GRAPES

SERVES 4

Active time: 20 min   Start to finish: 20 min

This variation on sole Véronique uses tiny Champagne grapes for the sauce—they have extremely delicate skins, so there's no need to peel them.

- 4 (6- to 7-oz) flounder or sole fillets
    All-purpose flour for dredging fish
- 2 to 3 tablespoons vegetable oil
- ¼ cup finely chopped shallot
- ⅔ cup sweet vermouth
- 7 oz stemmed Champagne grapes (1½ cups)
- 3 tablespoons unsalted butter, cut into tablespoon pieces
- 1 tablespoon fresh lemon juice

▶ Put oven rack in middle position and preheat oven to 250°F.

▶ Rinse fish and pat dry. Season both sides of fillets with salt and pepper, then dredge in flour, shaking off excess.

▶ Heat 2 tablespoons oil in a 12-inch heavy skillet over moderately high heat until it begins to smoke, then sauté 2 fillets, turning over once, until golden and just cooked through, about 4 minutes total. Transfer with a slotted spatula to a platter and keep warm, uncovered, in oven. Add more oil if necessary and sauté remaining 2 fillets in same manner, transferring to platter.

▶ Add shallot to skillet and cook over moderate heat, stirring, until softened, about 2 minutes. Add vermouth and simmer, scraping up any brown bits, 1 minute. Add grapes and cook over low heat, swirling skillet, until just heated through, 1 to 2 minutes.

▶ Remove skillet from heat and add butter, swirling until incorporated. Add lemon juice and season sauce with salt and pepper. Spoon sauce with grapes over fish and serve immediately.

FLOUNDER IN JALAPEÑO CREAM

SERVES 4

Active time: 20 min   Start to finish: 25 min

- 2 scallions, white parts finely chopped and greens reserved for another use
- 1 tablespoon unsalted butter
- 1 to 2 tablespoons finely chopped fresh jalapeño including seeds
- ½ cup heavy cream
- ½ teaspoon salt
- 4 (6- to 8-oz) pieces flounder fillet
- ⅛ teaspoon black pepper
- ½ cup quartered grape tomatoes
- 1 tablespoon chopped fresh cilantro

▶ Cook chopped scallions in butter in a 10-inch heavy skillet over moderate heat, stirring, until softened, 3 to 4 minutes. Add jalapeño (to taste), cream, and ¼ teaspoon salt and bring to a simmer.

▶ Pat fish dry, then sprinkle with pepper and remaining ¼ teaspoon salt. Fold each fillet in half crosswise. Put folded fish in sauce in skillet and cook at a bare simmer, covered, until fish is just cooked through, 5 to 6 minutes. Transfer fish to a platter and keep warm, covered with foil.

▶ Add tomatoes and cilantro to sauce in skillet along with any fish juices accumulated on platter and cook over moderately low heat until heated through, about 1 minute. Spoon sauce over fish.

KITCHEN NOTE

NOTHING BEATS THE SUCCULENCE OF A TOMATO FROM THE GARDEN. TODAY, THERE ARE HUNDREDS OF KINDS TO CHOOSE FROM, IN AN ARRAY OF COLORS, SHAPES, AND SIZES. ASK YOUR LOCAL GROWERS ABOUT **HEIRLOOMS** THEY MIGHT BE CULTIVATING—WONDERFUL OLD VARIETIES SUCH AS BURBANK, CHEROKEE PURPLE, AND OXHEART WON'T KEEP AS LONG AS HYBRIDS, BUT THEY MAKE UP FOR IT IN FLAVOR, TEXTURE, AND NUTRITION.

FISH WITH CURRIED CUCUMBER TOMATO WATER AND TOMATO HERB SALAD

SERVES 6

Active time: 35 min   Start to finish: 1¼ hr

For cucumber tomato water

- 1 (½-lb) cucumber, peeled and chopped (1½ cups)
- 1 (¼-lb) tomato, chopped (¾ cup)
- ¼ teaspoon curry powder (preferably Madras)
- ¼ teaspoon salt

For tomato herb salad

- 1 lemon
- 1 lb assorted small heirloom tomatoes, halved (larger ones quartered)
- ¼ cup loosely packed fresh parsley leaves
- 2 tablespoons thinly sliced fresh basil
- 1 tablespoon extra-virgin olive oil
- 2 teaspoons finely chopped fresh chives
- 1 teaspoon finely chopped fresh lemon balm (optional)
- ¼ teaspoon black pepper
- ¼ to ½ teaspoon sugar (to taste)
- ¼ teaspoon salt

For fish

- 6 (5- to 7-oz) mild white-fleshed fish fillets such as flounder, sea bass, or snapper
- 1 tablespoon extra-virgin olive oil

Make cucumber tomato water:

▸ Purée cucumber, tomato, curry powder, and salt in a blender until smooth, about 30 seconds.

▸ Line a fine-mesh sieve with a dampened paper towel and set over a large glass measure, then transfer cucumber mixture to sieve and let drain until liquid measures ⅔ cup, about 20 minutes.

▸ If liquid measures less than ⅔ cup, gently squeeze paper towel over sieve until liquid totals ⅔ cup. Discard solids and transfer liquid to a 2- to 3-quart saucepan.

▸ Boil cucumber tomato water until reduced to about ⅓ cup, then remove from heat and cool to room temperature, about 30 minutes.

Make tomato herb salad:

▸ Cut peel, including all white pith, from lemon with a sharp paring knife. Working over a bowl, cut segments free from membranes, letting segments fall into bowl, then chop segments, reserving juice in a cup.

▸ Gently toss lemon segments and reserved juice with remaining salad ingredients in a large bowl. Stir in cooled cucumber tomato water.

Bake fish:

▸ Put oven rack in middle position and preheat oven to 500°F.

▸ Rinse fish and pat dry. Brush fillets all over with oil and season with salt and pepper.

▸ Bake fillets in 1 layer in a lightly oiled shallow baking pan until just cooked through, 4 to 8 minutes, depending on thickness of fillets.

▸ Serve tomato herb salad on top of fish.

CATFISH IN SPICY TOMATO SAUCE

SERVES 6

Active time: 10 min   Start to finish: 25 min

- 1 (28-oz) can whole tomatoes in juice
- 1 tablespoon olive oil
- 2 garlic cloves, finely chopped
  Rounded ¼ teaspoon cayenne
- ⅜ teaspoon ground cinnamon
- ¼ teaspoon ground cumin
- ⅛ teaspoon ground allspice
- ⅛ teaspoon ground ginger
- 1¼ teaspoons salt
- 1½ teaspoons sugar
- 6 (5-oz) catfish fillets
- 3 tablespoons chopped fresh flat-leaf parsley

▸ Put oven rack in middle position and preheat oven to 400°F.

▸ Purée tomatoes with their juice in a blender. Heat oil in a 12-inch heavy skillet over moderate heat until hot but not smoking, then cook garlic, spices, and ¾ teaspoon salt, stirring, until garlic is golden, about 1 minute. Add tomato purée and sugar and briskly simmer, uncovered, stirring occasionally, until slightly thickened, 6 to 8 minutes.

▸ Pour sauce into a 13- by 9-inch baking dish. Pat fish dry and sprinkle with remaining ½ teaspoon salt. Arrange fillets in 1 layer on sauce, tucking each tail end under if necessary to fit, and bake until fish is just cooked through, 10 to 12 minutes. Serve sprinkled with parsley.

PEANUT-CRUSTED TROUT WITH PINEAPPLE CILANTRO RELISH

SERVES 4

Active time: 25 min   Start to finish: 25 min

- 1 large bunch fresh cilantro including stems
- ⅓ cup unsalted dry-roasted peanuts
- 1 teaspoon finely chopped peeled fresh ginger
- 1 garlic clove
- ½ teaspoon black pepper
- 3 tablespoons vegetable oil
- 2 tablespoons fresh lime juice
- 1¼ teaspoons salt
- 1 teaspoon finely chopped fresh serrano chile, including seeds
- 4 trout fillets with skin (1 to 1¼ lb total), pin bones removed
- 3 cups chopped peeled fresh pineapple (preferably labeled "extra sweet")
- 2 teaspoons Asian fish sauce

▸ Preheat broiler, then oil rack of a broiler pan.
▸ Chop enough cilantro stems to measure ½ cup, then transfer to a food processor along with peanuts, ginger, garlic, pepper, 2 tablespoons oil, 1 tablespoon lime juice, 1 teaspoon salt, and ½ teaspoon chile. Process until finely chopped, about 30 seconds, then transfer to a bowl. Do not clean processor.
▸ Pat fillets dry and arrange, flesh sides up, tightly on rack of broiler pan (fillets should just touch). Spread peanut mixture evenly over tops of fillets.
▸ Broil fish 3 to 4 inches from heat until lightly browned and just cooked through, about 4 minutes.
▸ While fish broils, chop enough cilantro leaves to measure 1 cup, then pulse in processor along with pineapple, fish sauce, remaining tablespoon each of oil and lime juice, remaining ¼ teaspoon salt, and remaining ½ teaspoon chile until combined.
▸ Serve fish topped with pineapple cilantro relish.

FISH TACOS

SERVES 6

Active time: 10 min   Start to finish: 10 min

- 1½ lb flounder fillets (preferably large)
- 2 tablespoons olive oil
- 1 teaspoon salt
- ½ teaspoon black pepper
- 1 cup mayonnaise
- ½ cup plain yogurt
- ½ teaspoon chipotle chile powder
- 1 (1-lb) bag coleslaw mix (8 cups)
- 12 (6- to 7-inch) corn tortillas (not low-fat)

Accompaniments: salsa; lime wedges

▸ Preheat broiler.
▸ Pat fish dry and place in a shallow baking pan, then brush fish with oil and sprinkle with ½ teaspoon salt and ½ teaspoon pepper. Broil fish 3 to 4 inches from heat, without turning, until opaque and just cooked through, about 4 minutes (depending on thickness of fillets).
▸ While fish cooks, make sauce by stirring together mayonnaise, yogurt, chipotle powder, and remaining ½ teaspoon salt in a small bowl. Toss together coleslaw mix with ½ cup sauce in a large bowl.
▸ Wrap stack of tortillas in dampened paper towels and microwave on high power until warm and pliable, 1 to 3 minutes. Discard paper towels and wrap tortillas in a cloth napkin to keep warm.
▸ Transfer fish to a platter and serve immediately with coleslaw and warm tortillas for making tacos.

Cooks' note:
• For additional texture and color, instead of broiling the fish, sauté lightly floured fillets in a skillet with hot oil over high heat until lightly golden, about 2 minutes per side.

BROILED SALMON WITH CITRUS YOGURT SAUCE

SERVES 6

Active time: 20 min   Start to finish: 35 min

For salmon

- 1 (3-lb) piece salmon fillet with skin (1 inch thick at thickest part; preferably center cut)
- ⅜ teaspoon salt
- ¼ teaspoon black pepper

For sauce

- 1 cup low-fat plain Greek yogurt or plain whole-milk yogurt (see cooks' note, below)
- 2 tablespoons extra-virgin olive oil
- 2 tablespoons water
- 1 teaspoon finely grated fresh lime zest (see Tips, page 8)
- 1 tablespoon fresh lime juice
- ½ teaspoon finely grated fresh orange zest
- 1 teaspoon fresh orange juice
- ¾ teaspoon salt
- ¼ to ½ teaspoon mild honey (to taste)

Special equipment: pliers (preferably needlenose)
Accompaniment: lime wedges

▸ Preheat broiler. Line rack of broiler pan with foil and lightly oil foil.
▸ Pat fish dry and check for bones by running your hand over fish from thinnest to thickest end. Remove any bones with pliers. Put fish, skin sides down, on rack of broiler pan and sprinkle with salt and pepper, then broil 4 inches from heat 7 minutes. Cover fish loosely with foil and continue broiling until just cooked through, 7 to 9 minutes more.
▸ While salmon broils, whisk together all sauce ingredients in a bowl until combined.
▸ Serve salmon with sauce.

Cooks' note:
• If you can't find Greek yogurt, buy regular plain whole-milk yogurt and drain it in a sieve or colander lined with a double thickness of paper towels, chilled, 1 hour.

KITCHEN NOTE

GREEK YOGURT (MADE FROM SHEEP'S MILK) IS STRAINED, SO IT'S EXTREMELY DENSE AND MUCH RICHER TASTING THAN AMERICAN YOGURT (MADE FROM COW'S MILK). IF YOU CANNOT FIND IT, LOOK FOR GREEK-STYLE YOGURT—IT'S MADE IN AMERICA (USUALLY FROM COW'S MILK), IS INCREASINGLY AVAILABLE IN SUPERMARKETS, AND HAS MANY OF THE QUALITIES OF GREEK YOGURT.

SALMON WITH ENDIVE, DILL, AND CREAM

SERVES 4

Active time: 20 min   Start to finish: 20 min

- 4 (6- to 7-oz) center-cut pieces salmon fillet with skin (1¼ inches thick), any pin bones removed
- ¾ teaspoon salt
- ½ teaspoon black pepper
- 1 tablespoon olive oil
- ½ cup finely chopped shallots
- 2 large Belgian endives (½ lb total), quartered lengthwise, cored, and cut crosswise into ½-inch pieces
- ⅓ cup dry white wine
- 1 cup heavy cream
- 2 tablespoons chopped fresh dill
- 1 tablespoon fresh lemon juice

▸ Preheat broiler. Line rack of a broiler pan with foil, then lightly oil foil.
▸ Pat salmon dry, then arrange, skin sides down, on rack of broiler pan. Sprinkle with ½ teaspoon salt and ¼ teaspoon pepper, then broil 4 to 5 inches from heat until almost cooked through, about 6 minutes. Keep warm, loosely covered with foil. (Fish will cook through from residual heat.)
▸ Meanwhile, heat oil in a 12-inch heavy skillet over moderately high heat until hot but not smoking, then sauté shallots, stirring, 1 minute. Add endives and sauté, stirring, until softened, 3 to 4 minutes. Add wine and boil over high heat, stirring, until liquid is reduced to 1 tablespoon, about 1 minute. Add cream and remaining ¼ teaspoon each of salt and pepper and boil, stirring occasionally, until liquid is thickened and reduced by half, 3 to 4 minutes. Stir in dill, lemon juice, and salt to taste. Serve salmon with sauce.

BROILED MACKEREL WITH GINGER AND GARLIC

SERVES 4
Active time: 20 min   Start to finish: 40 min

- 4 (8-oz) mackerel fillets
- 2 tablespoons minced peeled fresh ginger
- 2 tablespoons minced garlic
- 2 tablespoons fresh lime juice
- 1 tablespoon vegetable oil
- 1½ teaspoons salt
- 1½ teaspoons chili powder (not pure chile powder)
- 1 teaspoon turmeric
- 1 cup loosely packed fresh cilantro sprigs

Accompaniment: **lime wedges**

▶ Put fillets, skin sides down, in a lightly oiled large shallow baking pan. Stir together ginger, garlic, lime juice, oil, salt, chili powder, and turmeric in a small bowl until combined well, then rub onto mackerel flesh and marinate 10 minutes.
▶ Preheat broiler. Broil mackerel 5 to 6 inches from heat, without turning, until cooked through and lightly browned, 7 to 8 minutes. Transfer to plates with 2 spatulas and top with cilantro.

MAHIMAHI WITH BROWN-SUGAR SOY GLAZE

SERVES 4
Active time: 15 min   Start to finish: 20 min

- 6 scallions
- 3 tablespoons packed brown sugar
- 2½ tablespoons soy sauce
- 3 tablespoons fresh lemon juice
- 4 (6-oz) pieces skinless mahimahi fillet
- ½ teaspoon salt
- 1½ tablespoons vegetable oil

▶ Preheat oven to 200°F.
▶ Cut white and pale green parts of scallions crosswise into 2-inch pieces, then thinly slice enough scallion greens to measure 3 tablespoons.
▶ Stir together brown sugar, soy sauce, and lemon juice in a small bowl until sugar is dissolved.

▶ Pat fish dry and sprinkle with salt. Heat oil in a 12-inch nonstick skillet over moderately high heat until hot but not smoking, then cook fish on 1 side until browned, 3 to 4 minutes. Turn fish over and brown 1 minute. Add soy sauce mixture and simmer, covered, until fish is almost cooked through, about 3 minutes. Transfer fish with a slotted spatula to a heatproof platter and keep warm in oven. (Fish will cook through from residual heat.)
▶ Add 2-inch scallion pieces and juices from fish platter to sauce and boil, stirring occasionally, until glaze is very thick and reduced to less than ¼ cup, about 5 minutes. Spoon glaze over fish and sprinkle with scallion greens.

SHELLFISH

MUSSELS IN LAGER

SERVES 2 (MAIN COURSE) OR 4 (FIRST COURSE)
Active time: 30 min   Start to finish: 30 min

- ½ stick (¼ cup) unsalted butter
- 1 medium onion, chopped (1 cup)
- 2 celery ribs, cut into ¼-inch dice (1 cup)
- 1 cup drained canned diced tomatoes (from a 14- to 15-oz can)
- 3 garlic cloves, finely chopped
- 1 teaspoon chopped fresh thyme
- 1 Turkish or ½ California bay leaf
- ½ teaspoon salt
- ¼ teaspoon black pepper
- 2 cups lager such as Harp (16 fl oz; pour beer slowly into a measure; do not measure foam)
- 2 lb mussels (preferably cultivated), scrubbed well and beards removed
- 1 tablespoon Dijon mustard
- 2 tablespoons heavy cream
- ¼ cup chopped fresh flat-leaf parsley

Accompaniment: **crusty bread**

▶ Heat butter in a wide 5- to 6-quart heavy pot over moderately high heat until foam subsides, then cook onion, celery, tomatoes, garlic, thyme, bay leaf, salt, and pepper, stirring occasionally, until vegetables are softened, about 4 minutes.

▶ Add beer and bring just to a boil. Add mussels and cook, covered, stirring occasionally, until mussels open wide, 4 to 6 minutes, transferring them to a bowl as they open. (Discard any mussels that remain unopened after 6 minutes.) Remove pot from heat. Stir together mustard and cream in a bowl, then add mixture along with parsley to hot broth and whisk until combined. Discard bay leaf. Serve sauce over mussels.

MUSSELS WITH TOMATO BROTH
SERVES 4
Active time: 25 min   Start to finish: 25 min (not including making tomato sauce)

  3   garlic cloves, finely chopped
¼   teaspoon dried hot red pepper flakes (optional)
  3   tablespoons extra-virgin olive oil
  1   cup dry white wine
  1   cup tomato sauce (recipe follows)
  4   lb mussels (preferably cultivated), scrubbed well
        and beards removed

▶ Cook garlic and red pepper flakes in oil in a 6- to 8-quart heavy pot over moderately low heat, stirring, until garlic is pale golden, 1 to 2 minutes. Add wine and boil over high heat 2 minutes. Add tomato sauce and mussels and cook over moderately high heat, covered, stirring occasionally, until mussels just open wide, 6 to 8 minutes. (Discard any mussels that remain unopened after 8 minutes.) Serve immediately.

TOMATO SAUCE
MAKES ABOUT 5 CUPS
Active time: 15 min   Start to finish: 1½ hr

  2   medium onions, finely chopped
  4   garlic cloves, finely chopped
  6   tablespoons extra-virgin olive oil
  2   (28- to 32-oz) cans whole tomatoes in juice
  1   teaspoon salt, or to taste
  1   teaspoon sugar (optional), or to taste

▶ Cook onions and garlic in oil in a 4- to 5-quart heavy pot over moderately low heat, stirring, until softened, 6 to 8 minutes.

▶ Add tomatoes, including juice, and salt, then simmer gently, uncovered, stirring and mashing tomatoes with a fork occasionally, until sauce is thickened and reduced to about 5 cups, 1 to 1¼ hours.
▶ If tomato sauce tastes too acidic, add sugar and cook 5 minutes more.

Cooks' note:
• Sauce can be made ahead and cooled completely, uncovered, then chilled, covered, 5 days or frozen in an airtight container up to 3 months.

SEA SCALLOPS WITH MUSHROOMS AND SHERRY
SERVES 4
Active time: 30 min   Start to finish: 30 min

20   large sea scallops (1½ lb), tough ligament
        removed if attached
⅛   teaspoon black pepper
½   teaspoon salt
  2   tablespoons olive oil
½   stick (¼ cup) unsalted butter
  1   lb cremini mushrooms, quartered
⅓   cup finely chopped shallots
  2   garlic cloves, finely chopped
⅔   cup medium-dry Sherry
  1   tablespoon balsamic vinegar
  1   tablespoon soy sauce

▶ Pat scallops dry. Sprinkle with pepper and ¼ teaspoon salt.
▶ Heat oil in a 12-inch heavy skillet over moderately high heat until hot but not smoking, then cook scallops, turning over once, until browned well and just cooked through, 5 to 7 minutes total. Transfer to a platter and loosely cover.
▶ Heat 2 tablespoons butter in skillet over moderately high heat until foam subsides, then sauté mushrooms, stirring occasionally, until golden, about 4 minutes. Add shallots and garlic and sauté, stirring, 2 minutes. Add Sherry, vinegar, soy sauce, and remaining ¼ teaspoon salt and simmer, uncovered, stirring occasionally, 2 minutes. Meanwhile, cut remaining 2 tablespoons butter into small pieces.
▶ Remove skillet from heat and stir in butter until incorporated. Spoon sauce over scallops.

GREEN CURRY SHRIMP WITH NOODLES

SERVES 4

Active time: 35 min   Start to finish: 40 min

      1 cup chopped shallots (about 4)
      2 fresh lemongrass stalks (optional), 1 or 2 outer leaves
          discarded and lower 6 inches of stalks thinly sliced
      2 large garlic cloves, chopped
      1 tablespoon chopped peeled fresh ginger
      1 tablespoon finely chopped fresh cilantro stems
      1 to 2 tablespoons bottled Asian green curry paste
   1½ teaspoons sugar
     ¾ teaspoon salt
     ½ teaspoon turmeric
     ¼ cup water
     ¼ cup plus 2 tablespoons vegetable oil
      1 (13- to 14-oz) can unsweetened coconut milk (not
          low-fat)
   1¾ cups reduced-sodium chicken broth (14 fl oz)
     ¾ lb dried flat ⅜-inch-wide rice noodles or ½ lb dried
          flat ⅛-inch-wide stir-fry rice noodles
   1½ lb peeled and deveined large shrimp (21 to 25 per lb)
      2 to 3 teaspoons Asian fish sauce, or to taste

Accompaniment: **fresh cilantro sprigs**

▸ Purée shallots, lemongrass, garlic, ginger, and cilantro
stems in a blender with curry paste, sugar, salt, turmeric,
and water until as smooth as possible, about 1 minute.
▸ Heat oil in a 4-quart wide heavy pot over moderate heat
until hot but not smoking, then cook curry paste mixture,
stirring frequently, until it just begins to stick to bottom of
pot, 8 to 10 minutes. Add coconut milk and broth and
simmer, uncovered, stirring occasionally, until reduced to
about 3⅔ cups, 8 to 10 minutes.
▸ While sauce simmers, cook noodles in a 6-quart pot of
boiling salted water (see Tips, page 8), uncovered, stirring
occasionally, until tender, 4 to 6 minutes. Drain in a colander
and rinse under cold water. Drain noodles well and divide
among 4 large bowls.
▸ Add shrimp to sauce and simmer, stirring, until just cooked
through, 2 to 3 minutes. Remove from heat and stir in fish
sauce and salt and pepper to taste. Ladle shrimp and sauce
over noodles.

SHRIMP AND TASSO GUMBO

SERVES 6

Active time: 1¼ hr   Start to finish: 2¼ hr

      2 lb large shrimp in shell (21 to 25 per lb), peeled and
          shells reserved
    14 cups water
     ¼ cup vegetable oil
     ½ cup all-purpose flour
      2 medium onions, chopped
      2 celery ribs, chopped
      1 large green bell pepper, chopped
     ½ lb fresh or frozen pork tasso (Cajun-cured smoked meat;
          see Sources), thawed if frozen, trimmed and cut into
          ¼-inch pieces
   1½ teaspoons salt
     ½ teaspoon cayenne
    10 oz fresh or frozen baby okra, thawed if frozen, trimmed,
          and cut into ¼-inch-thick rounds (2 cups)
     ¾ cup thinly sliced scallion greens

Accompaniments: **white rice; hot pepper sauce**

▸ Simmer shrimp shells and water, uncovered, in an 8-quart
pot until liquid is reduced to about 12 cups, 15 to 20
minutes, then pour through a sieve set over a large bowl
and discard shells.
▸ Stir together oil and flour in a 10-inch heavy skillet
(preferably cast-iron) with a flat metal or wooden spatula,
then cook over moderately low heat (do not use a high-BTU
burner), scraping back and forth constantly (not stirring)
until roux is the color of milk chocolate, 30 to 45 minutes.
(As roux cooks, it may be necessary to lower the heat to
prevent scorching.) Add onions, celery, and bell pepper and
cook, scraping back and forth occasionally, until onion is
softened, about 8 minutes.
▸ Scrape roux mixture into cleaned 8-quart pot, then add
shrimp stock and bring to a boil, stirring occasionally.
Reduce heat, then add tasso, salt, and cayenne and simmer,
uncovered, 30 minutes. Add okra and simmer until tender,
5 to 8 minutes. Stir in shrimp and simmer until just cooked
through, 2 to 3 minutes. Stir in scallion greens and salt
to taste.

Cooks' notes:

• Andouille or other smoked pork sausage can be substituted for the tasso. Brown the sausage in a heavy skillet over moderate heat, stirring occasionally, then transfer to paper towels to drain. Stir into gumbo with scallions.

• Gumbo improves in flavor if made 1 day ahead without okra, shrimp, and scallion greens and cooled completely, uncovered, then chilled, covered. Reheat, then proceed with recipe, adding and cooking okra and shrimp.

SHRIMP CURRY

SERVES 4

Active time: 30 min   Start to finish: 30 min

    1 large onion, quartered
    1 (2-inch-long) piece fresh ginger, peeled
  ½ teaspoon salt
  ½ teaspoon sugar
  ¼ cup vegetable oil
1½ teaspoons curry powder (preferably Madras)
    1 to 2 fresh serrano chiles, halved lengthwise
    1 cup water
    1 (14-oz) can unsweetened coconut milk (not low-fat)
    1 tablespoon fresh lime juice
    1 lb large shrimp in shell (21 to 25 per lb)

Accompaniment: **basmati rice**
Garnish: **lime wedges**

▶ Pulse onion and ginger in a food processor until finely chopped. Cook onion mixture with salt and sugar in oil in a 12-inch heavy skillet over moderate heat, stirring frequently, until onion begins to brown, about 5 minutes. Stir in curry powder and chiles and cook, stirring frequently, 2 minutes. Stir in water, coconut milk, and lime juice and simmer, stirring occasionally, until thickened, 5 to 8 minutes.
▶ While sauce simmers, peel shrimp (devein if desired) and season with salt and pepper. Add shrimp to sauce and simmer, stirring occasionally, until shrimp are just cooked through, about 3 minutes. Add salt to taste and serve immediately.

SHRIMP AND AVOCADO IN TAMARIND SAUCE

SERVES 4

Active time: 40 min   Start to finish: 40 min

  ¼ cup vegetable oil
    1 large shallot, thinly sliced and separated into rings
  ¼ cup tamarind pulp (from a pliable block; see Sources)
  ½ cup boiling-hot water
    2 tablespoons sugar
    1 tablespoon soy sauce
    1 tablespoon Asian fish sauce
    3 tablespoons fresh lime juice
    2 firm-ripe California avocados
    1 tablespoon minced peeled fresh ginger
    1 garlic clove, minced
    2 (1½- to 2-inch-long) fresh Thai chiles or 1 serrano, stemmed and minced (including seeds)
  ¼ teaspoon salt
    1 lb large shrimp in shell (21 to 25 per lb), peeled, leaving tail and first segment of shell intact, and deveined
  ⅓ cup roasted salted peanuts, chopped

Accompaniment: **jasmine rice**

Fry shallot and make tamarind sauce:

▶ Heat oil in a 1-quart heavy saucepan over moderate heat until hot but not smoking, then fry shallot, stirring, until golden brown, about 2 minutes. Transfer with a slotted spoon to paper towels to drain. Reserve oil.
▶ Soak tamarind pulp in boiling-hot water in a small bowl until softened, about 5 minutes. Force pulp through a sieve into a bowl, discarding solids. Add sugar, soy sauce, fish sauce, and 1½ tablespoons lime juice and stir until sugar is dissolved.

Cut avocados and cook shrimp:

▶ Halve, pit, and peel avocados. Cut into 1½-inch chunks and toss with remaining 1½ tablespoons lime juice in a bowl.
▶ Transfer reserved oil to a 12-inch heavy skillet and heat over moderately high heat until hot but not smoking, then sauté ginger, garlic, chiles, and salt, stirring constantly, until fragrant, about 30 seconds. Add shrimp and sauté, turning over once, 2 minutes total. Stir in tamarind mixture and simmer until shrimp are just cooked through, 2 minutes more.
▶ Spoon shrimp and avocado over rice, then sprinkle with peanuts and fried shallot.

BEEF

BROILED STEAK WITH HORSERADISH CREAM

SERVES 4

Active time: 10 min   Start to finish: 20 min

- 1   (1-inch-thick) sirloin steak (1½ to 2 lb)
- ¾   teaspoon salt
- ¾   teaspoon black pepper
- ½   cup sour cream
- 2   tablespoons drained bottled horseradish

▶ Preheat broiler.

▶ Pat steak dry and sprinkle all over with ½ teaspoon salt and ½ teaspoon pepper.

▶ Broil steak on oiled rack of broiler pan 3 inches from heat 4 to 5 minutes per side for medium-rare. Transfer to a cutting board and let stand, loosely covered with foil, 5 minutes before slicing.

▶ Stir together sour cream, horseradish, and remaining ¼ teaspoon salt and ¼ teaspoon pepper in a small bowl and serve with steak.

FILETS MIGNONS WITH ORANGE FENNEL CRUST

SERVES 4

Active time: 15 min   Start to finish: 20 min

- ¼   cup fine dry bread crumbs
- ½   teaspoon fennel seeds, coarsely chopped
- ½   teaspoon finely grated fresh orange zest (see Tips, page 8)
- 2   tablespoons olive oil
- ¾   teaspoon salt
- ½   teaspoon black pepper
- 4   (1¼-inch-thick) filets mignons (beef tenderloin steaks; about 7 oz each)
- 4   teaspoons Dijon mustard

▶ Put oven rack in upper third of oven and preheat oven to 500°F.

▶ Stir together bread crumbs, fennel seeds, zest, 1 tablespoon oil, ¼ teaspoon salt, and ¼ teaspoon pepper in a small bowl until combined well.

▶ Pat steaks dry, then sprinkle all over with remaining ½ teaspoon salt and ¼ teaspoon pepper. Heat remaining tablespoon oil in a 12-inch heavy ovenproof skillet over moderately high heat until hot but not smoking, then sear steaks until browned well on bottom, 3 to 4 minutes. Remove skillet from heat and turn steaks over with a spatula. Spread top of each steak with 1 teaspoon mustard, then sprinkle evenly with bread crumb mixture. Transfer skillet to oven and roast steaks, without turning over, 5 minutes for medium-rare.

SUNDAY RIB ROAST

SERVES 4 TO 6

Active time: 15 min   Start to finish: 2¼ hr

- 1   (2-rib) tied prime beef rib roast (from small end; about 4½ lb trimmed)
- 1½   tablespoons kosher salt
- 1   teaspoon black pepper
- 2   tablespoons all-purpose flour
- 1½   tablespoons English dry mustard (preferably Colman's)

Special equipment: **an instant-read thermometer**
Accompaniment: **onion gravy (page 268)**

▶ Put oven rack in lower third of oven and preheat oven to 450°F.

▶ Put beef, fat side up, in a small roasting pan and sprinkle all over with salt and pepper. Stir together flour and mustard, then pat onto top and sides of roast to form a thick coating.

▶ Roast beef 20 minutes. Reduce oven temperature to 350°F and roast until thermometer inserted into center of meat registers 115°F, about 1¼ hours more. Transfer beef to a cutting board and let stand, uncovered, 25 minutes before slicing. (Internal temperature will rise to 125°F for medium-rare while meat stands.)

BOEUF À LA MODE
(Braised Beef and Onions)

SERVES 8

Active time: 15 min   Start to finish: 2¾ hr

Like any pot roast, this one tastes even better made ahead and reheated. Drizzle the pan juices over steamed potatoes or serve the sliced meat over noodles.

  2 (2-lb) well-marbled boneless beef chuck pot roasts
       (1½ inches thick)
  2 teaspoons ground allspice
  2 teaspoons salt
  1 teaspoon black pepper
1½ lb onions, halved lengthwise, then thinly sliced
       lengthwise (6 cups)
  6 large garlic cloves, finely chopped
  2 tablespoons finely chopped fresh flat-leaf parsley

Special equipment: **heavy-duty foil**

▶ Put oven rack in middle position and preheat oven to 400°F.

▶ Pat meat dry. Stir together allspice, salt, and pepper in a small bowl and rub all over meat.

▶ Spread half of onions and half of garlic in a 13- by 9-inch roasting pan and arrange meat on top. Spread remaining onions and garlic over meat. Tightly cover pan with foil and roast, turning meat over after 1 hour, until meat is very tender, about 2½ hours total.

▶ Skim fat from pan juices. Slice meat across the grain and sprinkle with parsley. Serve with onions and pan juices.

Cooks' note:

• Beef can be braised 2 days ahead. Cool meat in juices, uncovered, then slice and chill in juices, covered. Reheat, covered, in a preheated 350°F oven 30 to 40 minutes.

RIB-EYE STEAK WITH WARM TOMATO CORN SALAD

SERVES 6 TO 8

Active time: 30 min   Start to finish: 40 min

  3 (12- to 14-oz) boneless rib-eye steaks (1½ inches thick)
1½ teaspoons salt
  ¾ teaspoon black pepper
  1 tablespoon olive oil
  2 tablespoons unsalted butter
  1 medium onion, chopped
  1 Italian frying pepper, seeded and chopped
  2 garlic cloves, finely chopped
  1 teaspoon chili powder (not pure chile powder)
  2 cups corn (from 4 large ears)
  ½ lb cherry or grape tomatoes, halved
  ¼ cup chopped fresh basil
  1 tablespoon fresh lime juice

▶ Pat steaks dry and sprinkle with salt and pepper.

▶ Heat oil in a 12-inch heavy skillet over moderately high heat until hot but not smoking, then sauté steaks, turning over once, 10 to 12 minutes total for medium-rare. Transfer to a plate and keep warm, covered with foil.

▶ Pour off fat from skillet, keeping any brown bits in skillet, and return to moderately high heat. Add butter, onion, and frying pepper and sauté, stirring occasionally and scraping up brown bits, until onion is golden, about 6 minutes. Add garlic and chili powder and sauté, stirring, 1 minute. Stir in corn and cover skillet. Cook until corn is just tender, about 3 minutes. Remove lid, then add tomatoes and sauté, stirring, until tomatoes just begin to soften, about 2 minutes. Remove from heat and stir in any meat juices accumulated on plate, basil, lime juice, and salt to taste.

▶ Transfer steaks to a cutting board, then cut across the grain into ½-inch-thick slices. Serve with tomato corn salad.

KITCHEN NOTE

BEEF CHUCK IS THE SHOULDER AND ARM OF THE STEER, FROM THE NECK ALL THE WAY BACK THROUGH THE FIRST FIVE RIBS. CUTS FROM THAT MASSIVE SECTION INCLUDE CHUCK ROASTS, POT ROASTS, AND SHORT RIBS. THEIR TOUGHNESS IS TAMED BY LONG, MOIST COOKING. MAKE SURE THE CUT IS WELL MARBLED; IF IT'S TOO LEAN OR TOO THIN, IT WILL BECOME DRY WHEN COOKED.

BEEF PINWHEELS WITH ARUGULA SALAD

SERVES 4

Active time: 30 min   Start to finish: 1 hr (includes soaking skewers)

  1   (1½-lb) piece flank steak
  3   tablespoons olive oil
  ¼   teaspoon black pepper
  ½   teaspoon salt
  ¼   lb very thinly sliced prosciutto
  ¼   lb thinly sliced provolone
  ¾   lb arugula, stems discarded

Special equipment: **8 to 10 (6-inch-long) wooden skewers, soaked in water 30 minutes**
Accompaniment: **lemon wedges**

▶ Cover work surface with plastic wrap and put steak on it with a short side of steak nearest you. Holding a sharp knife parallel to work surface and beginning on a long side, using short slicing motions, butterfly steak by cutting it horizontally almost, but not all the way, in half, then open it like a book.
▶ Cover steak with a double thickness of plastic wrap (about 2 feet long) and, using the flat side of a meat pounder (or using a rolling pin), gently pound meat ¼ inch thick.
▶ Discard top sheets of plastic wrap and turn steak on plastic wrap so grain of meat is running left to right, then rub 1 tablespoon oil onto steak and sprinkle with pepper and ¼ teaspoon salt. Arrange prosciutto in a slightly overlapping layer on steak, then cover with cheese.
▶ Beginning with side nearest you, using plastic wrap as an aid and pressing slightly on filling, roll up steak tightly, then skewer steak crosswise at 1-inch intervals. Using a sharp knife, cut between skewers to make 1-inch-thick pinwheels. (End pieces will be about 1½ inches thick. Trim if desired.)
▶ Prepare grill for cooking over medium-hot charcoal or moderate heat for gas (see Tips, page 8).
▶ Grill pinwheels, cut sides down, on well-oiled grill rack, covered only if using a gas grill, turning over once (use a metal spatula to loosen), until beef is well browned outside but still pink inside and cheese is beginning to melt, 6 to 8 minutes total.
▶ Toss arugula with remaining 2 tablespoons oil and remaining ¼ teaspoon salt in a large bowl. Serve on a platter, topped with pinwheels.

Cooks' notes:
• Pinwheels can be formed (but not cooked) 1 day ahead and chilled on a platter, loosely covered with plastic.
• If you aren't able to grill outdoors, pinwheels can be broiled on well-oiled rack of a broiler pan 4 to 6 inches from heat, turning over once, 6 to 8 minutes total.

KITCHEN NOTE

WE PREFER WELL-SEASONED CAST-IRON **GRILL PANS** TO THOSE WITH NONSTICK SURFACES AND GENERALLY AVOID USING NONSTICK COOKING SPRAYS, OPTING INSTEAD TO LIGHTLY BRUSH THE PANS WITH VEGETABLE OIL. AS A GENERAL RULE, FOODS THAT ARE LESS THAT 1 INCH THICK WORK BEST IN A STOVE-TOP GRILL PAN BECAUSE THEY COOK QUICKLY AND CREATE LESS SMOKE.

SKIRT STEAK WITH RED-WINE SAUCE

SERVES 4

Active time: 15 min   Start to finish: 20 min

1½   lb skirt steak, cut into 4 pieces
  ¾   teaspoon salt
  ¼   teaspoon black pepper
  1   tablespoon vegetable oil
  ¾   cup dry red wine
  4   fresh thyme sprigs
  1   Turkish or ½ California bay leaf
  1   teaspoon sugar
  ½   teaspoon Worcestershire sauce
  2   tablespoons cold unsalted butter, cut into small pieces

▶ Pat steak dry and sprinkle all over with salt and pepper. Heat oil in a 12-inch heavy skillet over moderately high heat until hot but not smoking, then cook steaks, turning over once, 5 to 7 minutes total for medium-rare. Transfer to a platter.
▶ Pour off fat from skillet, then add wine, thyme, bay leaf, sugar, and Worcestershire sauce and bring to a boil, scraping up any brown bits from bottom of skillet. Continue to boil until reduced by about half, about 3 minutes. Add any meat juices accumulated on platter, then remove skillet from heat and discard bay leaf and thyme. Stir in butter and salt and pepper to taste and serve with steaks.

STOUT-BRAISED SHORT RIBS

SERVES 6

Active time: 35 min   Start to finish: 4½ hr

¼ cup packed dark brown sugar
1 tablespoon paprika (not hot)
1 tablespoon curry powder (preferably Madras)
2 teaspoons ground cumin
2 teaspoons black pepper
2 teaspoons salt
1 teaspoon dry mustard
4 to 4¼ lb beef short ribs, cut into 4-inch pieces
4 medium leeks (white and pale green parts only), chopped (2 cups)
3 tablespoons olive oil
4 medium carrots, chopped (2 cups)
3 celery ribs, chopped (1½ cups)
2 Turkish bay leaves or 1 California
¼ cup chopped garlic (5 to 6 large cloves)
1¾ cups beef broth (14 fl oz)
2 (12-oz) bottles stout such as Mackeson or Guinness
2 (14- to 15-oz) cans diced tomatoes

Special Equipment: **a 6-qt wide heavy nonreactive pot with a lid (see cooks' note, below)**
Accompaniment: **buttered egg noodles tossed with chopped fresh parsley**

▶ Put oven rack in lower third of oven and preheat oven to 375°F.
▶ Stir together brown sugar, paprika, curry powder, cumin, pepper, salt, and mustard in a small bowl until combined.
▶ Pat ribs dry and arrange in 1 layer in a shallow baking pan or a shallow dish, then generously coat all sides of ribs with spice mixture. Marinate, uncovered and chilled, 1 hour.
▶ Wash leeks in a bowl of cold water, agitating them, then lift out leeks and drain in a colander.
▶ Heat oil in pot over high heat until hot but not smoking, then quickly brown ribs on all 3 meaty sides (but not bone side) without crowding, in batches if necessary, about 1 minute per side. Transfer meat to a large plate, then add leeks, carrots, celery, and bay leaves to pot and cook over moderately low heat, stirring occasionally, until vegetables begin to soften, about 3 minutes. Add garlic and cook, stirring, 1 minute.

▶ Add broth, beer, and tomatoes with their juice, then add ribs with any juices and remaining spices accumulated on plate and bring liquid to a boil, uncovered. Cover pot and transfer to oven, then braise until meat is very tender, 2 to 2½ hours.
▶ Skim excess fat from surface of sauce. Discard bay leaves.

Cooks' notes:
• Stainless steel, enameled cast iron, and glass are nonreactive, but avoid pure aluminum and uncoated iron.
• Short ribs improve in flavor if braised 1 day ahead and cooled completely, uncovered, then chilled, covered. Reheat, covered, in a 350°F oven until hot, 1 to 1½ hours.

KITCHEN NOTE

WE PREFER MILD TURKISH **BAY LEAVES** TO THE CALIFORNIA VARIETY, WHICH CAN TASTE ALMOST MEDICINAL. OUR RECIPES CALL FOR HALF THE AMOUNT OF CALIFORNIA BAY LEAVES AS TURKISH. REMOVE BAY LEAF FROM A DISH BEFORE SERVING; ITS SHARP EDGES CAN SCRATCH THE THROAT.

MEATLOAF

SERVES 6

Active time: 15 min   Start to finish: 1¼ hr

2 lb meatloaf mix (beef, pork, and veal)
1 cup cooked oatmeal
1 cup finely chopped onion
⅓ cup finely chopped fresh parsley
¼ cup soy sauce
2 large eggs
2 teaspoons finely chopped garlic
½ teaspoon dried thyme
½ teaspoon black pepper
½ cup chili sauce (ketchup-based)

▶ Put oven rack in middle position and preheat oven to 350°F.
▶ Mix together all ingredients except chili sauce using your hands. Transfer mixture to a 13- by 9-inch glass baking dish and mound into a 10- by 5-inch oval loaf. Spread chili sauce over meatloaf and bake 1 hour.

CHIPOTLE BURGERS

SERVES 4

Active time: 20 min   Start to finish: 25 min

2   tablespoons canned chipotle chiles in *adobo*,
      including sauce
1   lb ground beef chuck
½   cup finely chopped onion
1   teaspoon salt
4   English muffins or hamburger buns, halved horizontally

▸ Prepare grill for cooking over medium-hot charcoal or moderate heat for gas (see Tips, page 8.)
▸ Meanwhile, open any whole chipotles and discard seeds, then mince chipotles.
▸ Mix chipotles (with sauce), beef, onion, and salt with your hands, then form mixture into 4 (¾-inch-thick) patties.
▸ Grill burgers on lightly oiled grill rack, covered only if using gas grill, turning over once, 4 minutes total for medium-rare. Grill English muffins, cut sides down, until grill marks appear, about 30 seconds. Serve burgers in English muffins.

Cooks' note:
• If you aren't able to grill outdoors, burgers can be cooked in a hot well-seasoned ridged grill pan over moderately high heat, turning over once, about 7 minutes total for medium-rare.

PORK

GRILLED JERK PORK WITH CURRIED PEACH RELISH

SERVES 6

Active time: 50 min   Start to finish: 10 hr (includes marinating)

For relish
1½   lb firm-ripe peaches
½   lb tomatoes
½   cup chopped red onion (1 medium)
1   tablespoon minced peeled fresh ginger
1   teaspoon kosher salt
1   tablespoon vegetable oil
1½   teaspoons curry powder
2   tablespoons sugar
1   tablespoon fresh lime juice

For pork
3   scallions (white and pale green parts only), trimmed
1   tablespoon chopped fresh thyme
2   teaspoons kosher salt
½   teaspoon ground allspice
¼   teaspoon black pepper
2   tablespoons fresh lime juice
1   tablespoon molasses (not robust or blackstrap)
1   teaspoon Scotch bonnet or habanero hot sauce
      (see Sources), or to taste
2   pork tenderloins (1¾ to 2 lb total)
2   tablespoons vegetable oil for basting

Special equipment: **an instant-read thermometer**

Make relish:
▸ Cut a shallow X in bottom of each peach and tomato with a sharp paring knife and blanch in 2 batches in a 4-quart pot of boiling water 10 seconds. Transfer peaches and tomatoes with a slotted spoon to a bowl of ice and cold water and let stand until cool enough to handle. Peel peaches and tomatoes, then halve peaches lengthwise and pit. Cut peaches into 1-inch pieces. Coarsely chop tomatoes.
▸ Cook onion, ginger, and salt in oil in a 3-quart heavy saucepan over moderate heat, stirring occasionally, until softened, 3 to 4 minutes. Add curry powder and cook, stirring constantly, 1 minute. Add peaches and tomatoes with any juices, sugar, and lime juice and simmer, uncovered, stirring occasionally, until mixture is thick and peaches are tender but still hold their shape, about 8 minutes. Transfer to a bowl and cool, uncovered, then chill, covered, at least 8 hours.

Marinate pork:
▸ Combine scallions, thyme, salt, allspice, pepper, lime juice, molasses, and hot sauce in a blender and blend until smooth. Put pork in a glass dish and rub all over with marinade. Marinate, covered and chilled, turning occasionally, 8 hours. Bring to room temperature before grilling.

Grill pork:
▸ Prepare grill for cooking over medium-hot charcoal or moderate heat for gas (see Tips, page 8).
▸ Discard any marinade remaining in dish, then brush pork lightly with oil and grill on lightly oiled grill rack, turning occasionally and basting frequently with oil, until thermometer inserted diagonally into center of meat registers 145°F, 15 to 25 minutes.

▶ Transfer pork to a cutting board and let stand 15 minutes before slicing. (Internal temperature will rise to about 155°F.) Serve pork with relish.

Cooks' notes:

• If you aren't able to grill outdoors, pork can be cooked in a hot lightly oiled well-seasoned large ridged grill pan until thermometer inserted diagonally into center of meat registers 145°F, 15 to 25 minutes.

• Relish can be made 1 week ahead and chilled, covered. Bring to room temperature before serving.

• Both the peach relish and the pork benefit from an overnight rest in the refrigerator; the relish mellows in flavor, and the pork becomes even more tender in the fiery marinade.

BBQ PORK TENDERLOIN

SERVES 4

Active time: 25 min   Start to finish: 35 min

1   lb pork tenderloin
1   medium onion, chopped
2   tablespoons olive oil
1   garlic clove, minced
¼   cup ketchup
¼   cup ketchup-style chili sauce
1   tablespoon Worcestershire sauce
2   teaspoons cider vinegar
½   teaspoon hot sauce such as Tabasco
1   cup water

Accompaniment: coleslaw

▶ Trim pork of excess fat and silver skin, then cut crosswise into ¼-inch-thick slices. Cut each slice into 3 strips.
▶ Cook onion in oil in a 4-quart heavy pot over moderate heat, stirring occasionally, until golden, about 5 minutes. Add garlic and cook, stirring, 1 minute. Add ketchup, chili sauce, Worcestershire sauce, vinegar, hot sauce, and water and simmer, uncovered, stirring occasionally, about 5 minutes.
▶ Add pork and simmer, covered, until pork is cooked through and tender, 8 to 10 minutes. Transfer pork with a slotted spoon to a bowl and cover to keep warm. Boil remaining sauce, stirring occasionally, until slightly thickened, about 3 minutes. Pour sauce over pork.

ORANGE-SOY-BRAISED PORK RIBS

SERVES 4 TO 6

Active time: 30 min   Start to finish: 3 hr

4   lb country-style pork ribs
½   teaspoon salt
1½   cups fresh orange juice
½   cup soy sauce
2   tablespoons sugar
2   tablespoons finely chopped peeled fresh ginger
1   tablespoon minced garlic (3 cloves)
½   teaspoon coarsely ground black pepper

Special equipment: a 17- by 11-inch flameproof roasting pan

▶ Put oven rack in middle position and preheat oven to 325°F.
▶ Sprinkle ribs evenly with salt.
▶ Bring orange juice, soy sauce, sugar, ginger, garlic, and pepper to a boil in roasting pan over moderately high heat, stirring until sugar is dissolved. Add ribs in 1 layer using tongs, turning to coat, and cover pan tightly with foil.
▶ Braise ribs in oven until very tender, about 2 hours. (If making ahead, see cooks' note, below.)
Before serving:
▶ Reduce oven temperature to 200°F.
▶ Transfer ribs to a baking dish, arranging them in 1 layer, and keep warm in oven.
▶ Skim fat from cooking liquid if desired, then make glaze by boiling liquid, uncovered, stirring occasionally, until syrupy and reduced to about ¾ cup, about 15 minutes. Brush glaze generously on ribs.

Cooks' note:

• Ribs can be braised 5 days ahead and cooled completely in cooking liquid, uncovered, then chilled, covering them once they are completely cold. To reheat, set roasting pan with ribs and cooking liquid over moderate heat, covered with foil. Simmer, covered, turning over once, until they are heated through, about 15 minutes, then transfer ribs to a baking dish and keep warm. Make glaze as directed.

PORK CHOPS WITH MUSTARD SAUCE

SERVES 4
Active time: 25 min   Start to finish: 25 min

- 4 (¾-inch-thick) pork chops
- ¾ teaspoon salt
- ½ teaspoon black pepper
- 2 tablespoons vegetable oil
- ¼ cup finely chopped shallots (1 to 2)
- 2 tablespoons unsalted butter
- ½ cup reduced-sodium chicken broth
- ¼ cup country-style Dijon mustard
- 2 tablespoons heavy cream
- 2 teaspoons fresh lemon juice

▶Put oven rack in middle position and preheat oven to 325°F.

▶Heat a dry 12-inch heavy skillet over moderately high heat until hot. Pat pork dry and sprinkle all over with salt and pepper. Add oil to hot skillet, swirling to coat, then brown chops, turning over once, about 8 minutes total. Transfer to a shallow baking pan, reserving skillet, and bake, uncovered, until cooked through, about 5 minutes. Let stand, loosely covered with foil, 5 minutes.

▶Meanwhile, pour off fat from skillet, then cook shallots in butter over moderate heat, stirring, until softened, 3 to 5 minutes. Add broth and any juices from baking pan and boil, scraping up any brown bits, 2 minutes. Add mustard and cream and return to a boil, then add lemon juice and simmer until sauce is slightly thickened, about 3 minutes.

▶Serve pork with sauce.

VIETNAMESE CARAMELIZED GRILLED PORK

SERVES 4
Active time: 20 min   Start to finish: 20 min

- 6 (¼-inch-thick) boneless pork loin chops
- ⅓ cup sugar
- ¼ cup finely chopped shallots (about 2)
- 1 tablespoon fresh lime juice
- 1 tablespoon Asian fish sauce
- ½ teaspoon salt

Accompaniment: **Vietnamese Rice Noodle Salad (page 265)**

▶Pound chops between 2 large sheets of plastic wrap with flat side of a meat pounder or with a rolling pin until less than ⅛ inch thick. Make several small ¼-inch-deep slits around edge of each chop to prevent curling, then halve chops lengthwise and transfer to a bowl.

▶Cook sugar in a dry 1-quart heavy saucepan over moderate heat, undisturbed, until it begins to melt. Continue to cook, stirring occasionally with a wooden spoon, until sugar is melted into a golden caramel. Add shallots, lime juice, fish sauce, and salt (caramel will harden) and cook, stirring constantly, until caramel is dissolved and shallots are softened, about 2 minutes. Pour sauce over pork and toss until coated well.

▶Heat a lightly oiled well-seasoned ridged grill pan over moderately high heat until hot but not smoking, then grill pork in batches, turning over once, until just cooked through, about 2 minutes per batch. (Discard any remaining sauce.)

STIR-FRIED PORK AND NAPA CABBAGE

SERVES 4
Active time: 45 min   Start to finish: 45 min

- 1 (1-lb) pork tenderloin
- 2½ tablespoons soy sauce
- 4 teaspoons cornstarch
- 1½ tablespoons sugar
- 2 tablespoons rice vinegar (not seasoned)
- ½ teaspoon salt
- 2 tablespoons water
- 2 lb Napa cabbage, quartered lengthwise, cored, and cut crosswise into 1½-inch pieces (10 cups)
- 2 tablespoons vegetable oil
- 1 tablespoon finely chopped garlic
- 1 tablespoon finely chopped peeled fresh ginger
- ¼ cup loosely packed fresh cilantro leaves

Accompaniment: **rice**

▶Trim off and discard any silver skin from pork (do not trim fat). Cut pork across grain into ¼-inch-thick slices, then toss with 1 tablespoon soy sauce, 2 teaspoons cornstarch, and 1 tablespoon sugar in a bowl.

▶Stir together vinegar, salt, remaining 1½ tablespoons soy sauce, and remaining ½ tablespoon sugar in a small bowl.

▶Stir together water and remaining 2 teaspoons cornstarch.

▸ Rinse cabbage in a large colander. Tap colander lightly, then transfer cabbage to a large bowl with water still clinging to leaves.

▸ Heat 1 tablespoon oil in a 12-inch nonstick skillet over high heat until hot but not smoking, then add pork in 1 layer as quickly as possible. Cook, undisturbed, until pork begins to brown, about 3 minutes, then turn over and cook, undisturbed, until browned but still pink in center, about 1 minute more. Transfer pork and any juices to a plate. Do not clean skillet.

▸ Heat remaining tablespoon oil in skillet over moderately high heat until hot but not smoking, then stir-fry garlic and ginger 30 seconds. Add half of cabbage and stir-fry over high heat until cabbage is wilted, 2 to 3 minutes. Stir in remaining cabbage (skillet will be very full) along with any water in bowl and soy sauce mixture, then cook, covered, stirring occasionally, until all of cabbage is tender, 4 to 5 minutes.

▸ Add pork along with any juices accumulated on plate and bring to a boil. Stir cornstarch mixture, then pour into skillet and boil, stirring, until sauce is slightly thickened, about 1 minute. Season with salt, then serve sprinkled with cilantro.

ITALIAN SAUSAGE WITH RED GRAPES

SERVES 6

Active time: 25 min   Start to finish: 25 min

  2   tablespoons olive oil
  2   lb sweet Italian sausage (about twelve 3- to 4-inch links)
  2   lb seedless red grapes, stemmed
  ¼   cup balsamic vinegar

Accompaniment: **sautéed greens with garlic**

▸ Heat oil in a 12-inch heavy skillet over moderate heat until hot but not smoking, then cook sausages, turning over once, until well browned, about 8 minutes total. Add grapes and cook, stirring occasionally, until sausages are cooked through and grapes are softened, 10 to 12 minutes. Stir in vinegar and salt and pepper to taste.

GRILLED ITALIAN SAUSAGE WITH WARM PEPPER AND ONION SALAD

SERVES 4

Active time: 45 min   Start to finish: 45 min

Luganega, a coiled slender Italian pork sausage, is sold at Italian markets and some supermarkets. If you can't find it, substitute any fresh Italian sausage.

  3   mixed large bell peppers, trimmed and quartered lengthwise
  1   large red onion, quartered lengthwise and separated into layers
  3   tablespoons extra-virgin olive oil
1½   tablespoons red-wine vinegar
  ½   teaspoon dried oregano, crumbled
  ½   teaspoon salt
  ⅛   teaspoon black pepper
  1   lb *luganega* or other fresh Italian sausage

Special equipment: **a perforated grill sheet (see Sources); 2 (10- to 12-inch-long) wooden or metal skewers**

▸ Prepare grill for cooking over medium-hot charcoal or moderate heat for gas (see Tips, page 8).

▸ Toss peppers and onion with 1 tablespoon oil. Grill on lightly oiled grill sheet set directly on grill rack, with grill covered only if using a gas grill, turning occasionally, until slightly softened and charred, 9 to 15 minutes (onion will cook faster), transferring to a bowl as cooked.

▸ Add vinegar, oregano, salt, pepper, and remaining 2 tablespoons oil to peppers and onion, tossing to coat. Let stand 10 minutes to allow flavors to develop.

▸ While vegetables stand, run skewers crisscrossed horizontally through sausage coil, securing ends. Grill directly over medium-hot charcoal (moderate heat for gas) on lightly oiled grill rack, covered only if using a gas grill, turning over once, until cooked through, 10 to 12 minutes total. (Thicker sausage may take longer.)

▸ Transfer vegetables to a platter and top with sausage.

Cooks' note:

• If you aren't able to grill outdoors, vegetables and sausage can be cooked in a hot lightly oiled well-seasoned ridged grill pan over moderately high heat.

POTATO- AND CHORIZO-STUFFED ANCHO CHILES

SERVES 4 (MAIN COURSE) OR 8 (FIRST COURSE)
Active time: 50 min   Start to finish: 9½ hr (includes soaking)

    8 large dried ancho chiles (3 to 4 oz total)
    1 (14- to 15-oz) can stewed tomatoes (with juice)
    ¾ teaspoon salt
    2 medium russet (baking) potatoes (1 lb total)
    ¼ lb Spanish chorizo (cured spiced pork sausage; not
        picante; see Sources), casing discarded and sausage
        finely chopped (1 cup)
    ¾ lb Monterey Jack cheese, cut into ⅓-inch cubes
        (2⅓ cups)

Special equipment: **an electric coffee/spice grinder**

▸ Rinse chiles, then cover with cold water in a bowl and soak, weighted with a sieve (to keep submerged), until completely rehydrated (most will turn a brighter red), about 8 hours. Do not drain chiles.
▸ Put oven rack in middle position and preheat oven to 350°F.
▸ Remove 1 chile from soaking liquid and, working over chile bowl and sieve, cut a slit down one side with scissors and let interior liquid and loose seeds drain into sieve. Carefully cut out seedpod, leaving stem intact and letting any easily loosened seeds fall into sieve, then discard seedpod. Repeat with remaining chiles, arranging seeded chiles, cut sides up, in 1 layer in a 13- by 9- by 2-inch (3-quart) baking dish.
▸ Reserve 1 cup chile-soaking liquid for sauce. Turn chile seeds out of sieve into a shallow baking pan and spread evenly, then toast in oven, stirring occasionally, until dry, fragrant, and a few shades darker, 8 to 10 minutes. Cool seeds in pan on a rack, then finely grind in grinder (you will have about 1 tablespoon).
▸ Purée tomatoes, including juice from can, in a blender with reserved soaking water, ground chile seeds, and ½ teaspoon salt until smooth, then transfer to a 3-quart heavy saucepan and boil, stirring occasionally, until sauce is thickened slightly and reduced to about 2 cups, 5 to 7 minutes.
▸ Peel potatoes and cut into ⅓-inch cubes (about 2½ cups). Cook in a 3-quart pot of boiling salted water (see Tips, page 8), uncovered, until tender but not falling apart, 6 to 8 minutes. Drain in a colander and rinse under cold water to stop cooking.

▸ Stir together potatoes, chorizo, cheese, and remaining ¼ teaspoon salt in a bowl, then fill chiles generously with stuffing (about ½ cup each; slit will not close over it). Pour sauce around (not over) chiles, then cover dish with foil and bake until sauce is bubbling all over, 35 to 45 minutes.

Cooks' note:
• Dish can be assembled (but not baked) up to 1 day ahead. Keep stuffed chiles in sauce chilled, covered. Add 5 to 10 minutes to baking time.

KITCHEN NOTE
ANCHO CHILE, THE DRIED FORM OF THE POBLANO, IS BRICK RED TO DARK MAHOGANY IN COLOR. IT IS WRINKLED AND MEDIUM-HOT TO HOT, WITH A COMPLEX, RAISINY FLAVOR. LOOK FOR ANCHOS THAT ARE PLIABLE AND AROMATIC.

LAMB

ROSEMARY LAMB CHOPS WITH SWISS CHARD AND BALSAMIC SYRUP

SERVES 4
Active time: 35 min   Start to finish: 35 min

For balsamic syrup
    ¾ cup balsamic vinegar
    ¼ teaspoon minced fresh rosemary
    ⅛ teaspoon black peppercorns
For chard
    1 bunch Swiss chard (1 lb)
    ¼ cup chopped red onion
    1 teaspoon finely chopped garlic
    1 tablespoon olive oil
    ½ teaspoon salt
    ¼ teaspoon black pepper
    1 tablespoon water
For lamb chops
    8 rib lamb chops (1¼ lb total), trimmed of all fat
    1 teaspoon finely chopped garlic
    ½ teaspoon salt
    ½ teaspoon finely chopped fresh rosemary
    ¼ teaspoon black pepper

Make syrup:

▶ Simmer all syrup ingredients in a 1- to 1½-quart nonreactive saucepan over moderate heat until just syrupy and reduced to about ¼ cup, about 8 minutes. Pour through a sieve into a small bowl, discarding rosemary and peppercorns.

Sauté chard:

▶ Cut stems and center ribs from chard leaves, discarding any tough portions, then cut stems and ribs into ¼-inch-thick slices. Stack chard leaves and roll into cylinders. Cut cylinders crosswise to make 1-inch-wide strips.

▶ Cook onion and garlic in oil in a 12-inch nonstick skillet over moderate heat, stirring occasionally, until onion begins to soften, about 4 minutes. Add chard stems and ribs, salt, and pepper and cook, stirring occasionally, until stems are just tender, about 6 minutes. Stir in chard leaves and water and cook, stirring occasionally, until tender, about 8 minutes.

Broil chops while chard cooks:

▶ Preheat broiler. Sprinkle chops with garlic, salt, rosemary, and pepper, then broil on a lightly oiled broiler pan, 4 to 5 inches from heat, turning over once, 6 to 7 minutes total for medium-rare. Serve chops and chard drizzled with syrup.

Cooks' note:

• Stainless steel and enameled cast iron are nonreactive, but avoid pure aluminum and uncoated iron.

EACH SERVING ABOUT 263 CALORIES AND 14 GRAMS FAT

TURKISH-STYLE LAMB BURGERS WITH WALNUT SAUCE

SERVES 4

Active time: 25 min   Start to finish: 45 min

For burgers

- 1 cup boiling-hot water
- ⅓ cup bulgur
- ¾ teaspoon salt
- 1 medium onion, quartered
- ¼ cup packed fresh cilantro leaves
- ¼ cup packed fresh flat-leaf parsley leaves
- 1 lb ground lamb
- ½ teaspoon paprika (not hot)
- ¼ teaspoon ground allspice
- ¼ teaspoon black pepper
- ¼ teaspoon cayenne

For sauce

- 1 small garlic clove
- ⅛ teaspoon salt
- ½ cup walnuts (1½ oz)
- ¼ cup water
- 1 teaspoon fresh lemon juice
- ⅛ teaspoon cayenne

For pitas

- 4 (4-inch) pita loaves
- 1 tablespoon olive oil
  Paprika (not hot) for dusting

Garnish: **fresh cilantro sprigs**

Soak bulgur for burgers:

▶ Pour boiling-hot water over bulgur with ½ teaspoon salt in a small bowl and soak 15 minutes, then drain in a sieve.

Make sauce while bulgur soaks:

▶ Mince garlic and mash to a paste with salt (⅛ teaspoon) using a large heavy knife, then transfer to a food processor and blend with remaining sauce ingredients until smooth. Transfer to a bowl.

Prepare burgers:

▶ Preheat broiler.

▶ Pulse onion and herbs in cleaned processor until finely chopped, then transfer to a bowl and stir in bulgur, lamb, paprika, allspice, pepper, cayenne, and remaining ¼ teaspoon salt until just combined. Form lamb mixture into 4 patties (4 inches in diameter).

Broil pitas and burgers:

▶ Arrange pitas on a baking sheet. Brush with oil, then lightly dust with paprika and season with pepper. Broil on lowest rack until toasted, 1 to 3 minutes (watch to prevent burning). Keep pitas warm, loosely covered with foil, while broiling burgers.

▶ Oil rack of a broiler pan and heat 4 inches from heat until hot, 3 to 5 minutes.

▶ Broil burgers on rack of broiler pan, turning over once, until cooked through, 5 to 7 minutes total. Serve burgers on pitas, topped with sauce.

LAMB AND POLENTA "LASAGNE"

SERVES 4

Active time: 25 min   Start to finish: 1¼ hr

- 2   (14- to 15-oz) cans stewed tomatoes
- ¾   teaspoon salt
- ½   plus ⅛ teaspoon ground allspice
- ¼   teaspoon black pepper
- 1   lb ground lamb (not lean)
- 1   lb ready-made plain polenta (in a plastic-wrapped roll)
- ½   lb whole-milk mozzarella, coarsely grated (about 1 cup)

▶ Put oven rack in middle position and preheat oven to 400°F.

▶ Drain 1 can tomatoes, reserving juice, then roughly break up tomatoes into ½-inch pieces with a spoon if necessary.

▶ Purée second can of tomatoes, including juice, with reserved juice (from other can), ¼ teaspoon salt, and ⅛ teaspoon allspice in a blender until smooth. Transfer tomato sauce to a 2-quart heavy saucepan and boil, uncovered, stirring occasionally, until reduced to about ½ cup, about 20 minutes. Remove from heat.

▶ Heat a dry 12-inch heavy skillet over moderate heat until hot, then brown lamb with pepper and remaining ½ teaspoon each of salt and allspice, stirring and breaking up lumps (but leaving meat slightly chunky), about 5 minutes. Add drained tomatoes and cook, stirring occasionally, until juices are absorbed, about 1 minute.

▶ Cut polenta into ¼-inch-thick slices with a sharp knife and cover bottom of a 9-inch ceramic or glass pie plate with half of polenta slices (overlapping slightly). Scatter half of lamb mixture over polenta, then top with half of mozzarella, then remaining polenta. Scatter remaining lamb on top and spread tomato sauce over meat, then top with remaining mozzarella.

▶ Bake, uncovered, until bubbling and beginning to brown, about 20 minutes. Let stand, loosely covered with foil, 15 minutes before serving.

CHICKEN

PAN-SEARED CHICKEN WITH TARRAGON BUTTER SAUCE

SERVES 4 TO 6

Active time: 30 min   Start to finish: 30 min

¼   cup finely chopped shallot (1 large)
½   stick (¼ cup) unsalted butter, cut into ½-inch cubes
⅓   cup dry white wine
2   lb thin-sliced skinless boneless chicken breasts (also called cutlets)
¾   teaspoon salt
⅜   teaspoon black pepper
3   tablespoons olive oil
¼   cup chopped fresh tarragon
1   tablespoon finely chopped fresh flat-leaf parsley
2   teaspoons fresh lemon juice

▶ Cook shallot in 1 tablespoon butter in a small heavy saucepan over moderate heat, stirring occasionally, until softened, about 2 minutes. Add wine and boil until most of liquid is evaporated, about 3 minutes. Set aside.

▶ Pat chicken dry and sprinkle all over with ½ teaspoon salt and ¼ teaspoon pepper. Heat oil in a 12-inch heavy skillet over moderately high heat until hot but not smoking, then sauté chicken in 3 or 4 batches, turning over once, until golden and just cooked through, about 2 minutes per batch. Transfer as cooked to a platter and keep warm, loosely covered with foil.

▶ Return shallot mixture to moderately low heat and add remaining 3 tablespoons butter, 1 cube at a time, whisking until incorporated. Remove from heat and whisk in tarragon, parsley, lemon juice, remaining ¼ teaspoon salt, and remaining ⅛ teaspoon pepper. Spoon sauce over chicken.

ROAST CHICKEN DINNER

SERVES 4

Active time: 15 min   Start to finish: 50 min

1   (3- to 3½-lb) chicken, quartered (see cooks' note, below) and wing tips discarded
2   tablespoons olive oil
2¼   teaspoons salt
1¾   teaspoons black pepper
1   lb boiling potatoes, cut into 1-inch wedges
2   zucchini (1 lb total), quartered lengthwise, then cut crosswise into 2½- to 3-inch lengths
1   medium onion, halved lengthwise, then cut crosswise into ¼-inch-thick slices
½   cup reduced-sodium chicken broth
1   tablespoon fresh lemon juice

Special equipment: a 17- by 12-inch flameproof roasting pan
Garnish: lemon wedges

▶ Put oven rack in upper third of oven and preheat oven to 500°F.

▶ Pat chicken dry, then toss with 1 tablespoon oil, 1¼ teaspoons salt, and 1 teaspoon pepper in a bowl. Arrange chicken, skin sides up, without pieces touching, in roasting pan, leaving a 2-inch border around edges of pan.

▶ Toss potatoes, zucchini, and onion with remaining tablespoon oil, remaining teaspoon salt, and remaining ¾ teaspoon pepper in same bowl, then spread in 1 layer around chicken, arranging zucchini skin sides up. Stir together broth and lemon juice and pour around chicken and vegetables.

▶ Roast, uncovered, until chicken is pale golden and cooked through, about 30 minutes.

▶ Remove pan from oven and preheat broiler. Broil chicken and vegetables 3 inches from heat until chicken is golden brown, about 6 minutes. Serve chicken and vegetables with pan juices.

Cooks' note:
• If you don't want to quarter a whole chicken, you can buy precut chicken quarters.

ROAST CHICKEN AND ASPARAGUS WITH TAHINI SAUCE

SERVES 4

Active time: 30 min   Start to finish: 30 min

2   lb asparagus, cut into 2-inch pieces
3   tablespoons olive oil
1¼ teaspoons salt
½   teaspoon black pepper
4   skinless boneless chicken breast halves (3 to 4 lb total)
⅓   cup well-stirred tahini (Middle Eastern sesame paste)
⅓   cup water
2   tablespoons fresh lemon juice
1   teaspoon sugar
1   garlic clove, minced

▸ Put oven racks in middle and lower thirds of oven and preheat oven to 450°F.
▸ Toss asparagus with 1 tablespoon oil, ¼ teaspoon salt, and ¼ teaspoon pepper in a 15- by 10-inch shallow baking pan. Roast on bottom rack, shaking pan once or twice, until just tender, about 10 minutes.
▸ Meanwhile, pat chicken dry and sprinkle all over with ½ teaspoon salt and remaining ¼ teaspoon pepper. Heat remaining 2 tablespoons oil in a 12-inch heavy ovenproof skillet (not nonstick) over moderately high heat until hot but not smoking, then brown chicken, turning over once, until golden, about 6 minutes total. Transfer skillet to middle of oven and roast until chicken is just cooked through, about 5 minutes.
▸ While chicken roasts, purée tahini, water, lemon juice, sugar, garlic, and remaining ½ teaspoon salt in a blender until smooth, about 1 minute. (Add more water if sauce is too thick.)
▸ Serve chicken and asparagus drizzled with some of sauce and with remaining sauce on the side.

KITCHEN NOTE

TAHINI, A MIDDLE EASTERN PASTE MADE OF SESAME SEEDS, SEPARATES WHEN IT SITS—THE OIL RISES TO THE TOP AND THE DENSE PASTE SETTLES TO THE BOTTOM—SO YOU MUST STIR IT BEFORE YOU USE IT. TAHINI CAN GO OFF, SO BUY IT FROM A PLACE WITH A HIGH TURNOVER, SUCH AS A MIDDLE EASTERN MARKET OR NATURAL FOODS STORE.

GRILLED LEMON CHICKEN

SERVES 4 TO 6

Active time: 30 min   Start to finish: 10 hr (includes marinating)

1   tablespoon finely grated fresh lemon zest (see Tips, page 8)
½   cup fresh lemon juice
½   cup vegetable oil
1   large egg
1   tablespoon salt
1   teaspoon poultry seasoning
¼   teaspoon white pepper
1   (3½-lb) chicken, cut into 8 serving pieces

Make marinade:
▸ Combine all ingredients except chicken in a blender and blend until emulsified.
Prepare chicken:
▸ Put chicken pieces in a large sealable plastic bag. Add marinade, then seal bag, forcing out excess air, and turn chicken once or twice to coat. Marinate, chilled, at least 8 hours. Bring chicken to room temperature 30 minutes before grilling and discard marinade.
To cook chicken using a charcoal grill:
▸ Open vents on bottom of grill and on lid. Light a large chimney starter of charcoal (80 to 100 briquettes). Leaving about one quarter of grill free of charcoal, bank lit charcoal across rest of grill so that coals are about 3 times higher on opposite side.
▸ When charcoal turns grayish white (15 to 20 minutes) and you can hold your hand 5 inches above rack for 3 to 4 seconds, sear chicken on lightly oiled grill rack over coals, uncovered, turning over occasionally, until browned, 4 to 8 minutes total. Move chicken to side of grill with no coals underneath and cook, covered with lid, turning over occasionally, until just cooked through, about 12 minutes for wings, 18 to 20 minutes for breasts, and 20 to 28 minutes for dark meat. Transfer chicken as cooked to a platter.
To cook chicken using a gas grill:
▸ Preheat all burners on high, covered, 10 minutes, then adjust heat to moderately high. Sear chicken on lightly oiled grill rack, uncovered, turning over once, until well browned, 4 to 8 minutes total. Turn off 1 burner (middle burner if there are 3) and arrange chicken on rack above shut-off burner. Cook, covered with lid and turning over occasionally, until just cooked through, about 12 minutes for wings, 18 to

20 minutes for breasts, and 20 to 28 minutes for dark meat. Transfer chicken as cooked to a platter.

Cooks' notes:

• Chicken can be marinated up to 1 day.
• If you aren't able to grill outdoors, chicken can be seared in batches in a hot well-seasoned ridged grill pan over moderately high heat, turning over occasionally, 10 to 12 minutes. Transfer chicken as seared to a large baking pan and bake, skin sides up, in middle of a preheated 375°F oven until just cooked through, 20 to 25 minutes.

APRICOT CHICKEN WITH ALMONDS
SERVES 4
Active time: 10 min   Start to finish: 30 min

    4 (6-oz) skinless boneless chicken breast halves
  5/8 teaspoon salt
  1/2 teaspoon black pepper
  1/3 cup sliced almonds
  1/2 cup apricot preserves
 1 1/2 tablespoons soy sauce
    1 tablespoon whole-grain mustard
    1 tablespoon unsalted butter

▸ Put oven rack in lower third of oven and preheat oven to 400°F. Lightly oil a 13- by 9-inch flameproof baking dish (not glass).
▸ Pat chicken dry and sprinkle all over with 1/2 teaspoon salt and 1/4 teaspoon pepper total, then arrange at least 1/4 inch apart in baking dish. Bake 10 minutes.
▸ While chicken bakes, toast almonds in a small baking pan in oven, stirring twice, until golden, 8 to 10 minutes.
▸ Meanwhile, cook apricot preserves, soy sauce, mustard, butter, remaining 1/8 teaspoon salt, and remaining 1/4 teaspoon pepper in a small saucepan over moderate heat, stirring, until preserves are melted. Pour sauce over chicken and continue to bake until chicken is just cooked through, about 10 minutes more.
▸ Turn on broiler and broil chicken 4 to 5 inches from heat, basting once, until chicken is glazed and browned in spots, about 3 minutes. Serve sprinkled with almonds.

SWEET-AND-SOUR CHICKEN THIGHS WITH CARROTS
SERVES 4 TO 6
Active time: 30 min   Start to finish: 1 1/4 hr

The Ashkenazic and Sephardic traditions feature dishes with sweet-and-sour combinations such as honey and lemon. Serve this chicken with potatoes or matzo farfel.

    8 small chicken thighs with skin and bones (2 1/2 to 2 3/4 lb total), trimmed of excess fat
    2 teaspoons salt
 1 1/4 teaspoons paprika (not hot)
  3/4 teaspoon cinnamon
  1/2 teaspoon black pepper
 1 1/2 tablespoons olive oil
    1 large onion, halved lengthwise, then cut lengthwise into 1/4-inch-wide strips
    1 lb carrots (6 medium), cut diagonally into 1-inch pieces
    2 tablespoons minced garlic
  1/2 cup water
  1/4 cup fresh lemon juice
    2 tablespoons mild honey
    1 tablespoon finely chopped fresh flat-leaf parsley
    1 tablespoon finely chopped fresh cilantro

▸ Pat chicken dry. Stir together 1 1/2 teaspoons salt with paprika, cinnamon, and pepper and rub onto chicken.
▸ Heat oil in a 12-inch heavy skillet over moderately high heat until hot but not smoking, then brown chicken in 2 batches, turning over once, about 10 minutes per batch. Transfer chicken as browned to a plate.
▸ Discard all but 3 tablespoons fat from skillet, then add onion and carrots. Sprinkle with remaining 1/2 teaspoon salt and pepper to taste and cook over moderate heat, stirring occasionally, until onion is softened and beginning to brown, 8 to 10 minutes. Add garlic and cook, stirring occasionally, 1 minute.
▸ Return chicken, skin sides up, to skillet, nestling it into vegetables. Stir together water, lemon juice, and honey until blended and add to skillet, then cook over moderately low heat, covered, until chicken is cooked through and carrots are tender, 25 to 30 minutes. Skim fat from sauce, then add salt to taste. Sprinkle with herbs just before serving.

CHILI AND HONEY CHICKEN LEGS

SERVES 4

Active time: 10 min   Start to finish: 45 min

The chili powder used here can be found in supermarkets and is made from a blend of spices—it is much milder than pure chile powder from New Mexico, which is very hot.

- 2 tablespoons chili powder (not pure chile powder)
- 1 tablespoon mild honey
- 1 tablespoon fresh lime juice
- 1 teaspoon salt
- ½ teaspoon black pepper
- 4 whole chicken legs (2 lb total), thighs and drumsticks separated

▶ Put oven rack in upper third of oven and preheat oven to 425°F. Line bottom of a 15- by 10-inch shallow baking pan with foil and set an oiled large metal rack in pan.

▶ Stir together chili powder, honey, lime juice, salt, and pepper in a large bowl, then add chicken and turn to coat completely.

▶ Transfer chicken to rack, arranging in 1 layer, then bake, turning over once, until cooked through, 30 to 35 minutes.

BRAISED CHICKEN WITH APPLES AND SAGE

SERVES 4

Active time: 20 min   Start to finish: 50 min

- 8 chicken thighs with skin and bones (3 lb)
- 1¼ teaspoons salt
- ½ teaspoon black pepper
- 1 tablespoon olive oil
- 1 tablespoon unsalted butter
- 1 tablespoon packed brown sugar
- 2 apples (preferably Gala; ¾ lb total), peeled, cored, and cut into ½-inch-thick wedges
- ½ cup chopped shallots (2 to 3)
- ⅔ cup reduced-sodium chicken broth
- 1 teaspoon cider vinegar
- ½ teaspoon chopped fresh sage

▶ Pat chicken dry and sprinkle all over with salt and pepper. Heat oil in a 12-inch heavy skillet over moderately high heat until hot but not smoking, then brown chicken well, starting with skin sides down and turning over once, 10 to 12 minutes total. Transfer chicken to a plate and pour off all but 1 tablespoon fat from skillet.

▶ Add butter, brown sugar, apples, and shallots to fat in skillet and cook over moderate heat, stirring occasionally, until apples are browned, about 5 minutes.

▶ Add broth, vinegar, and sage and deglaze skillet by boiling, stirring and scraping up any brown bits, 1 minute. Return chicken, skin sides up, to skillet along with any juices accumulated on plate. Reduce heat and simmer, loosely covered with foil, until chicken is cooked through and sauce is slightly reduced, 20 to 25 minutes.

CHICKEN WITH CHILAQUILES AND SALSA VERDE

SERVES 4 TO 6

Active time: 10 min   Start to finish: 10 min

- 1 cup sour cream
- 3 to 4 tablespoons milk
- 1¾ cups Mexican salsa verde (sometimes called tomatillo sauce; from a 16-oz jar)
- 1¾ cups reduced-sodium chicken broth (14 fl oz)
- 2½ to 3 cups coarsely shredded cooked chicken (from a 2-lb rotisserie chicken, skin removed)
- ¼ teaspoon salt
- ¼ teaspoon black pepper
- 6 cups coarsely crushed tortilla chips (not low-fat, baked, or flavored; from a 16-oz bag) plus broken chips remaining in bag (about 1 cup)
- ½ cup crumbled feta (2 oz)
- ¼ cup chopped fresh cilantro

▶ Stir together sour cream and just enough milk to get a thick pourable consistency.

▶ Bring salsa and broth to a boil in a 5- to 6-quart heavy pot over moderately high heat. Add chicken, salt, and pepper and cook, stirring, until chicken is heated through, 1 to 2 minutes, then stir in 6 cups tortilla chips and cook until chips are softened (but not mushy), about 1 minute.

▶ Transfer *chilaquiles* to a large platter. Sprinkle with feta, cilantro, and 1 cup broken chips and serve immediately, with thinned sour cream on the side.

ASSORTED FOWL

DUCK BREASTS WITH SWEET CHERRY SAUCE

SERVES 4
Active time: 1 hr   Start to finish: 1½ hr

1	tablespoon extra-virgin olive oil
½	cup chopped onion (1 small)
3	garlic cloves, crushed
1	tablespoon finely chopped shallot
1	teaspoon tomato paste
½	teaspoon black pepper
½	teaspoon ground cumin
	Scant ¼ teaspoon dried hot red pepper flakes
¾	teaspoon salt
½	cup coarsely chopped red bell pepper (½ medium)
1	plum tomato, coarsely chopped
¼	cup dry red wine
1½	to 2 tablespoons cider vinegar
2	tablespoons sugar
½	teaspoon Dijon mustard
1¼	lb dark sweet cherries such as Bing, quartered and pitted (3 cups)
2	(¾-lb) boneless Moulard duck breasts with skin (see Sources)
2	tablespoons water
1	tablespoon chopped fresh tarragon or chives

Special equipment: **an instant-read thermometer**

▶ Heat oil in a 2- to 3-quart heavy saucepan over moderate heat until hot but not smoking, then cook onion, garlic, and shallot, stirring occasionally, until golden, about 7 minutes.
▶ Add tomato paste, black pepper, cumin, hot pepper flakes, and ¼ teaspoon salt and cook, stirring, 30 seconds. Add bell pepper and tomato and cook, stirring occasionally, until softened, about 5 minutes.
▶ Stir in wine, vinegar (to taste), and sugar and simmer 1 minute. Stir in mustard, 1½ cups cherries, and remaining ½ teaspoon salt and simmer 1 minute.

▶ Purée mixture in a blender until very smooth, about 1 minute (use caution when blending hot liquids). Force cherry sauce through a fine-mesh sieve into a bowl and transfer ¼ cup sauce to a small bowl for glazing duck.
▶ Put oven rack in middle position and preheat oven to 450°F.
▶ Score duck skin in a crosshatch pattern with a small sharp knife and season duck all over with salt and pepper.
▶ Heat water in a 12-inch heavy ovenproof skillet over low heat until hot, then add duck, skin sides down. Cook duck, uncovered, over low heat, without turning, until most of fat is rendered and skin is golden brown, about 25 minutes.
▶ Transfer duck to a plate and discard all but 1 tablespoon fat from skillet. Brush duck all over with cherry sauce from small bowl and return to skillet, skin sides up.
▶ Roast duck in oven until thermometer registers 135°F (see cooks' note, below), about 8 minutes for medium-rare.
▶ Transfer duck to a cutting board and set skillet aside. Let duck stand, loosely covered with foil, 10 minutes.
▶ Immediately after covering duck, carefully pour off any fat from skillet, leaving any brown bits, and add remaining cherry sauce, stirring and scraping up any brown bits. Add remaining 1½ cups cherries. (Cherries will lose flavor if cooked; heat from skillet will warm sauce.)
▶ Holding a sharp knife at a 45-degree angle, cut duck into slices. Sprinkle with chopped herbs and serve with cherry sauce.

Cooks' note:
• The USDA recommends cooking duck breasts to an internal temperature of 170°F to ensure that any harmful bacteria are killed, but since we prefer the meat medium-rare, we cook it to only 135°F. Otherwise, the duck gets tough and livery.

KITCHEN NOTE

WHEN **PITTING CHERRIES**, A SMALL SHARP KNIFE WILL DO THE TRICK, BUT A CHERRY PITTER, WHICH LOOKS A BIT LIKE A HOLE PUNCH, IS MORE EFFICIENT. EITHER TOOL WORKS ON SWEET AS WELL AS SOUR CHERRIES, BUT BECAUSE SOUR CHERRIES ARE SO SOFT, YOU CAN JUST USE YOUR FINGERS.

THE SIMPLEST ROAST TURKEY

SERVES 8 TO 10

Active time: 20 min   Start to finish: 3 hr

This high-heat roasting method renders a tender bird. Note: We do not recommend this method for turkeys weighing more than 16 pounds. For birds weighing less than 14 pounds, check temperature earlier.

  1   **(14- to 16-lb) turkey, neck and giblets (excluding liver) reserved for turkey giblet stock (recipe follows)**
2½ **teaspoons salt (2 teaspoons if using a kosher bird)**
1½ **teaspoons black pepper**

Special equipment: pliers (preferably needlenose); a small metal skewer (optional); kitchen string; a 17- by 11½- by 2-inch flameproof roasting pan; a flat metal rack; an instant-read thermometer

▶ Remove any feathers and quills with pliers (kosher turkeys tend to require this more than others).
▶ Put oven rack in lower third of oven. Preheat oven to 450°F.
▶ Rinse turkey inside and out and pat dry. Mix salt and pepper in a small bowl and sprinkle it evenly in turkey cavities and all over skin. Fold neck skin under body and, if desired, secure with metal skewer. Tuck wing tips under breast and tie drumsticks together with kitchen string.
▶ Put turkey on rack in roasting pan. (Add 1 cup water if using a dark-colored metal pan.) Roast, rotating pan 180 degrees halfway through roasting, until thermometer inserted into fleshy part of each thigh (close to but not touching bone) registers 170°F, 1¾ to 2½ hours.
▶ Carefully tilt turkey so juices from inside large cavity run into roasting pan. Transfer turkey to a platter (do not clean roasting pan) and let stand 30 minutes. (Internal temperature of thigh meat will rise to 180°F while turkey stands.) Cut off and discard string from turkey.

Other cooking options:

Stuffed turkey: Twelve cups of stuffing will fill both cavities and leave you extra to bake separately. Just before roasting, spoon room-temperature stuffing loosely (stuffing expands as it cooks) into neck (smaller) cavity. Fold neck skin underneath body and secure with metal skewer. Loosely fill body (larger) cavity, and tie drumsticks together with kitchen string. If you don't want any stuffing to spill out, cover opening with a slice of fresh bread, tucking it inside cavity before tying drumsticks. Follow roasting directions above. (Timing for a stuffed bird may be slightly longer, but start checking the temperature at 1¾ hours.) Immediately transfer stuffing from body cavity to a shallow baking dish (separate from one for stuffing baked outside turkey). Take temperature of stuffing in neck cavity and if less than 165°F, add it to baking dish (with stuffing from body cavity). Bake (covered for a moist stuffing or uncovered for a crisp top) until thermometer registers a minimum of 165°F, 20 to 45 minutes.

Roast turkey breast: The same method used above can be applied to a whole turkey breast (instead of the entire bird). For a 6- to 8-lb breast (with skin and bone), reduce amount of salt to 1½ teaspoons and pepper to ¾ teaspoon. Use a V-rack instead of a flat rack. Roast, rotating pan 180 degrees halfway through roasting, until thermometer inserted into thickest part of each breast half (close to but not touching bone) registers 170°F, about 1 hour 10 minutes to 1½ hours. Let stand 30 minutes. (Internal temperature of breast will rise to 175°F–180°F while turkey stands.)

TURKEY GIBLET STOCK

MAKES 4 CUPS

Active time: 30 min   Start to finish: 3½ hr

       Neck and giblets (excluding liver) from turkey
  1   **tablespoon vegetable oil**
  1   **celery rib, coarsely chopped**
  1   **carrot, coarsely chopped**
  1   **onion, peeled and quartered**
 10   **cups water**
  1   **Turkish or ½ California bay leaf**
  1   **teaspoon black peppercorns**
  1   **teaspoon dried thyme, crumbled**
 ¼   **teaspoon salt**

▶ Pat neck and giblets dry. Heat oil in a 3-quart heavy saucepan over moderately high heat until hot but not smoking, then brown neck and giblets, 10 to 15 minutes. Add remaining ingredients and simmer, uncovered, until neck and giblets are very tender, about 3 hours. Pour stock through a large fine-mesh sieve into a bowl, reserving gizzard and heart for gravy if desired but discarding remaining solids. If using broth right away, let stand until fat rises to top, 1 to 2 minutes, then skim off and discard fat.

▸ If stock measures less than 4 cups, add water. If more, boil, uncovered, in clean pot until reduced to 4 cups.

▸ If not using stock right away, cool completely, uncovered, then chill, covered, before skimming fat (it will be easier to remove when cool or cold).

Pressure cooker option: Brown neck and giblets in a 6-quart pressure cooker, uncovered, according to procedure above. Reduce amount of water from 10 cups to 5 cups but keep remaining ingredients the same. Add remaining ingredients, seal pressure cooker with lid, and cook at high pressure according to manufacturer's instructions, 45 minutes. Put pressure cooker in sink (do not remove lid) and run cold water over lid until pressure goes down completely. Remove lid, then strain and measure stock according to procedure above.

Cooks' note:
• Stock can be chilled, covered, 3 days, or frozen 3 months.

TURKEY GIBLET GRAVY
MAKES ABOUT 4 CUPS
Active time: 20 min   Start to finish: 20 min (does not include making stock)

Roasting pan with juices from a (14- to 16-lb) roast turkey
Unsalted butter (less than ½ stick), melted, if turkey drippings yield less than ¼ cup
4 cups hot turkey giblet stock (recipe precedes)
¼ cup all-purpose flour
Reserved cooked giblets (optional), finely chopped

▸ Pour pan juices into a 1-quart glass measure (do not clean roasting pan), then skim off fat and reserve fat and juices separately. (If using a fat separator, pour pan juices into separator and let stand until fat rises to top, 1 to 2 minutes. Carefully pour pan juices from separator into 1-quart glass measure and reserve fat left in separator.) If there is less than ¼ cup reserved fat, add melted butter.

▸ Straddle roasting pan across 2 burners. Add 1 cup giblet stock to pan and deglaze pan by boiling over high heat, scraping up brown bits, about 1 minute. Add to glass measure with remaining 3 cups giblet stock.

▸ Whisk together reserved fat and flour in a 2-quart heavy saucepan and cook roux over moderately low heat, whisking, 3 minutes. Add hot stock to roux in a fast stream, whisking constantly to prevent lumps, then whisk in any turkey juices accumulated on platter and finely chopped giblets (if using). Simmer gravy, whisking occasionally, 10 minutes. Season with salt and pepper.

TURKEY JAMBALAYA
SERVES 6 (MAIN COURSE)
Active time: 35 min   Start to finish: 1 hr

2¾ lb smoked turkey drumsticks
2 tablespoons vegetable oil
1 medium onion, chopped
1 small green bell pepper, chopped
1 large celery rib, chopped
1 large garlic clove, finely chopped
1 (14- to 16-oz) can diced tomatoes in juice, drained
1¾ cups reduced-sodium chicken broth (14 fl oz)
1¼ cups water
½ teaspoon salt
½ teaspoon cayenne
2 cups long-grain white rice
½ cup chopped scallion greens

▸ Cut turkey meat off bone with a paring knife, then cut (or pull off) and discard tendons and skin from meat. Cut turkey into 1-inch pieces.

▸ Heat oil in a 6- to 7-quart wide heavy pot over moderately high heat until hot but not smoking, then cook onion, bell pepper, and celery, stirring frequently, until onion begins to brown, about 5 minutes. Add garlic and cook, stirring, 30 seconds. Add meat, tomatoes, broth, water, salt, and cayenne and bring to a boil, covered, over high heat. Stir in rice and bring to a full rolling boil. Cover pot, then cook over low heat until rice is tender and liquid is absorbed, about 20 minutes. Remove from heat and let stand, covered, 5 minutes. Stir in scallion greens.

Cooks' note:
• If removing tendons from the drumsticks seems too laborious, substitute 1½ lb smoked ham steak. Trim steak, discarding any bone, then cut into 1-inch pieces.

BREAKFAST, BRUNCH, AND SANDWICHES

BREAKFAST AND BRUNCH DISHES

MULTIGRAIN TOASTS WITH SCRAMBLED EGGS AND CANADIAN BACON

SERVES 6

Active time: 15 min   Start to finish: 20 min

- 7 tablespoons unsalted butter
- 6 slices multigrain bread
- 9 large eggs
- ¼ teaspoon salt
- ¼ teaspoon black pepper
- 6 oz sliced Canadian bacon, chopped
- 6 tablespoons sour cream
- 2 tablespoons chopped fresh chives

▶ Put oven rack in middle position and preheat oven to 450°F.

▶ Melt 6 tablespoons butter, then brush onto both sides of bread. Using a 2½-inch round cookie cutter or rim of a glass, cut out 1 round from center of each bread slice. Arrange bread slices (and cutout rounds) on a large baking sheet and toast in oven, without turning over, until golden, about 8 minutes. Transfer each toast (with round) to a plate.

▶ While bread toasts, lightly whisk together eggs, salt, and pepper in a bowl. Cook bacon in remaining tablespoon butter in a 12-inch nonstick skillet over moderately high heat, stirring occasionally, until lightly browned, 1 to 2 minutes. Add eggs and cook, undisturbed, until they begin to set around edge, about 1 minute, then cook, stirring occasionally with a spatula, until just set, about 1 minute more. Divide among toast holes and top with sour cream and chives.

ZUCCHINI, BACON, AND GRUYÈRE QUICHE

SERVES 6 TO 8

Active time: 20 min   Start to finish: 50 min (not including cooling)

- 1 (9-inch) refrigerated pie dough round (from a 15-oz package)
- ¼ lb sliced bacon, coarsely chopped
- 2 medium zucchini (¾ lb total), halved lengthwise, then cut crosswise into ⅛-inch-thick slices
- ½ teaspoon salt
- ¾ cup heavy cream
- ¾ cup whole milk
- ¼ teaspoon black pepper
- 3 large eggs
- 2 oz Gruyère, coarsely grated (1 cup)

Special equipment: a 9½-inch deep-dish pie plate

▶ Put oven rack in middle position and preheat oven to 450°F.

▶ Fit pie dough into pie plate and lightly prick all over. Bake according to package instructions, then transfer crust in pie plate to a rack.

▶ Reduce oven temperature to 350°F.

▶ While crust bakes, cook bacon in a 12-inch heavy skillet over moderately high heat, stirring occasionally, until just crisp, about 6 minutes. Transfer bacon with a slotted spoon to a paper-towel-lined plate, reserving fat in skillet.

▶ Add zucchini and ¼ teaspoon salt to fat in skillet and sauté over moderately high heat, stirring frequently, until zucchini is tender and starting to brown, about 5 minutes, then transfer with slotted spoon to a plate.

▶ Heat cream, milk, pepper, and remaining ¼ teaspoon salt in a 1- to 2-quart saucepan until mixture reaches a bare simmer, then remove from heat.

▶ Whisk together eggs in a large heatproof bowl, then gradually whisk in hot cream mixture until combined. Stir in bacon, zucchini, and cheese and pour into piecrust. Bake until filling is just set, 25 to 30 minutes. Transfer quiche in pan to rack to cool slightly, about 20 minutes.

ARUGULA AND FONTINA FRITTATA

SERVES 4

Active time: 15 min   Start to finish: 20 min

1 garlic clove, halved
1½ tablespoons extra-virgin olive oil
5 oz baby arugula (7 cups packed)
6 large eggs
½ teaspoon salt
¼ teaspoon black pepper
¼ lb Fontina, rind discarded and cheese cut
        into ½-inch cubes

▸ Preheat broiler.

▸ Cook garlic in oil in a 10-inch well-seasoned cast-iron or other ovenproof skillet over moderate heat, stirring occasionally, until golden, about 2 minutes. Discard garlic and add arugula, then cook, stirring frequently, until wilted, 1 to 2 minutes.

▸ Whisk together eggs, salt, and pepper until combined, then pour over arugula in skillet and cook, undisturbed, over moderate heat until almost set, 5 to 6 minutes. Sprinkle cheese evenly on top and broil 4 to 5 inches from heat until eggs are just set and cheese is melted, 1 to 2 minutes.

POACHED EGGS WITH TOMATO CILANTRO SAUCE

SERVES 4

Active time: 30 min   Start to finish: 35 min

In Mexico, this breakfast dish is called huevos ahogados, *meaning "drowned eggs," since the eggs are served in soup bowls with a lot of sauce.*

1 teaspoon distilled white vinegar
2 lb tomatoes, coarsely chopped
2 large garlic cloves, coarsely chopped
1 small fresh green serrano chile, coarsely chopped
1 teaspoon salt, or to taste
½ teaspoon sugar, or to taste
1 cup water
¼ cup plus 1 tablespoon olive oil
¼ cup chopped fresh cilantro plus additional for sprinkling
8 (½-inch-thick) slices of baguette
8 large eggs

▸ Put oven rack in middle position and preheat oven to 350°F.

▸ Fill a deep 12-inch skillet with 1½ inches cold water. Add vinegar and bring to a simmer.

▸ Meanwhile, purée tomatoes, garlic, chile, 1 teaspoon salt, ½ teaspoon sugar, and 1 cup water in a blender until smooth, then pour through a medium-mesh sieve into a bowl, pressing hard on and then discarding solids.

▸ Heat ¼ cup oil in a 12-inch heavy skillet over moderately high heat until hot but not smoking, then carefully pour in tomato sauce (it will splatter). Stir in cilantro and briskly simmer, uncovered, stirring occasionally, until sauce is slightly thickened, about 10 minutes. Stir in salt and sugar to taste, then reduce heat to low.

▸ While sauce simmers, put baguette slices in a shallow baking pan and brush with remaining tablespoon oil and season lightly with salt and pepper. Bake until just crisp on top, about 10 minutes. Keep toasts warm in turned-off oven.

▸ Meanwhile, break eggs, 2 at a time, into a cup, then slide eggs into simmering water, spacing them in skillet, and poach at a bare simmer until whites are firm but yolks are still runny, 4 to 5 minutes.

▸ Gently transfer eggs with a slotted spoon to soup bowls and season with salt. Spoon sauce generously over eggs and sprinkle with cilantro. Serve with toasts.

Cooks' note:
• The eggs in this recipe will not be fully cooked, which may be of concern if salmonella is a problem in your area. Cook eggs until fully set if desired.

KITCHEN NOTE

YOU MIGHT HAVE HEARD THAT BROWN **EGGS** ARE MORE FLAVORFUL THAN WHITE EGGS, BUT THAT'S NOT TRUE. THE COLOR IS DETERMINED SIMPLY BY THE BREED OF THE CHICKEN IT COMES FROM. ONE THING THAT DOES HAVE AN IMPACT ON FLAVOR, THOUGH, IS WHAT THE CHICKENS ARE FED, WHICH EXPLAINS THE POPULARITY OF EGGS FROM FREE-RANGE AND/OR ORGANIC BIRDS.

TOMATO AND CHEDDAR SOUFFLÉS

SERVES 4

Active time: 25 min   Start to finish: 45 min

- 2 tablespoons unsalted butter plus 1 teaspoon, melted
- ½ oz Parmigiano-Reggiano, finely grated with a rasp (½ cup)
- 4 (¼-inch-thick) center-cut slices from a small tomato
- 2 tablespoons all-purpose flour
- 1 cup whole milk
- ⅛ teaspoon salt
- ⅛ teaspoon black pepper
- ⅛ teaspoon cayenne
- 2 oz coarsely shredded sharp Cheddar (½ cup) plus 2 tablespoons for sprinkling
- 2 large eggs, separated

Special equipment: **4 (6-oz) ovenproof custard cups or ramekins**

▸ Put oven rack in middle position and preheat oven to 400°F.

▸ Brush custard cups with 1 teaspoon melted butter (total), then coat each with 1 tablespoon Parmigiano-Reggiano. Put 1 tomato slice in bottom of each cup and arrange cups in a shallow baking pan.

▸ Heat remaining 2 tablespoons butter in a 1½-quart heavy saucepan over moderate heat until foam subsides, then whisk in flour. Cook roux, whisking, 1 minute, then whisk in milk, salt, pepper, and cayenne. Bring to a boil over moderate heat, whisking constantly, and boil until thickened, 3 to 4 minutes. Remove from heat and whisk in ½ cup Cheddar, 2 tablespoons Parmigiano-Reggiano, and yolks.

▸ Beat whites with a small pinch of salt using an electric mixer until they just hold stiff peaks. Fold one third of whites into cheese sauce to lighten, then fold in remaining whites gently but thoroughly. Divide mixture among cups and sprinkle with remaining 2 tablespoons each of Parmigiano-Reggiano and Cheddar.

▸ Bake soufflés until puffed and golden, 17 to 20 minutes. Serve (in cups) immediately.

BELGIAN BUTTERMILK WAFFLES WITH GLAZED BANANAS

MAKES 8 WAFFLES

Active time: 30 min   Start to finish: 30 min

For waffles

- 2 cups all-purpose flour
- 2 tablespoons sugar
- 2 teaspoons baking powder
- 1 teaspoon baking soda
- ¾ teaspoon salt
- 2 cups well-shaken buttermilk
- ¾ stick (6 tablespoons) unsalted butter, melted and cooled to room temperature
- 2 large eggs
  Vegetable oil for waffle iron

For topping

- 2 tablespoons unsalted butter
- 2 firm-ripe large bananas, cut diagonally into ⅓-inch-thick slices
- 1¼ cups pure maple syrup

Special equipment: **a waffle iron (preferably Belgian-style)**
Accompaniment: **sour cream or whipped cream**

Make waffles:

▸ Put oven rack in middle position and put a large metal rack directly on it. Preheat oven to 250°F and preheat waffle iron.

▸ Whisk together flour, sugar, baking powder, baking soda, and salt in a large bowl.

▸ Whisk together buttermilk, melted butter, and eggs in another bowl, then whisk into flour mixture until just combined.

▸ Brush hot waffle iron lightly with vegetable oil and pour a slightly rounded ½ cup of batter into each waffle mold (see cooks' note, below). Cook according to manufacturer's instructions until golden and cooked through, about

3 minutes. Transfer waffles as cooked to rack in oven to keep warm, arranging in 1 layer to stay crisp. Make more waffles in same manner.

Make topping while last batch of waffles cooks:
▶ Heat butter in a 12-inch heavy skillet over moderately high heat until foam subsides, then add banana slices in 1 layer and cook until golden, about 1 minute per side. Remove from heat and add syrup to skillet.
▶ Spoon bananas over waffles, then drizzle with warm syrup before serving.

Cooks' note:
• If using a regular waffle iron (not Belgian), batter will yield about 14 waffles using ⅓ cup per waffle.

GRIDDLE CAKES WITH MARMALADE AND CLOTTED CREAM
SERVES 4
Active time: 25 min   Start to finish: 25 min

½ cup all-purpose flour
½ cup quick-cooking oats
 2 teaspoons sugar
 1 teaspoon baking powder
½ teaspoon baking soda
¼ teaspoon salt
 1 cup well-shaken buttermilk
 1 large egg, lightly beaten
 5 tablespoons unsalted butter, melted and cooled slightly

Accompaniments: **marmalade or jam; clotted cream or crème fraîche**

▶ Put oven rack in middle position and preheat oven to 200°F. Warm 4 plates in oven.
▶ Heat a well-seasoned griddle or heavy skillet (preferably cast-iron) over moderately low heat until hot.
▶ While griddle heats, whisk together flour, oats, sugar, baking powder, baking soda, and salt, then whisk in buttermilk, egg, and 3 tablespoons butter until combined.
▶ Brush hot griddle with some of remaining butter, then spoon 3 tablespoons batter per oatcake onto hot griddle and cook until bubbles appear on surface, edges are set, and undersides are golden, 1 to 2 minutes. Flip cakes with a large spatula and cook until tops spring back when pressed

gently, 1 to 2 minutes more. Transfer as cooked to plates in oven and loosely cover with foil. Brush griddle with butter between batches if necessary.
▶ Brush griddle cakes with any remaining butter and serve immediately.

BROWNED ONION KUGELS
SERVES 6 TO 8 (MAIN COURSE) OR 12 (SIDE DISH)
Active time: 30 min   Start to finish: 1¼ hr

A kugel is traditionally baked in a single large pan, but using a muffin tin is a bit more elegant—and produces an abundance of tasty browned edges. Serve the kugels as a main brunch dish or an accompaniment to pot roast or baked chicken.

 6 oz medium dried egg noodles (1¾ cups)
 1 stick (½ cup) unsalted butter
 3 cups chopped onions (2 large)
1¼ cups sour cream
1¼ cups small-curd cottage cheese (10 oz)
 1 tablespoon poppy seeds
 4 large eggs
 1 teaspoon salt
¼ teaspoon black pepper

Special equipment: **a muffin tin with 12 (½-cup) cups**

▶ Put oven rack in middle position and preheat oven to 425°F.
▶ Cook noodles in a 6- to 8-quart pot of boiling salted water (see Tips, page 8), uncovered, until al dente, about 5 minutes. Drain in a colander and rinse under cold water, then drain well.
▶ Melt butter in a 12-inch heavy skillet over moderate heat and brush muffin cups with some of butter. Add onions to remaining butter in skillet and cook, stirring occasionally, until well browned, about 20 minutes. Transfer onions to a large bowl and stir in noodles, sour cream, cottage cheese, and poppy seeds. Lightly beat eggs with salt and pepper, then stir into noodle mixture until combined well.
▶ Divide mixture among muffin cups and bake until puffed and golden, 20 to 25 minutes. Loosen edges of kugels with a thin knife and cool kugels in pan 5 minutes before serving.

SANDWICHES

SPICED BEEF AND ONION PITAS WITH PARSLEY SAUCE

SERVES 4
Active time: 30 min   Start to finish: 30 min

For sauce

- 3 cups loosely packed fresh flat-leaf parsley leaves (from 2 bunches)
- 2 tablespoons cider vinegar
- 2 tablespoons water
- 1 tablespoon chopped shallot
- 1 teaspoon sugar
- ½ teaspoon salt
- ¼ teaspoon black pepper
- ¼ cup olive oil

For beef and onion pitas

- 4 (6-inch) pita loaves with pockets
- ¼ cup olive oil or vegetable oil
- 1 lb white onions, quartered lengthwise, then cut lengthwise into ¼-inch-wide wedges
- ¾ teaspoon ground coriander
- ½ teaspoon ground cumin
- ½ teaspoon salt
- ¼ teaspoon black pepper
- 1 lb sliced stir-fry beef (top round) or ⅓-inch-thick top round steaks, cut into ⅓-inch-wide strips

Make sauce:
▶ Purée all sauce ingredients in a blender until smooth.

Make beef and onion pitas:
▶ Toast pitas 1 at a time directly on rack of a gas burner over high heat, turning with tongs, until heated through but still flexible (pitas may puff), about 1 minute, then wrap in foil to keep warm. (Alternatively, wrap untoasted pitas in foil and warm in a preheated 300°F oven or toaster oven.)
▶ Heat 1 tablespoon oil in a 12-inch heavy skillet over moderately high heat until hot but not smoking, then sauté half of onions, stirring occasionally, until browned but still crisp, 4 to 5 minutes. Transfer to a large plate. Sauté remaining onions in 1 tablespoon oil in same manner and transfer to plate (reserve skillet).
▶ Stir together coriander, cumin, salt, and pepper in a bowl. Pat beef dry and toss with spices. Heat 1 tablespoon oil in

skillet over moderately high heat, then sauté half of beef, stirring, until browned but still pink inside, 1 to 1½ minutes. Transfer beef to plate with onions. Sauté remaining beef in remaining tablespoon oil in same manner, transferring to plate.

To serve:
▶ Halve pitas and fill with beef and onions. Serve sauce on the side.

KITCHEN NOTE

NAMED AFTER A SMALL VILLAGE IN SOMERSET, **CHEDDAR** HAS BEEN THE MOST WIDELY CONSUMED AND POPULAR CHEESE IN ENGLAND SINCE THE ELIZABETHAN PERIOD AND HAS BEEN COPIED THROUGHOUT THE WORLD. THIS PRESSED, UNCOOKED, SEMI-HARD CHEESE HAS A HARD RIND AND IS TRADITIONALLY MADE FROM WHOLE COW'S MILK THAT HAS BEEN MIXED WITH THE SKIMMED CREAM FROM THE PREVIOUS EVENING'S MILKING.

GRILLED CHEDDAR AND BACON SANDWICHES WITH MANGO CHUTNEY

SERVES 4
Active time: 25 min   Start to finish: 25 min

- 8 (¼-inch-thick) slices whole-grain bread
- 1½ tablespoons unsalted butter, softened
- 4 teaspoons mango chutney
- 6 oz thinly sliced Cheddar (preferably Colby or Longhorn)
- 8 cooked bacon slices, halved crosswise

▶ Spread 1 side of each bread slice with butter. Turn over 4 slices and spread with chutney, then divide cheese and bacon among them. Top with remaining bread slices, buttered sides up.
▶ Heat a dry 12-inch heavy skillet over moderate heat until hot, then cook sandwiches, 2 at a time, pressing occasionally and turning over once, until bread is golden brown and cheese is melted, about 5 minutes per batch.

ROAST BEEF AND WATERCRESS WRAPS WITH ANCHOVY ROSEMARY MAYONNAISE

SERVES 4

Active time: 15 min   Start to finish: 15 min

1   garlic clove
⅔   cup mayonnaise
2   teaspoons anchovy paste
1½   teaspoons fresh lemon juice
1½   teaspoons finely chopped fresh rosemary
⅛   teaspoon black pepper
4   (10-inch) flour tortillas or sandwich wraps
1   lb thinly sliced rare roast beef (from deli counter)
6   oz watercress, coarse stems discarded

▶ Mince garlic with a large heavy knife, then mash to a paste with a pinch of salt using flat side of knife. Whisk together garlic paste, mayonnaise, anchovy paste, lemon juice, rosemary, and pepper in a small bowl.

▶ Toast tortillas 1 at a time directly on burner (gas or electric) over moderately high heat, turning over and rotating with tongs, until slightly puffed and browned in spots but still flexible, about 30 seconds each. Transfer to a clean kitchen towel as toasted and stack, loosely wrapped in towel.

▶ Spread mayonnaise (about 2 tablespoons, or more to taste) on top of each tortilla, then divide roast beef and watercress among tortillas, covering about half of rounds. Tuck in sides of tortillas and roll up tightly to enclose filling, then cut in half.

GRILLED MONTEREY JACK AND CORN QUESADILLAS

SERVES 2 TO 4

Active time: 20 min   Start to finish: 20 min

¼   lb Monterey Jack cheese, coarsely grated (about 1½ cups)
1   cup frozen corn, thawed
2   tablespoons mayonnaise
2   scallions, thinly sliced crosswise
2   tablespoons chopped fresh cilantro
1   tablespoon chopped canned chipotle chiles in *adobo*
4   (8-inch) flour tortillas
1   tablespoon vegetable oil

Special equipment: **a well-seasoned ridged grill pan**

▶ Stir together cheese, corn, mayonnaise, scallions, cilantro, and chiles in a small bowl. Lightly brush 1 tortilla with some of oil. Turn tortilla over and spread ½ cup filling over half, then fold other half over to form a half-moon. Assemble 3 more quesadillas in same manner.

▶ Heat lightly oiled grill pan over moderate heat until hot, then cook quesadillas, 2 at a time, turning over once, until cheese is melted, about 4 minutes per batch. Transfer to a cutting board and cut in half.

PASTA AND GRAINS

PASTA

PASTA SHELLS WITH SUMMER VEGETABLE SAUCE

SERVES 6 (MAIN COURSE)

Active time: 35 min   Start to finish: 35 min

5   tablespoons olive oil
1   medium onion, chopped
1   lb eggplant, peeled and cut into ½-inch cubes
1   large red bell pepper, cut into ⅓-inch pieces
1   lb zucchini, cut into ½-inch cubes
¾   lb cherry tomatoes, halved
2   garlic cloves, chopped
2   (3-inch) fresh thyme sprigs plus 1 teaspoon chopped fresh thyme leaves
¾   teaspoon salt
¼   teaspoon black pepper
1   lb medium pasta shells
2   tablespoons finely chopped fresh flat-leaf parsley
1   (6-oz) log soft mild goat cheese (¾ cup)

▸ Heat 3 tablespoons oil in a 12-inch heavy skillet over moderately high heat until hot but not smoking, then sauté onion, stirring frequently, until lightly browned, about 4 minutes. Add eggplant, bell pepper, and remaining 2 tablespoons oil and cook, stirring occasionally, until eggplant begins to soften, about 5 minutes. Add zucchini, tomatoes, garlic, thyme sprigs, salt, and pepper, then reduce heat and simmer briskly, uncovered, stirring occasionally, 15 minutes. Season with salt and discard thyme sprigs.
▸ While sauce simmers, cook pasta in a 6- to 8-quart pot of boiling salted water (see Tips, page 8), uncovered, until al dente.
▸ Meanwhile, sprinkle parsley and chopped thyme on a small plate. Roll goat cheese log in herbs to coat well.
▸ Drain pasta in a colander and transfer to a large shallow bowl. Spoon sauce over pasta and serve topped with slices of goat cheese.

LINGUINE WITH WHITE CLAM SAUCE

SERVES 4 (MAIN COURSE) OR 8 (FIRST COURSE)

Active time: 25 min   Start to finish: 35 min

Although they're not technically clams, cockles work best in this dish, since they're very small and have tender, sweet flesh. You can identify them by their tiny size (about ½ to 1 inch across) and green-tinged shells.

⅓   cup extra-virgin olive oil
1   medium onion, chopped
6   garlic cloves, finely chopped
¾   teaspoon dried hot red pepper flakes
¼   teaspoon dried oregano, crumbled
⅓   cup dry white wine
⅓   cup bottled clam juice
1   lb linguine
2   lb small cockles (up to 1 inch across; 5 to 6 dozen), scrubbed well
2   tablespoons cold unsalted butter, cut into ½-inch cubes
⅓   cup chopped fresh flat-leaf parsley

Accompaniments: **extra-virgin olive oil for drizzling; dried hot red pepper flakes**

▸ Heat oil in a 5- to 6-quart heavy pot over moderately high heat until hot but not smoking, then sauté onion, stirring, until golden, about 4 minutes. Add garlic, red pepper flakes, and oregano and cook, stirring occasionally, until garlic is golden, about 2 minutes. Stir in wine and clam juice and boil, uncovered, stirring occasionally, until slightly reduced, about 3 minutes.
▸ Cook pasta in a 6- to 8-quart pot of boiling salted water (see Tips, page 8), uncovered, until al dente, then drain in a colander.
▸ While pasta cooks, stir cockles into sauce and simmer, covered, stirring occasionally, until cockles open wide, 4 to 6 minutes. (Discard any cockles that remain unopened after 6 minutes.) Remove from heat and stir in butter until melted.
▸ Add pasta to cockles along with parsley and salt to taste, then toss with sauce until combined well.

Cooks' note:
• You can substitute bottled baby clams in the shell (see Sources) for the cockles. Stir clams into sauce and cook until just heated through.

KITCHEN NOTE

ITALIAN BOTTLED BABY CLAMS IN THE SHELL ARE THAT RARE FIND FOR HOME COOKS: A CULINARY SHORTCUT THAT DOESN'T REQUIRE SACRIFICING FLAVOR OR TEXTURE. THE SMALL WHOLE CLAMS ARE BRIEFLY COOKED, THEN BOTTLED IN A SOLUTION OF THEIR OWN JUICE, SALT, AND A TOUCH OF CITRIC ACID.

CAVATAPPI WITH BUTTERNUT SQUASH

SERVES 4 (MAIN COURSE)
Active time: 30 min   Start to finish: 30 min

 1 lb dried *cavatappi* (ridged corkscrew pasta) or penne rigate
1¾ lb butternut squash, peeled, seeded, and cut into 1-inch pieces (about 3½ cups)
 3 garlic cloves, finely chopped
 1 tablespoon olive oil
 1 cup water
 1 teaspoon finely chopped fresh sage
 ½ teaspoon salt
 3 tablespoons unsalted butter, cut into ½-inch cubes
 2 oz finely grated Parmigiano-Reggiano (1 cup; see Tips, page 8) plus additional for sprinkling

▶ Cook pasta in a 6- to 8-quart pot of boiling salted water (see Tips, page 8), uncovered, until al dente.
▶ While heating water for pasta, pulse squash in a food processor until coarsely chopped. Cook garlic in oil in a 12-inch heavy skillet over moderate heat, stirring, until pale golden, about 1 minute. Add squash, water (1 cup), sage, and salt and simmer, covered, until squash is tender, 5 to 7 minutes. Add butter and stir until incorporated.
▶ Reserve 1 cup pasta-cooking water, then drain pasta in a colander and return to pot. Stir in squash mixture, cheese, and pepper to taste until combined well. Season with salt and add some of reserved cooking water to moisten if necessary.

RED-WINE SPAGHETTI WITH BROCCOLI

SERVES 4 (MAIN COURSE) OR 8 (FIRST COURSE)
Active time: 35 min   Start to finish: 35 min

This recipe was inspired by a dish that chef Alessandro Giuntoli made when he was at Osteria del Circo, in New York City.

1¾ lb broccoli, thick stems discarded
 1 lb spaghetti
 1 (750-ml) bottle red wine (preferably Zinfandel)
 1 teaspoon sugar
 4 garlic cloves, finely chopped (2 tablespoons)
 ½ teaspoon dried hot red pepper flakes
 ⅓ cup extra-virgin olive oil
 ¾ teaspoon salt
 ½ teaspoon black pepper
 1 oz finely grated Parmigiano-Reggiano (½ cup; see Tips, page 8)

Accompaniment: finely grated Parmigiano-Reggiano

▶ Cut broccoli into 1-inch-wide florets (with ½ inch of stem). Blanch in a 6- to 8-quart pot of boiling salted water (see Tips, page 8), uncovered, 2 minutes. Transfer with a slotted spoon to a large colander to drain, reserving broccoli-cooking water in pot, then transfer broccoli to a bowl.
▶ Return cooking water to a boil and cook spaghetti, stirring occasionally, 5 minutes (pasta will not be fully cooked). Drain in colander and return empty pot to stovetop. Add wine and sugar to pot and boil vigorously 2 minutes. Add spaghetti and shake pot to prevent pasta from sticking. Gently stir with tongs until coated and boil over high heat, stirring occasionally, until most of liquid is absorbed, about 6 minutes (pasta will be al dente).
▶ Immediately after adding spaghetti to wine mixture, cook garlic and red pepper flakes in oil in a deep 12-inch heavy skillet over moderately low heat, shaking skillet occasionally, until garlic is pale golden, about 5 minutes. Add broccoli, salt, and pepper and cook, stirring, 1 minute.
▶ Increase heat to high and pour spaghetti mixture into skillet, tossing with tongs to combine (skillet will be very full). Cook, stirring, until all of wine is absorbed, about 2 minutes. Remove from heat and stir in cheese. Serve immediately.

WHOLE-WHEAT SPAGHETTI WITH BROCCOLI, CHICKPEAS, AND GARLIC

SERVES 4 (MAIN COURSE)

Active time: 15 min   Start to finish: 25 min

- 6 garlic cloves, chopped (about ¼ cup)
- ½ teaspoon dried hot red pepper flakes
- ¼ cup extra-virgin olive oil plus additional for drizzling
- 2 (10-oz) packages frozen chopped broccoli (not thawed)
- ¾ teaspoon salt
- 1 (15-oz) can chickpeas, rinsed and drained
- ½ lb whole-wheat spaghetti

Accompaniments: **finely grated Parmigiano-Reggiano (see Tips, page 8); lemon wedges (optional)**

▶Cook garlic and red pepper flakes in oil in a 12-inch heavy skillet over moderate heat, stirring, until garlic is golden, about 1 minute. Add broccoli and salt and cook, breaking up frozen chunks and stirring occasionally, until broccoli is thawed and crisp-tender, 5 to 7 minutes. Stir in chickpeas and cook until heated through.

▶Cook pasta in a 6- to 8-quart pot of boiling salted water (see Tips, page 8), uncovered, until al dente. Reserve ½ cup pasta-cooking water, then drain pasta in a colander. Add pasta and reserved cooking water to broccoli and chickpeas in skillet and cook over moderate heat, tossing, until combined well. Serve drizzled with additional olive oil.

COUSCOUS WITH SPICED ZUCCHINI

SERVES 4 TO 6 (SIDE DISH)

Active time: 25 min   Start to finish: 25 min

- 1 cup reduced-sodium chicken broth
- 1 teaspoon salt
- ¾ cup plain couscous
- 2 tablespoons extra-virgin olive oil
- 1 medium onion, chopped
- 1 garlic clove, finely chopped
- 1 lb zucchini, cut into ½-inch cubes
- ¾ teaspoon ground coriander
- ½ teaspoon chili powder (not pure chile powder)
- ¼ teaspoon ground cumin
- ¼ teaspoon black pepper
- ¼ cup chopped fresh mint
- 1 tablespoon fresh lemon juice

▶Bring broth with ¼ teaspoon salt just to a boil in a small saucepan, then pour over couscous in a bowl and let stand, covered, 5 minutes. Fluff with a fork and set aside until ready to use.

▶Heat oil in a 10-inch heavy skillet over moderately high heat until hot but not smoking, then sauté onion with ¼ teaspoon salt, stirring occasionally, until golden, about 6 minutes. Add garlic and sauté, stirring, until fragrant, about 1 minute. Add zucchini and remaining ½ teaspoon salt and sauté, stirring occasionally, until just tender, about 5 minutes. Reduce heat to moderately low, then stir in coriander, chili powder, cumin, and pepper and cook, stirring frequently, 2 minutes. Gently stir zucchini mixture into couscous and cool to warm or room temperature. Just before serving, stir in mint and lemon juice.

PENNE RIGATE WITH MIXED GREENS AND PINE NUTS

SERVES 6 (MAIN COURSE)

Active time: 10 min   Start to finish: 25 min

- 1 lb penne rigate
- 3 tablespoons unsalted butter
- 3 tablespoons olive oil
- ¼ cup pine nuts (1¼ oz)
- 1 teaspoon chopped garlic
- 2 (8- to 10-oz) bags mixed salad greens with radicchio (often labeled "Italian" or "Mediterranean"; 16 to 20 cups)
- ½ teaspoon salt
- ½ teaspoon black pepper
- 1 oz finely grated Parmigiano-Reggiano (½ cup; see Tips, page 8), plus additional for serving

▶Cook penne in a 5- to 6-quart heavy pot of boiling salted water (see Tips, page 8), uncovered, until al dente or according to package directions, then drain in a colander.

▶Combine butter, oil, and pine nuts in cleaned and dried pot and cook over moderately high heat, stirring, until nuts are pale golden, about 3 minutes. Add garlic and cook, stirring, until garlic is golden, about 1 minute. Stir in greens and cook, stirring, until they wilt, about 3 minutes. Add penne, salt, and pepper and toss to coat. Stir in cheese and serve immediately, with additional cheese on the side.

MACARRONES CON CREMA Y QUESO
(Macaroni with Cream and Cheese)
SERVES 4 (MAIN COURSE) OR 6 (FIRST COURSE)
Active time: 40 min   Start to finish: 40 min

- ¾ lb fresh poblano chiles (about 4)
- ½ large white onion, cut lengthwise into ¼-inch-wide strips (1¾ cups)
- ½ teaspoon salt
- 2 tablespoons unsalted butter
- ½ fresh serrano chile, minced (1 teaspoon), including seeds
- 2 large garlic cloves, minced
- ½ teaspoon dried oregano (preferably Mexican), crumbled
- 6 oz dried *cavatappi* (ridged corkscrew pasta) or penne rigate
- ⅔ cup *crema* or crème fraîche
- ¼ lb *queso fresco* or mild feta, crumbled (1 cup)

▶ Lay poblanos on their sides on racks of gas burners, then turn flames on moderately high. Roast poblanos, turning occasionally with tongs, until skins are blistered and charred, 4 to 6 minutes. (Alternatively, broil poblanos on rack of a broiler pan about 2 inches from heat, turning occasionally with tongs, 8 to 10 minutes.) Transfer poblanos immediately to a large bowl and cover tightly. Let steam 10 minutes, then peel or rub off skins and discard stems, seeds, and ribs. Cut poblanos into ¼-inch-thick strips.

▶ Cook onion with salt in butter in a 12-inch heavy skillet over moderately low heat, stirring occasionally, until onion is golden, 10 to 12 minutes. Add poblanos, serrano, garlic, and oregano and cook, stirring, until fragrant, about 1 minute. Remove from heat.

▶ While onion is browning, cook pasta in a large pot of boiling salted water (see Tips, page 8), uncovered, until tender, 14 to 15 minutes. Reserve ¼ cup pasta-cooking water, then drain pasta in a colander. Add pasta to chile mixture along with *crema* and reserved cooking water. Increase heat to high and cook, tossing, until pasta is coated well, about 1 minute. Stir in cheese.

KITCHEN NOTE

DRIED **PASTA** WORKS WELL WITH ALL TYPES OF SAUCES BUT HOLDS UP PARTICULARLY WELL TO HEAVIER MEAT OR CREAM-BASED SAUCES. FRESH PASTA IS BEST PAIRED WITH A LIGHTER SAUCE, SUCH AS BROWNED BUTTER AND SAGE.

ACINI DI PEPE WITH SPINACH AND FETA
SERVES 6 (SIDE DISH)
Active time: 20 min   Start to finish: 20 min

Acini di pepe, *the Italian term for "peppercorns," also refers to tiny pearls of pasta. This dish goes well with lamb chops or grilled chicken.*

- ½ lb *acini di pepe* or orzo (1¼ cups)
- 2 tablespoons olive oil
- 2 tablespoons unsalted butter
- 3 garlic cloves, minced (1 tablespoon)
- ¼ teaspoon dried hot red pepper flakes
- 3 scallions, chopped
- 1 (10-oz) package chopped frozen spinach, thawed and squeezed dry
- ½ cup crumbled feta (3 oz; preferably French)

Accompaniment: **lemon wedges**

▶ Cook pasta in a 4- to 6-quart pot of boiling salted water (see Tips, page 8), uncovered, stirring occasionally, until al dente, then drain well in a coarse-mesh sieve. Transfer to a bowl and keep warm, covered.

▶ Meanwhile, heat oil and butter in a 12-inch heavy skillet over moderately high heat until hot but not smoking, then sauté garlic, red pepper flakes, and scallions, stirring occasionally, until garlic is golden, about 2 minutes. Add spinach and cook, stirring, until heated through, about 4 minutes.

▶ Toss pasta with spinach mixture and feta until combined. Season with salt and pepper.

TAGLIATELLE WITH CHESTNUTS, PANCETTA, AND SAGE

SERVES 4 (MAIN COURSE) OR 6 TO 8 (FIRST COURSE)

Active time: 30 min   Start to finish: 30 min

- 3 oz pancetta (Italian unsmoked cured bacon), chopped (scant 1 cup)
- 1 tablespoon extra-virgin olive oil
- 1 small onion, finely chopped
- 4 garlic cloves, minced
- 2 tablespoons finely chopped fresh sage
- 8 oz bottled peeled roasted whole chestnuts, coarsely crumbled (1½ cups)
- ½ lb dried flat egg pasta such as tagliatelle or fettuccine
- 2 oz finely grated Parmigiano-Reggiano (1 cup; see Tips, page 8)
- 2 tablespoons unsalted butter
- 1 tablespoon finely chopped fresh flat-leaf parsley

▶ Cook pancetta in oil in a 12-inch heavy skillet over moderate heat, stirring frequently, until beginning to brown, 3 to 4 minutes. Add onion and cook, stirring frequently, until beginning to brown, 2 to 3 minutes. Add garlic and 1 tablespoon sage and cook, stirring, 1 minute. Stir in chestnuts and remove from heat.

▶ Cook pasta in a 6- to 8-quart pot of boiling salted water (see Tips, page 8), uncovered, according to package directions. Reserve 1½ cups pasta-cooking water, then drain pasta in a colander and add to pancetta mixture in skillet. Add 1 cup reserved cooking water along with cheese and butter and cook, tossing constantly, over high heat until pasta is coated well (add more reserved water if necessary), about 1 minute. Add salt and pepper to taste and serve sprinkled with parsley and remaining tablespoon sage.

KITCHEN NOTE

PANCETTA, WHICH COMES FROM THE PORK BELLY AND IS SALT-CURED (NOT SMOKED), ADDS LOTS OF FLAVOR TO WINTER DISHES. LOOK FOR **PANCETTA** AT ITALIAN MARKETS AND SPECIALTY FOODS SHOPS. IT KEEPS IN THE REFRIGERATOR FOR A WEEK OR IN THE FREEZER FOR THREE MONTHS. IN A PINCH, BACON CAN BE SUBSTITUTED (THOUGH IT WILL HAVE A SMOKY FLAVOR).

GRAINS

SAVORY FARRO TART

SERVES 8 (FIRST COURSE)

Active time: 15 min   Start to finish: 1¼ hr

Farro *is often said to be the Italian word for "spelt," but it is actually a different strain of wheat.*

- 1 cup *farro* (see Sources)
- 2 tablespoons unsalted butter plus additional for buttering dish
- 2 tablespoons fine dry bread crumbs
- 2 garlic cloves, chopped
- 30 oz whole-milk ricotta (3¼ cups)
- 1 whole large egg plus 2 large yolks
- 1¼ oz finely grated Parmigiano-Reggiano (⅔ cup; see Tips, page 8)
- ¼ cup coarsely chopped fresh flat-leaf parsley
- ¾ teaspoon salt
- ½ teaspoon black pepper
- ½ teaspoon freshly grated nutmeg

Special equipment: **a 9-inch shallow ovenproof dish such as a glass pie plate**

▶ Cook *farro* in a 2- to 3-quart saucepan of boiling salted water (see Tips, page 8) until just tender, about 10 minutes. Drain in a sieve and cool to room temperature.

▶ Put oven rack in middle position and preheat oven to 375°F. Butter dish and lightly coat with bread crumbs, knocking out excess crumbs.

▶ Melt butter (2 tablespoons) in a small heavy skillet over low heat and cook garlic, stirring, 1 minute, then transfer to a medium bowl. Stir in *farro*, ricotta, whole egg, yolks, Parmigiano-Reggiano, parsley, salt, pepper, and nutmeg until combined well.

▶ Spoon mixture into dish and bake until just set and top is pale golden, 35 to 45 minutes. Cool to warm on a rack. Cut into wedges and serve.

BUTTERNUT SQUASH POLENTA

SERVES 4 (SIDE DISH)
Active time: 25 min   Start to finish: 25 min

- ¾ cup finely chopped onion (1 medium)
- 5 tablespoons unsalted butter
- 1 (12-oz) package frozen butternut squash purée
(sometimes called winter squash; 1½ cups), thawed
- 2½ cups water
- 2 cups whole milk
- 1¼ teaspoons salt
- ¼ teaspoon black pepper
- ¾ cup instant polenta
- 1 oz finely grated Parmigiano-Reggiano (½ cup; see Tips, page 8)

▶ Cook onion in 3 tablespoons butter in a 10-inch heavy skillet over moderate heat, stirring, until very soft, about 8 minutes. Stir in squash and cook, stirring occasionally, 2 minutes.

▶ Bring water, milk, salt, and pepper to a boil in a 4-quart heavy pot. Add polenta in a thin stream, whisking. Cook polenta at a bare simmer, stirring with a long-handled whisk and turning down heat as needed to prevent spattering, 5 minutes.

▶ Stir in squash mixture and cook, stirring, 3 minutes. Remove from heat, then stir in cheese and remaining 2 tablespoons butter. Serve immediately.

CUMIN HERB RICE PILAF

SERVES 6 (SIDE DISH)
Active time: 15 min   Start to finish: 30 min

- 1½ teaspoons cumin seeds
- 1 large bunch scallions, white part thinly sliced
(¼ cup) and enough greens finely chopped to
measure ⅓ cup
- 2 tablespoons olive oil
- 1¼ cups long-grain white rice
- 1 cup reduced-sodium chicken broth
- ¾ cup water
- ¾ teaspoon salt
- ¼ teaspoon black pepper
- ⅓ cup finely chopped fresh flat-leaf parsley

▶ Cook cumin seeds and white part of scallions in 1 tablespoon oil in a 2-quart heavy saucepan over moderately low heat, stirring occasionally, until scallions are softened, 1 to 2 minutes.

▶ Add rice and cook, stirring frequently, 1 minute. Stir in broth, water, salt, and pepper and bring to a boil over high heat. Cover pan, then reduce heat to low and cook until liquid is absorbed and rice is tender, about 15 minutes. Remove from heat and let stand, covered, 5 minutes.

▶ Fluff rice with a fork and toss with scallion greens, parsley, and remaining tablespoon oil.

CINNAMON-SPICED RICE

SERVES 6 TO 8 (SIDE DISH)
Active time: 15 min   Start to finish: 45 min

- 1 medium onion, chopped
- 3 garlic cloves, chopped
- ¾ teaspoon cumin seeds
- 1 (2½- to 3-inch) cinnamon stick
- 2 tablespoons olive oil
- 1½ cups long-grain white rice
- 2¼ cups reduced-sodium chicken broth (18 fl oz)
- ¾ teaspoon sugar
- ¾ teaspoon black pepper
- 1 teaspoon salt

▶ Cook onion, garlic, cumin seeds, and cinnamon stick in oil in a 2- to 3-quart heavy saucepan over moderate heat, stirring, until onion is beginning to soften, about 3 minutes. Add rice and cook, stirring, until grains become slightly translucent, about 2 minutes.

▶ Stir in broth, sugar, pepper, and salt and bring to a boil. Reduce heat and simmer, covered, until rice is tender and liquid is absorbed, about 15 minutes. Remove from heat and let stand, covered, 10 minutes. Fluff rice with a fork and discard cinnamon stick.

BULGUR, APRICOT, AND PINE NUT DRESSING

SERVES 8 (SIDE DISH)

Active time: 20 min   Start to finish: 50 min

¼   cup extra-virgin olive oil
⅔   cup pine nuts (3½ oz)
1   large onion, finely chopped (1½ cups)
1   cup coarse bulgur (5½ oz; see Sources)
1¾ cups water
½   cup dried apricots (preferably California; 3 oz), finely chopped
½   teaspoon salt
¼   teaspoon black pepper
4   oz feta, coarsely crumbled (¾ cup)
½   cup chopped fresh flat-leaf parsley

▶ Heat oil in a 4-quart heavy pot over moderate heat until hot but not smoking, then cook pine nuts, stirring constantly, until golden, 2 to 3 minutes. Transfer with a slotted spoon to paper towels to drain.

▶ Add onion to pot, then reduce heat to moderately low and cook, stirring occasionally, until softened but not browned, about 6 minutes. Add bulgur and cook, stirring, 1 minute. Stir in water, apricots, salt, and pepper and bring to a boil. Remove pan from heat and let stand, covered, until bulgur is tender, about 30 minutes. Stir in nuts, feta, parsley, and salt and pepper to taste.

Cooks' note:

• Bulgur can be made, without nuts, feta, and parsley, 1 day ahead and chilled, covered. Reheat in a heavy saucepan over moderately low heat, stirring occasionally, before adding remaining ingredients.

KITCHEN NOTE

WE PREFER THE STRONG, TANGY TASTE OF CALIFORNIA **DRIED APRICOTS** TO THAT OF THE INSIPIDLY SWEET TURKISH VARIETY. OFTEN LABELED "MEDITERRANEAN," TURKISH APRICOTS ARE SMALLER AND DRIED WHOLE, AFTER THE PITS HAVE BEEN SLIPPED OUT. THE CALIFORNIA KIND ARE ALWAYS CUT IN HALF BEFORE THEY ARE PITTED.

POLENTA AND SAUSAGE STUFFING

SERVES 8 (SIDE DISH)

Active time: 1 hr   Start to finish: 1½ hr

This stuffing uses polenta two ways—half of it is left creamy, while the other half gets browned, for a contrast of texture.

½   stick (¼ cup) unsalted butter plus additional for buttering pans
6½ cups water
2   teaspoons salt
2   cups quick-cooking polenta (11 oz)
1   lb sweet Italian sausage, casings discarded
2   tablespoons olive oil
1   medium onion, chopped
1   large garlic clove, minced
2   cups reduced-sodium chicken broth (16 fl oz)
½   cup finely chopped fresh flat-leaf parsley
2   oz finely grated Parmigiano-Reggiano (1 cup; see Tips, page 8)

▶ Butter a 15- by 10-inch shallow baking pan. Bring 6 cups water with salt to a boil in a 4-quart heavy pot, then add polenta in a stream, stirring with a long-handled spoon, and simmer, stirring constantly, 5 minutes (polenta will be very thick). Add 3 tablespoons butter and stir until butter is incorporated. Spread polenta in buttered pan and chill, uncovered, until firm, about 15 minutes.

▶ While polenta chills, cook sausage in 1 tablespoon oil in a 10-inch heavy skillet over moderately high heat, breaking up lumps, until no longer pink, about 3 minutes, then transfer with a slotted spoon to a large bowl. Add onion to skillet and cook over moderate heat, stirring occasionally, until browned, about 3 minutes; add garlic and cook, stirring, until fragrant, about 30 seconds. Stir in remaining ½ cup water, scraping up any brown bits from bottom of skillet, then add onion mixture and chicken broth to sausage.

▶ Preheat broiler. Melt 1 tablespoon butter with remaining tablespoon oil in a small saucepan. Invert polenta onto a large cutting board, then cut half of it into ½-inch cubes (reserve remainder) and toss with butter mixture in a medium bowl. Return polenta cubes to baking pan, spreading evenly, and broil 3 to 4 inches from heat until golden brown in patches, 8 to 12 minutes.

▶ Put oven rack in upper third of oven and preheat oven to 450°F. Butter a 13- by 9-inch baking dish (3-quart).

▶ Coarsely mash remaining polenta with a potato masher and add to sausage mixture. Add broiled polenta cubes, parsley, ½ cup cheese, and pepper to taste and toss until combined well. Transfer to baking dish. Sprinkle top of stuffing with remaining ½ cup cheese and bake, covered tightly with a sheet of buttered foil (buttered side down), until heated through, about 20 minutes. Remove foil and bake until top is lightly browned, 10 to 15 minutes more.

Cooks' note:

• Stuffing, without parsley and cheese, can be prepared (but not baked) 1 day ahead and chilled, covered. Bring to room temperature, then stir in parsley and cheese before proceeding.

LOUISIANA SHRIMP RICE DRESSING

SERVES 8 TO 10 (SIDE DISH)
Active time: 45 min   Start to finish: 1¼ hr

3½ cups water
 2 teaspoons salt
 2 cups long-grain white rice
 2 medium onions, chopped
 2 celery ribs, chopped
 1 medium green bell pepper, chopped
 2 tablespoons vegetable oil
 2 tablespoons unsalted butter
 2 large garlic cloves, finely chopped
 2 (28-oz) cans whole tomatoes in juice
 1 cup water
 ½ teaspoon cayenne
1½ lb large shrimp in shell (21 to 25 per lb), peeled, deveined, and cut crosswise into ½-inch pieces
 1 cup thinly sliced scallion greens (from 1 bunch)

▶ Bring water and ½ teaspoon salt to a boil over high heat in a 4-quart heavy pot, then stir in rice. Cover pot, then reduce heat to low and cook until liquid is absorbed and rice is tender, about 15 minutes. Remove from heat and let stand, covered, 5 minutes. Fluff rice with a fork, then keep covered.
▶ While rice cooks, cook onions, celery, and bell pepper in oil and butter in an 8-quart wide heavy pot over moderately low heat, stirring occasionally, until bell pepper is softened, 10 to 12 minutes. Add garlic, tomatoes with their juice, water, cayenne, and remaining 1½ teaspoons salt and simmer, uncovered, breaking up tomatoes with a wooden spatula and stirring frequently to prevent scorching, until very thick, 45 to 50 minutes. Add shrimp and simmer, stirring frequently, until just cooked through, 2 to 3 minutes. Add scallion greens and rice and stir until combined well, then season with salt if desired.

Cooks' note:

• Rice and tomato sauce, without shrimp and scallions, can be made 3 days ahead and cooled completely, uncovered, then chilled separately in airtight containers. Reheat rice in a colander or large sieve set over a pot of boiling water, covered with a dampened paper towel. Reheat sauce in pot before proceeding.

VEGETABLES

ASPARAGUS WITH OLIVE AND ORANGE BUTTER

SERVES 4
Active time: 10 min   Start to finish: 15 min

- **2 lb asparagus, ends snapped off and discarded**
- **2 tablespoons unsalted butter**
- **2 tablespoons fresh orange juice**
- **2 to 3 teaspoons black olive paste**

▶ Cut asparagus into 2-inch-long pieces and cook in a 4-quart wide pot of boiling salted water (see Tips, page 8), uncovered, until just crisp-tender, 4 to 5 minutes. Drain in a colander.
▶ Melt butter in a 12-inch heavy skillet over moderately high heat, then whisk in juice and olive paste (to taste) until blended. Add asparagus and salt and pepper to taste, tossing to coat.

GREEN GODDESS GREEN BEANS

SERVES 6
Active time: 25 min   Start to finish: 30 min

- **1½ lb green beans, trimmed**
- **⅓ cup coarsely chopped fresh flat-leaf parsley**
- **¼ cup mayonnaise**
- **¼ cup sour cream**
- **1½ teaspoons red-wine vinegar**
- **½ teaspoon fresh lemon juice**
- **½ teaspoon anchovy paste**
- **¼ teaspoon salt**
- **¼ teaspoon black pepper**

▶ Cook beans in a 6- to 8-quart pot of boiling salted water (see Tips, page 8), uncovered, until just tender, 6 to 8 minutes. Drain in a colander and immediately transfer to a bowl of ice and cold water to stop cooking. When beans are cool, drain in colander and pat dry.
▶ Purée parsley, mayonnaise, sour cream, vinegar, lemon juice, anchovy paste, salt, and pepper in a blender until smooth. Transfer to a bowl and toss with beans.

Cooks' note:
• Sauce can be made 1 day ahead and chilled, covered.

KALE WITH GARLIC AND BACON

SERVES 8
Active time: 50 min   Start to finish: 1 hr

- **2½ lb kale (about 4 bunches), tough stems and center ribs cut off and discarded**
- **10 bacon slices (½ lb), cut into ½-inch pieces**
- **4 garlic cloves, finely chopped**
- **2 cups water**

▶ Stack a few kale leaves and roll lengthwise into a cigar shape. Cut crosswise into ¼-inch-wide strips with a sharp knife. Repeat with remaining leaves.
▶ Cook bacon in a 6- to 8-quart wide heavy pot over moderate heat, stirring occasionally, until crisp, then transfer with a slotted spoon to paper towels to drain. Pour off and discard all but 3 tablespoons fat from pot, then cook garlic in remaining fat over moderately low heat, stirring, until pale golden, about 30 seconds. Add kale (pot will be full) and cook, turning with tongs, until wilted and bright green, about 1 minute. Add water and simmer, partially covered, until just tender, 6 to 10 minutes. Toss with bacon and salt and pepper to taste.

Cooks' note:
• Large kale leaves are easy to cut in the manner described in this recipe. If all you can find are small leaves, just coarsely chop them.

GREEN BEANS WITH LEMON AND PINE NUTS

SERVES 8

Active time: 30 min   Start to finish: 30 min

1½ lb green beans, trimmed and cut diagonally into
        ½-inch pieces
¼   cup pine nuts, toasted (see Tips, page 8)
2   tablespoons finely chopped fresh flat-leaf parsley
1½ teaspoons finely grated fresh lemon zest (see Tips,
        page 8)
4   teaspoons extra-virgin olive oil

▶ Cook beans in a 4-quart pot of boiling salted water (see Tips, page 8), uncovered, until just tender, about 5 minutes, then drain well in a colander. Transfer to a bowl and toss with nuts, parsley, zest, oil, and salt and pepper to taste.

BRUSSELS SPROUTS WITH CHESTNUTS

SERVES 8

Active time: 25 min   Start to finish: 35 min

2   tablespoons unsalted butter
¾   teaspoon salt
½   teaspoon black pepper
1¼ cups water
2   lb Brussels sprouts, trimmed and halved
        lengthwise (8 cups)
1   cup heavy cream
⅔   cup bottled roasted whole chestnuts (4 oz),
        coarsely crumbled

▶ Bring butter, salt, pepper, and 1 cup water to a boil over high heat in a deep 12-inch heavy skillet, then add Brussels sprouts and simmer, partially covered, stirring occasionally, until crisp-tender, 6 to 8 minutes. Remove lid and boil over moderately high heat until water is evaporated and sprouts are lightly browned, 3 to 4 minutes. Add cream and remaining ¼ cup water and bring to a boil, stirring. Add chestnuts, then reduce heat and simmer, stirring occasionally, until heated through, about 2 minutes.

SOUTHWESTERN SUCCOTASH

SERVES 8

Active time: 40 min   Start to finish: 1 hr

This colorful side dish's bold flavors make it a great accompaniment to grilled meats.

3   fresh poblano chiles (¾ lb total)
2   tablespoons olive oil
1   medium onion, cut into ⅓-inch pieces
1   medium red bell pepper, cut into ⅓-inch pieces
2   garlic cloves, finely chopped
½   teaspoon black pepper
½   teaspoon cumin seeds
1¼ teaspoons salt
2   cups fresh corn (from 3 to 4 ears)
1   lb tomatoes, cut into ⅓-inch pieces
1   lb yellow squash, cut into ⅓-inch pieces
¼   cup heavy cream
1   tablespoon fresh lime juice
3   tablespoons chopped fresh cilantro

▶ Lay chiles on their sides on racks of gas burners, then turn flames on moderately high. Roast chiles, turning with tongs, until skins are blistered, 5 to 7 minutes. (Alternatively, broil chiles on rack of a broiler pan about 2 inches from heat, turning occasionally with tongs, 8 to 10 minutes.) Transfer chiles immediately to a large bowl and cover tightly. Let steam 10 minutes, then peel or rub off skins and discard stems, seeds, and ribs. Cut chiles into ⅓-inch pieces.
▶ Heat oil in a 12-inch heavy skillet over moderately high heat until hot but not smoking, then sauté onion and red bell pepper, stirring occasionally, until golden, about 6 minutes. Add garlic, black pepper, cumin seeds, and ¼ teaspoon salt and sauté, stirring, until garlic is fragrant, about 1 minute.
▶ Add corn, tomatoes, squash, and ½ teaspoon salt and cook over moderately high heat, covered, stirring occasionally, until vegetables are just tender and have exuded liquid, 8 to 10 minutes. Remove lid and continue to cook, stirring occasionally, until most of liquid is evaporated, about 5 minutes.
▶ Stir in chiles, cream, lime juice, 2 tablespoons cilantro, and remaining ½ teaspoon salt and continue to cook, stirring occasionally, until liquid is slightly thickened, about 3 minutes. Sprinkle with remaining tablespoon cilantro.

ROASTED CORN WITH CHIPOTLE MAYONNAISE

SERVES 6 (SNACK OR SIDE DISH)
Active time: 15 min   Start to finish: 25 min

- 6 ears corn, shucked
- ½ cup mayonnaise
- 4 teaspoons finely chopped canned chipotle chiles in *adobo*
- 6 lime wedges

Special equipment: **a large cast-iron skillet or griddle**

▶ Add corn to a 6- to 8-quart pot of boiling water. Return water to a boil, then cover and remove from heat. Let stand 10 minutes. Transfer corn with tongs to paper towels to drain.

▶ Stir together mayonnaise and chiles in a small bowl.

▶ Heat skillet over moderately high heat until hot, then roast corn in 2 batches, turning occasionally with tongs, until blackened in spots, about 5 minutes per batch. Cut corn crosswise into 2-inch sections with a sharp knife and serve with mayonnaise and lime wedges.

KITCHEN NOTE

WHEN SHOPPING FOR **CORN**, EXAMINE THE EARS CAREFULLY. THE STEMS SHOULD LOOK RECENTLY CUT; THE HUSKS SHOULD BE VIBRANT GREEN AND SLIGHTLY DAMP; AND THE BROWN SILK SHOULD FEEL SLIGHTLY STICKY. IF YOU CAN'T SERVE IT RIGHT AWAY, STORE IT, UNHUSKED, IN A PLASTIC BAG IN THE COLDEST PART OF THE FRIDGE.

SCALLION CORNMEAL FRITTERS

MAKES 18 FRITTERS
Active time: 25 min   Start to finish: 25 min

- 1 large egg, lightly beaten
- 1 cup whole milk
- 1⅓ cups yellow cornmeal (preferably stone-ground)
- 1 teaspoon baking powder
- ½ teaspoon salt
- 2 tablespoons finely chopped scallion greens
  About ½ cup vegetable oil

▶ Put oven rack in middle position and preheat oven to 200°F.

▶ Whisk together egg, milk, cornmeal, baking powder, salt, and scallions in a bowl until combined.

▶ Heat ¼ inch oil in a 10-inch heavy skillet over moderately high heat until hot but not smoking. Fill a ¼-cup measure half full with batter and carefully spoon it into skillet, then form 4 more fritters in skillet and fry, turning over once, until golden, 3 to 4 minutes total. Transfer to paper towels to drain briefly, then keep warm in 1 layer in a shallow baking pan in oven. Make more fritters in same manner (do not crowd skillet; last batch will make only 3 fritters).

WILTED CABBAGE WITH MUSTARD AND HORSERADISH

SERVES 4
Active time: 15 min   Start to finish: 30 min

- 3 tablespoons unsalted butter
- 1 large onion, halved lengthwise and thinly sliced
- 2 to 2½ lb green cabbage, quartered, cored, and cut crosswise into ¼-inch-thick strips (12 cups)
- ¾ teaspoon salt
- 1 cup water
- 1 tablespoon coarse-grain mustard
- 1 teaspoon bottled horseradish
- 1 teaspoon all-purpose flour

▶ Heat butter in a 12-inch heavy skillet over moderately high heat until foam subsides, then sauté onion, stirring occasionally, until lightly browned, about 5 minutes. Stir in cabbage, salt, and ½ cup water and cook, covered, stirring occasionally, until cabbage is just tender, about 12 minutes. Transfer to a serving dish.

▶ Whisk together mustard, horseradish, and flour in skillet, then add remaining ½ cup water and whisk until combined well. Simmer 2 minutes, then stir into cabbage mixture. Season with salt and pepper.

PEAS WITH BACON AND DILL

SERVES 4 TO 6
Active time: 20 min   Start to finish: 20 min

    4   thick bacon slices, cut crosswise into ¼-inch pieces
    1   small onion, chopped
    2   (10-oz) packages frozen baby peas (not thawed)
    ½   cup water
    1   teaspoon salt
    ⅛   teaspoon black pepper
    2   tablespoons chopped fresh dill
    1   tablespoon unsalted butter

▶ Cook bacon in a 10-inch heavy skillet over moderate heat, stirring occasionally, until browned, about 5 minutes. Spoon off all but 2 tablespoons fat from skillet (but leave bacon in skillet), then add onion and cook, stirring frequently, until beginning to soften, 3 to 4 minutes. Add peas, water, salt, pepper, and 1 tablespoon dill and cook, covered, stirring occasionally, until peas are tender, 5 to 8 minutes. Stir in butter and remaining tablespoon dill.

CURRIED OKRA WITH CHICKPEAS AND TOMATOES

SERVES 4 (MAIN COURSE) OR 6 (SIDE DISH)
Active time: 20 min   Start to finish: 35 min

 1¼   lb small fresh okra, left untrimmed, or 2 (10-oz)
       packages frozen whole okra (not thawed)
 1½   tablespoons vegetable oil
    1   medium onion, chopped
    2   garlic cloves, finely chopped
    4   teaspoons finely chopped peeled fresh ginger
    2   teaspoons curry powder
    1   (14- to 15-oz) can whole tomatoes in juice, tomatoes
       chopped, reserving juice
    1   (19-oz) can chickpeas, drained and rinsed (2 cups)
    ⅔   cup water
    ¾   teaspoon salt
    ¼   teaspoon black pepper

Accompaniment: **basmati rice**

▶ If using fresh okra, trim, leaving tops intact, being careful not to cut into pods.

▶ Heat oil in a 12-inch heavy skillet over moderately high heat until hot but not smoking, then sauté onion and garlic with ginger and curry powder, stirring, 2 minutes. Add tomatoes with their juice, chickpeas, and water and boil, uncovered, stirring occasionally, 3 minutes. Stir in okra, salt, and pepper and simmer, covered, stirring occasionally, until okra is tender, about 10 minutes.

ROASTED POTATO WEDGES WITH ROSEMARY BUTTER

SERVES 4
Active time: 10 min   Start to finish: 40 min

 1½   tablespoons olive oil
    2   lb russet (baking) potatoes (preferably organic;
       about 4 medium)
    1   teaspoon kosher salt
    ¼   teaspoon black pepper
 1½   tablespoons unsalted butter
    1   teaspoon finely chopped fresh rosemary

▶ Put oven rack in lower third of oven and preheat oven to 500°F. Oil bottom of a 15- by 10- by 1-inch baking pan with ½ tablespoon oil.
▶ Cut each potato lengthwise into 8 wedges and toss with salt, pepper, and remaining tablespoon oil in a large bowl. Arrange potato wedges, flat sides down, in baking pan, then cover pan tightly with foil and roast 10 minutes. Remove foil and roast 10 minutes more. Loosen potatoes with a metal spatula, then turn over onto other flat sides and roast until tender and golden, about 10 minutes.
▶ While potatoes roast, melt butter with rosemary in a small saucepan over moderately low heat. Loosen potatoes with spatula, then transfer to a serving dish or plates and spoon rosemary butter over them.

BUBBLE AND SQUEAK
(Fried Potatoes and Cabbage)

SERVES 4

Active time: 15 min   Start to finish: 35 min

1 lb russet (baking) potatoes, peeled and cut into
    1½-inch pieces
¾ stick (6 tablespoons) unsalted butter
1 lb Savoy cabbage, cored and thinly sliced
¾ teaspoon salt
¼ teaspoon black pepper

▸ Cover potatoes with cold salted water (see Tips, page 8) by 1 inch and bring to a boil, then boil, uncovered, until tender when pierced with a sharp knife, about 18 minutes. Drain in a colander.

▸ Heat butter in a 10-inch heavy nonstick skillet over moderately high heat until foam subsides, then sauté cabbage with salt and pepper, stirring frequently, until tender, about 5 minutes.

▸ Add potatoes, mashing and stirring them into cabbage while leaving some lumps and pressing to form a cake. Cook, without stirring, until underside is crusty and golden, about 10 minutes. Serve immediately.

FRIED POTATOES WITH OREGANO AND PARMESAN

SERVES 4

Active time: 20 min   Start to finish: 30 min

¼ cup extra-virgin olive oil
1½ lb Yukon Gold potatoes (about 5), peeled and halved
    lengthwise, then cut crosswise into ¼-inch-thick slices
1 large onion, halved lengthwise, then sliced lengthwise
    (¼ inch thick)
¾ teaspoon dried oregano, crumbled
½ teaspoon salt
¼ teaspoon black pepper
3 tablespoons finely grated Parmigiano-Reggiano
    (see Tips, page 8)

▸ Heat oil in a 12-inch nonstick skillet over moderately high heat until hot but not smoking, then add potatoes, onion, oregano, salt, and pepper and reduce heat to moderate. Cook, covered, stirring and turning potatoes occasionally,

until almost tender, about 10 minutes. Remove lid and cook, stirring and turning potatoes over 3 or 4 times, until browned, 8 to 10 minutes more. Add salt and pepper to taste, then transfer to a shallow bowl and sprinkle with cheese.

BALSAMIC ROASTED POTATO WEDGES

SERVES 4 TO 6

Active time: 10 min   Start to finish: 35 min

4 large yellow-fleshed potatoes such as Yukon Gold
    (2 lb total), scrubbed well
2½ tablespoons extra-virgin olive oil
1 teaspoon kosher salt
¼ teaspoon black pepper
2½ tablespoons balsamic vinegar

▸ Put oven rack in lower third of oven and preheat oven to 450°F.

▸ Halve each potato lengthwise, then cut each half lengthwise into 4 wedges. Toss potato wedges with oil, salt, and pepper in a 17- by 11-inch shallow baking pan (about 1 inch deep) and arrange in 1 layer. Roast potatoes, turning over once, until golden brown and cooked through, 20 to 25 minutes.

▸ Sprinkle with 2 tablespoons vinegar, shaking pan to distribute vinegar evenly, then roast until vinegar is evaporated, about 3 minutes.

▸ Serve sprinkled with remaining ½ tablespoon vinegar and salt to taste.

POTATO AND BLUE CHEESE GRATIN

SERVES 4

Active time: 10 min   Start to finish: 40 min

1½ lb medium yellow-fleshed potatoes, such as
    Yukon Gold
1 cup heavy cream
1 garlic clove, finely chopped
½ teaspoon salt
¼ teaspoon black pepper
⅓ cup crumbled blue cheese (1 oz)

Special equipment: **an adjustable-blade slicer; a 10-inch heavy skillet with a flameproof handle**

▶ Put oven rack in upper third of oven and preheat oven to 425°F.

▶ Peel potatoes and slice ⅛ inch thick with slicer, then toss with cream, garlic, salt, and pepper in skillet. Cover with foil and roast until potatoes are very tender, about 25 minutes.

▶ Remove from oven and preheat broiler. Remove foil and sprinkle potatoes with cheese. Broil until top is browned, 2 to 3 minutes.

KITCHEN NOTE

OUR RECIPES CALL FOR COMMON ORANGE-FLESHED **SWEET POTATOES**, SUCH AS THE BEAUREGARD, JEWEL, AND GARNET VARIETIES. SWEET POTATOES ARE NOT YAMS, EVEN IF THEY ARE LABELED AS SUCH AT THE MARKET.

SWISS CHARD WITH RAISINS AND PINE NUTS

SERVES 4
Active time: 25 min   Start to finish: 30 min

1½	lb Swiss chard (preferably rainbow or red; from 2 bunches)
½	cup pine nuts (2½ oz)
¼	cup olive oil
1	medium onion, finely chopped
¼	cup golden raisins, finely chopped
1	cup water

▶ Tear chard leaves from stems, then coarsely chop stems and leaves separately.

▶ Toast pine nuts in oil in a 6- to 8-quart wide heavy pot over moderate heat, stirring constantly, until golden, 1½ to 2 minutes, then transfer with a slotted spoon to paper towels to drain and season with salt.

▶ Cook onion in oil remaining in pot, stirring occasionally, 1 minute, then add chard stems and cook, stirring occasionally, 2 minutes. Add raisins and ½ cup water and simmer, covered, until stems are softened, about 3 minutes. Add chard leaves and remaining ½ cup water and simmer, partially covered, stirring occasionally, until leaves are tender, about 3 minutes. Season with salt and pepper.

▶ Serve sprinkled with pine nuts.

ROASTED SWEET POTATOES WITH LIME SYRUP AND CHIVES

SERVES 8
Active time: 30 min   Start to finish: 45 min

These potatoes caramelize slightly in the oven, which gives them a sweet crunch as their flesh remains creamy. Lime syrup lends them addictive acid and tart notes, and fresh chives add a faint onion flavor.

3½	lb sweet potatoes, peeled and cut into ½-inch cubes (10 cups)
½	stick (¼ cup) unsalted butter, melted
¾	teaspoon salt
½	teaspoon black pepper
¼	cup water
2	tablespoons sugar
1	tablespoon fresh lime juice
½	teaspoon finely grated fresh lime zest (see Tips, page 8)
2	tablespoons finely chopped fresh chives

▶ Put oven racks in upper and lower thirds of oven and preheat oven to 450°F.

▶ Toss potatoes with butter, salt, and pepper in a bowl until coated well, then spread in 1 layer in 2 (15- by 10- by 1-inch) baking pans and roast, uncovered, switching position of pans halfway through roasting, until potatoes are tender and undersides are browned, 15 to 20 minutes.

▶ While potatoes roast, bring water, sugar, and lime juice to a boil in a very small saucepan, stirring until sugar is dissolved, then simmer until reduced to about 3 tablespoons, 3 to 4 minutes. Toss potatoes with syrup and zest in a large bowl, then sprinkle with chives.

Cooks' note:
• Potatoes can be roasted and syrup made 1 day ahead. Chill separately in airtight containers. Reheat potatoes in a single roasting pan in oven, and heat syrup in a small saucepan until hot. Toss together, then toss with zest and sprinkle with chives.

SWEET-POTATO PURÉE WITH SMOKED PAPRIKA

SERVES 8
Active time: 15 min   Start to finish: 1½ hr

It is critical that you use smoked—not regular—paprika in this dish. Whether you use sweet or hot, you will end up with irresistible potatoes.

3   lb sweet potatoes
½   stick (¼ cup) unsalted butter, cut into ½-inch
    cubes and softened
⅓   cup heavy cream
¼   teaspoon sweet or hot smoked paprika (see Sources)
¼   teaspoon salt, or to taste
⅛   teaspoon cayenne, or to taste

▸ Put oven rack in middle position and preheat oven to 400°F.
▸ Prick each potato once with a fork, then bake potatoes in a foil-lined shallow baking pan until tender, about 1 hour. When cool enough to handle, peel, then cut away any eyes or dark spots. Purée potatoes with butter, cream, paprika, salt, and cayenne in a food processor until smooth.

Cooks' note:
• Purée can be made 1 day ahead and chilled in an airtight container. Reheat in a double boiler or a metal bowl set over a saucepan of simmering water, stirring occasionally.

TOMATO BREAD PUDDING

SERVES 6 TO 8
Active time: 20 min   Start to finish: 1 hr

5   cups (1-inch) cubes country-style bread
    (from 1 loaf), crusts discarded
1   stick (½ cup) unsalted butter, melted
1   (14½-oz) can whole tomatoes in juice
⅔   cup water
⅔   cup packed light brown sugar

1   tablespoon tomato paste
¾   teaspoon salt
½   teaspoon hot pepper sauce such as Tabasco

▸ Put oven rack in middle position and preheat oven to 400°F.
▸ Toss bread cubes with butter in a 13- by 9-inch baking dish until coated.
▸ Purée tomatoes with their juice in a blender 5 seconds, then transfer to a small saucepan along with water, brown sugar, tomato paste, salt, and hot sauce. Bring mixture just to a simmer, then pour over bread cubes, stirring to combine. Bake, uncovered, until edges are beginning to caramelize, 35 to 40 minutes.

BUTTERNUT SQUASH WITH SHALLOTS AND SAGE

SERVES 4
Active time: 20 min   Start to finish: 25 min

2   tablespoons olive oil
3   shallots, halved lengthwise, then cut crosswise into
    ¼-inch-thick slices (¾ cup)
1   (1¾-lb) butternut squash, peeled, halved lengthwise,
    seeded, and cut into ½-inch cubes (4 cups)
½   cup reduced-sodium chicken broth or water
1   tablespoon packed brown sugar
½   teaspoon finely chopped fresh sage
½   teaspoon salt
1   teaspoon balsamic vinegar
¼   teaspoon black pepper

▸ Heat oil in a 12-inch heavy skillet over moderate heat until hot but not smoking, then cook shallots and squash, stirring, until shallots are softened, about 5 minutes.
▸ Add broth, brown sugar, sage, and salt, stirring until sugar is dissolved. Simmer, covered, stirring occasionally, until squash is tender, 8 to 10 minutes. Remove from heat and stir in vinegar, pepper, and salt to taste.

MAIN COURSE SALADS

MELON, ZUCCHINI, AND CHICKEN SALAD

SERVES 4

Active time: 25 min   Start to finish: 25 min

In this perfect no-cook dish you can substitute crumbled bacon for the chicken or just omit the meat altogether.

- 2 medium zucchini (¾ lb total)
- 1 teaspoon salt
- 2 (3-inch-wide) wedges honeydew melon, seeded and rind removed
- 1 whole smoked chicken breast (1 lb), skinned and thinly sliced crosswise with a knife
- 1 (½-lb) piece Parmigiano-Reggiano
- ¼ cup packed fresh mint leaves, cut crosswise into thin shreds
- ¼ cup extra-virgin olive oil
- ¼ cup fresh lime juice

Special equipment: **an adjustable-blade slicer**

▸ Cut zucchini crosswise diagonally into ⅛-inch-thick slices using slicer and transfer to a colander set over a bowl. Sprinkle with salt, tossing to coat, and let stand 5 minutes, then rinse under cold water. Arrange in 1 layer on paper towels and pat dry.
▸ Cut melon wedges lengthwise into ⅛-inch-thick slices using slicer.
▸ Divide melon, zucchini, and chicken among 4 plates. Shave about one fourth of cheese into curls with a vegetable peeler and divide curls and mint among the 4 plates. Drizzle each plate with oil and lime juice. Season with salt and pepper. Serve immediately.

SALMON PLATTER WITH CAPER DRESSING

SERVES 4

Active time: 35 min   Start to finish: 40 min

- 6 oz small boiling potatoes
- 1¼ teaspoons salt
- ¼ cup fresh lemon juice
- 2 tablespoons drained bottled capers, rinsed and finely chopped, plus additional whole capers for sprinkling
- 1½ teaspoons Dijon mustard
- 1½ teaspoons sugar
- ½ cup extra-virgin olive oil
- 1 small red onion, halved lengthwise, then very thinly sliced crosswise
- 1 firm-ripe California avocado
- ½ seedless cucumber (usually plastic-wrapped), thinly sliced crosswise
- ¾ lb thinly sliced smoked salmon
- ½ lb sliced pumpernickel bread, cut into triangles

▸ Peel potatoes and cut into ¼-inch-thick slices, then transfer to a 2-quart saucepan and cover with water by 1 inch. Add ½ teaspoon salt and bring to a boil. Reduce heat and simmer, partially covered, until potatoes are tender, 5 to 8 minutes. Drain in a colander, then transfer to a bowl.
▸ Meanwhile, whisk together lemon juice, chopped capers, mustard, sugar, and remaining ¾ teaspoon salt until sugar and salt are dissolved, then whisk in oil until emulsified.
▸ Toss potatoes gently with ¼ cup dressing. Toss onion with ¼ cup dressing in another bowl and let stand 5 minutes.
▸ Peel and pit avocado, then cut into ¼-inch-thick slices.
▸ Arrange potatoes, avocado, cucumber, onion, salmon, and bread on a large platter and sprinkle with whole capers. Drizzle with some dressing and serve remainder on the side.

CURRIED EGG SALAD

SERVES 4

Active time: 15 min   Start to finish: 40 min

⅓	cup mayonnaise
1	tablespoon fresh lime juice
1½	teaspoons curry powder
1	teaspoon Dijon mustard
¼	teaspoon salt
⅛	teaspoon cayenne
6	hard-boiled large eggs, chopped
1	cup diced (¼ inch) Granny Smith apple (from 1 apple)
⅓	cup finely chopped red onion
¼	cup chopped fresh cilantro

▶ Whisk together mayonnaise, lime juice, curry powder, mustard, salt, and cayenne in a bowl until combined. Add eggs, apple, onion, and cilantro and stir to combine.

SPINACH SALAD

SERVES 4 TO 6

Active time: 20 min   Start to finish: 40 min

6	bacon slices, cut into 1-inch pieces
2	medium shallots, halved and thinly sliced lengthwise (¾ cup)
¼	cup olive oil
6	tablespoons red-wine vinegar
	Scant ½ teaspoon salt
¼	teaspoon black pepper
1	lb curly spinach (about 20 cups), coarse stems discarded
4	hard-boiled large eggs, chopped

▶ Cook bacon in a 12-inch skillet over moderate heat, stirring occasionally, until golden and crisp, about 8 minutes. Transfer with a slotted spoon to paper towels to drain. Add shallots and oil to bacon fat in skillet and cook over moderately high heat, stirring occasionally, until softened and browned, about 3 minutes. Remove skillet from heat and add vinegar, stirring and scraping up any brown bits from bottom of skillet.
▶ Stir in salt and pepper and immediately pour dressing over spinach, tossing to coat. Serve sprinkled with eggs and bacon.

KITCHEN NOTE

TO HARD-BOIL EGGS, PUT THE EGGS INTO A LARGE HEAVY POT AND COVER THEM WITH 1½ INCHES OF COLD TAP WATER. PARTIALLY COVER THE POT AND BRING THE WATER TO A ROLLING BOIL. REDUCE THE HEAT TO LOW, COVER THE POT COMPLETELY, AND COOK THE EGGS FOR 30 SECONDS. REMOVE FROM THE HEAT AND LET THE EGGS STAND IN THE HOT WATER, STILL COVERED, FOR 15 MINUTES. THEN RUN THE EGGS UNDER COLD WATER FOR ABOUT 5 MINUTES—THIS STOPS THE COOKING AND PREVENTS YOLK DISCOLORATION.

SIDE SALADS

FENNEL AND ENDIVE SALAD WITH ORANGE VINAIGRETTE

SERVES 6

Active time: 15 min   Start to finish: 30 min

1	navel orange
1½	tablespoons white-wine vinegar
¼	teaspoon salt, or to taste
¼	teaspoon black pepper
3	tablespoons olive oil
2	medium fennel bulbs (sometimes called anise; 2 lb total), stalks discarded
2	Belgian endives, trimmed

Special equipment: **an adjustable-blade slicer**

▶ Finely grate enough zest from orange (see Tips, page 8) to measure 2 teaspoons, then squeeze 1 tablespoon juice into a large bowl. Whisk in zest, vinegar, salt, pepper, and oil until combined well.
▶ Cut fennel bulbs lengthwise into very thin slices with slicer. Halve endives lengthwise, then halve crosswise and cut lengthwise into ¼-inch-wide strips. Add endives and fennel to vinaigrette and toss to combine. Chill, covered, 15 minutes to allow flavors to develop.

CAESAR SALAD

SERVES 6

Active time: 25 min Start to finish: 25 min

1 large garlic clove, halved lengthwise
¾ to 1 cup extra-virgin olive oil
1 (3-oz) Portuguese roll or a 7-inch piece of baguette,
      cut into ¾-inch cubes
8 anchovy fillets packed in oil, drained
1 large egg
2 tablespoons fresh lemon juice
3 hearts of romaine (an 18-oz package), leaves
      separated but left whole
1 oz finely grated Parmigiano-Reggiano (½ cup;
      see Tips, page 8)

Special equipment: **a very large salad bowl (preferably
wooden)**

▶ Season salad bowl by rubbing a cut half of garlic and
1 teaspoon oil onto bottom and side of bowl (reserve garlic).
▶ Heat ¾ cup oil with both halves of reserved garlic over
moderately high heat, turning garlic until golden, 1 to
2 minutes, then discard garlic. Add bread cubes and
sauté, turning occasionally, until golden on all sides,
about 2 minutes. Transfer croutons to paper towels to
drain. Pour oil through a small fine-mesh sieve into a
heatproof measure, then add enough additional olive
oil to total 6 tablespoons and reserve.
▶ Put anchovies in salad bowl and mash to a paste using
2 forks. Whisk in egg and lemon juice, then add reserved
oil in a slow stream, whisking until emulsified. Add salt
to taste.
▶ Add romaine leaves to dressing and toss to coat. Add
croutons and toss briefly.
▶ Divide salad among 6 large plates, then sprinkle with
cheese and pepper to taste. Serve immediately.

Cooks' notes:
• The egg in this recipe is not cooked, which may be of
concern if salmonella is a problem in your area.
• Although the croutons are best warm, they can be fried
1 hour ahead.

ESCAROLE AND EDAMAME SALAD

SERVES 4

Active time: 25 min Start to finish: 25 min

2 cups frozen shelled *edamame* (soybeans; 9 oz)
1 tablespoon red-wine vinegar
½ teaspoon sugar
¾ teaspoon salt
¼ teaspoon black pepper
3 tablespoons extra-virgin olive oil
1½ lb escarole, trimmed and cut crosswise into
      very thin strips (8 cups)
⅓ cup finely chopped fresh mint
1¾ oz finely grated Parmigiano-Reggiano (⅔ cup;
      see Tips, page 8)

▶ Cook *edamame* in a 3-quart saucepan of boiling salted
water (see Tips, page 8), uncovered, 5 minutes. Drain in
a sieve and rinse under cold water to stop cooking. Drain
edamame again and pat dry.
▶ Whisk together vinegar, sugar, salt, and pepper in a small
bowl until sugar and salt are dissolved. Add oil in a slow
stream, whisking until combined.
▶ Toss together *edamame*, escarole, and mint in a large bowl.
Add cheese and drizzle salad with dressing, then toss again.
Serve immediately.

PARSLEY AND CABBAGE SALAD

SERVES 6

Active time: 15 min Start to finish: 15 min

3 tablespoons extra-virgin olive oil
1 tablespoon sour cream
1 tablespoon cider vinegar
1 tablespoon water
½ teaspoon anchovy paste
¼ teaspoon salt
⅛ teaspoon black pepper
½ Savoy or green cabbage, cored, cut into 3 wedges,
      and thinly sliced crosswise (6 to 8 cups)
2 cups fresh flat-leaf parsley leaves

▶ Whisk together oil, sour cream, vinegar, water, anchovy
paste, salt, and pepper in a large bowl. Add cabbage and
parsley and toss until coated.

ROASTED POTATO AND OKRA SALAD
SERVES 6
Active time: 40 min   Start to finish: 1 hr

  2 lb small potatoes such as fingerling, red, or
      yellow-fleshed
  1 large bunch scallions, white parts halved lengthwise
      and remainder reserved for another use
  2 large fresh rosemary sprigs plus ½ teaspoon
      chopped fresh rosemary
  ¼ cup olive oil
2¼ teaspoons salt
  1 teaspoon black pepper
  ¾ lb small (2- to 3-inch) okra
  2 cups shelled fresh fava beans (2½ lb in pods) or
      shelled fresh or frozen *edamame* (soybeans;
      1½ lb in pods if fresh)
  1 cup corn (from 1 to 2 ears)
1½ tablespoons fresh lemon juice
  1 tablespoon finely chopped shallot

Roast potatoes and okra:
▶ Put oven rack in middle position and preheat oven to
450°F.
▶ Halve potatoes lengthwise and toss with scallion pieces,
rosemary sprigs, 2 tablespoons oil, ¾ teaspoon salt, and
½ teaspoon pepper. Spread potato mixture in a large roasting
pan and roast, stirring once, 20 minutes. Stir potatoes and
add okra to pan, tossing to coat. Continue to roast until okra
and potatoes are tender, about 30 minutes more.
Cook beans and corn while potatoes roast:
▶ Cook beans in 1 quart of boiling water in a 4-quart pot,
uncovered, 3 minutes, then immediately transfer with a
slotted spoon to a bowl of ice and cold water to stop cooking.
Reserve bean-cooking water. Gently peel off skins from beans.
▶ Return cooking water to a boil and add 1 teaspoon salt,
then cook corn until tender, about 4 minutes. Drain corn
in a sieve and immediately transfer to bowl of ice and
cold water to stop cooking. Drain corn again.
Make dressing and assemble salad:
▶ Whisk together lemon juice, shallot, chopped rosemary,
remaining 2 tablespoons oil, and remaining ½ teaspoon each
of salt and pepper in a large bowl until combined. Discard
rosemary sprigs, then add hot potatoes and okra to dressing
along with beans, corn, and salt to taste, tossing to combine.
Cool salad to warm before serving.

Cooks' note:
• Be aware that fava beans can cause a potentially fatal
reaction in some people of Mediterranean, African, and
Pacific Rim descent.

KITCHEN NOTE

A JAPANESE TREAT, **EDAMAME** ("ED-AH-*MAH*-
MAY") ARE YOUNG, TENDER GREEN SOYBEANS
THAT ARE BOILED AND OFTEN EATEN STRAIGHT
FROM THE POD. BOTH FROZEN EDAMAME IN THE
POD AND FROZEN SHELLED EDAMAME ARE NOW
WIDELY AVAILABLE.

CHERRY TOMATO AND LEMON SALAD
SERVES 4
Active time: 20 min   Start to finish: 35 min

  2 large lemons
  1 tablespoon sugar
  1 lb cherry or grape tomatoes (3 cups), halved or,
      if large, quartered
  3 tablespoons chopped fresh chives
  2 teaspoons extra-virgin olive oil
  ½ teaspoon salt
  ¼ teaspoon black pepper

▶ Finely grate enough zest (see Tips, page 8) from 1 lemon to
measure 2 teaspoons. Trim ends of both lemons, then stand
lemons on a cut side and cut peel, including all white pith,
from lemons with a sharp paring knife (discard peel). Cut
segments free from membranes, then cut segments
crosswise into ¼-inch pieces. Toss lemon segments gently
with sugar in a bowl.
▶ Stir in remaining ingredients and zest, then let stand,
covered, at room temperature 15 minutes (to allow flavors
to develop).
EACH SERVING ABOUT 70 CALORIES AND 3 GRAMS FAT

LENTIL SALAD WITH TOMATO AND DILL

SERVES 4 TO 6

Active time: 25 min   Start to finish: 35 min

- 1 cup dried lentils (preferably small French lentils)
- 1 large garlic clove, chopped
- 1 teaspoon salt, or to taste
- ¾ lb tomatoes, diced (2 cups)
- 4 large scallions, thinly sliced (¾ cup)
- ¼ cup chopped fresh dill
- ¼ cup thinly sliced fresh basil
- 3 tablespoons red-wine vinegar, or to taste
- ¼ cup extra-virgin olive oil
- ¼ teaspoon black pepper

▶ Bring 4 cups water to a boil in a 2-quart heavy saucepan with lentils, garlic, and ½ teaspoon salt, then reduce heat and simmer, uncovered, until lentils are just tender, 15 to 25 minutes. Drain in a large sieve, then transfer to a large bowl.
▶ Toss hot lentils with tomatoes, scallions, dill, basil, vinegar, oil, pepper, and remaining ½ teaspoon salt, or to taste.

VIETNAMESE RICE NOODLE SALAD

SERVES 4

Active time: 15 min   Start to finish: 15 min

- ¼ lb thin rice noodles
- ¼ cup rice vinegar (not seasoned)
- 1 tablespoon sugar
- 1 tablespoon Asian fish sauce
- ¼ teaspoon salt
- 1 medium carrot, coarsely shredded
- 2 scallions, thinly sliced crosswise
- 1 cup loosely packed mixed fresh cilantro, mint, and/or basil leaves, torn if large
- ¼ cup chopped unsalted dry-roasted peanuts

▶ Soak noodles in hot water 10 minutes, then drain in a large sieve.
▶ Cook noodles in a 4-quart pot of boiling water, uncovered, until tender, about 1 minute. Drain in sieve and rinse under cold water until cold. Drain well and pat noodles dry.
▶ Whisk together vinegar, sugar, fish sauce, and salt in a large bowl until sugar and salt are dissolved. Add noodles, carrot, scallions, herbs, and peanuts, tossing to combine.

KITCHEN NOTE

ALSO CALLED RICE VERMICELLI, DRIED **RICE STICK NOODLES** ARE THIN AND OFF-WHITE AND ARE SOLD IN WIDE, WIRY SKEINS. THEY SHOULD BE SOFTENED IN WATER BEFORE USE.

BARLEY AND CORN SALAD WITH BASIL CHIVE DRESSING

SERVES 4 TO 6

Active time: 25 min   Start to finish: 25 min

- 2 cups plus 1 tablespoon water
- ¾ teaspoon salt
- 1 cup quick-cooking barley
- 2 cups corn (from about 4 ears)
- ⅓ cup olive oil
- ⅓ cup chopped fresh basil
- 3 tablespoons chopped fresh chives
- 1½ tablespoons red-wine vinegar
- ¼ teaspoon sugar
- ¼ teaspoon black pepper
- 3 Belgian endives (about 1 lb total), trimmed and sliced crosswise ½ inch thick

▶ Bring 2 cups water with ¼ teaspoon salt to a boil in a 1½-quart saucepan. Stir in barley, then reduce heat and simmer, covered, until barley is tender, about 10 minutes.
▶ While barley simmers, blanch corn in a 1½- to 2½-quart saucepan of boiling water 1 minute, then drain in a large sieve and rinse under cold running water to stop cooking. Drain again and pat dry, then transfer to a large bowl.
▶ Remove barley from heat (when tender) and let stand, covered, 5 minutes.
▶ While barley stands, pulse oil, basil, chives, vinegar, sugar, pepper, remaining tablespoon water, and remaining ½ teaspoon salt in a blender until herbs are finely chopped.
▶ Drain barley well in large sieve and add to corn in bowl, then add endives and dressing, tossing to combine.

QUINOA AND BULGUR SALAD WITH FETA

SERVES 4 (SIDE DISH)
Active time: 20 min   Start to finish: 40 min

Not technically a grain, but rather the seed of an herb, quinoa hails from South America. (It is often called a "supergrain" because it contains more protein than any grain.) Bulgur comes from the hulled, cracked berries of whole wheat, and has a nutty flavor.

⅓   cup quinoa (see Sources)
4   cups water
1½   teaspoons salt
⅓   cup medium bulgur
2   tablespoons olive oil
2   tablespoons fresh lemon juice
¾   teaspoon dried mint, crumbled
¼   teaspoon black pepper
4   brine-cured black olives such as Kalamata, pitted and cut into slivers
2   radishes, quartered and thinly sliced
2   oz feta, coarsely crumbled (½ cup)
1   head Bibb lettuce, cut into ¼-inch strips (4 cups)

▸ Wash quinoa in 3 changes of cold water in a bowl, draining in a sieve between changes of water.
▸ Stir together quinoa, 4 cups water, and ¾ teaspoon salt in a 2- to 3-quart saucepan and simmer, uncovered, until quinoa is just tender and germ starts to separate from grain, about 20 minutes. Drain well in sieve, then transfer to a medium bowl.
▸ While quinoa simmers, cover bulgur with warm water by 2 inches and soak until tender and chewy, about 10 minutes. Drain well in sieve, then stir into drained quinoa. Cool grains completely, about 20 minutes.
▸ While grains cool, stir together oil, lemon juice, mint, pepper, and remaining ¾ teaspoon salt in a small bowl and let stand 15 minutes, then stir into grains along with olives, radishes, feta, and lettuce. Serve immediately.

Cooks' note:
• Grains can be made 1 day ahead and chilled, covered. Bring to room temperature while dressing stands.

SAUCES AND CONDIMENTS

ASIAN DIPPING SAUCE
MAKES ABOUT ⅔ CUP
Active time: 10 min   Start to finish: 10 min

Often served with summer rolls or grilled meats, this sauce is also great over rice.

- 3 tablespoons packed light brown sugar
- ¼ cup Asian fish sauce
- 3 tablespoons fresh lime juice
- 1 or 2 thinly sliced fresh Thai chiles (1 to 2 inches long) or ¼ teaspoon dried hot red pepper flakes
- 1 garlic clove, thinly sliced

▸ Stir together all ingredients in a bowl.

Cooks' note:
• Sauce keeps, covered and chilled, 1 week.

SPICY HAZELNUT SAUCE
MAKES ABOUT 1¼ CUPS
Active time: 15 min   Start to finish: 20 min

Serve this sauce over baked or sautéed white-fleshed fish.

- ⅔ cup hazelnuts (3 oz), toasted (see Tips, page 8) and any loose skins rubbed off in a kitchen towel
- ½ cup warm water
- 1 small garlic clove, minced
- ½ teaspoon salt
- ½ cup finely chopped fresh cilantro
- 2 teaspoons red-wine vinegar
- ¼ teaspoon cayenne
- ¼ cup olive oil

▸ Purée nuts with water, garlic, salt, cilantro, vinegar, and cayenne in a blender or food processor until smooth. With motor running, add oil in a slow stream, blending until emulsified.

CRANBERRY QUINCE SAUCE
MAKES ABOUT 5 CUPS
Active time: 30 min   Start to finish: 2½ hr

This sauce provides a sweet and tart contrast to rich meat or poultry.

- 1¾ lb quinces (2 large)
- 4 cups water
- 1½ cups sugar
- 1 (12-oz) bag fresh or frozen cranberries (do not thaw; 3½ cups)

Special equipment: **an 8-inch square of cheesecloth; kitchen string**

▸ Peel, quarter, and core quinces, reserving peel and cores, then cut quarters into ¼-inch pieces. Tie up peel and cores in cheesecloth. Bring water and sugar to a boil in a 4-quart heavy pot, stirring until sugar is dissolved, then add quince and cheesecloth bundle and simmer, partially covered, until quince is tender, about 1½ hours. Add cranberries and simmer, uncovered, stirring occasionally, until cranberries burst and soften, 8 to 10 minutes.
▸ Drain mixture in a large medium-mesh sieve set over a bowl, discarding cheesecloth bundle and reserving cranberry solids, then return cooking liquid to pot and boil, uncovered, until syrupy and reduced to about 1½ cups, 5 to 10 minutes. Stir together syrup and cranberry mixture in bowl, then cool to room temperature.

Cooks' note:
• Sauce can be made 3 days ahead and chilled in an airtight container.

KITCHEN NOTE

TO TOAST NUTS, PUT THEM IN A SHALLOW BAKING PAN IN THE MIDDLE OF A PREHEATED 350°F OVEN UNTIL GOLDEN, 4 TO 10 MINUTES.

ONION GRAVY

MAKES ABOUT 2¼ CUPS
Active time: 30 min   Start to finish: 30 min

　1　tablespoon vegetable oil
　1　tablespoon unsalted butter
　1　medium onion, thinly sliced
1½　tablespoons all-purpose flour
1¼　cups water
　1　cup canned beef broth
　1　tablespoon Worcestershire sauce
　¼　teaspoon black pepper

▶ Heat oil and butter in a 12-inch heavy skillet over moderately high heat until foam from butter subsides, then sauté onion, stirring frequently, until softened and browned, about 15 minutes. Add flour and cook, stirring, 1 minute. Stir in water, broth, Worcestershire sauce, and pepper, then reduce heat and simmer, stirring and scraping up any brown bits, until gravy is slightly thickened, 8 to 10 minutes. Add salt and additional Worcestershire sauce to taste if desired.

BEURRE BLANC

MAKES ABOUT 1 CUP
Active time: 15 min   Start to finish: 20 min

　¼　cup dry white wine
　¼　cup white-wine vinegar
　2　tablespoons finely chopped shallot
　⅓　cup heavy cream
　¼　teaspoon salt
　⅛　teaspoon white pepper, or to taste
　2　sticks (1 cup) unsalted butter, cut into
　　　tablespoon-size pieces and chilled

▶ Boil wine, vinegar, and shallot in a 2- to 3-quart heavy saucepan over moderate heat until liquid is syrupy and reduced to 2 to 3 tablespoons, about 5 minutes. Add cream, salt, and white pepper and boil 1 minute. Reduce heat to moderately low and add a few tablespoons butter, whisking constantly. Add remaining butter a few pieces at a time, whisking constantly and adding new pieces before previous ones have completely liquefied (the sauce should maintain consistency of hollandaise), lifting pan from heat occasionally to cool mixture.

▶ Remove from heat, then season with salt and pepper and pour sauce through a medium-mesh sieve into a sauceboat, pressing on and then discarding shallot. Serve immediately.

Cooks' note:
• Wine mixture can be reduced, and cream and seasoning added, up to 1 hour ahead. Boil cream 1 minute before adding butter.

THYME GARLIC BUTTER

MAKES ABOUT ½ CUP
Active time: 15 min   Start to finish: 3 hr (includes chilling)

　1　garlic clove
　½　teaspoon salt
　1　stick (½ cup) unsalted butter, softened
　3　tablespoons chopped fresh flat-leaf parsley
　2　teaspoons chopped fresh thyme
　2　teaspoons finely grated fresh lemon zest
　　　(see Tips, page 8)
　¼　teaspoon black pepper

▶ Mince garlic and mash to a paste with salt using a heavy knife. Transfer to a food processor along with remaining ingredients and blend.
▶ Roll into a 6-inch log in a sheet of plastic wrap, twisting ends closed. Chill, covered, at least 2 hours for flavors to develop. Bring to room temperature before using.

GREEN OLIVE AND PIMIENTO RELISH

MAKES ABOUT 2 CUPS
Active time: 15 min   Start to finish: 45 min

1½　cups pimiento-stuffed green olives (7 oz),
　　　drained, patted dry, and finely chopped
　2　garlic cloves, minced
　1　cup chopped fresh cilantro
　5　tablespoons extra-virgin olive oil
　1　teaspoon whole-grain Dijon mustard

▶ Stir together all ingredients and let stand 30 minutes to allow flavors to develop.

CONCORD GRAPE JAM

MAKES 6 OR 7 (½-PINT) JARS

Active time: 2¾ hr   Start to finish: 1 day (includes time for flavors to develop)

    5 lb Concord grapes, stemmed
    5 cups sugar
    3 tablespoons fresh lemon juice

Special equipment: **7 (½-pt) canning jars with lids and screw bands; a boiling-water canner, or an 8- to 10-qt deep pot plus a flat metal rack; an instant-read thermometer; a food mill fitted with fine disk**

Sterilize jars and lids:

▶ Wash jars, lids, and screw bands in hot soapy water, then rinse well. Dry screw bands. Put jars on rack in canner and add enough water to cover by 2 inches. Bring to a boil, covered, then boil for 10 minutes. Remove from heat, leaving jars in water. Heat lids in water to cover by 2 inches in a small saucepan until thermometer registers 180°F (do not let boil). Remove from heat, leaving lids in water. Keep jars and lids submerged in hot water, covered, until ready to use.

Cook and can jam:

▶ Chill 2 small plates (for testing jam).

▶ Slip skins from grapes and purée skins with 1 cup sugar in a food processor, then transfer to a 4- to 6-quart wide heavy pot. Stir in lemon juice, peeled grapes, and remaining 4 cups sugar and boil over moderate heat, stirring frequently and skimming foam, until pulp is broken down, about 20 minutes. Force jam through food mill set over a large bowl. Discard remaining solids. Return jam to pot and cook at a slow boil, skimming foam occasionally and stirring frequently as mixture thickens to prevent scorching, 35 minutes, then test for doneness.

▶ To test jam, remove from heat, then drop a teaspoonful on a chilled plate and chill 1 minute. Tilt plate: Jam should remain in a mound and not run. If jam runs, continue cooking at a slow boil, testing every 5 minutes, until done, up to 25 minutes more.

▶ Remove jars and lids from water, reserving water in canner. Drain jars upside down on a clean kitchen towel 1 minute, then invert. Ladle jam into jars, leaving ¼ inch of space at top.

Seal, process, and store jars:

▶ Wipe off rims of filled jars with a clean damp kitchen towel, then top with lids and firmly screw on screw bands. Put sealed jars on rack in canner and, if necessary, add enough hot water to cover jars by 2 inches. Bring to a boil, covered. Boil jars 10 minutes, then transfer with tongs to a towel-lined surface to cool.

▶ Jars will seal as they cool; if you hear a ping, it signals that the vacuum formed at the top of the jar has made the lid concave. Remember that you may or may not be around to hear that ping (some jars make the sound after you remove them from water, and others in same batch may take a few hours); the important thing is for jars to eventually have concave lids. Preserves will thicken as they cool.

▶ After jars have cooled 12 to 24 hours, press center of each lid to check that it's concave, then remove screw band and try to lift off lid with your fingertips. If you can't, lid has a good seal. Replace screw band. Promptly put any jars that haven't sealed properly in the refrigerator and use them first.

Cooks' notes:

• Let jam stand in jars at least 1 day for flavors to develop.

• Jam keeps in sealed jars in a cool dark place 5 to 6 months.

PICKLED ONIONS

MAKES ABOUT 2 CUPS

Active time: 25 min   Start to finish: 1 week (includes chilling)

    10 oz medium (1-inch) boiling onions, peeled (about 16)
    1½ cups malt vinegar
    ½ cup water
    3 tablespoons packed dark brown sugar
    2 tablespoons pickling spice
    1 (1-inch) piece fresh ginger, peeled and sliced

▶ Cover onions with water in a 2- to 3-quart heavy saucepan, then bring to a simmer and cook 5 minutes. Drain in a colander and transfer to a clean heatproof jar. Simmer remaining ingredients in saucepan 5 minutes, then pour over onions. Cool completely, uncovered. Chill, covered, 1 week to allow flavors to develop.

Cooks' note:

• Pickled onions can be chilled up to 3 weeks.

PICKLED PEACHES

MAKES 6 PINTS

Active time: 1½ hr Start to finish: 1½ days (includes chilling)

These sweet-and-sour peaches perk up the flavor of ham and fried chicken; they are also very good with vanilla ice cream.

1	(1,000-mg) vitamin C tablet (to prevent discoloration), crushed to a powder
6½	cups cold water
24	firm-ripe small peaches (6 to 7 lb)
2½	cups sugar
1¼	cups distilled white vinegar
4	teaspoons pickling spice
¼	teaspoon kosher salt

Special equipment: **6 (1-pt) canning jars with lids and screw bands; a boiling-water canner, or a 10- to 12-qt deep pot plus a flat metal rack; an instant-read thermometer**

Prepare peaches:

▸Dissolve vitamin C powder in 6 cups water in a large bowl (to acidulate water).

▸Cut a shallow X in bottom of each peach with a sharp paring knife and blanch in 4 batches in a 5- to 6-quart pot of boiling water 10 to 15 seconds. Transfer with a slotted spoon to a large bowl of ice and cold water and let stand until cool enough to handle. Peel peaches, then halve lengthwise and pit. Add peaches to acidulated water and let stand 10 minutes, then drain well in a colander.

▸Toss peaches with sugar in a 6-quart wide heavy pot and chill, covered, at least 8 and up to 12 hours.

Sterilize jars and lids:

▸Wash jars, lids, and screw bands in hot soapy water, then rinse well. Dry screw bands. Put jars on rack in canner and add enough water to cover jars by 2 inches. Bring to a boil, covered, then boil 10 minutes. Remove from heat, leaving jars in water. Heat lids in water to cover by 2 inches in a small saucepan until thermometer registers 180°F (do not let boil). Remove from heat, leaving lids in water. Keep jars and lids submerged in hot water, covered, until ready to use.

Cook and can peaches:

▸Add vinegar, spice, salt, and remaining ½ cup water to peaches (sugar will have dissolved and will have drawn out

peach juices) and bring to a boil over moderate heat, skimming foam. Reduce heat and simmer until peaches are barely tender, about 3 minutes.

▸Remove jars and lids from water, reserving water in canner. Drain jars upside down on a clean kitchen towel 1 minute, then invert and divide peaches among jars using a slotted spoon. Return peach-cooking liquid to a boil, then pour into jars, leaving ¼ inch of space at top. Run a thin knife between peaches and sides of jars to eliminate air bubbles.

Seal, process, and store jars:

▸Wipe off rims of filled jars with a clean damp kitchen towel, then top with lids and firmly screw on screw bands. Put sealed jars on rack in canner and, if necessary, add enough hot water to cover jars by 2 inches. Bring to a boil, covered. Boil jars 20 minutes, then transfer with tongs to a towel-lined surface to cool.

▸Jars will seal as they cool; if you hear a ping, it signals that the vacuum formed at the top of the jar has made the lid concave. Remember that you may or may not be around to hear that ping (some jars make the sound after you remove them from water, and others in same batch may take a few hours); the important thing is for jars to eventually have concave lids.

▸After jars have cooled 12 to 24 hours, press center of each lid to check that it's concave, then remove screw band and try to lift off lid with your fingertips. If you can't, the lid has a good seal. Replace screw band. Promptly put any jars that haven't sealed properly in the refrigerator and use them first.

Cooks' note:

• Peaches keep in sealed jars in a cool dark place 6 months.

KITCHEN NOTE

BEFORE USING **HOME-CANNED GOODS**, CHECK THE JAR AGAIN TO MAKE SURE THE LID IS CONCAVE, SIGNIFYING THAT THE VACUUM SEAL IS STILL PRESENT. IF YOU CAN REMOVE THE LID WITHOUT HAVING TO PRY IT OFF WITH A CAN OPENER, DO NOT USE THE CONTENTS. (IF YOU HAVE MADE YOUR OWN PRESERVES, PROMPTLY PUT ANY JARS THAT HAVEN'T SEALED IN THE FRIDGE AND USE THEM FIRST.)

DESSERTS

CAKES

CHOCOLATE YOGURT CAKE

MAKES 1 LOAF

Active time: 20 min   Start to finish: 2 hr (includes cooling)

- ¾ stick (6 tablespoons) unsalted butter, softened, plus additional for greasing pan
- ⅔ cup unsweetened Dutch-process cocoa powder plus additional for dusting pan
- 1¾ cups all-purpose flour
- 1½ teaspoons baking powder
- ¾ teaspoon salt
- ½ teaspoon baking soda
- 1 cup plain whole-milk yogurt
- ⅓ cup water
- 1 teaspoon vanilla
- 1¼ cups sugar
- 2 large eggs

Special equipment: **an 8½- by 4½- by 2½-inch loaf pan (6-cup capacity)**

▶ Put oven rack in middle position and preheat oven to 350°F. Generously butter loaf pan, then dust with cocoa powder, knocking out excess.

▶ Whisk together flour, baking powder, salt, baking soda, and ⅔ cup cocoa in a bowl. Whisk together yogurt, water, and vanilla in another bowl.

▶ Beat ¾ stick butter with sugar in a large bowl using an electric mixer at medium speed until light and fluffy. Add eggs 1 at a time, beating well after each addition. Reduce speed to low and add half of flour mixture. Add yogurt mixture, then add remaining flour mixture and mix until just combined.

▶ Transfer batter to pan and bake until a wooden pick or skewer inserted in center comes out clean, about 1 hour. Cool in pan on a rack 15 minutes, then turn out onto rack to cool completely.

BLUEBERRY PUDDING CAKE

SERVES 6 TO 8

Active time: 15 min   Start to finish: 50 min

- ⅓ cup plus ½ cup sugar
- ¼ cup water
- 1 tablespoon fresh lemon juice
- 1 teaspoon cornstarch
- 10 oz blueberries (2 cups)
- 1 cup all-purpose flour
- 1¾ teaspoons baking powder
- 1 teaspoon salt
- 1 large egg
- ½ cup whole milk
- 1 stick (½ cup) unsalted butter, melted and cooled slightly
- 1 teaspoon vanilla

▶ Put oven rack in middle position and preheat oven to 375°F. Butter a 9-inch square baking pan.

▶ Stir together ⅓ cup sugar with water, lemon juice, and cornstarch in a small saucepan, then stir in blueberries. Bring to a simmer, then simmer, stirring occasionally, 3 minutes. Remove from heat.

▶ Whisk together flour, baking powder, salt, and remaining ½ cup sugar in a medium bowl.

▶ Whisk together egg, milk, butter, and vanilla in a large bowl, then add flour mixture, whisking until just combined.

▶ Spoon batter into baking pan, spreading evenly, then pour blueberry mixture evenly over batter (berries will sink). Bake until a knife inserted in center of cake portion comes out clean, 25 to 30 minutes. Cool in pan on a rack 5 minutes.

Cooks' note:
• Cake can be made 1 day ahead and cooled completely, uncovered, then kept, wrapped well in foil, at room temperature.

CARDAMOM APPLE ALMOND CAKE

SERVES 8

Active time: 35 min   Start to finish: 2½ hr (includes cooling)

Designed for Passover, matzo meal takes the place of flour, and, because the cornstarch in confectioners sugar isn't kosher, we powdered granulated sugar in an electric coffee/spice grinder and mixed it with potato starch.

For cake

    Vegetable oil for greasing pan
½ cup matzo meal (not cake meal) plus additional for dusting
1 cup slivered almonds (4½ oz), toasted (see Tips, page 8) and cooled
    Scant ½ teaspoon ground cardamom
½ teaspoon salt
5 large eggs, separated, at room temperature for 30 minutes
1 cup granulated sugar
2 Granny Smith apples, peeled and coarsely grated

For powdered sugar

⅓ cup granulated sugar
½ teaspoon potato starch

Special equipment: a 9- to 9½-inch (24-cm) springform pan; an electric coffee/spice grinder

▸ Put oven rack in middle position and preheat oven to 350°F. Oil springform pan and dust with matzo meal, knocking out excess.
▸ Pulse almonds in a food processor with cardamom, ½ cup matzo meal, and ¼ teaspoon salt until finely ground. (Be careful not to pulse to a paste.)
▸ Beat yolks in a large bowl with an electric mixer at medium-high speed until smooth, then add ¾ cup sugar, 1 tablespoon at a time, beating, and beat until mixture is very thick and pale, 2 to 3 minutes. Stir in nut mixture, then apples. Beat whites and remaining ¼ teaspoon salt in another bowl with cleaned beaters at medium speed until they hold soft peaks. Add remaining ¼ cup sugar, a little at a time, beating, and beat until whites just hold stiff peaks. Stir one fourth of whites into yolk mixture to lighten, then fold in remaining whites gently but thoroughly. Scrape batter into pan and rap pan once on work surface to eliminate any large air bubbles.
▸ Bake cake until puffed, browned, and top springs back

when touched, 40 to 45 minutes. Transfer to a rack and cool completely in pan (cake will sink slightly in center). Run a knife around edge of cake to loosen, then remove side of pan.
Make powdered sugar:
▸ Grind sugar in coffee/spice grinder until powdered, then stir together with potato starch in a bowl. Sift some of powdered sugar over cake before serving and reserve remainder for another use.

Cooks' notes:
• Cake can be made 1 day ahead and cooled completely, then kept, covered with foil, at room temperature.
• Cardamom loses flavor and aroma quickly, so be sure to store it in an airtight container in a cool dry place.

CRANBERRY WALNUT UPSIDE-DOWN CAKE

SERVES 8

Active time: 30 min   Start to finish: 2¼ hr (includes cooling)

For topping

½ stick (¼ cup) unsalted butter
¾ cup packed light brown sugar
1¾ cups fresh or frozen cranberries (7 oz; do not thaw if frozen)
¾ cup coarsely chopped walnuts (3 oz), toasted (see Tips, page 8)

For cake

1½ cups all-purpose flour
1½ teaspoons baking powder
1 teaspoon baking soda
½ teaspoon salt
1 stick (½ cup) unsalted butter, softened
¾ cup sugar
2 large eggs
½ teaspoon vanilla
¾ cup well-shaken buttermilk

Special equipment: a well-seasoned 10-inch cast-iron skillet
Accompaniment: lightly sweetened whipped cream

Make topping:
▸ Melt butter in skillet over moderate heat, then swirl to coat bottom and side of skillet and stir in brown sugar. Simmer, stirring, until sugar is dissolved, 1 to 2 minutes, then

sprinkle cranberries and walnuts evenly over butter mixture and remove from heat.

Make cake:

▸ Put oven rack in middle position and preheat oven to 350°F.

▸ Whisk together flour, baking powder, baking soda, and salt. Beat together butter and sugar in a large bowl with an electric mixer at high speed until light and fluffy, 4 to 6 minutes. Add eggs 1 at a time, beating well after each addition. Beat in vanilla. Reduce speed to low and add flour mixture alternately in batches with buttermilk, beginning and ending with flour mixture and mixing until just combined. (Do not overmix.)

Bake cake:

▸ Heat topping in skillet over moderately high heat until it starts to bubble, then gently spoon batter over topping and spread evenly. Quickly transfer to oven and bake until cake is golden brown and a wooden pick or skewer inserted in center comes out clean, 25 to 30 minutes. Cool cake in skillet on a rack 15 minutes. Run a thin knife around inside edge of skillet, then invert a serving plate over skillet and invert cake onto plate. Cool completely on plate on rack, about 1 hour. Serve cake at room temperature.

Cooks' note:

• Cake can be made 1 day ahead and kept, wrapped in plastic wrap, at room temperature.

KITCHEN NOTE

DO NOT SUBSTITUTE AMERICAN-STYLE, OR "NATURAL," UNSWEETENED COCOA POWDER FOR DUTCH-PROCESS OR VICE VERSA. REGULAR COCOA POWDER IS ACIDIC, SO IT MUST BE COMBINED WITH AN ALKALINE INGREDIENT SUCH AS BAKING SODA TO CREATE CARBON DIOXIDE BUBBLES, WHICH CAUSE LEAVENING. DUTCH-PROCESS COCOA HAS AN ALKALINE SOLUTION ADDED TO THE BEANS DURING ROASTING AND MUST BE COMBINED WITH AN ACID, SUCH AS BAKING POWDER. IF WE DON'T SPECIFY, EITHER TYPE WILL WORK.

CHOCOLATE ESPRESSO SPELT CAKE
SERVES 8
Active time: 20 min   Start to finish: 1¼ hr

When measuring spelt flour, be sure to spoon it into the measuring cup and level it off to prevent packing it down; this will keep the cake light.

1½ sticks (¾ cup) unsalted butter, softened, plus additional for greasing pan

¾ cup unsweetened Dutch-process cocoa powder plus additional for dusting pan and cake

1 cup boiling-hot water

1½ tablespoons instant-espresso powder (see Sources)

1½ teaspoons vanilla

1 teaspoon baking soda

½ lb Medjool dates (12 to 14), pitted and coarsely chopped (1½ cups)

2 cups spelt flour (see Sources)

2 teaspoons baking powder

¾ teaspoon salt

1 cup packed dark brown sugar

2 large eggs

Special equipment: **a 9- to 9½-inch (24-cm) springform pan**
Accompaniment: **lightly sweetened whipped cream**

▸ Put oven rack in middle position and preheat oven to 350°F. Butter springform pan, then lightly dust with cocoa powder, knocking out excess.

▸ Stir together boiling-hot water, espresso powder, vanilla, and baking soda in a bowl, then add dates, mashing lightly with a fork, and steep until liquid cools to room temperature, about 10 minutes.

▸ Whisk together spelt flour, cocoa powder, baking powder, and salt in another bowl. Beat together butter and brown sugar with an electric mixer at medium-high speed until pale and fluffy. Add eggs 1 at a time, beating until just combined. Beat in date mixture (batter will look curdled), then reduce speed to low and add flour mixture, mixing until just combined.

▸ Spoon batter into springform pan, smoothing top, and bake until a wooden pick or skewer inserted in center comes out clean, about 50 minutes to 1 hour. Cool cake in pan on a rack 5 minutes, then remove side of pan and cool cake to warm or room temperature.

PUMPKIN SPICE BUNDT CAKE WITH BUTTERMILK ICING

SERVES 12

Active time: 30 min   Start to finish: 1¾ hr (includes cooling)

This cake tastes even better a few days after it's baked, so it's perfect to have on hand over the holidays, when guests tend to drop in unexpectedly.

For cake

1½   sticks (¾ cup) unsalted butter, softened, plus
        additional for greasing bundt pan
2¼   cups all-purpose flour plus additional for dusting pan
  2   teaspoons baking powder
  1   teaspoon baking soda
  1   teaspoon cinnamon
  ¾   teaspoon ground allspice
  ½   teaspoon salt
1¼   cups canned solid-pack pumpkin (from a 15-oz can;
        not pie filling)
  ¾   cup well-shaken buttermilk
  1   teaspoon vanilla
1¼   cups sugar
  3   large eggs

For icing

  2   tablespoons plus 2 teaspoons well-shaken buttermilk
1½   cups confectioners sugar

Special equipment: **a 10-inch nonstick bundt pan (3 qt)**

Make cake:

▶ Put oven rack in middle position and preheat oven to 350°F. Generously butter bundt pan, then dust with flour, knocking out excess.
▶ Whisk together flour (2¼ cups), baking powder, baking soda, cinnamon, allspice, and salt in a bowl. Whisk together pumpkin, buttermilk (¾ cup), and vanilla in another bowl.
▶ Beat together butter (1½ sticks) and sugar in a large bowl with an electric mixer at medium-high speed until pale and fluffy, 3 to 5 minutes, then add eggs and beat 1 minute. Reduce speed to low and add flour and pumpkin mixtures alternately in batches, beginning and ending with flour mixture and mixing until batter is just smooth.
▶ Spoon batter into pan, smoothing top, then bake until a wooden pick or skewer inserted in center comes out clean, 45 to 50 minutes. Cool cake in pan on a rack 15 minutes,

then invert rack over cake and invert cake onto rack. Cool 10 minutes more.

Make icing:

▶ While cake cools, whisk together buttermilk and confectioners sugar until smooth. Drizzle icing over warm cake, then cool cake completely. Icing will harden slightly.

Cooks' note:

• Cake can be made 3 days ahead and kept in an airtight container at room temperature.

COOKIES

MINI BLACK-AND-WHITE COOKIES

MAKES ABOUT 5 DOZEN COOKIES

Active time: 1 hr   Start to finish: 1½ hr

This is a miniature version of a New York favorite—a cakey cookie with sweet half-moons of vanilla and chocolate icing.

For cookies

1¼   cups all-purpose flour
  ½   teaspoon baking soda
  ½   teaspoon salt
  ⅓   cup well-shaken buttermilk
  ½   teaspoon vanilla
  7   tablespoons unsalted butter, softened
  ½   cup sugar
  1   large egg

For icings

2¾   cups confectioners sugar
  2   tablespoons light corn syrup
  2   teaspoons fresh lemon juice
  ½   teaspoon vanilla
  4   to 6 tablespoons water
  ¼   cup unsweetened Dutch-process cocoa powder

Special equipment: **a small offset spatula**

Make cookies:

▶ Put oven racks in upper and lower thirds of oven and preheat oven to 350°F. Butter 2 large baking sheets.
▶ Whisk together flour, baking soda, and salt in a bowl. Stir together buttermilk and vanilla in a cup.

▸ Beat together butter and sugar in a large bowl with an electric mixer at medium-high until pale and fluffy, about 3 minutes, then add egg, beating until combined well. Reduce speed to low and add flour mixture and buttermilk mixture alternately in batches, beginning and ending with flour mixture, and mixing just until smooth.

▸ Drop rounded teaspoons of batter 1 inch apart onto baking sheets. Bake, switching position of sheets halfway through baking, until tops are puffed, edges are pale golden, and cookies spring back when touched, 6 to 8 minutes total. Transfer to a rack to cool completely.

Make icings while cookies cool:

▸ Stir together confectioners sugar, corn syrup, lemon juice, vanilla, and 2 tablespoons water in a small bowl until smooth. If icing is not easily spreadable, add more water, ½ teaspoon at a time. Transfer half of icing to another bowl and stir in cocoa, adding more water, ½ teaspoon at a time, to thin to same consistency as vanilla icing. Cover surface with a dampened paper towel, then cover bowl with plastic wrap.

Ice cookies:

▸ With offset spatula, spread white icing over half of flat side of each cookie. Starting with cookies you iced first, spread chocolate icing over other half.

Cooks' note:

• Once icing is dry, cookies keep, layered between sheets of wax paper or parchment, in an airtight container at room temperature 4 days.

FIG SWIRLS

MAKES ABOUT 4 DOZEN COOKIES
Active time: 1 hr Start to finish: 7¼ hr (includes chilling)

The swirls are attained with a specific skill: slice and bake. You'll get a little sweet pastry and a little filling in every bite.

For pastry dough

1¾ cups all-purpose flour
¼   teaspoon baking powder
¼   teaspoon baking soda
¼   teaspoon salt
1   stick (½ cup) unsalted butter, softened
4   oz cream cheese at room temperature
1   large egg yolk
1   teaspoon vanilla

For filling

1   cup packed soft dried Mission figs (8 oz), hard tips discarded
¾   cup mild honey
2   tablespoons fresh orange juice
2   teaspoons grated fresh orange zest
½   teaspoon cinnamon

Make pastry dough:

▸ Whisk together flour, baking powder, baking soda, and salt in a bowl.

▸ Pulse butter, cream cheese, yolk, and vanilla in a food processor until smooth, then add flour mixture and pulse until dough just forms a ball.

▸ Halve dough and form each half into a roughly 6- by 2-inch rectangle. Chill, wrapped in plastic wrap, until firm, about 1½ hours.

Make filling:

▸ Purée figs, honey, juice, zest, and cinnamon in cleaned food processor until almost smooth.

Make logs:

▸ Roll out 1 piece of dough between 2 sheets of wax paper into a 10- by 8-inch rectangle (about ⅓ inch thick), with a long side facing you. Remove top sheet of wax paper and gently spread one fourth of fig mixture over bottom half of dough, leaving a ¼-inch border. Using wax paper as an aid, roll dough, jelly-roll style, halfway, enclosing fig mixture. Flip dough, with wax paper. Remove paper. Spread with one third of remaining fig mixture and roll in same manner to form an S-shaped log. Make another log with remaining piece of dough and filling. Chill logs, wrapped in wax paper, until firm, at least 4 hours.

Bake cookies:

▸ Put oven rack in middle position and preheat oven to 375°F.

▸ Cut logs crosswise into ⅓-inch-thick slices and arrange slices about 2 inches apart on lightly buttered baking sheets. Bake until pastry is pale golden, 12 to 15 minutes. Transfer to racks to cool.

Cooks' notes:

• Unbaked logs can be chilled up to 3 days.

• Cookies keep, layered between sheets of wax paper or parchment, in an airtight container at room temperature 1 week.

COCONUT MACAROONS

MAKES 4 COOKIES

Active time: 10 min Start to finish: 45 min

Butter and flour for preparing baking sheet and foil
1 **large egg white**
1 **tablespoon sugar**
¼ **teaspoon vanilla**
⅛ **teaspoon almond extract**
¾ **cup sweetened flaked coconut**

▸ Put oven rack in middle position and preheat oven to 300°F. Butter a baking sheet, then line with foil and lightly butter and flour foil, knocking off excess flour.
▸ Stir together egg white, sugar, vanilla, almond extract, and a pinch of salt until combined, then stir in coconut. Divide coconut mixture into fourths, then drop in 4 mounds (about 2 inches apart) onto baking sheet.
▸ Bake until tops are pale golden in spots, 15 to 20 minutes, then carefully lift foil with cookies from baking sheet and transfer to a rack to cool completely, about 15 minutes. Peel macaroons from foil.

EACH COOKIE ABOUT 74 CALORIES AND 5 GRAMS FAT

GRANOLA CHOCOLATE CHIP COOKIES

MAKES 18 LARGE (4-INCH) COOKIES

Active time: 20 min Start to finish: 35 min

1 **cup all-purpose flour**
½ **teaspoon baking soda**
½ **teaspoon salt**
1 **stick (½ cup) unsalted butter, softened**
⅓ **cup packed light brown sugar**
⅓ **cup granulated sugar**
½ **teaspoon vanilla**
1 **large egg**
1 **cup granola (chop clusters if large)**
¾ **cup semisweet chocolate chips (4½ oz)**

▸ Put oven racks in upper and lower thirds of oven and preheat oven to 375°F.
▸ Whisk together flour, baking soda, and salt in a small bowl. Beat together butter, sugars, and vanilla in a medium bowl with an electric mixer at high speed until pale and fluffy, about 3 minutes, then beat in egg until combined well.

Reduce speed to low, then add flour mixture and mix until just combined. Stir in granola and chocolate chips.
▸ Drop 18 mounds (about 2 level tablespoons per mound) of batter about 2 inches apart onto 2 ungreased large baking sheets, then pat each mound into a 2½-inch round.
▸ Bake cookies, switching position of sheets halfway through baking, until pale golden, about 13 minutes. Cool on sheets 1 minute, then transfer to racks to cool completely.

PEANUT TUILES

MAKES ABOUT 4 DOZEN COOKIES

Active time: 1¼ hr Start to finish: 1½ hr

5 **tablespoons unsalted butter, cut into pieces**
½ **cup sugar**
3 **tablespoons light corn syrup**
1 **tablespoon heavy cream**
½ **cup all-purpose flour**
¼ **teaspoon salt**
¾ **cup salted roasted or cocktail peanuts, chopped**

Special equipment: **an 18- by 13-inch nonstick bakeware liner such as Silpat; a small offset spatula**

▸ Put oven rack in middle position and preheat oven to 350°F. Line baking sheet with nonstick liner.
▸ Combine butter, sugar, corn syrup, and cream in a 2-quart heavy saucepan and bring to a boil over moderate heat, stirring constantly. Add flour and salt and cook, stirring constantly, until batter is slightly thickened, about 1 minute. Stir in peanuts.
▸ Working in a small batch of 6 cookies, drop level teaspoons of batter about 3 inches apart on lined baking sheet. Bake until golden and bubbly, 5 to 7 minutes. Cool on baking sheet on a rack 1½ minutes. Quickly but carefully flip cookies over with offset spatula. Working quickly, roll 1 cookie around handle of a wooden spoon and immediately slide cookie onto rack to cool completely. Repeat with remaining cookies. (If cookies become too hard to roll, return them to oven briefly.) Wipe down bakeware liner with a paper towel and make more cookies in same manner.

Cooks' note:
• Cookies keep in an airtight container at room temperature 1 week.

CRUNCHY PECAN COOKIES
MAKES ABOUT 42 COOKIES
Active time: 15 min   Start to finish: 1¼ hr

- 6 oz pecans (1½ cups)
- 1 cup sugar
- ¼ cup potato starch
- ¼ teaspoon salt
- Scant ¼ teaspoon cinnamon
- 3 large egg whites, lightly beaten

Special equipment: **parchment paper**

▸ Put oven rack in middle position and preheat oven to 375°F. Line a large baking sheet with parchment paper.
▸ Coarsely chop 1 cup pecans and set aside. Pulse remaining ½ cup pecans in a food processor with sugar, potato starch, salt, and cinnamon until finely ground (be careful not to pulse to a paste), then stir into egg whites. Stir in chopped pecans.
▸ Drop ½ tablespoons of batter 2 inches apart on baking sheet and bake until cookies are lightly browned and slightly puffed, 15 to 17 minutes. Slide parchment onto a rack and cool cookies completely (cookies will crisp as they cool), then remove from parchment. Bake and cool 2 more parchment-lined sheets of cookies in same manner.

Cooks' note:
• Cookies can be made 1 week ahead and kept in an airtight container at room temperature.

CRANBERRY OAT BARS
MAKES 24 BARS
Active time: 20 min   Start to finish: 1¼ hr

- 1¼ sticks (10 tablespoons) unsalted butter, softened, plus additional for greasing baking pan
- 1½ cups old-fashioned rolled oats
- 1 cup packed light brown sugar
- 2 large eggs
- 2 tablespoons whole milk
- 2 teaspoons vanilla
- 1 cup all-purpose flour
- ½ teaspoon freshly grated nutmeg
- ½ teaspoon salt
- ½ teaspoon baking soda
- 1½ cups pecans (6 oz), chopped
- 1⅓ cups dried cranberries, chopped

▸ Put oven rack in middle position and preheat oven to 350°F. Generously butter a 9-inch square baking pan.
▸ Toast oats in another baking pan, stirring occasionally, until pale golden, about 12 minutes.
▸ Beat butter (1¼ sticks) and brown sugar with an electric mixer at medium-high speed until light and fluffy, about 2 minutes. Beat in eggs, milk, and vanilla. Whisk together flour, nutmeg, salt, and baking soda, then beat into butter mixture until incorporated. Stir in oats, pecans, and cranberries. Spread in buttered pan.
▸ Bake until golden and a wooden pick or skewer inserted in center comes out clean, 30 to 35 minutes. Cool in pan on a rack 20 minutes, then cut into bars.

KITCHEN NOTE

IF YOU LOVE TO MAKE COOKIES, YOU MIGHT WANT TO PICK UP A COUPLE OF PROPER **BAKING SHEETS**. THEY HAVE ONLY ONE OR TWO LIPPED SIDES FOR HANDLING, WHICH ALLOWS YOU TO SLIDE COOKIES QUICKLY AND EASILY FROM SHEET TO COOLING RACK. WE PREFER MEDIUM-WEIGHT LIGHT-COLORED (NOT NONSTICK) ALUMINUM BAKING SHEETS. IF YOU USE DARK METAL PANS, INCLUDING NONSTICK ONES, YOUR BAKED GOODS WILL PROBABLY BROWN MORE AND THE COOKING TIMES MAY BE SHORTER. WE ARE NOT HUGE FANS OF INSULATED COOKIE SHEETS; COOKIES TEND TO TAKE SOMEWHAT LONGER TO BAKE ON THEM.

PIES AND TARTS

SWEET-POTATO PIE WITH GINGERSNAP PECAN CRUST

SERVES 8
Active time: 45 min   Start to finish: 3¾ hr (includes cooling)

For crust

- 5 tablespoons unsalted butter, melted, plus additional for buttering pie plate
  Flour for dusting pie plate
- 1 cup finely crushed gingersnap cookies (5 oz; twenty 2-inch cookies)
- ½ cup finely chopped pecans (2 oz), toasted (see Tips, page 8)
- 2 tablespoons sugar
- ⅛ teaspoon salt

For filling

- 2 lb sweet potatoes (4 medium)
- ½ cup sugar
- ⅓ cup water
- 3 large eggs
- ½ teaspoon cinnamon
- ¼ teaspoon salt
- ⅔ cup whole milk
- 1 tablespoon dark rum
- ½ teaspoon vanilla

Special equipment: **a 10-inch glass or ceramic pie plate (6-cup capacity)**
Accompaniments: **lightly sweetened whipped cream; toasted pecans**

Make crust:

▸ Put oven rack in middle position and preheat oven to 350°F. Butter and flour pie plate, knocking out excess flour.
▸ Toss together all crust ingredients in a bowl with a fork until crumbs are moistened, then press evenly onto bottom and up side of pie plate. Bake crust 6 minutes, then cool on a rack.

Make filling:

▸ Increase oven temperature to 400°F.
▸ Prick each sweet potato once with a fork. Roast in a foil-lined shallow baking pan until tender, about 1 hour. Remove from oven and reduce oven temperature to 375°F. Halve potatoes lengthwise and cool.

▸ While potatoes cool, cook sugar in a dry 8-inch heavy skillet over moderate heat, undisturbed, until it begins to melt. Continue to cook, stirring occasionally with a fork, until sugar melts into a deep golden caramel. Remove from heat. Carefully pour water down side of skillet (mixture will bubble and steam vigorously), then return to heat and simmer, stirring, until hardened caramel is completely dissolved. Remove from heat.
▸ When potatoes are cool enough to handle, peel, then cut away any eyes or dark spots. Purée potatoes in a food processor until smooth, then add eggs, cinnamon, and salt and blend until smooth. Add milk, caramel, rum, and vanilla, and blend until combined well.
▸ Pour filling into crust. Bake until filling 2 inches from edge is slightly puffed and center trembles slightly when gently shaken, 40 to 50 minutes (top may crack; filling will continue to set as it cools). If the crust begins to brown too much before the filling is done, crimp a ring of foil or use a pie shield to protect it. Cool pie on rack about 1 hour. Serve warm or at room temperature.

Cooks' notes:
• Crust can be made 2 days ahead and cooled completely, then kept, covered with plastic wrap, at room temperature.
• Sweet potatoes can be baked 1 day ahead and chilled, covered. Bring to room temperature before peeling.

KITCHEN NOTE

MANY OF OUR RECIPES CALL FOR **"LIGHTLY SWEETENED" WHIPPED CREAM** AS AN ACCOMPANIMENT. WHEN WHIPPING YOUR CREAM, IT'S BEST TO USE CONFECTIONERS SUGAR OR SUPERFINE GRANULATED SUGAR; BOTH DISSOLVE QUICKLY INTO THE CREAM AND DON'T LEAVE ANY SUGARY GRIT.

KIWI TART

SERVES 8

Active time: 15 min   Start to finish: 45 min

- 1 (9-inch) round of refrigerated pie dough (from a 15-oz package), unrolled or unfolded
- 6 oz cream cheese, softened slightly
- 2 tablespoons sugar
- 2 tablespoons milk
- 1 teaspoon finely grated fresh lemon zest (see Tips, page 8)
- ½ teaspoon vanilla
- 3 firm-ripe kiwifruit, peeled and thinly sliced

Special equipment: **an 8¾- to 9¼-inch tart pan (1 inch deep) with a removable bottom; pie weights or raw rice**

▶ Put oven rack in middle position and preheat oven to 450°F.

▶ Fit dough into tart pan, leaving a ½-inch overhang, then fold overhang inward and press against side of pan to reinforce edge. Lightly prick bottom and side of shell with a fork.

▶ Line shell with foil and fill with pie weights. Bake until edge is pale golden, about 10 minutes. Carefully remove weights and foil and bake shell until golden all over, about 5 minutes more. Cool shell in pan on a rack, about 20 minutes.

▶ Meanwhile, beat together cream cheese, sugar, milk, zest, and vanilla in a bowl with an electric mixer until creamy and smooth, 2 to 3 minutes.

▶ Spread cream cheese filling in cooled shell and top with kiwi slices.

Cooks' note:

• Tart can be made 4 hours ahead and chilled, covered. Bring to room temperature before serving.

KITCHEN NOTE

ALWAYS **MEASURE TART PANS AND PIE PLATES** ACROSS THE TOP, NOT ACROSS THE BOTTOM.

BANOFFEE PIE

SERVES 8

Active time: 30 min   Start to finish: 3½ hr

- 2 cups canned sweetened condensed milk (21 oz)
- 1 (9-inch) round of refrigerated pie dough (from a 15-oz package)
- 3 large bananas
- 1½ cups chilled heavy cream
- 1 tablespoon packed light brown sugar

Special equipment: **a 9-inch pie plate (preferably deep-dish)**

▶ Put oven rack in middle position and preheat oven to 425°F.

▶ Pour condensed milk into pie plate and stir in a generous pinch of salt. Cover pie plate with foil and crimp foil tightly around rim. Put in a roasting pan, then add enough boiling-hot water to reach halfway up side of pie plate, making sure that foil is above water. Bake, refilling pan to halfway with water about every 40 minutes, until milk is thick and a deep golden caramel color, about 2 hours. Remove pie plate from water bath and transfer toffee to a bowl, then chill toffee, uncovered, until cold, about 1 hour.

▶ While toffee chills, clean pie plate and bake piecrust in it according to package instructions. Cool piecrust completely in pan on a rack, about 20 minutes.

▶ Spread toffee evenly in crust and chill, uncovered, 15 minutes.

▶ Cut bananas into ¼-inch-thick slices and pile over toffee.

▶ Beat cream with brown sugar in a clean bowl with an electric mixer until it just holds soft peaks, then mound over top of pie.

Cooks' notes:

• Toffee can be chilled up to 2 days (cover after 1 hour).

• Toffee-filled crust can be chilled up to 3 hours.

FROZEN DESSERTS

BRANDIED PEACH PARFAITS

SERVES 4

Active time: 20 min   Start to finish: 1½ hr

- 1   lb firm-ripe peaches
- 1   tablespoon fresh lemon juice
- 3   tablespoons brandy
- ½   cup sugar
- 1   pt vanilla ice cream, softened

Special equipment: **4 (4-oz) parfait or other tall narrow glasses**

▸ Cut a shallow X in bottom of each peach with a sharp paring knife and blanch in a 3-quart saucepan of boiling water 10 seconds. Transfer peaches with a slotted spoon to a bowl of ice and cold water and let stand until cool enough to handle. Peel peaches, then halve lengthwise and pit. Cut peaches into 1-inch pieces, then toss with lemon juice and 2 tablespoons brandy in a bowl.
▸ Cook sugar in a dry 9- to 10-inch heavy skillet over moderately low heat, stirring slowly with a fork (to help sugar melt evenly), until melted and pale golden. Cook caramel, without stirring, swirling skillet, until deep golden. Carefully add peach mixture (caramel will harden and steam vigorously) and cook, stirring frequently, until caramel is dissolved and peaches are tender, about 5 minutes. Transfer to a bowl and cool to room temperature, stirring occasionally, 10 to 15 minutes, then stir in remaining tablespoon brandy.
▸ Spoon 2 tablespoons peach mixture into each glass, then top with a small scoop of ice cream. Repeat with another layer of peaches and ice cream and spoon remaining peaches on top. Serve immediately.

Cooks' note:
• Brandied peaches keep, covered and chilled, 1 week.

BANANA ICE CREAM SANDWICHES

SERVES 4

Active time: 10 min   Start to finish: 2 hr

This treat is a great make-ahead dessert.

- ½   cup chilled heavy cream
- ¼   cup *dulce de leche*
- 1   ripe medium banana
- ½   teaspoon fresh lime juice
- 4   (7-inch) flour tortillas (not low-fat)
- 1   tablespoon unsalted butter, melted

Accompaniment: **chocolate sauce**

▸ Put oven rack in middle position and preheat oven to 350°F.
▸ Beat cream with an electric mixer until it just holds stiff peaks. Reduce speed to low and mix in *dulce de leche*, banana, and lime juice until combined. Freeze until firm but not frozen hard, at least 45 minutes.
▸ Brush tortillas with butter on both sides. Spread out on a baking sheet and toast, turning over once, until golden, 12 to 16 minutes total. Cool tortillas completely, about 20 minutes.
▸ Divide cream mixture between 2 tortillas and top with remaining 2 tortillas. Freeze on baking sheet, loosely covered with foil, until frozen, about 1 hour. To serve, cut each sandwich in half.

CANTALOUPE GRANITA

SERVES 4

Active time: 10 min   Start to finish: 50 min (includes freezing)

- 2   cups coarsely chopped cantaloupe (from ½ melon, seeded)
- ¼   cup sugar, or to taste
- ½   tablespoon fresh lemon juice, or to taste
- 1   cup ice cubes

▸ Purée all ingredients in a blender until smooth, then pour into a 13- by 9-inch metal pan and freeze until mixture becomes a firm slush, at least 40 minutes. Scrape with a fork and serve in chilled glasses.

AVOCADO GELATO

MAKES ABOUT 1 QUART

Active time: 20 min   Start to finish: 2¾ hr (includes freezing)

Though avocado may seem unusual as a sweet, it's commonly used as a dessert ingredient in Latin America. Its dense, velvety texture produces a gelato of exceptional smoothness.

We call for a crushed vitamin C tablet here, which is the trick to retaining the bright green color of the avocados without affecting their flavor.

  2 **cups whole milk**
 ¾ **cup sugar**
  3 **(4- by 1-inch) strips fresh orange zest (see Tips, page 8)**
  2 **tablespoons cornstarch**
  2 **firm-ripe California avocados (1 to 1¼ lb total)**
  1 **(500-mg) vitamin C tablet, crushed to a powder**

Special equipment: **an ice cream maker**

▶ Bring 1¾ cups milk, ½ cup sugar, zest, and a pinch of salt to a simmer in a 2-quart heavy saucepan over moderate heat. Whisk together cornstarch and remaining ¼ cup milk in a small bowl until smooth, then whisk into simmering milk. Bring to a boil, whisking constantly, and boil 1 minute. Transfer mixture to a metal bowl, then set bowl in a larger bowl of ice and cold water and stir frequently until cooled completely, 10 to 15 minutes. Discard zest.
▶ Quarter, pit, and peel avocados, then purée with vitamin C and remaining ¼ cup sugar in a food processor until smooth. Add milk mixture and blend well.
▶ Freeze avocado mixture in ice cream maker. Transfer to an airtight container and put in freezer to harden, about 1 hour.

Cooks' note:
• Ice cream can be made 1 week ahead.

RHUBARB SORBET WITH VANILLA RHUBARB COMPOTE

SERVES 6

Active time: 35 min   Start to finish: 3 hr (includes chilling)

For sorbet

  2 **lb rhubarb stalks, trimmed and cut into 1-inch-long pieces (about 7 cups)**
1⅔ **cups sugar**
  2 **tablespoons light corn syrup**

For compote

 ¾ **cup sugar**
1½ **cups water**
 ½ **lb rhubarb stalks, trimmed and cut diagonally into ¼-inch-thick slices (about 1 cup)**
  2 **drops vanilla**

Special equipment: **an ice cream maker**

Make sorbet:

▶ Toss together rhubarb, sugar, and corn syrup in a 4-quart heavy pot and let stand, stirring occasionally, 30 minutes (to macerate).
▶ Cook mixture over low heat, stirring frequently, until rhubarb has released about 2 cups liquid, 10 to 15 minutes. Increase heat and simmer, stirring frequently, until rhubarb is very tender, 12 to 15 minutes.
▶ Purée mixture in 2 batches in a blender until very smooth (use caution when blending hot liquids). Transfer purée to a bowl, then set bowl in a larger bowl of ice and cold water and stir occasionally until cold, 10 to 15 minutes. Freeze purée in ice cream maker, then transfer to an airtight container and put in freezer to harden, at least 1 hour.

Make compote while purée chills:

▶ Simmer sugar and water in a 2- to 3-quart saucepan, stirring, until sugar is dissolved. Add rhubarb slices and return just to a simmer, then remove pan from heat and stir in vanilla gently (to avoid breaking up rhubarb). Cool mixture to room temperature, gently stirring once or twice, about 30 minutes. Chill, covered, until ready to use.
▶ Let sorbet soften at room temperature 5 minutes, then serve with compote.

Cooks' note:
• Sorbet and compote can be made 3 days ahead.

FRUIT FINALES

AMARETTI-STUFFED PEACHES

SERVES 8
Active time: 15 min   Start to finish: 1½ hr

½   stick (¼ cup) unsalted butter, softened
 1   cup coarsely crumbled *amaretti* (Italian almond
       macaroons, preferably Lazzaroni brand;
       about 16; see Sources)
2½ tablespoons all-purpose flour
 2   tablespoons sugar
⅛   teaspoon salt
 1   large egg
 8   firm-ripe small peaches (about 2 lb), halved
       lengthwise and pitted

Accompaniment: **mascarpone cheese or crème fraîche**

▸ Put oven rack in middle position and preheat oven to 350°F.
▸ Melt 2 tablespoons butter and pour into a 13- by 9-inch glass or ceramic baking dish.
▸ Pulse ¾ cup crumbled *amaretti* in a food processor until finely chopped, then add flour, sugar, salt, and remaining 2 tablespoons butter. Blend until butter is incorporated, then add egg and blend until smooth.
▸ Scoop out just enough peach pulp from center of each peach half with a melon-ball cutter or a small spoon to create a 1-inch-deep cavity. Arrange peaches, cut sides up, in baking dish, then brush skins with melted butter from dish. Divide *amaretti* mixture among cavities, then sprinkle remaining ¼ cup crumbled *amaretti* over filling. Bake until filling is puffed and crisp, 40 to 50 minutes. Serve warm or at room temperature.

KITCHEN NOTE

THE ITALIAN ALMOND-FLAVORED MACAROONS KNOWN AS **AMARETTI** ARE MADE WITH SUGAR, EGG WHITES, AND ALMOND FLAVORING. *AMARETTI* APPEAR DELICATE, BUT WHILE THEIR TEXTURE IS LIGHT AND AIRY, THEY PACK A HEARTY CRUNCH.

BERRY TOAST CUPS

SERVES 4
Active time: 35 min   Start to finish: 40 min

¾   lb berries, trimmed and thinly sliced if
       using strawberries
 2   tablespoons fruit liqueur such as triple sec
       or crème de cassis
 1   teaspoon vanilla
 3   tablespoons sugar
 8   slices firm white sandwich bread
 2   tablespoons unsalted butter, melted
½   cup chilled heavy cream

Special equipment: **a 3-inch round biscuit or cookie cutter; a muffin tin with at least 8 (⅓- to ½-cup) muffin cups**

▸ Put oven rack in middle position and preheat oven to 400°F.
▸ Combine berries, liqueur, vanilla, 2 tablespoons sugar, and a pinch of salt in a bowl and let macerate at room temperature, stirring occasionally, 20 minutes.
▸ While berries macerate, cut out 8 rounds from bread using cookie cutter, then roll each round with a rolling pin, pressing firmly, into a flat 3¼-inch round. Generously brush muffin cups with some butter and press bread rounds onto bottom and up side of cups. Brush with remaining butter and toast until bottoms are golden, about 10 minutes.
▸ While bread cups toast, beat cream with remaining tablespoon sugar using an electric mixer at high speed until it just holds soft peaks.
▸ Transfer 2 toast cups to each of 4 plates, then divide berry mixture among toast cups and top with whipped cream and any leftover liquid from berries.

BROILED PLUMS WITH MANGO SORBET

SERVES 4
Active time: 15 min   Start to finish: 20 min

½   lb plums (about 2 medium), pitted and cut into
       ½-inch wedges
 1   tablespoon sugar
¼   teaspoon vanilla
⅛   teaspoon cinnamon
 3   tablespoons water
 2   cups (1 pt) fat-free mango sorbet

▶ Preheat broiler. Toss plums with sugar, vanilla, and cinnamon in a 1½- to 2-quart (9- to 10-inch round) gratin or other flameproof shallow dish (not glass). Let plums stand 5 minutes in dish to macerate.

▶ Add water to dish and broil plums 6 to 8 inches from heat, gently stirring once or twice, until fruit is softened, 7 to 10 minutes. Serve fruit and juice from pan topped with sorbet.

Cooks' note:
• Plums can be broiled 2 hours ahead and divided among serving dishes while still warm.

EACH SERVING ABOUT 162 CALORIES AND LESS THAN 1 GRAM FAT

APRICOT PANDOWDY
SERVES 6
Active time: 15 min   Start to finish: 45 min

A pandowdy is a homey American dessert of cooked fruit covered with a piecrust or biscuit crust that is often cut up halfway through baking and pushed into the fruit. We leave the crust whole here for a quicker and easier version.

1½ lb fresh apricots, quartered lengthwise and pitted
 1 tablespoon cornstarch
 ½ cup plus 1 tablespoon sugar
 2 tablespoons unsalted butter
 1 (10-inch) round of refrigerated pie dough (from a 15-oz package), unrolled or unfolded
 1 tablespoon milk

▶ Put oven rack in middle position and preheat oven to 400°F.

▶ Toss apricots with cornstarch and ½ cup sugar until coated.

▶ Heat butter in a 10-inch heavy skillet over moderate heat until foam subsides, then stir in apricot mixture. Bring to a boil, stirring frequently, then immediately transfer to a 9-inch pie plate.

▶ Fold pie dough into quarters and trim 1 inch from rounded edge. Unfold (trimmed round should be 8 inches in diameter) and put on top of fruit. Brush pastry with milk and sprinkle with remaining tablespoon sugar.

▶ Bake until apricot filling is bubbling and crust is golden, about 20 minutes. Cool 10 minutes before serving.

GELATINS AND PUDDINGS

LEMON GELATIN WITH RASPBERRIES
SERVES 4
Active time: 30 min   Start to finish: 5½ hr (includes chilling)

 4 large lemons
 2 cups cold water
 1 (¼-oz) envelope unflavored gelatin (2¼ teaspoons)
⅔ cup sugar
 6 oz raspberries (1¼ cups), picked over

Special equipment: **4 (6- to 8-oz) juice glasses**

▶ Remove all zest from lemons in strips with a vegetable peeler, then remove and discard any white pith from zest using a paring knife. Reserve lemons.

▶ Boil zest and 1¾ cups water in a 2-quart saucepan over high heat, uncovered, until water is bright yellow, about 5 minutes. Remove from heat, then discard zest and keep lemon water warm, covered.

▶ Meanwhile, sprinkle gelatin over remaining ¼ cup water in a small bowl and let stand 1 minute to soften.

▶ Squeeze ⅔ cup lemon juice from lemons into a bowl, then stir in sugar until dissolved. Pour through a fine-mesh sieve into a large glass measure, then add warm lemon water and stir in gelatin mixture until dissolved.

▶ Pour about ¼ cup lemon mixture into each glass and chill until set, about 2 hours. Reserve remaining lemon mixture at room temperature.

▶ Spoon some raspberries over each serving, then top with reserved lemon mixture and chill until set, 3 hours more.

Cooks' note:
• Dessert can be chilled up to 1 day. Juice from raspberries may color gelatin.

EACH SERVING ABOUT 136 CALORIES AND LESS THAN 1 GRAM FAT

STICKY TOFFEE PUDDING

SERVES 6 TO 8

Active time: 25 min   Start to finish: 1¼ hr

- 2 sticks (1 cup) unsalted butter, softened, plus additional for greasing pan
- 1 cup self-rising cake flour plus additional for flouring pan
- 1 cup pitted dates (5 oz), finely chopped
- 1⅓ cups water
- 1¼ cups packed dark brown sugar
- 1 large egg
- ⅛ teaspoon salt

▶ Put oven rack in middle position and preheat oven to 350°F. Butter and flour an 8- by 2-inch round cake pan, knocking out excess flour.

▶ Simmer dates in 1 cup water in a 1-quart heavy saucepan, covered, until soft, about 5 minutes. Remove from heat and let stand, covered, 5 minutes.

▶ Beat together 1 stick butter and ¼ cup brown sugar in a large bowl with an electric mixer at medium-high speed until light and fluffy, about 4 minutes. Beat in egg until combined. Reduce speed to low, then add flour and salt and mix at low speed until just combined. Add dates (with soaking liquid) and mix until just combined well.

▶ Pour batter into cake pan and bake until a wooden pick or skewer inserted in center comes out clean, about 30 minutes.

▶ Meanwhile, melt remaining stick butter in a 2-quart heavy saucepan over moderate heat and stir in remaining cup brown sugar, remaining ⅓ cup water, and a pinch of salt. Boil over moderately high heat, uncovered, stirring occasionally, until sugar is dissolved and sauce is reduced to about 1¼ cups, 2 to 8 minutes. Remove from heat and cover.

▶ Transfer pudding in pan to a rack and poke all over at 1-inch intervals with a chopstick. Gradually pour half of warm sauce evenly over hot pudding. Let stand until almost all of sauce is absorbed, about 20 minutes.

▶ Run a thin knife around edge of pan. Invert a plate over pudding and invert pudding onto plate. Pour remaining warm sauce over pudding and serve immediately.

Cooks' notes:
• Pudding, soaked with half of sauce, can stand at room temperature up to 2 hours. Reheat in pan in a preheated

300°F oven 10 minutes. Warm remaining sauce before pouring over pudding.
• Don't be concerned if pudding cracks a bit when you invert it onto plate; it will taste just as good.

BLACK RICE PUDDING

SERVES 8

Active time: 10 min   Start to finish: 2 hr (includes cooling)

Chinese black rice, sometimes called forbidden rice, works well for this recipe, but if you live near a Southeast Asian market you can use this same method with the more traditional Thai black sticky rice. If you can't find any kind of black rice, substitute brown rice (not quick-cooking)—it will result in a thicker, light-colored pudding but will still be delicious.

- 3 cups water
- 1 cup black rice
     A scant ½ teaspoon salt
- ½ cup sugar
- 1 (13½- to 15-oz) can unsweetened coconut milk, stirred well

▶ Bring water, rice, and ¼ teaspoon salt to a boil in a 4-quart heavy pot, then reduce heat to low and simmer, covered with a tight-fitting lid, 45 minutes (rice will be cooked but still wet). Stir in sugar, 1½ cups coconut milk, and remaining scant ¼ teaspoon salt and bring to a boil over high heat, then reduce heat to low and simmer, uncovered, stirring occasionally, until mixture is thick and rice is tender but still slightly chewy, about 30 minutes.

▶ Remove from heat and cool to warm or room temperature, stirring occasionally, at least 30 minutes. Just before serving, stir pudding and divide among 4 bowls. Stir remaining coconut milk and drizzle over pudding.

Cooks' note:
• Rice pudding keeps, covered and chilled, 5 days.

ORANGE COEURS À LA CRÈME WITH STRAWBERRY RASPBERRY SAUCE

SERVES 6

Active time: 30 min   Start to finish: 8½ hr (includes chilling)

You can find the Neufchâtel cheese called for here next to the cream cheese at your supermarket.

Don't be alarmed by the holes in your coeur à la crème molds—they allow liquid to drain out of the bottom so the hearts will be firm enough to hold their shape.

⅓ cup 1% cottage cheese
1   teaspoon finely grated fresh orange zest (see Tips, page 8)
⅓ cup plus 2 tablespoons sugar
4   oz Neufchâtel cheese
¾ cup plain low-fat yogurt
5   oz strawberries, quartered (1 cup)
3   oz raspberries (⅔ cup)
1   tablespoon Grand Marnier or other orange-flavored liqueur

Special equipment: **cheesecloth; 6 (3-inch) heart-shaped** *coeur à la crème* **molds (see Sources)**

▸ Cut 6 (8- by 6-inch) rectangles of cheesecloth without unfolding it. Rinse with cold water and wring dry. Line molds with damp cheesecloth, allowing it to hang over sides, and put molds in a shallow baking pan.

▸ Purée cottage cheese with zest and ⅓ cup sugar in a food processor or blender until very smooth, then add Neufchâtel cheese and purée until smooth. Add yogurt and pulse just until blended, then divide mixture among molds. Cover tops of molds with a sheet of plastic wrap and chill until firm, at least 8 hours.

▸ Purée berries with liqueur and remaining 2 tablespoons sugar in a food processor, then force through a fine-mesh sieve set into a bowl, discarding seeds.

▸ Invert molds onto dessert plates and remove cheesecloth. Serve *coeurs à la crème* drizzled with sauce.

Cooks' notes:

• If you don't have molds, cut 6 (12-ounce) paper cups to make shorter cups, 2 to 3 inches high. With a wooden pick, poke about 10 holes in bottom of each cup, enlarging holes slightly with pick. Line cups with dampened cheesecloth.

• *Coeurs à la crème* and sauce can be made 2 days ahead and chilled separately, covered.

EACH SERVING ABOUT 159 CALORIES AND 6 GRAMS FAT

SOURCES

INGREDIENTS

Amaretti—Italian markets.

Asian dried tangerine peel—Asian markets.

Baby octopus—Freshfish4u.com (877-474-3474).

Blackberry syrup—CoffeeAM.com (800-803-7774) and Kalustyan's (212-685-3451; kalustyans.com).

Black mustard seeds—Kalustyan's (212-685-3451; kalustyans.com).

Boquerones—specialty foods shops, La Tienda (tienda.com), and The Spanish Table (spanishtable.com).

Bottled baby clams in the shell—some Italian markets and D. Coluccio & Sons (718-436-6700).

Cellophane, glass, or mung bean noodles—Asian markets and Uwajimaya (800-889-1928).

Chinese black vinegar—Asian markets, Kam Man Food Products (212-571-0330), and Uwajimaya (800-889-1928).

Chinese pickled mustard greens—some Asian markets and Uwajimaya (800-889-1928).

Chinese sweet bean paste—Uwajimaya (800-889-1928).

Chinese wheat noodles—some Asian markets.

Coarse bulgur (cracked wheat)—Middle Eastern markets and Kalustyan's (212-685-3451; kalustyans.com).

Confit duck legs—butcher shops, some supermarkets, and D'Artagnan (800-327-8246; dartagnan.com).

Crème fraîche—cheese shops, specialty foods shops, and some supermarkets.

Dandelion greens—farmers markets and specialty produce markets.

Dried ancho chiles—Latino markets, many supermarkets, Chile Today-Hot Tamale (800-468-7377), and Kitchen/Market (888-468-4433; kitchenmarket.com).

Dried California apricots—many specialty foods shops, natural foods stores, and The Apricot Farm (800-233-4413; apricot-farm.com).

Dried French green lentils—specialty foods shops and some supermarkets.

Dried hot Indian red chiles—Kalustyan's (212-685-3451; kalustyans.com).

Dried porcini mushrooms—specialty foods shops.

Farinha de mandioca—some Latino markets and Sendexnet (866-736-3396; sendexnet.com).

Farro—Far Away Foods (farawayfoods.com).

Fine-quality fermented soy sauce—Uwajimaya (800-889-1928).

Fresh bay leaves—specialty foods shops and farmers markets.

Fresh curry leaves—Indian or Asian markets (may be labeled "*meetha neem*" or "*kari patta*").

Fresh or dried epazote—Kitchen/Market (888-468-4433; kitchenmarket.com).

Guanabana purée—Latino markets.

Instant espresso powder—specialty foods shops, some supermarkets, and The Baker's Catalogue (800-827-6836; bakerscatalogue.com).

Italian chickpea flour—many specialty foods shops and D. Coluccio & Sons (718-436-6700).

Lapsang souchong tea leaves—some supermarkets and Upton Tea Imports (800-234-8327; uptontea.com).

Lavash **bread**—Middle Eastern markets.

Live blue crabs—The Crab Place (877-328-2722; crabplace.com).

Malagueta **peppers**—some Latino markets and Sendexnet (866-736-3396; sendexnet.com).

Mirin—Uwajimaya (800-889-1928).

Mochiko (sweet rice flour)—Asian markets and Uwajimaya (800-889-1928).

Moulard duck breasts—D'Artagnan (800-327-8246; dartagnan.com).

Orange-flower water—specialty foods shops and Kalustyan's (212-685-3451; kalustyans.com).

Organic or sustainably raised boneless pork loin roast—some supermarkets, some specialty foods shops, and Niman Ranch (866-808-0340; nimanranch.com).

Panko (Japanese bread crumbs)—some supermarkets and Uwajimaya (800-889-1928).

Pearl (Israeli) couscous—Middle Eastern markets, specialty foods shops, and Kalustyan's (212-685-3451; kalustyans.com).

Peeled cooked whole chestnuts—specialty foods shops and some supermarkets.

Pomegranate molasses—Middle Eastern markets and Kalustyan's (212-685-3451; kalustyans.com).

Pork fatback with skin—some specialty foods shops and Niman Ranch (866-808-0340; nimanranch.com).

Quinoa—natural foods stores, many supermarkets, and Ethnicgrocer.com.

Rabbit—butcher shops, specialty foods shops, and some supermarkets (may require special order).

Raw green (hulled) pumpkin seeds—natural foods stores, specialty foods shops, and some supermarkets.

Raw peanuts in shell—Asian and Indian markets.

Salt cod—many fish markets, La Tienda (tienda.com), and The Spanish Table (spanishtable.com).

Scotch bonnet or habanero hot sauce—most supermarkets and Kitchen/Market (888-468-4433; kitchenmarket.com).

SOURCES

Sea salt (flaky sea salt and Sicilian sea salt)—specialty foods shops and SaltWorks (800-353-7258; saltworks.us).

Seaweed—seafood shops by special request.

Semolina—Italian markets and Far Away Foods (farawayfoods.com).

Serrano ham—La Tienda (tienda.com).

Shelled unsalted Persian pistachios—Kalustyan's (212-685-3451; kalustyans.com).

Sicilian olives—Italian markets.

Slab bacon—some specialty foods shops and butcher shops.

Smoked paprika—Kalustyan's (212-685-3451; kalustyans.com).

Sour cherries (fresh)—farmers markets; (frozen)—Friske Orchards (231-599-2604).

Spanish chorizo—Latino markets, specialty foods shops, some supermarkets, La Tienda (tienda.com), and The Spanish Table (spanishtable.com).

Spanish Mahón cheese—specialty foods shops, La Tienda (tienda.com), and The Spanish Table (spanishtable.com).

Spelt flour—natural foods stores.

Tamarind—Kalustyan's (212-685-3451; kalustyans.com).

Tasso—Cajun Grocer (888-272-9347; cajungrocer.com).

Thai red curry paste—many supermarkets and Temple of Thai (templeofthai.com).

Unsweetened passion-fruit purée (*maracuyá*)—Latino markets and some supermarkets.

Urfa and Maras pepper—Kalustyan's (212-685-3451; kalustyans.com).

Whole green cardamom pods—Middle Eastern markets and Kalustyan's (212-685-3451; kalustyans.com).

Wild salmon—specialty foods shops and Wild Edibles (212-687-4255; wildedibles.com).

Yellow or green garlic chives—Asian markets.

EQUIPMENT

5- to 6-oz ramekins—some cookware shops and Bridge Kitchenware (800-274-3435; bridgekitchenware.com).

9 1/4-inch flan ring—some cookware shops and Bridge Kitchenware (800-274-3435; bridgekitchenware.com).

Coeur à la crème molds—some cookware shops and Bridge Kitchenware (800-274-3435; bridgekitchenware.com).

Japanese Benriner—cookware shops and Uwajimaya (800-889-1928).

Metal cannoli tubes—New York Cake Supplies (800-942-2539).

Perforated grill sheet—cookware shops and stores such as Kmart and Bed Bath & Beyond.

Silpat nonstick bakeware liner—cookware shops and The Baker's Catalogue (800-827-6836; bakerscatalogue.com).

Wooden *tamis* (sieve)—Bridge Kitchenware (800-274-3435; bridgekitchenware.com).

INDEX

☺ INDICATES RECIPES THAT CAN BE PREPARED IN 30 MINUTES OR LESS, ACTIVE TIME

➴ INDICATES RECIPES THAT ARE LOW-FAT

ᐯ INDICATES VEGETARIAN RECIPES

289

INDEX

INDEX

TABLE SETTING ACKNOWLEDGMENTS

All items shown in photographs but not listed below are from private collections.

Jacket (front and back)
Plates—La Cafetiere (646-486-0667). Ramekins, spatula, and glasses—Broadway Panhandler (212-966-3434).

Frontispiece
Page 2: Spoon by iittala—MoMA Design Store (800-793-3167). Bowl by Mud Australia—ABC Carpet & Home (212-473-3000).

Sketches of Spain
Page 12: Black ceramic dishes—The Conran Shop (866-755-9079; www.conran.com).
Page 13: Wine bottles, square ceramic flower boxes, cake stand, and black oven dish—The Conran Shop.

Page 14, lower right: Black ceramic pan—The Conran Shop.

Page 22: Purple water glass—The Conran Shop.

Page 23: White plate—The Conran Shop.

Rewriting the Classics
Page 37: Flock dish—Designers Guild (011-44-20-7351-5775; www.designersguild.com).

Page 39: Pink plate—Branksome China (011-44-14-2565-2010; branksomechina.co.uk). Pewter charger—Nordic Style (011-44-20-7351-1755; nordicstyle.com).

Page 40, left: White plate—Designers Guild.

Page 40, right: Blue cotton shirt—Paul Smith (212-627-9770; paulsmith.co.uk).

Page 42: Linen "Deco" dice tablecloth—Jane Sacchi Linens (011-44-20-7349-7020; janesacchi.com). "Ceremony" table runner and "Ceremony" wine glasses by Linea Home—House of Fraser (011-44-20-7963-2000; houseoffraser.co.uk). Water glasses, Champagne flutes, and red-wine glasses—The Conran Shop (866-755-9079; www.conran.com). Ceramic pods (vases)—Sophie Cook Ceramics (011-44-20-8694-8363; sophiecook.com). White bowl and platter—David Mellor (011-44-20-7730-4259; davidmellordesign.co.uk).

Page 45: Trifle dish—The General Trading Company (011-44-20-7730-0411; generaltrading.co.uk).

La Dolce Via
Page 54: Dinner plate—La Cafetiere (646-486-0667).

Pages 56–57: Glasses and orange bowl—Broadway Panhandler (212-966-3434). Napkins, green bowl, and gray bowl—La Cafetiere.

Passion Pink
Page 64: "Dip" side plates and wine glasses—Nicole Farhi (212-223-8811). Dinner plates—Joan Platt (212-876-9228).

Page 65: Glasses—Nicole Farhi.

Page 68: "Dip" dinner plate—Nicole Farhi.

Page 69: Spoon—Global Table (212-431-5839).

Masala Magic
Page 72: Turquoise plate—Calvin Klein (212-292-9000).

Page 73: Purple bowl—ABC Carpet & Home (212-473-3000).

Orange Crush
Page 84: "Cesana" wineglasses—Armani Casa (212-334-1271). Bottles and folding chairs—Rooms & Gardens (202-362-3777). "Lapierre Como" tablecloth by The Silk Trading Co.—ABC Carpet & Home (212-473-3000). Orange linen cocktail napkins—Takashimaya New York (800-753-2038).

Cool and Bright
Page 104: Verana dinner plate—heathceramics.com.

Twilight Zone
Page 132: Vintage wooden trestle table—Paula Rubenstein (212-966-8954). Vintage chandelier—The Lively Set (212-807-8417).

Page 133: Nadia small glass tumbler—Juliska (888-414-8448).

Page 134: Egala small white porcelain dipping bowls—Armani Casa (212-334-1271). "Sand Collection" glazed pumice dinner plate—Nicole Farhi (212-223-8811). White wine goblet—Dean & DeLuca (212-226-6800).

Page 136, left: Natural beeswax candles—ABC Carpet & Home (212-473-3000). Blue Murano cocktail glasses—Nicole Farhi.

Page 136, right: "Sand Collection" glazed aqua dinner plate—Nicole Farhi.

A New Tradition
Pages 158-171: Wharton Esherick Museum (610-644-5822).

The Recipe Compendium
Page 197: Bowl—H. Groome (631-204-0491).

CREDITS

We gratefully acknowledge the photographers listed below. With a few exceptions, their work was previously published in *Gourmet*.

Quentin Bacon: Fresh, pp. 90–97. Cool and Bright, pp. 104–109. All Photographs © 2005.

Matthew Hranek: Sketches of Spain, pp. 12–23. In Bloom, pp. 98–103. Easy Living, pp. 110–115. A New Tradition, pp. 158–171. All Photographs © 2005.

John Kernick: Beginning to See the Light, pp. 116–121. A Midday Feast, pp. 172–177. All Photographs © 2005.

David Loftus: Rewriting the Classics, pp. 36–45. Dinner at Moro, pp. 46–51. All Photographs © 2005.

Geoff Lung: Chez Nous, pp. 30–35. A Little Bit Country, pp. 150–157. All Photographs © 2005.

Martyn Thompson: Jacket and endsheets. La Dolce Via, pp. 52–63. License to Chill, pp. 140–143. In the Mood, pp. 144–149. Christmas Present, pp. 178–187. All Photographs © 2005.

Mikkel Vang: Carrot Pachadi, p. 11. Supper Samba, pp. 24–29. Passion Pink, pp. 64–71. Masala Magic, pp. 72–75. Chilled Zucchini Soup, p. 83. Orange Crush, pp. 84–89. A Plateful of Summer, pp. 122–127. Dinner Gets Crackin', pp. 128–131. Twilight Zone, pp. 132–139. All Aglow, pp. 188–195. All Photographs © 2005.

Romulo Yanes: Pickled Peaches, p. 2. Bay Scallops, p. 6. Orange Soy Baby Back Ribs, p. 197. Street Food, pp. 76–81. All Photographs © 2005.

If you are not already a subscriber to *Gourmet* magazine and would be interested in subscribing, please call *Gourmet*'s toll-free number, (800) 365-2454 or e-mail subscriptions@gourmet.com.

If you are interested in purchasing additional copies of this book or other *Gourmet* cookbooks, please call (800) 245-2010.